Optimizing the Aging, Retirement, and Pensions Dilemma

Optimizing the Aging, Retirement, and Pensions Dilemma

MARIDA BERTOCCHI
SANDRA L. SCHWARTZ
WILLIAM T. ZIEMBA

WILEY

John Wiley & Sons, Inc.

Published by John Wiley & Sons, Inc., Hoboken, New Jersey.
Published simultaneously in Canada.

For general information on our other products and services or for technical support, please contact our Customer Care Department within the United States at (800) 762-2974, outside the United States at (317) 572-3993 or fax (317) 572-4002.

Wiley also publishes its books in a variety of electronic formats. Some content that appears in print may not be available in electronic books. For more information about Wiley products, visit our web site at www.wiley.com.

Library of Congress Cataloging-in-Publication Data:

Bertocchi, Marida.
   Optimizing the aging, retirement, and pensions dilemma / Marida Bertocchi, Sandra L. Schwartz, William T. Ziemba.
       p. cm. – (Wiley finance series)
   Includes bibliographical references and index.
   ISBN 978-0-470-37734-5 (cloth)
   1. Retirement–Economic aspects.   2. Retirement income–Planning.   3. Pensions.
   I. Schwartz, S. L. (Sandra L.), 1943–   II. Ziemba, W. T.   III. Title.
   HD7105.3.B475 2010
   332.024′014–dc22
                                                              2009031715

Printed in the United States of America

10 9 8 7 6 5 4 3 2 1

To my nieces and nephews

—Marida

*To Rachel who makes us so proud, and to Ruth
who lives the social security dream*

—Bill and Sandra

Contents

Acknowledgments

First, we would like to thank Costanza Torricelli and Mariana Brunetti, John M. Mulvey and Zhuojuan Zhang, Charles Sutcliffe, Enrico Biffis and David Blake, Rachel Ziemba, and Vittorio Moriggia for contributing their knowledge and time to write new chapters for this book. Their breadth of knowledge expanded and strengthened this book.

Sandra would like to thank the women of the pilates coffee group for letting her practice her ideas on them.

Our editors at John Wiley & Sons in the United States, Bill Falloon, Meg Freeborn, Kevin Holm, and Tiffany Carbonier; and in the UK, Caitlin Cornish, and Aimee Dibbens, have been very helpful throughout the process of producing this book.

This research was supported in part by the Italian research grant of the Ministry of Education and Research "Financial innovations and demographic changes: new products and pricing instruments with respect to the stochastic factors aging" (coordinator Bertocchi).

Special thanks go to various universities which extended useful facilities to Sandra and William during the final stages of the preparation of this book; thanks especially go to St. Catherines College and the Mathematical Institute, Oxford University, the ICMA Centre University of Reading, 7 Cities, *Wilmott* magazine, the business school at the National Technological University of Singapore, the Toulouse School of Economics, the University of Bergamo, and the University of Venice.

Preface

May you live in interesting times.

Paradoxically, this ancient Chinese saying is both a blessing and a curse. Interesting times are challenging times. In regards to many economic, social and political issues, we can affirm that these are interesting times. Planning for retirement, however, is one of these issues which can be encapsulated in the observation that there is good news and bad news: the good news is that we are living longer, the bad news is we have to pay for it.

In 2009, we are in the worst economic crisis since the 1930s, with large losses in pensions, incomes, and savings. Renewal from the crisis will require a global shift in consumption and saving patterns. These are indeed very interesting times, if you look at issues in economics and finance, but especially for pensions and retirement. Old adages like stocks for the long run and the safety of index and exchange-traded funds have not worked to protect asset values. Moreover, losses of retirement assets in the near term have coincided with job losses and reductions in value of other assets, including property. Almost all asset classes have become increasingly correlated as credit has contracted and economic growth has slowed sharply. Many individuals and investment vehicles charged with saving for retirement looked to make up gaps in financing by shifting into different asset allocations. Major corrections in corporate bonds, exchange traded and private equity, and alternative assets mean that making up the shortfall may be prolonged as individuals face the risk of elevated unemployment for a long period.

This book began as an attempt to fill the gap identified by the OECD and others on the need to improve financial education for retirement. As originally envisioned, this was mainly a question of wealth and asset liability allocation over time. Ensuring sufficient resources for retirement encompasses a complex set of decisions involving tax issues, assumptions of future salaries and potential loss of income with change of jobs, asset allocation for defined contribution (DC) pension plans, longevity, interest rates, inflation and, on retirement, whether to buy an annuity. All this in the face of changing demographics and social factors, including increased life expectancy and the switch to defined contribution pension plans. All of these issues require careful individual decision making in the face of increasing risk.

The shortcomings of individuals in providing for their retirement are legion: insufficient savings, inability to access and deal with risk, lack of understanding of asset allocation, inability to read and understand reports from their pensions, lack of determination of the funds needed to retire, lack of understanding of longevity risk, and so on. This book will help individuals plan better for retirement, making use of government and corporate entities to help them while assessing the risks to their own balance sheets. It also addresses some of the macro economic issues such as whether an economy can effectively save without investing in productive assets. Rather than setting a retirement age, we suggest that society as a whole to consider retirement a phase that depends on ability to work, gets phased in, and lasts a limited time until expected death. This would be a reversion to long-held life cycle ideals. In doing so, we would likely need to create a path for work that could continue as strength declines.

All that said, the scope of this book has been expanded to include a discussion of the current worldwide economic crisis and how that impacts retirement savings. We are sitting on a potential retirement time bomb, but there is still time to defuse it—and that is what this book is about.

PART One

The Aging Population: Issues for Retirement

CHAPTER 1

Issues in Retirement

We begin by discussing the changing demographics and the evolution of retirement.

O ver the course of decades we have evolved a hodge-podge of promises and policies relating to retirement. Our image of retirement has evolved from that of an infirm old age into a picture of ceasing work at a vigorous middle age, perhaps 60, having a life of leisure activities in a nice home with easy access to health care when it is needed and no financial worries. A confluence of issues have put this idyllic picture at risk. First is demographics: we are living longer. Second is affordability. Both public and private retirement provisions are at risk.

Roots of the Problem

Social provision for retirement grew over the decades, without prior planning, as a series of responses to a variety of economic and social issues. The roots of the growing *retirement and pension* problem come from a number of areas:

1. The social desire to avoid poverty in the aged population, to insure income when one is too old to work.
2. The entitlement to leisurely old age meets up with changing demographics, age distribution becoming top heavy with fewer workers to support each retiree.
3. The attempt to put off labor negotiations by trading off current income for retirement income This led to company pensions.

   Number 1 is both a reflection of a charitable instinct and the social trends of the elderly living independently of their families, who have often scattered to other regions and no longer directly support them. This was the beginning of social security legislation. This is important; even though economics is considered the selfish science, nevertheless a social instinct exists.

Number 2 became a problem over time. This is the modern feeling that one should not need to work all of one's life. This led to various methods of shifting income into the future. When retirement benefits were first granted, the population was younger, originally few people were eligible and the benefits were modest. The program grew far beyond its roots into a full-blown provision for retirement income.

Number 3 is akin to the subprime crisis: business put off to the future the hard decisions and gave in to labor in the short term to avoid the longer-term issues of labor-management relations—this was good for neither and has left the economy deprived of real innovation, with huge unpayable debt and further distrust.

All jurisdictions and corporations have attempted to tinker with the problem: programs have been changed in marginal, efficiency-improving ways. Countries might, for example, increase the number of years used to calculate the base of the social security payment (for example, France went from counting the best 10 years to the best 25). These tactics do not solve the problem but they do ameliorate it. (See Chapter 8.)

In this chapter we look first at the changing demographics. Then we explore the evolution of the concept of retirement and the assets available on retirement. We conclude with a road map for the rest of the book.

1.1   LONGEVITY AND CHANGING DEMOGRAPHICS ACROSS THE WORLD

Let's look at a compilation of various tables from the UN cited in Haas (2007). Together these paint a vivid picture of changing demographics. Table 1.1 shows that fertility rates have dropped below replacement in all countries in the survey except India. Japan was the earliest in the late 1950s; China was the latest through severe penalties for families with more than one child, a policy that began in 1979 and dropped the country below replacement beginning in the 1990s.

Table 1.2 shows the rapid growth in life expectancy from 1960–1965 to 2000–2005. There has been an average increase of 14.5 years in a 40-year period. In China the increase was more than 30 years and India almost 25. Russia added less than one year, so leaving it out would raise the average to more than 16 years. All these years are essentially added to retirement under current cultural expectations!

Table 1.3 presents the percent of the population over 65 in 1950, 2000, and projections for 2050. The numbers are astounding. On average almost

TABLE 1.1 Fertility Rates by Country over Time

Country	Years 2000–2005	Years Fell below Replacement
Germany	1.32	1970–1975
Japan	1.33	1955–1960
Russia	1.33	1965–1970
UK	1.66	1970–1975
France	1.87	1975–1980
China	1.70	1990–1995
US	2.04	1970–1975
India	3.07	2025–2030 (projected)

Source: Haas (2007).

TABLE 1.2 Life Expectancy

Country	1950–1955	2000–2005	% Increase
Japan	63.9	81.9	28.17
France	66.5	79.4	19.40
UK	69.2	78.3	13.15
Germany	67.5	78.6	16.44
US	68.9	77.3	12.19
China	40.8	71.5	75.25
Russia	64.5	65.4	1.40
India	38.7	63.1	63.05

Source: Haas (2007).

TABLE 1.3 Population over 65 by Country over Time, %

Country	1950	2000	2050
India	3.3	4.9	14.8
US	8.3	12.3	20.6
Russia	6.2	12.3	23.0
UK	10.7	15.9	23.2
China	4.5	6.8	23.6
France	11.4	16.3	27.1
Germany	9.7	16.4	28.4
Japan	4.9	17.2	35.9
Average	7.4	12.8	24.6

Source: Haas (2007).

TABLE 1.4 Median Age by Country over Time

Country	1950	2000	2050	Overall % Change
Japan	22.3	41.3	52.3	134.53
India	20.4	23.4	38.7	89.71
China	23.9	30.1	44.8	87.45
Russia	25.0	36.4	43.5	74.00
US	30.0	35.3	41.1	37.00
Germany	35.4	40.0	47.4	33.90
France	34.5	38.0	45.5	31.88
UK	34.6	37.7	42.9	23.99
Average	28.3	35.3	44.5	64.1

Source: Haas (2007).

25% of the population of these countries is projected to be over 65 in 2050. Already in 2000 the average (unweighted) is 12.8% so that would be a doubling of the proportion in the 65+ age bracket.

Table 1.4 presents the median age for selected countries in 1950, 2000, and projections for 2050. Again, the numbers are astounding. On average (unweighted), the median age is expected to rise from 28.3 in 1950 to 44.5 in 2050. The four countries that started with the lowest median ages have the highest increases: in the case of Japan more than doubling. The western countries starting out with median ages above 30 have lower increases, but still the level is significant.

Table 1.5 considers these numbers another way, presenting the support ratio by country, the number of workers per person over 65. In line with

TABLE 1.5 Support Ratios by Country over Time

Country	1950	2000	2050
India	17.2	12.4	4.5
US	7.8	5.4	3.0
Russia	10.5	5.6	2,6
UK	6.2	4.1	2.6
China	13.8	10.0	2.6
France	5.8	4.0	2.1
Germany	6.9	4.2	2.0
Japan	12.1	4.0	1.4

Source: Haas (2007).

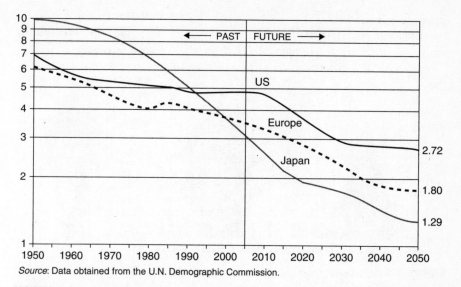

Source: Data obtained from the U.N. Demographic Commission.

FIGURE 1.1   Ratio of Population Aged 20–65 to Population Aged 65 and Older
Source: Siegel (2008).

the above numbers, this ratio goes from an average of about 10 in 1950 to 6.2 in 2000 and down to 2.6 in 2050. Figure 1.1 dramatically shows the changing age distributions over time in the three regions, the US, Europe and Japan.

Looking at the support ratios, it is indeed frightening to realize how few workers would be supporting the retirees. However, there have been times in the past when an aging population was also a concern. Europe in the 1920s to 1950s after much loss of population from two wars projected that problems would arise from an aging population. For example, in the UK they worried that the percentage over 65 would rise from 7.2% in 1931 to 17.5% in the late 1970s. This did not happen, of course, but as these tables show, we cannot think of all these older people as being unproductive and no longer contributing to their own support. A vigorous older age must mean a more productive 65-year-old! We will come back to this issue later.

Figure 1.2 shows most dramatically the impact of aging on the working age distribution. This is for Japan at three points of time, 1950, 2005, and projected for 2050 as the shape evolves from a tree to a kite. Children are generally less costly to support, and there is a long history of tax incentives and community support for child rearing including schools and after school activities. While in the older years, health care and other costs expand.

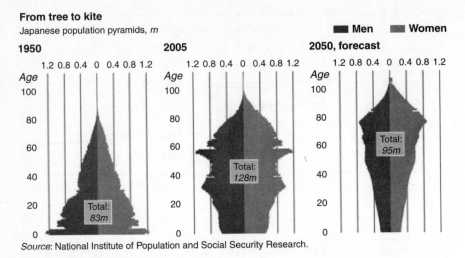

From tree to kite

Japanese population pyramids, *m*

Men **Women**

1950 **2005** **2050, forecast**

Source: National Institute of Population and Social Security Research.

FIGURE 1.2 Changing Age Distribution in Japan, 1950, 2005, 2050 est
Source: The Economist, 2007.

Initially, when people retired out of necessity, the costs of support were lower. Now with the expectation of an active retirement the costs are greater.

Biffis and Blake in Chapter 10 consider financial instruments to insure individuals and pension schemes against longevity risk.

1.2 THE EVOLUTION OF RETIREMENT

People used to work as long as they could, often till they dropped. In order to *retire* in good health, there must be funds available to support the activities of the nonworking years.

When retirement came from necessity, and before modern health care, the requirements of the retired were minimal—keeping them comfortable and fed. Now people are retiring younger and in more vigorous health, so their consumption requirements are higher, and also modern health care is able to offer more services for the elderly and that too costs more.

The first income security insurance program was established by Otto von Bismarck in 1881. In part this was a response to social unrest at the time. This plan paid out the insurance at 70, at which age few working males were still alive (though at that time Bismarck himself was 74). The purpose was to offer protection from poverty when workers physically could no longer work and to protect widows and orphans of working males who died young from loss of income. The minimum age was lowered to 65 in 1916 and became the initial standard of the US social security program.

There were some limited occupational plans in the 19th century. Belgium had compulsory insurance for seamen in 1844 and Italy in 1861. The UK had early plans for customs and civil servants (1859) and paid 1.67% of salary per year of employment up to two-thirds of salary, and blue collar plans paid about half the rate. Bismarck's plan was the first with broad coverage (40% in 1889 and 54% by 1895) (Clark, Munnell, and Orszag 2006). The destruction of net worth in wartime and depression led Europeans to push for more public income security plans.

Originally when the retirement age was set at 65, the majority of people had already died. Then with slightly increased life spans, retirement was possibly the last 10% of adult life; about 40 years of work followed by perhaps 5 years of retirement. Now the ratio of working life to retirement has been squeezed on both sides. The average age at retirement has declined, and the life span has increased. Now in some countries people work only 30 years followed by 30 years of retirement (OECD 2008). The average rate of employment in OECD countries for ages 55–64 is 48% (and only 25% in France, 70% in Switzerland).

In 1880 75% of men older than 64 were working, by 1950 it was 47% and by 1998 less than 20%. Later people began to expect 10 years of retirement after 40 years of work. Clearly, for many people, retirement is more attractive than working. The ability to be idle for such spans of life was helped by the growth in pensions and income support. In 1961, when social security was amended to allow early retirement at 62 at a lower benefit there was a spike in people commencing retirement. But with a remaining life expectancy of more than two decades this is a huge waste of talent.

A study in 1930 looking forward to 1990 foresaw those 64+ would represent 12.6% of the population (underestimating the population growth). The report was not concerned as retirement needs were thought to be minimal (physical needs, health, comfort) so they underestimated the changes in expectation.

Some 75% of retirees go from full-time work to no work, while in the past people would hang onto some work as long as they could, moving into supervisory positions even on the farm.

The changes in the last 60 years in the US are striking: In 1910 the average retirement age for men was 75, in 1940 it was 68, by 2001 it was about 62. In 1960 men were expected to spend 50 of their 68 years of life in paid work. In 2000 they worked for only 38 of their 76 years. As recently as 1965, about two-thirds of workers did not begin drawing social security benefits until they were 65 or older. Now, more than half retire at 62 or younger, and three-quarters receive their first benefit checks before they are

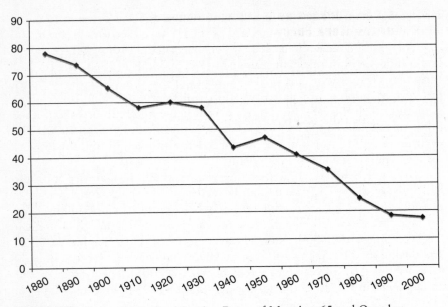

FIGURE 1.3 Labor Force Participation Rates of Men Age 65 and Over by
Decade, Percent
Source: Short (2006).

65 (Toner and Rosenbaum 2005). The notion of an active retirement has
been invented, and retirement has become a 20-year stage in life. Company
pensions clearly encompass three aspects: insurance (being old is like a disability), compensation (reward for a faithful career), and severance (payment
to allow termination). Together these factors have led to an increase in the
liabilities of the overall system. Under the social insurance program, workers earn entitlement to family benefits upon retirement, disability, or death.
This breaks down into retired workers (61%), disabled workers (10%),
families of retired and disabled workers (12%), and survivors of deceased
workers (17%) (Schwartz and Ziemba 2007).

  The trend toward earlier retirement and longer years of retirement will
need to be reversed. Policies are being put in place to foster this transition.
It is predicted that by 2030 at the latest, the age at which full retirement
benefits start will have risen to the mid-70s in all developed countries, and
benefits for healthy pensioners will be substantially lower than they are
today. Indeed, fixed retirement ages for people in reasonable physical and
mental condition may have been abolished to prevent the pensions burden
on the working population from becoming unbearable.

1.2.1 Older Workers as a Growing Share of the Work Force

The Labor Force is Aging: The Bureau of Labor Statistics (BLS) forecasts that, by 2014, the share of workers over 55 in the labor force will be 20%, up from the 15% in 2007. Most of these will be in the service sector, where most of the job growth will be. In part they will be replacing young people (BLS 2004). Also the BLS reported that, rather than retiring, over one-half of older workers are continuing to work in "bridge" jobs. This represents two forces: those who cannot afford to retire and those who want to explore other career paths and just want to keep active. The trend to greater workforce participation will increase as social security shortages will mean lower benefits especially for those who retire earlier (see Figure 1.3). Growing reliance on individual savings such as in 401(k)s and owner occupied houses will also make it more difficult to fund retirement. The BLS predicts that "traditional retirements will be the exception rather than the rule." We explore these issues in this book.

1.3 PROVISION FOR RETIREMENT

Individuals save to provide for retirement in a variety of ways: public pensions, occupational pensions (defined benefit (DB) and defined contribution (DC), which can be either protected or unprotected), and personal retirement savings. The role of pension assets on financial markets and economic stability provides a macro aspect to the retirement issue.

1.3.1 The Earliest Pensions

Providing retirement for the military goes back at least to ancient Rome. Military service could be long: up to 20 years. Beginning at the time of Marius (about 100 BCE), legionaries often were granted allotments of land upon retirement and by the time of Caesar Augustus, they could expect a payment of 12,000 sesterces on retirement versus an annual salary of about 900. Also they encouraged retirement communities, often encouraging retired military to settle down where they had served (thus avoiding the return of large numbers of unemployed soldiers). The remains of one such community are found in the Moroccan desert. These were complete towns with civic areas, hospitals, baths, physicians (see Gowans, 2007).

In the seventeenth century, if a Plymouth colonist was wounded defending the community against Indians, as he was unable to work, he was so to speak *retired* and would receive a pension to support him and his family. The pensions were funded by tax collections.

The first major retirement program in the US was that for the Union soldiers after the Civil War. It was a generous pension program replacing up to 30% of income (similar to social security) and reached 1 million participants by 1902. By 1900 21% of white males 55 and older were on pension. As well, by 1900 this pension program represented 30% of the federal budget.

1.3.2   Early Corporate Pensions

In 1875, the American Express railroad company established the first private pension plan in America. This is followed by banks, utility companies, and manufacturing companies that established company-funded retirement plans. Railroads used limited pensions for long-time employees as a way to encourage workers to retire for concerns about safety. Mandatory retirement was easier than dealing individually with the health of each employee. GE, DuPont, and Westinghouse were also early providers of pensions. Their retirement plans aimed at encouraging loyalty as they were investing a lot in human capital.

Corporate pensions were given a boost from the tax code. By 1926, employee benefits were virtually fully tax-deductible.

To contain wartime inflation, the Wage and Salary Act of 1942 froze wages. Firms then offered pensions and other benefits in their attempts to attract employees. Also pension contributions lowered the firm's taxes. In 1950 at General Motors, Charles Wilson created a company-run pension plan. He thought it would improve employee relations, though initially the United Auto Workers union objected. Wilson thought that lifetime employment with large corporations would be standard, and this was one way to build loyalty. At the time, pension benefits were usually not vested in the individual and so would be lost if the worker left the company. He did not foresee that these pensions would become a huge burden on the company (as of December 2008 GM had $13.6 billion in unfunded pension liabilities, the salaried and hourly pensions together have $84.5 billion in assets and $98.1 billion in liabilities).

The growth of corporate pensions and health insurance arose as a *bribe* to prevent labor unrest without huge increases in wages. For salaried employees they helped to defer income and minimize the effect of high marginal tax rates. In both cases they represented short-term solutions that created longer-term problems. Pension promises remind one of the Sufi story—when asked to teach an elephant to talk, Nasrullah struck a bargain with the king setting the due date many years down the road . . . knowing that something else would intervene in the meantime and he would not have to fulfill the promise. After all, the king was old and likely to die, or forget the promise. Barring bankruptcy, there is no simple way to avoid the corporate pension promises.

Between 1940 and 1950, the share of civilian workers covered by private pensions increased from about 7% to nearly 20%, while private health insurance rose from 10% to 50%. Many of the early pensions were pay-as-you-go defined benefit, and Drucker (1950) highlighted the problems of these pensions in an article called *The Mirage of Pensions*. When new DB pensions are started, even if firms make the ongoing payments, what hamstrings them are huge legacy costs associated with current employees. By 1960, private pensions grew to cover 30% of the labor force (23 million up from 3.7 million). In 1990, for example, about 57% of workplace pension benefits went to the wealthiest 20% of households. The next decades saw both regulation of private pensions and the establishment of various forms of individual tax deferred savings plans.

In 1973 the UAW won the right to a full pension with early retirement to commence after 30 years of work. This created an additional problem as initially pensions were net of social security. Retiring early meant the worker was not yet eligible for social security so received an enhanced pension to include social security benefits. Later, pensions became to be in addition to social security.

Lowenstein (2008) presents three cases of corporate and agency pensions and shows how they have led to problems in the economy and to problems in the relations between unions and the organizations they work for. The cases discuss how pension debt brought General Motors, the New York subways, and the city of San Diego to the brink of bankruptcy. So what can we learn from these three cases?

- In the mid-twentieth century the growth in corporate pensions came as a reaction to wage and price controls as they were outside the controlled sphere.
- American business has paid a high price for avoiding a public social safety net. Unions would add a *fringe* at a low level one year, such as supplemental payments while laid off, and then after a couple rounds of negotiating have the benefit up to 95% of salary for six months.
- Company pensions originally had social security benefits subtracted, and later they became additional to social security but both are taxable benefits.
- But when times were good, the fact that benefits reduced corporate tax liabilities pushed benefits higher . . . unfortunately, sometimes it is better to pay the tax! And when times are bad, there are no taxes!

- San Diego raises another issue regarding civic sponsorship: if a city invests in a team by building a stadium, for instance, should they not have representation on the board akin to ownership which in turn would prevent a team from just leaving the city and moving elsewhere? Indeed why not?
- Early bankruptcies led to the creation of the pension retirement insurance corporation... but the problem has grown too massive for this to help... the pension and health care promises are too large... Pension Benefit Guaranty Corporation has become the insurer of the weak as strong companies do not provide pensions.

These pensions tend to be based on the last few years' salary, so employees are allowed to work extra overtime in the last years in order to increase their pensions. In a similar fashion, some UK professors close to retirement with low salaries, because they did not move to other universities, are moving in their final years to capture short-term higher salaries and much higher long run pensions and final buyouts. A 62-year-old getting a £20,000 raise receives a £10,000 yearly pension increase each year plus a much higher retirement lump sum payment (£30,000) when taking mandatory retirement at 65. Chapter 8 discusses a possible shift to lifelong versus final salary pensions. In this scheme you can adjust total pension or keep it constant. This would avoid the incentive to change jobs just to increase pensions.

By 1980, 83% of large- and medium-sized companies offered DB pension plans and almost all companies provided health care coverage for full-time employees and their families. By 2003, only 33% of large corporations were offering DB pensions and only 58% of private employers offered any health insurance. The success of this welfare capitalist model was based on the global dominance of US business. After World War II the US represented about half of all global production. From this strength, business was able to set prices and obtain surpluses to fund these benefits. They were then able without pain to make promises to workers for future income in the form of DB pensions. Starting gradually in the 1960s and gaining speed later, this dominance was challenged. No longer able to set oligopolistic prices, the surplus was hard to maintain. Once they faced international competition, these economic rents were at risk, but it took some time for the realization to hit home, and the promises continued. But industries did fall and the promises were broken: steel, airlines, now automobiles (see, e.g., Morris 2006).

To highlight how open ended the pension promise is, Lowenstein notes a GM retiree who started work in 1926 and died in 2006 at 111 having received pension and health benefits for 48 years! A similar example comes from the US social security program, which began in the mid-1930s.

Ida May Fuller of Ludlow, Vermont, received the first social security check 00-000-001 on January 31, 1940. She lived to age 100 and collected $22,889 having made contributions of $24.75. Here we see the first overhang or deficit created by initial social security recipients who were already well into their working years when the program was implemented. By 2001, one in six Americans were receiving monthly benefit checks either as elderly, disabled, or children whose parents had died (Schwartz and Ziemba 2007).

1.3.3 Total Assets on Retirement

The current 2007–2008 economic situation reminds us that in times of crisis savings disappear. Institutions for saving have always been precarious, especially for the lower income groups. Some countries turned to the development of postal savings to make safe savings accounts available to low income people. The UK was the first to establish postal savings in 1861; at the time banks catered to the wealthy and were not accessible to all. Later, the post office offered insurance and annuities. There are still a number of countries where postal savings provides an important means of saving. The US provided similar postal savings from 1910 to 1966. Japan's is the most famous. Its post office was the world's largest savings bank with 198 trillion yen (US$1.7 trillion) of deposits as of 2006 and more now in 2009, especially in dollars, with a higher valued yen. It is now in a 10-year process of privatization. For an additional example, Brazil's national postal service in 2002 formed a partnership with the largest private bank in the country (Bradesco) to provide financial services at post offices. This is a reminder of how important is the evolution of the financial system.

Munnell et al. (2009a) show that retirement savings fall short of expectations. Her typical worker with preretirement income of $50,000 contributing 6% annually matched by 3% from the employer should have about $320,000 but the actual was only $75,000. They have defined a National Retirement Risk Index (NRRI) based on the resources available for retirement. They estimated that if people work to age 65 and annuitize *all* their assets, 44% will still be at risk to be unable to maintain their standard of living. When health care costs are included, 61% are at risk. Table 1.6 shows the wealth of a typical preretirement household. We will return to discuss some of these asset classes later.

1.3.4 The Contribution of Various Assets at Retirement

Popular financial advice suggests that households should strive to replace 65–85% of preretirement income in retirement (Butrica, Goldwyn, and Johnson

TABLE 1.6 Wealth of a Typical Household Approaching Retirement (55–64), 2007

Source of Wealth	Amount ($)	% Total
Primary house	$138,600	20
Business assets	15,900	2
Financial assets	29,600	4
401(k)/IRA	50,500	7
Defined benefit	122,100	18
Social Security	298,900	44
Other nonfinancial assets	21,000	3
Total	676,500	100

Source: Munnell et al. (2009a).

2005), but there appears to be little scientific basis for this estimate. A proper lifetime asset-liability analysis using multiperiod stochastic programming is suggested in Ziemba (2003); see also Consigli (2007) and Chapters 9 and 14–16 in this volume. Housing and health care are two of the largest categories of expenditure. About 25% of older people have mortgages—some have refinanced them for retirement while those who do not qualify for mortgages might fund some of their retirement with reverse mortgages.

The overall role of social security in funding retirement is ambiguous. While a poll found that only 20% of Americans who are not yet retired expect social security to be their major source of income when they stop working, 39% of retirees said that it was their major source of income. On the other hand social security appears to be becoming less important in overall funding (see Table 1.7). Leland and Wilgoren (2005) reported in the *New York Times* on the role of social security for the elderly. They

TABLE 1.7 Major Sources of Financial Support in Retirement

52%	401(k) defined contribution plans, Individual Retirement Accounts, and Keogh plans for the self-employed
31%	Company pension plans that pay guaranteed retirement benefits
30%	Equity built up in a home
27%	Social Security

Source: Gallup Poll, April 2007.

found that the lowest third of the population rely on social security for more than 90% of their income; while the wealthiest third relies on social security for less than 50% of their income and the middle third for 50–90%. Thus the lowest third who really depend on social security face a relatively large decline in standard of living as social security strives to replace about half or less of their preretirement income, and they typically have been unable to garner other savings to fill the gap. To highlight the difference, Leland and Wilgoren report on two brothers which captures the range in benefits: one who had held a variety of low-paying jobs receives $502 a month; the other and his wife, who had steady careers at the local school district, collect a combined $2,400.

Social security regulations now have declining income replacement rates. From 2000 to 2030 income replacement is set to decline for low earners from 55.5% to 49.1%; for medium earners 41.2% to 36.5% and for maximum earners 27.3% to 24%. In that same period Medicare premiums will amount to more of the social security benefit, going from 6% to 9.2% with further increases set bring it to 13.6% in 2050. Further erosion will occur through taxation of benefits. With all the various deductions and adjustments the replacement rate in 2050 will be only 26.9% for those retiring at 65 and 20.8% for those retiring at 62.

Where is the rest of the income coming from? In 2001, about half of all US families owned a tax-favored retirement account with median balance of $29,000. Older households had somewhat larger tax-favored savings, with a median value of $55,000 for the 59% of families age 55–64 who had such accounts. As expected, tax-favored savings are concentrated among high-income households; the top 20% of the income distribution held two-thirds of the retirement savings accounts. The heavy reliance on social security among retirees up through the middle of the income distribution, the shift away from DB pensions, and increased use of 401(k) plans amplifies the importance of payout options that convert savings into guaranteed incomes during retirement (Reno 2005).

To improve income in retirement there have been shifts toward both working part time and working longer (5% greater share) as well as receiving marginally more from employer pensions and out of social security and other assets in the period 1980 to 2000 (Social Security Administration). At the same time there has been a great shift from DB (from 60 to 15%) to DC (from 18% to 55%) pensions (with a shift from 22% to 30% covered by both). This shows an increase in financial risk for the retired.

Total savings falling though a greater share of net worth is in housing equity. Alicia Munnell, who heads the retirement research center at Boston College states: "Nobody is enjoying much in terms of growth in net worth. No one has enough to support themselves in retirement for 20 years." This is supported by the Fed's 2004 survey, which reports that just under half of all families held retirement accounts. The typical family's savings (including retirement accounts) fell to $23,000, down $7,000 from three years earlier. For households headed by a retired person, the typical savings fell from $34,400 to $26,500. Also, the 95% of Americans 55 to 64 who had any savings at all typically had $78,000, which is only about 1.5 times their median annual earnings.

Rich and Porter (2006) reported that housing wealth is increasingly funding retirement via reverse mortgages (the income of many of the elderly does not qualify them for normal mortgages). From 2001 to 2004 household net worth barely increased, to $93,100 from $91,700. While total savings dropped by 23%, the value of homes rose 22%. Just over 69% of Americans owned their own homes in 2004 (76% for retiree households). The median value of their homes jumped to $160,000 in 2004 from $131,000 three years before, a rise of 22% (for retirees value $130,000). While few plan to draw equity from their homes it is an insurance policy that more and more are calling on.

Roadmap

In Part I, Chapter 2 investigates a variety of macro economic costs for retirement and highlights the important shift from DB to DC pension schemes, which shifts a lot of the risk from employers to employees and thus retirees. Chapter 3 looks at the various pillars of retirement and various reforms including proposals for reforming social security, pensions in trouble before the crisis. Chapter 4 defines various asset classes and presents their historical returns and risks. Chapter 5 explores the 2007–2009 economic crisis and its impact on retirement assets.

Part II includes more in-depth analyses of some of these issues. Chapter 6 investigates the role of population aging in savings behavior. They discover that savings rates have a hump shape, starting out low and then increasing before declining. This can be explained by considering that young workers in establishing themselves in their careers are both creating skills and thus building up a higher expected stream of income in the future and are investing in homes, and as we have seen, home ownership is an important component of expected retirement income. Chapter 7 presents a continuous time model of intergenerational surplus management applicable for life and other insurance companies, pension funds, and other organizations. Chapter 8 analyzes the shift from final salary to career average pensions and uncovers a number of advantages in career average schemes including improved pension equity among different types of workers and the possibility of reducing the disincentive to continued work after peak income has been earned. Chapter 9 presents a stochastic programming model to help the DB pension system survive. It uncovers substantial industry concentration of the DB problem with industry problems and pension funding issues impacting each other, something that is confirmed by the bankruptcies in the auto industry. Policy simulations help create rules for the troubled industries. Chapter 10 evaluates using capital markets to more effectively deal with the longevity risk imposed on pensions and insurance companies which could both offer additional capacity and liquidity to the market, as well as more transparency. Chapter 11 looks at the long-term retirement funding of national and state-level governments, which have been adopting two strategies: contributing more money and increasing their risk profile in the hopes of boosting returns. Chapter 12 looks broadly at issues relating to decumulating assets on retirement and includes a study of the risks of own company stock, and options related to housing, annuities, insurance, etc.

Part III brings the various issues together in an all-encompassing modeling framework. Chapter 13 discusses some of the important lessons in successful investment for the long term including lessons from endowment management and the great investors. Chapter 14 describes a successful case study of the development of a multiperiod stochastic programming model for the Siemen's Austria pension plan, which has been in use since 2000 for pension plans and regulators. Chapters 15 and 16 construct and then implement a similar model for individuals, asset-liability planning over time.

Chapter 17 summarizes the key issues in the aging-retirement dilemma. Innovation in concepts of retirement and retirement funding is needed. Caring for the elderly and the infirm is a societal problem, not just a family problem. Indeed it is a mark of how civilized a society is. Moreover, it is a key job creation opportunity and a mark of real services. We are now at a key time to reevaluate retirement in its economic and social aspects. So the question is in order to deal with these issues we will need to change the social contract that has led to the expectation of a long, leisurely retirement.

REFERENCES

Bureau of Labor Statistics. 2004. Labor Market Projections, BLS:2004–14.

Butrica, B., J. H. Goldwyn, and R. W. Johnson. 2005. *Understanding Expenditure Patterns in Retirement*. CRR WP 2005-03.

Consigli, G. 2007. Asset-liability management for individual investors. *Handbook of Asset and Liability Modeling, Volume 2: Applications and Case Studies*, S. A. Zenios, W. T. Ziemba (eds.), Handbooks in Finance Series, North Holland, 751–827.

Drucker, P. F. 1950. The mirage of pensions, *Harper's Monthly*, February.

The Economist. 2007. Japan's changing demography. Cloud, or silver linings? July 26.

Gowans, A. 2007. Good retirement community takes a complicated recipe. May 7. www.theromanway.org/phpBB/viewtopic.php?t=374.

Haas, M. L. 2007. A geriatric peace? *International Security* 32(1):112–147.

Leland, J., and J. Wilgoren. 2005. Living with Social Security: Small dreams and safety nets. *New York Times*, June 19.

Lowenstein, R. 2008. *While America Aged.* New York: Penguin Press.

Morris, C. R. 2006. *Apart at the Seams: The Collapse of Private Pension and Health Care Protections.* Century Foundation Press. www.socsec.org/publications. asp?pubid=553.

Munnell, A. H., F. Golub-Sass, and D. Muldoon. 2009a. An update on 401(k) plans: insights from the 2007 SCF. CRR Number 9-5.

Munnell, A., A. Webb, F. Golub-Sass, and D. Muldoon. 2009b. Long-term care costs and the National Retirement Risk Index. April, IB#9-7 CRR, Boston College.

OECD. 2008. Improving financial education and awareness on insurance and private pensions.

Reno, V. 2005. Payouts in individual accounts pose new questions. TIAA-CREF Policy Brief.

Rich, M., and E. Porter. 2006. Increasingly, the home is paying for retirement. *New York Times*, February 24.

Schwartz, S. L., and W. T. Ziemba. 2007. ALM in Social Security. In *Handbook of Asset and Liability Modeling, Volume 2: Applications and Case Studies.* S. A. Zenios and W. T. Ziemba (eds.). Handbooks in Finance Series, North Holland: 1069–1117.

Short, J. 2006. Confederate veteran pensions, occupation, and men's retirement in the new south. *Social Science History* 30(1):75–101.

Siegel, J. 2008. *Stocks for the Long Run,* 4th ed. McGraw-Hill.

Toner, R., and D. E. Rosenbaum. 2005. In overhaul of Social Security, age is the elephant in the room. *New York Times*, June 12.

Ziemba, W. T. 2003. *The Stochastic Programming Approach to Asset Liability and Wealth Management.* AIMR.

CHAPTER 2

The Various Costs of Pensions: Macro and Micro

Since the goods and services one wants to consume in retirement must come out of current production, the macro issues are crucial.

A growing systemic problem is that retirement money whether pension or social security, is thought of as *locked away* when it needs to be invested in R&D, infrastructure, and so on. Toyota could spend twice as much developing new cars as GM because GM's funds were tied up in pensions and health care and lobbying. So by its nature, funding pensions, though necessary to fulfill promises, exacerbates the problem. This is a micro problem of finding and funding real investment.

In the previous chapter we explored the demographics and the evolution of retirement. In this chapter we will look at some of the costs, macro and micro, of retirement as now envisioned

2.1 GOVERNMENTAL COST OF RETIREMENT

The governmental cost of retirement takes two forms. One is the direct cost of social pensions in the budget, the other is the taxes forgone as a result of company and individual tax-deferred pension plans.

In 2005 the average OECD spending on pensions was 7% of GDP. Countries above 10% were Austria, France, Germany, Greece, and Italy, and all of these saw spending continue to grow. Spending in Japan, Poland, and Portugal continued to grow and reached 10%. Six countries with high spending have reformed their systems and in the future will spend less (Austria, Finland, France, Germany, Italy, and Sweden). Finland, Luxembourg, Netherlands, New Zealand, and Norway have reduced expenditures. Hungary is relatively high, and as they are unwilling to have a progressive, redistributive system to improve the level of those in poverty, it must increase the level of the highest earners. This is costly, and it will approach 17.5% in 2050 (see Martin and Whitehouse, 2008).

The World Bank is concerned that the needed high rate of contributions could lead to avoidance of the formal economy and tax evasion. Often pensions redistribute income to the relatively well off, and tend to lower economic growth by reducing savings. The World Bank recommends a three-tier system. One tier is a fully funded defined contribution (DC) private pension for each worker. Another tier is a public pension plan directly for alleviating poverty in old age. The third tier is a voluntary corporate or personal savings. These tiers are investigated in Chapter 3.

2.2   PENSIONS AND CAPITAL FORMATION

Singh (1996) considers the debate on pay as you go (PAYG) versus fully funded systems focusing on the relationship between funded private pensions, the development of capital markets, savings, capital formation, and economic growth. It appears that the emerging markets invest the funds locally to help develop their capital markets. (See Reisen 1994 and Chapter 11). Developed countries might also invest in the emerging markets!

While capital markets in emerging economies grew from less than $100 billion to $1,000 billion between 1982 and 1992, the markets still represented a small percentage of GDP. At the same time the industrial countries saw markets grow from $3 trillion to $10 trillion. Chile, which experimented with market-based DC individual pension plans, did not have capital market growth out of the range of the other emerging markets, so there are a variety of ways to increase capital markets.

The next link is whether increased capital markets lead to capital formation and growth. Singh (1996) quotes Keynes:

> As the organisation of investment markets improves, the risk of the predominance of speculation does, however, increase. In one of the greatest investment markets in the world, namely, New York, the influence of speculation is enormous. Speculators may do no harm as bubbles on a steady stream of enterprise. But the position is serious when enterprise becomes the bubble on a whirlpool of speculation. When the capital development of a country becomes the by-product of the activities of a casino, the job is likely to be ill done.

Allen and Gale (1995) compare the economic results of stock market versus bank saving in the US and Germany. During the oil price shock of the 1970s, the US market fell to half and stayed there for a decade. Households that had invested in stocks for retirement needed to sell shares to pay for retirement and reduce their consumption. Then in the 1980s the trend reversed, and the market effectively doubled, and the standard of living went up. The key is the volatility. Meanwhile in Germany, where the funds were in bank accounts and debt instruments, the value of bank savings neither declined dramatically nor increased dramatically, and retirees were able to consume as they had planned with little volatility.

Do strong capital markets fuel savings and investment and promote growth? During the period 1970–1989, because of takeovers, equity markets in the US and UK had a negative effect on investment. In Germany and Japan the effect was net positive but small. In the four countries, the main source of growth was retained earnings. The companies prefer internal financing and debt over new shares (Singh 1996).

Table 2.1 looks at the role of pension assets and liabilities as a percentage of corporate market capitalization for the world's 500 largest corporations. The column that shows the deficit as a percent of the total debt plus the deficit (this total can be considered the total debt of the corporation) is a way of viewing how companies have funded assets from the pension deficit. This ratio is quite high in Japan, the UK, and France. Behind the averages is a variety of leveraging: in Japan, in the UK, one-third of the companies relied for half of their financing on pension liability, for Japan it was more than 20%. Chapter 9 looks at a model to save GM's pension.

TABLE 2.1 Pension Liabilities and Deficits of the World's 500 Largest Companies, 2004

Country	Number of Companies	Pension Liabilities (bil euro)	Pension Deficit (bil euro)	Liabilities to Market Cap Average (%)	Deficits to debt + deficit (%)
USA	167	727	72	20.5	7.5
Japan	58	294	126	29.0	26.7
UK	42	360	59	35.2	15.5
Germany	18	166	79	40.5	21.7
Canada	17	44	4	18.3	6.6
France	17	52	19	15.0	15.8
Switzerland	11	65	8	13.5	9.3
Hong Kong	1.7	0.2	3.4	0.0	
Other	38	117	24		

Source: Clark, Munnell, and Orszag (2006).

2.3 REGULATING CORPORATE PENSIONS

The provision of retirement funding began ad hoc without planning. In the beginning, corporate pensions were unregulated. Firms were able to use their essentially notational pension obligations as internal financing and to purchase their own shares and boost the share value. There were twin incentives when regulation did begin. One was to insure that the promises could be met and the other was to avoid overfunding and thus tax avoidance. In the US, the UK, and Canada, companies are responsible for underfunding but must return any overfunding,

After the 2000 crisis, funding rules changed and became more tight: In the US, upper interest increased from 105% to 120% thus lowering funding requirements. Also there are longer correction periods in Ireland and possibly Canada.

2.3.1 US Regulations

Initially pensions were very loosely regulated. Tax exemption was granted to qualifying plans, and contributions and earnings were tax exempt. However, there were abuses, and beginning in the 1950s there was some regulation.

In 1958, Congress enacted the Welfare and Pension Disclosure Act under the Department of Labor, which required full disclosure of all private pension plans. Though patterned on the regulation of securities, the essential difference was that corporation committees not individuals are responsible for the employees' participation. This act required submission of a plan including benefits and type of administration. For plans with more than 100 participants an annual report was also required. This was later replaced by the Employee Retirement Income Security Act (ERISA) of 1974.

The bankruptcy of Studebaker left behind empty pension promises. Their plan was established in 1950 after bargaining with the UAW. It granted prior service credit that amounted to an unfunded liability of about $18 million. Over time the promised benefits were increased, creating more unfunded liabilities, each time added past service benefits. Each future liability was amortized over a 30-year period. When Studebaker closed its South Bend auto plant in 1963, they were unable to pay their promised pensions. Employees that were age 60 or older (about 3,600) got full pension benefits; they had first claim on the pension assets and received in total $21.5 million leaving only $2.5 million for the remaining workers. Those 40–59 (4,000) with ten years service got a lump sum payment worth only about 15% of the value of their benefits. The average age of this group was 52 and averaged about 23 years of service. The rest, with no vested rights (2,900) got nothing. The company consolidated its remaining production at its Hamilton,

Ontario, plant. See, for example, Bonsall (2000) for a history of Studebaker and its bankruptcy.

After the Studebaker case, ERISA was enacted in 1974. Though pension plans are not required, once established, they are regulated. ERISA regulates vesting, minimum funding requirements, and survivor benefits. The Pension Benefit Guaranty Corporation (PBGC) was established by ERISA to provide termination insurance for defined benefit (DB) plans but not at the full benefits.

Prior to ERISA, pensions were not vested and were not provided to employees who left before retirement age. Currently vesting is generally after five years service. DC contributions are vested after three years. Regulations have been changed over the years making it more difficult for firms to plan pension obligations and have in part led to the freezing of DB plans and their replacement with DC plans (more on this later).

Initially, the requirements allowed much funding latitude, and firms could amortize liabilities over 30 years. Pension liabilities would be calculated annually and amortized, and assets were also amortized, the account had to stay in balance each year. Until 2006 these accounts were notational credit balances, also the amortization was tightened from 30 to 7 years and a mark-to-market was required rather than smoothing of valuations over a five year period. As of 2008 those plans are required to remain fully funded. If the account is not fully funded the difference is amortized over seven years. Multi-employer pension plans (generally industry plans) are more loosely regulated than individual accounts. See, for example, ERISA regulations available on their web site.

Plan balances were regulated to fall between 100% of actuarial and 150% of current liabilities. The the different accounting principles result in vastly different commitments and provide different degrees of protection for employees, different impacts on corporate profit, and result in different tax payments. (See Kopcke 2006). With the lower limit, many plans were in excess, and they were then prevented from further contributions. Unfortunately much of the gain was from market prices and was later lost. There were also taxes on reversion of funds from the plans, for instance, when taken over by corporate raiders. The accounting types include

ABO (accumulated benefit obligation): the present value of the earned pension based on current salary and service; this is the pension that would be paid at retirement if the employee ceased working but was vested in the plan.

PBO (projected benefit obligation): the present value of the earned pension based on projected salary up to retirement but not including credit for additional years of service.

CCR (constant contribution rate): contribute a fixed percentage of salary to smooth out the annual contributions.

> An example: an employee with 15 years of service, $68,000 annual salary, assume an additional 15 years of service and final salary of $140,000, pension would be $70,000 (half of final salary), for 20 years, discount rate = 5%. The present value in 15 years of the promised pension is $830,000. ABO: pension would be $17,000, that is, half of current salary scaled back to service credit of half the 30 years for a full pension. This will require $202,000 in 15 years. The present value today is $97,000. PBO: pension would be $35,000, half of final salary scaled back to current service credit of half of the 30 years. This would require $400,000 in 15 years, for a present value of $200,000

Looking at the first year of service, the ABO would require $1,600 and the PBO would require $6,400. These amounts are vastly different, and notice that the PBO would still be funded at only half the required amount at the end of 30 years service! The ABO funding would increase steeply as the employee continues work going from 5% to 47% for employees near retirement. The ABO and PBO funding options are shown in Figure 2.1; note that the scales are different. Figure 2.2 compares the rate of asset accumulation under the two funding strategies.

A rapidly growing company might contribute to the ABO level or avoid a DB plan altogether; a more mature company would likely use the PBO. However, when funding at PBO the employer takes on a variety of risks, including variation in labor costs and in the return making this option more costly. As the older plans mature, the ratio of PBO to ABO is approaching one: in 1990 it was 125% and in 2004 it was only 107%. In 1985 the ratio of active employees to retirees was 80:20, in 2004. it was approximately 50:50 (CIEBA 2004).

The commitment to DB plans is thus high, between one-and-one-half and four times wages. Compare this with national accounts replacement costs for capital (plant and equipment, software, inventories) at four times wages and salaries. Clearly this amount of funds would be tempting to the corporation as a source of internal financing, especially as US companies prefer internal financing to debt financing. Kopcke (2006) analyses the strategic options, but it is clear that as regulation increased in an attempt to protect retiree rights and giving fewer options to the corporations their incentive to opt out of DB plans has grown.

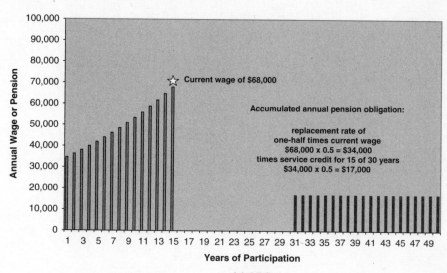

(a) ABO

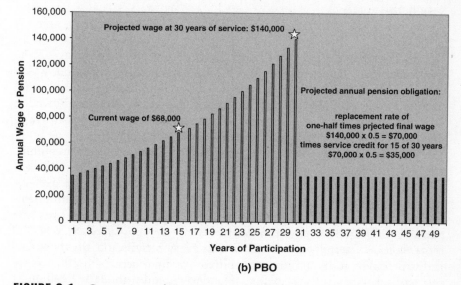

(b) PBO

FIGURE 2.1 Comparison of Two Funding Strategies for an Employee with 15 Years Service
Source: Kopcke (2006).

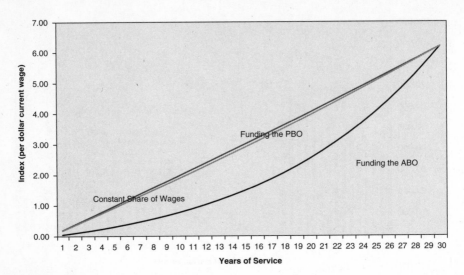

FIGURE 2.2   Comparing the Asset Accumulation under ABO and PBO for an Employee with 15 Years Service
Source: Kopcke (2006).

Another set of regulations beginning in 1986 related to caps on the salaries covered. The limits started at $200,000 indexed for inflation, which grew to $235,840 in 1993. Then Congress lowered the limit to $150,000 and to $200,000 in 2002. So while there was indexing, firms were not allowed to take this into account. These regulations made the plans more expensive to maintain (Munnell, Golub Sass, and Muldoon, 2009).

The PBGC is not government funded. It charges insurance premiums, holds assets from plans that are taken over, any unfunded liabilities it can recover, and investment income. The single-employer program protects 34.0 million workers and retirees in 28,800 pension plans. The multiemployer program protects 9.9 million workers and retirees in 1,540 pension plans. In 2009, PBGC pays retirement benefits to approximately 631,000 retirees of 3,800 terminated defined benefit pension plans. Initially the PBGC invested heavily in bonds but then shifted heavily to stocks in 2007. It estimates that the auto sector plans are underfunded by about $77 billion of which $42 billion would be guaranteed by PBGC. In the fiscal year ending September 39, 2008 it lost 23% and by April 30, 2009 it was $33.5 billion in deficit. At that time its asset allocation was 30% equities, 68% bonds, and 2% in alternatives, which were inherited from failed pension plans (PBGC 2009). It had been reported that they targeted an allocation of 45% equities, 45% bonds, and 10% alternatives (Wei, 2008).

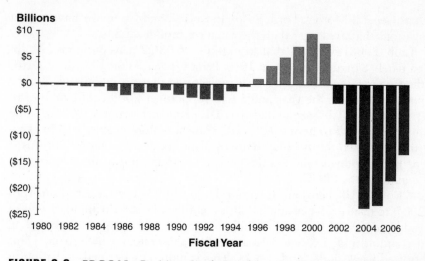

FIGURE 2.3   PBGC Net Position, Single-Employer Program, FY 1980-FY 2007
Source: PBGC (2007).

When PBGC takes over a fund there is a maximum payment, which is adjusted annually and is currently set at $4,312.50 a month (or $51,750 a year) for workers retiring at age 65.[1]

At the end of 2006, the PBGC estimated that the total underfunding in single-enployer insured DB plans on a termination basis was approximately $225 billion. After that they ceased publishing the estimates in their Annual Management Report. They are found in the Pension Insurance Data Book where the estimation limitations are described. Figure 2.3 shows the PBGC net position from 1980 to 2007.

It is hard to access what is actually happening to PBGC balances as it takes many years for bankruptcy to lead to the actual takeover of retirement plans of the bankrupt companies. For example, in September 2008 they took over the Rand McNally plan ($26.4 mil, 72% funded) from bankruptcy plans filed at the end of 2007.

In July 2008 when equity prices were down only 10% for the year, Credit Suisse issued a pensions report: The value of pension plans for S&P 500 companies has plunged by $170 billion even before the large third and fourth quarter declines. This reduced a $60 billion surplus from 2007 to a $110 billion deficit. The funded status of pensions appears on company balance sheets and must be marked-to-market annually. Some companies,

---

[1]In contrast, the Bank of England's pension scheme switched out of stocks and into index-linked gilts.

such as General Motors, Ford, Eastman Kodak, and Goodyear have benefit obligations that are larger than their market capitalizations.

Taub (2008) estimates that from 07Q2 to 08Q2 pension funds lost approximately $1 trillion or about 10%. Peter Orszag, at the time the director of the Congressional Budget Office conjectured that the cumulative decline in pension assets in the year and a half to October 2008 could amount to $2 trillion,. The CBO estimated that DB plans lost about 15%, dropping from 99% funded to about 92%. DC plans are more heavily weighted toward stocks (two-thirds plus) than DB plans so, declined more. But this is borne by individuals whereas the decline in funding ratios must be met by companies or the PBGC.

When the UK Pension Protection Fund (PPF) was established on April 6, 2005, to insure DB pension liabilities totaling about $1 trillion, they were already in deficit of about $134 billion. The PPF will charge plans based on underfunding and insolvency risk instead of a flat rate in which strong plans subsidized weak underfunded ones. This is more fair but makes the job of insurance more difficult as the weak must pay making them weaker (*The Economist* 2005).

2.3.2 Corporate Bankruptcies Leave a Trail of Broken Promises

Ralph Nader (2004) compiled a list of broken pension promises:

Change plan rules: Switch to a *cash balance* pension plan costing long-service salaried employees as much as half of their expected pensions, for example AT&T.

Shift plan on sale of subsidary: The law allows a parent company to transfer pension funds to the spun-off subsidiary; for example, Dresser-Rand, a division of Halliburton, took over the return funds from Halliburton which denied the employees their full early retirement pensions.

Reclassifying employees: Reclassifying employees as contractors as was done by Allstate to their staff insurance agents.

Changes after taking retirement: For example, GM cut back lifetime health insurance for its retirees after they accepted early retirement packages.

Own company stock in 401(k): MCI/WorldCom were told that the company stock was a sound investment, though the executives knew the company was inflating its books and they were selling their own company stock.

Time (2005) also wrote an article entitled "The Broken Promise" highlighting some of the ways in which DB plans could be abrogated.

Following United Airlines and USAirways, Delta and Northwest turned to bankruptcy court to cut costs and delay pension-fund contributions. In all, the pension funds of those airlines are short $22 billion.

On October 8, the largest US auto-parts maker, Delphi Corp., filed for bankruptcy protection, seeking to cut off medical and life-insurance benefits for its retirees. Its pension funds are short $11 billion. United Auto Workers leadership let GM rescind $1 billion worth of health-care benefits for its retirees.

From 1988 to 2004, the share of employers with 200 or more workers offering retiree health insurance plunged, from 66% to 36%.

Polaroid is an interesting case. Starting in 1988, employees contributed 8% of their salary to an employee stock-ownership plan (ESOP) created to stop a takeover as well as provide a retirement benefit as a supplement to their pension. However, from 1995 to 1998, the company lost $359 million. They sought bankruptcy protection at a time when its shares were virtually worthless, having fallen from $60 in 1997 to less than the price of a Coke in October 2001. The trustee sold the ESOP shares for 9 cents. A $300 million retirement account of 6,000 employees was wiped out. Many lost between $100,000 and $200,000. In 2002 Polaroid was sold to One Equity Partners for $255 million, a fraction of its value. In part, the buyers financed their purchase with $138 million of Polaroid's own cash. Employees each got a check for $4 and lost tens of thousands of dollars in ESOP contributions, health benefits, and severance payments. Polaroid quickly returned to profitability and the new managers received $12.08 a share (*Time*, 2005).

2.3.3 Comparing Regulation of Occupational Pension Schemes in the EU and the United States

Vesting of plans makes it possible to have labor mobility and also foster security of employment.

In France employers and employees must participate in plans that are industry- and sector-wide, and in turn vesting is immediate.

Disclosure of pension entitlements and rules vary among countries as shown in Table 2.2.

- The UK and Ireland require comprehensive disclosure of information; however, there still is a gap in understanding among plan members. In the UK membership in a scheme is not mandatory, but pensions are important as state pensions are low.

TABLE 2.2 Vesting Periods in the EU and US

Length of Vesting	Countries
Immediate	Denmark, France, Finland, Spain, Sweden
1 year	Belgium, Netherlands
2 years	UK
5 years	Austria, Greece, Ireland, Italy, United States
10 years	Germany, Luxembourg
None prescribed	Portugal

Source: Cooper (2000).

- Portugal requires only the publication of the scheme's constitution in the State Gazette.
- Italy only requires that the supervisory board receive an annual report, and there is no prescribed disclosure to plan members.
- Sweden only requires that unfunded liabilities be reported.

Portugal, Italy, and Sweden have limited communication, but the schemes are state run with high replacement rates. In other countries members receive information regularly (Cooper 2000). Minimum funding requirements are in Table 2.3. Insurance regulation includes an extra margin for solvency and possibly would help level out the funding level counter cyclically. Cooper also suggests that extra reserves could be required for volatile assets. Countries differ also on how they treat underfunded plans. In the US the amount of unfunded liability must appear on the balance sheet as primary debt, but history has shown that only about 10 cents on the dollar is recovered. However, in the UK, unpaid contributions are treated as deferred pay and is considered part of the debt along with other creditors.

Some form of insolvency insurance is generally available to protect the security of the plans, but these forms of insurance differ widely. For example in Austria, firms must put aside 50% of pension liabilities as a balance sheet item, but in case of bankruptcy this might provide little aid. Cooper points out that none of the protection schemes actually charges market value for the insurance provided, so the insurance agencies have limited reserves.

Another dimension on which countries differ is the role of member representation. In the UK and Ireland pensions are viewed as benefits provided and so controlled by the company. In continental Europe, there is member representation and often state representation as well (Cooper, 2000).

TABLE 2.3 Minimum Funding Requirements

Country	MFR Calculation Method	Basis	Amortization
Austria	None, mostly book reserves		
Belgium	ABO, assets quasi-market value pension funds regulated as insurance companies	7% immediate	
Denmark	None, defined contribution provision		
Finland	Mutual insurance within pooled scheme		
France	Mutual insurance within pooled scheme		
Germany	Regulated as insurance companies		
Greece	None		
Ireland	IBO	Run off	3.5 years
Italy	None		
Luxembourg	Newly introduced		
Netherlands	ABO	4% real	
	Greater of book or market value of bonds		
	Market value of equity and property		
Portugal	ABO	4.5%	Immediate
Spain	PBO with 4% margin	6%	10 years
Sweden	None, liabilities are effectively insured		
UK	IBO	Run off	5, or 1 year
	Asets market value		
US	ABO	Market	10 years
	Assets market value		

Source: Cooper (2000).

2.4 DC VS. DB: SHIFTING THE RISKS

As the cracks became apparent in DB plans, private plans have shifted to DC; this shifts many risks onto individual financial planning, making planning for retirement and more difficult.

Early corporate pensions were all DB. DC plans were introduced to help small businesses and the self-employed provide tax-sheltered savings for retirement. This is not at all the same as guaranteeing pensions but the possibility of individual accounts lulled people into thinking that they provided a reasonable substitute for DB pensions. While, historically, the large viable firms have stayed with their DB plans, they have proven to be a burden, especially when markets fall and the contribution level is high. By shifting to DC plans the investment risk is passed on to the employee.

The acceptance of DC alternatives has allowed the large firms that had been providing DB pensions to close them down and replace them with DC plans. Watson Wyatt predicts that by 2014 there will be more money in DC plans than in DBs. The regulation of DC plans is straightforward; basically the firm deposits the money in the individual accounts, and that's the end of the liability. There are advantages of DC plans: avoidance of the credit risk of bankruptcy; and improved labor mobility. But against these advantages there are a number of shortcomings.

Pierlot (2008) discusses the various risks and their distribution on a continuum; see Table 2.4 and Figure 2.4.

TABLE 2.4 Comparing Risk Allocation in DB and DC Plans

Risk	Description	DB Member	DC Member	DB Employer	DC Employer
Longevity	Risk of outliving pension savings		yes		
	Risk of increased cost			yes	
Investment	Volatility		yes	yes	
	Risk of need to consume savings		yes	yes	
Funding	Risk that obligations may fluctuate or increase	sometimes	yes	yes	
Sufficiency	Risk delay or having to accept lower standard of living	yes	yes		
Security	Risk pension won't be paid	yes			
Fiduciary	Risk of liability for failure of due standard			yes	yes

Source: Pierlot (2008).

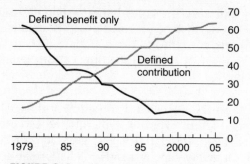

FIGURE 2.4 US Worker Participation in Retirement Plans by Type
Source: The Economist (2008), Employee Benefit Research Institute.

The types of pensions are:

1. Traditonal DB: employer promises benefits and funds plan; most of risk to employer, except if funding too high; but the employer may have layoffs or cease payment.
2. Public Sector DB: these are jointly sponsored so members have some risk, as salary can vary with funded status and benefits can be reduced; however, most of the risk is still borne by employer.
3. Cash Balance: acts like a DC plan, as there are individual accounts, but employer takes risk of minimum return.
4. Hyprid (DB/DC): can vary.
5. Union (member) funded DB: managed by unions and multiple employers contribute (auto industry), so for employers risk similar to DC plan, union bears risk of promised benefits.
6. Traditional DC: members bear risk.

Pierlot suggests the design of a DB that operates like a DC one. (See Figure 2.5). Employers contribute as in a DC plan, but members know their

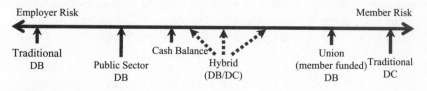

FIGURE 2.5 The Pension Risk Continuum
Source: Pierlot (2008).

balances so they can vary the contribution especially toward the end of one's career. They could also be operated as self-funded pensions, including funding toward a target.

There are a number of issues related to the shift from DB to DC (*The Economist*, 2008):

- Contributions to DC plans tend to be lower than DB plans, and the administrative costs are typically higher. In the UK, the average level of employers' payments into DB schemes, as of October 2007, was 14.2%; in DC schemes, the average was only 5.8%. Employees contribute 3% of their salaries to DC schemes, making a total of 8.8%, versus 19.1% for DB plans. In the US total DC contributions in 2009 were slightly higher at 9.8%.

- Participation rates are also lower: 61%, compared with 90% for final-salary schemes. Not only are workers undersaving, they are also turning down the contributions of their employers (about 6% which could add up to $300,000 over 40 years (assuming an average salary of $25,000 and an investment return of 7%).

- After 40 years of contributions, retirement income might be half of that of final salary DB plans. Unless the retirees are required to purchase an annuity, the money is likely to run out before death (US, Germany, and Australia do not have such requirements).

- Watson Wyatt estimates that the median 25 year old contributing at the British DC rate would earn a pension of about 30% of his final salary versus 66% for DB plans. Though partially offset by their lower contributions they also have investment risk; for about 5% of them, the pension would be worth just 15% of their final salary.

- A survey of 65 big US DC plans by *Pensions & Investments* magazine in 2008 found that 26% of their assets were in the parent company's shares. DB plans, with professional advice, would not have been so exposed (see Section 12.1 for an analysis of the optimality of own company stock).

- The employees in DC plans are not prepared for the complex investment decisions that combine the need to forecast lifetime earnings, asset returns, dynamic asset allocations, tax rates, inflation, and longevity. Rather than choose among many funds, they decide not to choose at all.

- Employees are heavily influenced by recent market conditions. US workers who began DC plans in 2000, at the height of the bull market, allocated 72% of their portfolio to the stock market; those who joined in 2003, after the long bear market, allocated just 48%. Once these decisions are made, inertia sets in; less than 10% of plan members in schemes run by Vanguard, a fund management group, change their asset allocation every year.

- The structure of the plans offered do not help in the decision making. Typically they focus on contributions not end goals. Over two-thirds of European plans surveyed by Mercer, had no formal objectives or goals.

- One study offered three groups of employees a choice of two funds. One group was offered an equity and bond fund, a second group an equity and balanced fund, and the final group a bond fund and a balanced fund. The most common option was a 50/50 split between the two funds, but that led to the second group having an equity weighting in their portfolio of 73% and the third group a weighting of just 35%.

In 2005, only 20% of the private sector work force still participated in DB plans versus about 40% in the mid-1980s. This represents 30,000 DB plans left, down from 112,000 in 1985, and that number will likely drop to zero in a decade. Many were in declining, old-line industries. There were then about 700,000 401(k) tax plans. US federal, state, and local government employees are also covered by DB plans. It has been estimated that unfunded liabilities of state and local DB plans are even higher than in the private sector, and these are typically the fastest-growing budget items (Morris 2006).

2.4.1 Pensions, Corporate Earnings, and Tax Deferral

Accounting procedures are complicated. There is the pull of various interests: governments want to create retirement security, and so they allow tax deferral on contributions to pensions, but at the same time they want to prevent pensions from being used as a tax loophole and encouraging too much money to be set aside in the pension accounts. In the end it is hard to avoid pension fund performance from affecting corporate earnings. Net liabilities flow through to the profit and loss statement. When earnings are over target, reducing liabilities, this is equivalent to a gain in profits and shortfalls increase liabilities and thus lower profits. Interest rates also affect liabilities. Lowered interest rates increase liabilities as the earnings potential of the fund declines. An example is United Airways. The problem was not the returns to fund management but the low contributions and the role of the interest rate on projected liabilities. Tax rules prevent firms from holding excessive contributions in the good times to cover expected shortfalls in the bad times. To prevent volatility in profits due to pension fund performance, ERISA allows a number of smoothing rules.

When plans are terminated, ERISA rules attempt an fair distribution, pro rata distribution. On termination, any unfunded liabilities disappear from the balance sheet thus immediately benefiting the corporation and its other creditors. Long-term employees often lose significant benefits upon a conversion.

- In 2004, of United's underfunded $9.8 billion pension, just $6.6 billion was guaranteed.
- Sears Holdings stopped further accruals to its pension plans after December 31, 2005. Retirees won't be affected.
- IBM and Motorola stopped offering new hires traditional pensions. IBM had already watered down pension plans for current staff. Avaya stopped accruals to its pension plan at the start of 2004.
- In 2005, GM had 2.5 retirees for every current worker.
- In the 1990s, big US steel companies with heavy pension obligations buckled under to global competition, including lean US minimills.
- In 2007 IBM moved to enroll all employees in its 401(k) and will offer its 127,000 financial advice on ALW management. Their plan comes at a cost of $50 million (Lusardi 2007).

Munnell et al. (2009) show that while the percent of private sector workers covered by a pension remains at about 50%, the type of pension has been changing dramatically from DB to DC; see Figure 2.6.

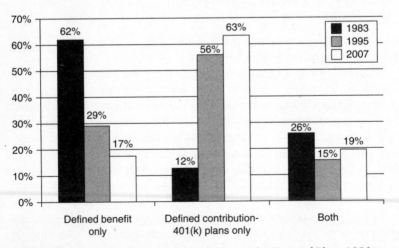

FIGURE 2.6 Workers with Pension Coverage by Type of Plan, 1983, 1995, 2007
Source: Munnell et al. (2009a).

The shift from DB to DC began in about 1981 with a number of regulatory changes:

- The ability to convert savings and profit-sharing accounts to 401(k); these plans were initially seen as supplementary.
- New 401(k) plans.
- Halt of new DB plans and terminations of existing DB due to bankruptcy as well as regulatory changes.

Longevity made lifetime annuities more expensive at the same time that interest rates were declining.

2.5   FREEZING PENSION PLANS

Butricia et al. (2009) model the impact on pension income of boomers of accelerating the transition of DB to DC. In the extreme scenario, private sector sponsors would, over the next five years, freeze all plans and a third of state and local plans. This would reduce average incomes at age 67. The impact would hit those in the 1961 to 1965 cohort highest as their pensions would be frozen with little tenure while they would have more time to make adjustments and accumulate DC pensions and personal savings.

There are a number of types of freezes:

Hard freeze freezes all accruals, only accrued benefits are paid on retirement, 85% are this type.

Soft freeze allows current employees to earn additional benefits from salary increase but not service, rarely used.

Closed freezes close to new entrants; about 13% are of this type.

A study by Munnell and Soto (2007) identified the firms that are most likely to freeze their pension plans:

- Plans with high credit balances
- Plans that are underfunded
- Plans where the actuarial liability is greater than the current liability
- Firms with poor credit ratings
- Non-union firms and firms with limited coverage of employees in the plan
- Firms facing global competition
- Firms with limited R&D
- Plans with large legacy costs

2.6   WHERE DO WE GO FROM HERE?

In 2009, the *New York Times* asked a number of experts their opinion of the future of retirement, and here are some of their comments:

- Alicia Munnell suggests the need for a new tier of retirement income as the 401(k) was not designed as a primary pension vehicle but as a supplement to a DB pension. The new tier would be designed to replace about 20% of preretirement income. She recommends something patterned after the Thrift Savings Plan offered to federal government employees. It is a low fee plan offered as part of the retirement package similar to the plans of TIAA-CREF or a 401(k). TSP had $191 billion under management for 4+ million participants with an overhead of only 30 cents per $1,000. Participants can choose among a group of funds or lifecycle funds that vary the allocations among asset classes depending on time horizon. Participants can change their allocations frequently. The allocations of the assets among the various funds for the Lifecycle funds is presented in Table 2.5. The name refers to the target years, for example L2040 means that the funds are needed around 2040. The government securities and fixed income funds had good returns; however, the record of the equity funds during the current crisis was at least as poor as other funds. Recognizing the risk, Munnell suggests that it would be useful to research guarantees and risk sharing.
- Teresa Ghilarducci, chairwoman of economic policy analysis at the New School for Social Research, the author of *When I'm 64: The Plot Against Pensions and the Plan to Save Them*, echoes Munnell. She calls the 401(k) a failed experiment with individual accounts for retirement. She suggests

TABLE 2.5 TSP Lifecycle Funds: Allocations among Various Funds, %

	Returns	Allocations				
	2008	L2040	L2030	2020	2010	Income
Government Securities Fund	3.75%	5	16	27	43	74
Barclays US Debt Index Fund	5.45%	10	9	8	7	6
Barclays Equity Index Fund	−36.11%	43	38	34	27	12
Barclays Extended Market Index Fund	−38.32%	18	16	12	8	3
Barclays EAFE Index Fund	−42.43%	25	21	19	15	5

Source: TSP (2008).

a guaranteed retirement account to which all workers and employers contribute 2.5%. For this they could get a refundable tax credit of $600. These would be credited to a lifetime pension with a guaranteed real 3% annual rate of return. Any surplus would be distributed among the funds. These accounts would insure that retirees not outlive their savings, nor would inflation reduce their buying power. Added to social security a full-time worker making $40,000 per year contributing into the plan for 40 years would receive roughly 71 of their preretirement income.

- David C. John, a senior fellow at the Heritage Foundation, comments that "401(k) plans will probably be replaced by 401(k) plans." His plans would modify 401(k)s with automatic enrollment, availability of phased annuity investments, and a change in the tax code that would deposit the tax benefits directly to the accounts to encourage more saving.
- Thomas C. Scott, chief executive officer of Scott Wealth Management and the author of *Fasten Your Financial Seatbelt* suggests that the future will borrow from the past as people prefer pensions they can count on rather than the dream of becoming a "401(k) millionaire." He expects to see new, more conservative financial products and government initiatives to encourage voluntary savings plans. While annuities are a good idea, only 5.5% of families owned an annuity because they tend to be complex.
- Jacob F. Kirkegaard, a fellow at the Peterson Institute for International Economics, expresses a concern that the tax breaks for 401(k) savings, amounting to $46 billion in 2007, go to the relatively well off 40% of the population. So he would like to see a plan that would extend to everyone and not favor risky investments.

REFERENCES

Alva, M. 2005. Corporate pensions going away as old firms decline, struggle; Sound companies move to 401(k)s as weak ones dump pensions on gov't (A). *Investor's Business Daily* May 26.

Allen, F., and D. Gale. 1995. A welfare comparison of intermediaries and financial markets in Germany and the US. *European Economic Review* 39.

Bonsall, T. E. 2000. *More than They Promised: The Studebaker Story.* Stanford University Press.

Butrica, A., H. M. Iams, K. E. Smith, and E. J. Toder. 2009. The disappearing defined benefit pension and its potential impact on the retirement incomes of boomers. CPP WP#2009-2

Clark, G. L., A. H. Munnell, and J. M. Orszag (eds.). 2006. *The Oxford Handbook of Pensions and Retirement Income.* Oxford University Press.

Committee on Investment of Employee Benefit Assets (CIEBA). 2004. The US pension crisis: Evaluation and analysis of emerging defined benefit pension issues. Association for Financial Professionals, March.

Cooper, D. 2000. The regulation of occupational pension schemes in the EU and U.S. Working Paper, City University.

The Economist 2005. Pension safety net, a premium price. July 14.

The Economist 2008. The trouble with pensions: Falling short. June 12.

Kopcke, R. W. 2006. Managing the risk in pension plans and recent pension reforms. Public Policy Discussion Paper 06-7. Federal Reserve Bank of Boston.

Lusardi, A. 2007. "401(k) Pension Plans and Financial Advice: Should Companies Follow IBM's Initiative?", Technical Note, Dartmouth.

Martin, J. P., and E. Whitehouse. 2008. Reforming retirement-income systems: Lessons from the recent experiences of OECD countries. Institute for the Study of Labor. DP No. 3521 (May).

Morris, C. R. 2006. Apart at the seams: The collapse of private pension and health care protections Century Foundation Press. www.socsec.org/publications.asp?pubid=553.

Munnell, A., A. Golub-Sass, and N. Karamcheve. 2009. Strange but True: Free loan from Social Security. CRR IB#9-6, Boston College.

Munnell, A. H., F. Golub-Sass, and D. Muldoon. 2009. An Update on 401(k) plans: insights from the 2007 SCF. CPP, Boston College.

Munnell, A. H., and M. Soto. 2007. Why are companies freezing their pensions? CRR WP 2007-22.

Nader, R. 2004. A trail of broken promises: Pension rights. CounterPunch www.counterpunch.org/nader03092004.html.

New York Times. 2009. So much for the 401(k). What's next? roomfordebate.com, March 25.

PBGC. 2009. PBGC deficit climbs. PBGC. 2007. Annual Management Report. May 20.

Pierlot, J. 2008. A pension in every pot: Better pensions for more Canadians. C. D. Howe Institute, No. 275, November.

Reisen, H. 1994. On the wealth of nations and retirees. *Finance and the International Economy*. In *Amex Bank Review Prize Essays*. Oxford University Press.

Singh, A. 1996. Pension reform, the stock market, capital formation and economic growth. A critical commentary on the World Bank's proposal. CEPA Working Paper.

Taub, S. 2008. The Bear Ate My Pension: $2 Trillion Worth, CFO.com, October 7.

Time. 2005. The broken promise, October 23.

Wei, S. 2008. Uncle Sam stocks up. *Wall Street Journal*, March 26.

CHAPTER 3

The Various Pillars of Retirement: Social Security, Company Pensions, Supplementary Pensions, and Private Savings

The typical household approaching retirement is at risk of having inadequate assets for a retirement that is similar to the life style they experienced while working. They face a variety of risks in different degrees depending on the structure of their assets and, especially, the form of pension plans and retirement savings they have been able to accumulate while working. These risks are shared in different degrees between the retiree, the employer, and even the government; and this varies across countries. This chapter explores the pillars of retirement and how they vary among countries.

3.1 PILLARS OF RETIREMENT

Key features of a national retirement package include adequacy versus income insurance; public versus private and corporate versus industry; or union versus individual responsibility. Most packages include a mix of these. These features give us the pillars or tiers of provision for retirement. From an economic point of view it might be best to consider the broadest categories:

1. Mandatory redistributive so that each individual attains a minimum income at retirement
2. Mandatory insurance that relates to income while working
3. Voluntary corporate or individual plans retirement savings
4. Personal savings

Number 2 comprises all defined benefit type programs both governmental, like social security, and corporate defined benefit (DB) pension plans where mandated. Sometimes corporate defined contribution plans (DC) are also included here, but there is a growing movement to classify these in number 3 (private savings) along with supplemental corporate saving programs as the risk is borne by the employee.

Social security, which combines parts of 1 and 2, is where demographics and public finance are most explosively entwined. In public perception it stands for a guarantee of income for retirement and the expectation that this promise will be fulfilled. The other pillars are occupational plans and personal savings. Fulfilling current expectations of publicly guaranteed income in retirement could cripple most nations. There are weaknesses or uncertainty in each of the other pillars as well. While default would be disruptive, large company pension plans or insurance companies can and have gone bankrupt leaving recipients without funds or avoiding bankruptcy by reneging on their obligations. Personal savings are hard to accumulate and to manage for the average worker. Thus social security is the main pillar that most people rely on. Changes in social security present a moral dilemma for governments since the public expects to receive the promised benefits.

Each of these can be classified as public-private, DB-DC, mandatory-voluntary, means tested-not means tested.

Different countries face varying degrees of vulnerability in their funds for retirement, and each came to the current reliance on social security by different paths. For comparison across countries we use the OECD Pension Tiers:

1. The safety net: redistribution (minimum standard of living): all OECD countries have some form of redistributive pension, which may relate to years of work but not earnings, may be means tested or a flat rate overall, all are mandatory and publicly funded.
2. DB depends on earnings. Two countries (Ireland and New Zealand) lack this tier. Four countries have point systems (French occupational and German, Norwegian, and Slovak public plans): contributions accumulate points, and on retirement these are converted to DB when multiplied by a point value. Four have private occupational schemes (Netherlands and Sweden have explicit DB; Iceland and Switzerland have set the rate of contribution, minimum rate of return, and annuity rate, which together determine the DB). Next are the DC plans, which are converted into pensions on retirement.
3. Supplementary (employer or individual).

One issue is that while social security schemes originally were intended as number 1, a safety net, they have become number 2, insurance based on income, thus creating a larger liability. Interestingly, in Europe number 2 is occupational while in North America it is governmental.

OECD reports annually on pensions of the member countries. They compare countries based on income replacement rates (gross and net); pension wealth (gross and net); various core objectives (progressivity and link with earnings); and pension levels two weighted averages: pension levels and wealth and structure. For a description of how pensions work over the range of incomes, the OECD looks at mean earnings and .5, .75, 1.5, and 2 times those earnings. Earnings overtime are standardized to a percentage of the average earnings at each time.

Table 3.1 shows the gross replacement rates from mandatory pensions by earner category for the OECD countries. These are for men. The average gross replacement rate from mandatory pensions is 59% but this varies up to 90% for Greece and down to 34.4% for the UK. For low earners this is 73% rising to 120% in Denmark, and the lowest is Germany at 40%. High earners in Ireland receive the lowest rate. The net replacement, after tax, averages about 11% higher at 70%, For low earners the average net replacement rate is 83%; this is lowest in the Anglophone countries at 76% and highest in the Nordic countries at 95%. A few countries have a lower income replacement rates for women: Italy at 78%, Poland at about 73%; Mexico which starts a the same rate as men but tapers off to 83% at the mean earner. Several things are reflected here: women typically retire five years earlier (at 60 rather than 65) and live longer. However, they typically earn less than men so on net end up with lower retirement income.

Taxation is also important in determining net replacement. On net, Greece and Turkey replace more than the wage. Reforms have lowered the total promised social pensions by about 22% for men and 25% for women.

Pension wealth at retirement is a unique measure applied by the OECD, which encompasses the age of eligibility, life expectancy, and the revaluation or indexation of benefits. Luxemburg has highest at 18 times annual earnings for men and 22 for women (US$587,000). The lowest is found in Ireland, Mexico, New Zealand, UK, and the United States at six times earnings. Eligibility is 65 for most countries, 67 for the US, Iceland, and Norway. And less than 65 for the Czech Republic, France (60), Hungary, Korea, the Slovak Republic, and Turkey. See OECD (2005) *Pensions at a Glance: Public Policies Across OECD Countries*. See the 2007 report for an update.

The length of career makes a difference in some countries. On average, five years less results in 5% lower replacement rate. However in the US the maximum is reached after 35 years so a change in five years does not affect the rate.

The OECD average additional life expectancy at 65 is 16.9 for men and 21.6 for women. For the model, they assume 3.5% yearly return on DC pensions.

TABLE 3.1 Gross Replacement Rates by Income Group

	Median	0.5	0.75	1	1.5	2
Greece	95.7	95.7	95.7	95.7	95.7	95.7
Luxembourg	90.3	99.8	92.1	88.3	84.5	82.5
Denmark	83.6	119.6	90.4	75.8	61.3	57.1
Netherlands	81.7	80.6	81.5	81.9	82.4	82.6
Spain	81.2	81.2	81.2	81.2	81.2	67.1
Austria	80.1	80.1	80.1	80.1	78.5	58.8
Iceland	80.1	109.9	85.8	77.5	74.4	72.9
Hungary	76.9	76.9	76.9	76.9	76.9	76.9
Korea	72.7	99.9	77.9	66.8	55.8	45.1
Turkey	72.5	72.5	72.5	72.5	72.5	72.5
Italy	67.9	67.9	67.9	67.9	67.9	67.9
Sweden	63.7	79.1	66.6	62.1	64.7	66.3
Finland	63.4	71.3	63.4	63.4	63.4	63.4
Switzerland	62.0	62.5	62.1	58.4	40.7	30.5
Poland	61.2	61.2	61.2	61.2	61.2	61.2
Norway	60.0	66.4	61.2	59.3	50.2	42.7
Slovak Republic	56.7	56.7	56.7	56.7	56.7	56.7
Czech Republic	54.3	78.8	59.0	49.1	36.4	28.9
Portugal	54.3	70.4	54.5	54.1	53.4	52.7
France	51.2	63.8	51.2	51.2	46.9	44.7
Canada	49.5	75.4	54.4	43.9	29.6	22.2
Australia	47.9	70.7	52.3	43.1	33.8	29.2
New Zealand	46.8	79.5	53.0	39.7	26.5	19.9
US	43.6	55.2	45.8	41.2	36.5	32.1
Belgium	40.7	57.3	40.9	40.4	31.3	23.5
Germany	39.9	39.9	39.9	39.9	39.9	30.0
Ireland	38.2	65.0	43.3	32.5	21.7	16.2
Japan	36.8	47.8	38.9	34.4	29.9	27.2
Mexico	36.6	52.8	37.3	35.8	34.4	33.6
UK	34.4	53.4	37.8	30.8	22.6	17.0
OECD	60.8	73.0	62.7	58.7	53.7	49.2

Source: OECD (2007).

The types of pension systems are shown in Table 3.2. Some of the countries are evolving pension systems beyond the traditional DB/DC types. There are variants of points schemes. The points systems of France (occupational schemes) and Germany, Norway, and the Slovak Republic (public schemes) are converted on retirement by a pension point variable. The plans of Italy, Poland, and Sweden earn a notational interest rate and then are converted at retirement based on life expectancy. These schemes are discussed below. Switzerland has a hybrid system in which there is a mandatory DC scheme

TABLE 3.2 Pension Systems in OECD Countries

Country	Tier 1	Tier 2
Australia	Targeted	Private DC
Austria	Targeted	Public DB
Belgium	Minimum credit	Public DB
Canada	Basic + targeted	Public DB
Czech Republic	Basic	Public DB
Denmark	Basic + targeted	public + private DC
Finland	Targeted	Public DB
France	Targeted + minimum	Public DB + points
Germany	Social	Public
Greece	Minimum	Public DB
Hungary	–	Public DB + private DC
Iceland	Targeted	Private DB
Ireland	Basic	–
Italy	Social assistance	Public notational accounts
Japan	Basic	Publi DBc
Korea	Basic	Public DB
Luxembourg	Basic + minimum	Public DB
Mexico	Targeted	Private DC
Netherlands	Basic	Private DB
New Zealand	Basic	–
Norway	Basic + targeted	Public points
Poland	Targeted	Public notational accounts + private DC
Portugal	Minimum	Public DB
Slovak Republic	Minimum	Public DB
Spain	Minimum	Public DB
Sweden	Targeted	Public notational accounts + private DB + DC
Switzerland	Targeted	Public DB + private defined credits
Turkey	Minimum	Public DB
UK	Basic + targeted	Public DB
US	Targeted	Public DB

Source: Queisser et al. (2007).

and a minimum rate of return, so the plan mimicks a DB plan (Queisser et al. 2007).

The balance between Tier 1 and 2 and public and private mandatory pensions is shown in Table 3.3. Some of the countries with high private mandatory pensions may be experiencing hardship with the fall in the market; for instance, in Austria it has been suggested that they revert to public pensions only. This table obscures some of the aspects of the different

TABLE 3.3 The Balance between Tier 1 and 2 and Public and Private Mandatory Pensions, OECD Countries

	First Tier			Second Tier						
	Resource Tested	Basic	Minimum	Tier 1	Public	Private DB	Private DC	T Public	T Private	RR
Mexico		11.9	4.3	16.2			83.9	32.3	83.9	36.6
Iceland	5.7	13.3		19.0		81.0		38.0	81.0	80.1
Netherlands		38.2		38.2		61.8		76.4	61.8	81.7
Denmark	12.5	31.5		44.0			56.0	88.0	56.0	83.6
Slovak Republic			0.2	0.2	45.3		54.5	45.7	54.5	56.7
Australia	45.8			45.8			54.2	91.6	54.2	47.9
Poland			0.3	0.3	48.8		50.9	49.4	50.9	61.2
Sweden			4.7	4.7	49.0	26.4	20.0	58.4	46.4	63.7
Hungary				0.0	65.9		34.1	65.9	34.1	76.9
Switzerland	0.1		0.4	0.1	68.4	31.5		68.6	31.5	62.0
Norway		30.1	0.1	30.5	58.5		11.1	119.5	11.1	60.0
Greece				0.1	99.9			100.0	0.0	95.7
Luxembourg		13.4	0.1	13.5	86.6			100.0	0.0	90.3
Spain			0.2	0.2	99.8			100.0	0.0	81.2

Country								
Austria				0.0	100.0	100.0	0.0	80.1
Korea		52.0		52.0	48.1	100.0	0.0	72.7
Turkey			0.8	0.8	99.2	100.0	0.0	72.5
Italy	0.1			0.1	99.9	100.0	0.0	67.9
Finland			1.5	1.5	98.5	100.0	0.0	63.4
Czech Republic		17.2		17.2	82.8	100.0	0.0	54.3
Portugal			3.5	3.5	96.5	100.0	0.0	54.3
France	1.3		1.9	3.2	96.8	100.0	0.0	51.2
Canada	16.5	34.5		51.0	49.0	100.0	0.0	49.5
New Zealand		100.0		100.0		100.0	0.0	46.8
United States				0.0	100.0	100.0	0.0	43.6
Belgium			5.4	5.4	94.6	100.0	0.0	40.7
Germany	1.1			1.1	98.9	100.0	0.0	39.9
Ireland		100.0		100.0		100.0	0.0	38.2
Japan		40.2		40.2	59.8	100.0	0.0	36.8
UK	0.5	50.8	33.9	85.2	15.0	100.0	0.0	34.4
OECD	2.8	1.9	17.8	22.5	58.7	87.8	18.9	60.8

Source: Adapted from OECD (2007).

structures as it considers only Tier 1 and 2 mandatory plans. So it appears that all the US pensions are public since the only thing that is mandated is social security and that is income based. Also in Canada the only mandated plans are public while many people have company and personal accounts. In Europe, private plans and even private supplemental plans are sometimes mandated. In Denmark and Sweden components of Tier 2 private DC plans include occupational schemes. In France the public pension includes both the state (59.3%) and the occupational (37.5%) components.

In many countries individuals need to have voluntary savings to make up the gap to the average OECD replacement rate of 58.7%. Twelve countries have mandatory plans that fall below the average: France, the Czech Republic, Canada, Australia, US, Belgium, Germany, New Zealand, Mexico, Japan, Ireland, and the UK are the countries with gaps varying from about 7.5% for France to 28% for the UK. Voluntary plans also improve the replacement rate in other countries. Approximate values for coverage of voluntary private pension plans is shown in Table 3.4.

TABLE 3.4 Coverage of Voluntary
Private Pensions

Country	Coverage (%)
Canada	64
Germany	63
US	55
Ireland	52
UK	51
Norway	45
Japan	45
Belgium	45
Spain	40
Czech Republic	40
Austria	40
Hungary	30
Slovak Republic	26
Luxembourg	24
New Zealand	22
Finland	22
France	20
Italy	10
Portugal	5

Source: Adapted from OECD (2007).

3.2 REFORMING OECD PENSIONS

In recent decades, all countries have been reforming the structure of income in retirement. Raising the age of pensions was the most common reform. This countered the past lowering of the age: the average fell from 64.5 in 1958 to 62.2 in 1993 for men and from 61.8 to 60.7 for women. The aim is to have an OECD full benefit pension age of 65 (or 67 in Denmark, Germany, Iceland, Hungary, US, UK). However, the effective age is often lower, so policy is directed toward raising the age and increasing labor force participation among older workers. Reinforcing the trend in higher employment rates for older people since the 1990s, the UK Labor government has stated its aim is to get up to one million more older workers back into employment. But this has obscured some very real problems involved in extending working lives.

Other changes include extending the number of years over which the pension is calculated. For example France went from best 10 to best 25. Other countries (Finland, Poland, Slovak Republic, and Sweden) are changing to using lifetime earnings (as does Canada). See Table 3.5. The Eastern European and Central Asian countries are also moving toward lifetime earnings. Chapter 8 analyzes the move toward lifetime earnings for faculty pensions in the UK.

Another strategy has been to revalue past income, essentially deflating it by inflation. This can lower the pension by 40%. In turn the pension itself is to be only partially indexed to inflation versus wage growth.

Some countries are moving from DB to DC (Hungary, Mexico, Poland, Slovak Republic, Sweden). Some have gone from DB to notional accounts (Italy, Poland, Sweden). A final reform is to turn the pension into an annuity; this will create an automatic adjustment to further longevity changes. Martin and Whitehouse (2008) provide simulations of how the various reforms affect the income replacement rates of low and average workers.

3.3 CHANGING ROLE OF PRIVATE PENSIONS

Some countries—Hungary, Mexico, Poland, the Slovak Republic, and Sweden—have no mandatory private pensions to substitute for part of the public pensions. Iceland, Switzerland, and the UK have required these private pensions since at least the 1980s. In Denmark, the Netherlands, and Sweden industrial agreements provide coverage for at least 80% of the workforce. (Martin and Whitehouse 2008, p. 14). Other countries have private pensions, though not mandatory. See Figure 3.1. In some of the countries, the total replacement is less than originally.

TABLE 3.5 Earnings Measure and Valorization for Earnings-Related Schemes in the High Income OECD Countries

High-Income OECD Countries	Earnings Measure	Valorization
Australia	n.a.	n.a.
Austria	Best 15 years, moving to 40 years	Yes, to be decided (earnings probable)
Belgium	Lifetime average	Prices
Canada	Lifetime average, excluding 15% of worst years	Average earnings
Denmark	n.a.	n.a.
Finland	Final 10 years, moving to lifetime average	50% of prices and 50% of average earnings, moving to 80% of prices and 20% of average earnings
France	Best 20 years, moving to 25 years (public)	Prices (public)
	Lifetime average (occupational points)	Prices (occupational)
Germany	Lifetime average (points)	Average earnings; adjustment for changes in contributions and potential contribution to voluntary pensions
Greece	Final 5 years	Pension increases of public sector workers
Iceland	Lifetime average (occupational)	Fixed rate
Ireland	n.a.	n.a.
Italy	Lifetime average (notional accounts)	Moving to an average of GDP growth over 5 years
Japan	Lifetime average	Average earnings
Korea, Rep. of	Lifetime average	Average earnings
Luxembourg	Lifetime average	Average earnings
Netherlands	Lifetime average for approx. two-thirds, and final for one-third of schemes (occupational)	Average earnings (occupational)
New Zealand	n.a.	n.a.
Norway	Best 20 years (points)	Average earnings
Portugal	Best 10 out of final 15 years, moving to lifetime average	75% prices and 25% average earnings with maximum real growth of 0.5%

TABLE 3.5 (*Continued*)

High-Income OECD Countries	Earnings Measure	Valorization
Spain	Final 15 years	Prices up to 2 years before retirement
Sweden	Lifetime average (notional accounts) Final (occupational scheme)	Average earnings with adjustment for demographics (notional accounts)
Switzerland	Lifetime average (public scheme)	Average earnings
	Lifetime average (occupational)	Minimum interest rate specified
United Kingdom	Lifetime average	Average earnings
US	Best 35 years	Average earnings up to age 60; prices from age 62 to 67

Source: Martin and Whitehouse (2008).

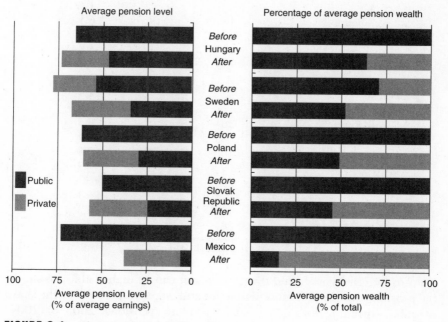

FIGURE 3.1 Changing Role of Private Pensions
Source: OECD (2007).

TABLE 3.6 Pension Contribution Rates (Employee and Employer) as well as the Share of Public Spending for Old-Age and Survivors' Pensions, 2003 or 2004

Country	Pension Contribution 2004	Public Spending 2003
Australia	n.a.	4.1
Austria	22.8	13.2
Belgium	16.4	9.3
Canada	9.9	4.4
Czech Republic	28	8
Denmark	n.a.	7.2
Finland	21.4	6.4
France	24	12.3
Germany	19.5	11.7
Greece	20	12.4
Hungary	26.5	8.7
Iceland	n.a.	4.2
Ireland	n.a.	3.7
Italy	32.7	13.9
Japan	13.9	9.3
Korea	9	1.4
Luxembourg	16	6.5
Mexico	n.a.	1.2
Netherlands	28.1	5.8
New Zealand	n.a.	4.5
Norway	n.a.	7.4
Poland	32.5	12.4
Portugal	n.a.	10.5
Slovak Republic	26	6.5
Spain	28.3	8.4
Sweden	18.9	10.8
Switzerland	9.8	7.2
Turkey	20	n.a.
UK	n.a.	6.1
US	12.4	6.3
OECD (21)	20	7.7

Source: Adapted from OECD (2007).

Costs to the worker and the government can be high. Table 3.6 shows the pension contribution rates (employee and employer) as well as the share of public spending for old-age and survivors' pensions, 2003 or 2004. Hungary: 26.5% gross earnings, higher than OECD average of 20% in 2004, since then contributions have increased to 33.5%. In the period 1994–2004, only a few countries have significantly increased their contribution rates: Canada almost doubled, Korea increased by 50%, Finland increased by 15%, and France by 12%. Surprisingly, a few countries actually lowered their contributions: Japan and the Netherlands by 15%, Hungary by 13%, the Slovak Republic by almost 9%. The share of the budget varied little in the period 1990–2003 except for Poland up 7%, the Slovak Republic up 6.5%, Portugal up 5%; while Luxembourg and New Zealand were down about 3%.

3.3.1 Summarizing Pension Reforms in the OECD

An OECD (2007) report investigates four dimensions: financial (how much less will future benefits be), distributional impact across earning groups; structure between public and private and incentives to continue to work. Most countries have been increasing the retirement age to 65 (US, Iceland and Norway to 67) for men; many are also making the retirement age for women equal to that of men. France has the lowest eligibility at 60.

Penalties for early retirement and increases in the number of contribution years are also being instated (OECD, 2006). Some countries are paying bonuses or higher accrual rates to those who work longer.

Countries are also increasing the span over which the pension is calculated (France from top 10 to top 25 years; Austria from 15 to 40; most now use lifetime earnings).

Some countries are switching from DB to DC plans as part of their public plans, and some are adjusting to a points system which has a similar effect. Also, to dampen the effects of inflation, some countries are moving from indexation on wages to partial indexation on prices. Other countries are moving from PAYG to prefunding pensions, increasing ceilings, etc.

Still even with the reforms, the proportion of GDP spent on pensions has increased; for the OECD on average it increased from 6.7% in 1990 to 7.7% in 2003. Italy is the highest, growing from 10.2 to 13.9. Austria is also high, going from 11.9 to 13.2. A few countries have seen declines, notably New Zealand (−2.9) and Finland (−1.7).

There has been a growing role for private pensions. In 11 countries, the private pensions provide a part of the mandatory pension. Voluntary pensions also play a role, which is substantial (coverage >25%) in 13 countries.

There were a number of salient issues:

1. Countries are reforming, some still lag behind (all have made some changes).
2. Reforms are slow.
3. Countries need more private savings.
4. Some still encourage early retirement.
5. There is greater risk of poverty in old age.

3.4 PLANS FOR REFORMING SOCIAL PENSIONS

The ideas to reform social pensions encompass three main approaches one changes the contribution rates, benefit payout and age to retirement, the other seeks to improve the return on the funds held in trust by exploiting the equity risk premium and a third seeks to break the link to a fixed monetary payout. This section follows the discussion in Schwartz and Ziemba (2007).

To rephrase the problem in the case of the US: in the beginning there was an extra return to early participants and the ratio of dependents to supporters was very low. This windfall is in the very nature of a PAYG system as early retirees will not have contributed to the fund for their entire working life thus creating an immediate *deficit* This continued in effect while coverage expanded and while the population was growing. Geanakopolos, Mitchell, and Zeldes (1998) estimated that the transfer to those born before 1917 was $15.7 trillion. Now with a more stable population and greatly improved life expectancy, the bonus is dropping, and the return on contributions is falling to the steady state rate first identified by Samuelson (1958) as the rate of growth of total wages—labor growth plus productivity improvements. This has led to the consideration of ways to improve the return to cover all the economy including the return to capital. For this there would need to be a direct way for social security savings to tap into capital formation. This has led to the proposals for investment of funds in the stock market. Unfortunately there is not a direct link between stock market investment and capital formation. This gives rise to two opposing views: that investing some of the contributions will improve the accumulation in the social security accounts and the other attesting that the impact will be nil as the added investment would raise share prices and benefit current owners and later depress prices just when people would need the funds. So part of the issue is how to deal not just with the financial issues of allocating the funds but also the real economic effects of creating sufficient goods and services to meet the needs of the retired.

One important aspect of the debate is the types of risks faced by retirees: longevity risk; spousal survivorship risk; inflation risk; investment risk, and, specifically, how they are borne. For example, a life annuity is a financial product that allows a retiree to shift longevity risk and investment risk to an insurance company but opens up credit risk.

3.4.1 Increase Contributions, Cut Benefits, Extend Working Life

Public pension plans around the world face the same demographic challenges as the US social security system. In many cases the demographics of comparable countries have even higher dependency ratios. Almost universally the reforms have been met with protests.

Increasing reserve funds by increasing the contribution rate would provide security that the system will not default, but this is a drain on the system similar to a tax increase. It is possible that slower growth in some European countries is due to increased contribution rates that lowers consumption and growth. Model simulations at the OECD (2005) show that with the proposed types of reforms (increased retirement age, lower payouts, increased contribution rates) only about a 1% increase in private savings would be expected.

Lowering the liability by increasing the retirement age. In the US the retirement age is set to increase from 65 to 67. However, there are obstacles to extending the age of retirement. In Japan and many European countries, one of the biggest is a pay scale that increases with age. In France and Germany 50- to 65-year-olds earn 60–70% more than 25- to 30-year-olds. In Britain where they earn about the same, employment of older people is higher. This is seen in a growing disparity of unemployment rates among 55- to 64-year-olds in various European countries: in 1990 it was roughly even at about 7% while in 2003 it was only 3.3% in Britain and 9.7% in Germany (some of this may be related to the reunification of east and west).

There is a correlation between the average retirement age and the rate of employment of older workers. In Sweden with the highest average retirement age of almost 64 the labor force participation rate of the 55–64 age group is almost 70% while in Poland with the lowest average the retirement age of 57 has a participation rate of about 25%. The other countries fall in between. Switzerland is an anomaly with a retirement age of 61 but a participation rate of almost 70%, equal to Sweden; (*The Economist*, 2006).

There are social aspects that limit the extension of the working age. In some countries like China, early retirement is institutionalized to provide a good career path for younger workers with women retiring at 50 and men at 55. On the other hand, later retirement might also mean that younger workers would end up supervising older ones.

Switzerland increases the state pension by SFr5,000 ($3,825) per year for people who stay at work for up to five years beyond the statutory retirement age. This has been effective: more than 60% of all 55- to 64-year-olds are in work, compared with less than 30% in Italy and Belgium. In Britain a person cannot receive a pension and a salary from the same employer and in the US, pension plans often withhold benefits from a retired person who is rehired or works for more than 40 hours a month. In Japan companies rehire retired employees on one-year renewable contracts. (*The Economist* 2006)

Chateau and Chojnicki (2008) take the population distribution in 2000 and advance it to 2050 with assumptions on survival, fertility, and

TABLE 3.7 The Dependency Ratio in Three European Countries

		2000	2005	2010	2020	2040	2050
Germany	60+ to 20–59	41%	46%	47%	56%	77%	81%
	65+ to 20–64	26%	31%	34%	38%	58%	57%
France	60+ to 20–59	38%	38%	42%	52%	67%	71%
	65+ to 20–64	27%	28%	28%	35%	49%	51%
UK	60+ to 20–59	38%	39%	43%	48%	63%	66%
	65+ to 20–64	26%	27%	28%	33%	46%	47%

Source: Chateau and Chojnicki (2008).

immigration. Their dependency ratios for Germany, France, and the UK are in Table 3.7.

Their estimation shows the improvement in the dependency ratios if retirement is postponed as it would give some time for society and the structure of work to adapt to the need to work longer and postpone retirement.

A good retirement scheme should not discourage workers who want to continue to work.

3.4.2 Use the Contributions to Buy Stocks instead of Government Bonds

Some suggest that the trouble with public pensions is that they are invested in government bonds rather than equities, which in the long term earn an additional 4% more per year. See Chapter 11 for a discussion the the sovereign pension plans.

Some countries have moved to invest their social pensions in equities. Canada did this in 1997. The government was cognizant of the desire of Canadians to preserve the Canadian pension plan yet needed higher assets. In 1997 the federal and provincial governments adopted a balanced approach to reform to bring the plan to sustainability, a manageable contribution rate of 9.9% (up from 1.8% when it was established in 1966). There was limited change in benefits, a moderate increase in contribution rates, and the creation of an asset pool to be invested in the markets and managed at arm's length from government for the best possible rates of return. This moved the CPP from a PAYG system to partially funded system. The market investment policy is implemented by an independent organization, the Canada Pension Plan Investment Board, set up in 1998 investing by 1999. The CPPIB reflects a fundamental policy change in policy. Prior to the CPPIB, the policy was to invest surplus funds in provincial government bonds at the federal government's investment rate. This was an undiversified portfolio with an interest rate subsidy to the provinces much like the US social security trust fund. The CPPIB investment policy is similar to other large public pension plans in Canada, such as the Ontario Teachers' Pension Plan and the Ontario Municipal Employees' Retirement System. It invests in a diversified portfolio of market securities (including international) under investment rules that require the prudent management of pension plan assets in the interests of plan contributors and beneficiaries and is free to hire its own independent professional managers. The CPP is transitioning to have 20% prefunded by 2017 though the creation of the CPP reserve fund. Their goal is a 4.41% real (inflation-adjusted) return.

The OECD (2005) report on Ageing and Pension System Reform points out that the shift from public pensions to market based ones also shifts risk to the individual. The report recommends that the government minimize this risk by facilitating new financial instruments including issuing more long-term debt and index-linked bonds. This might increase the cost of carrying the debt. They also observe the need to deal with longevity risks; see Chapter 10 for more on this.

Alternatively, pension assets could be invested in socially relevant projects to expand productivity and capacities in goods and services that will be consumed by the elderly—investment in health care and health care research, public transit, and other infrastructure projects.

Those who advocate for equities state that "stocks have never lost value over the long term." However, this is a statement of a stock index or the market overall. Individual stocks have lost value and companies have gone bankrupt. The odds are against individuals investing successfully. They tend to pick investments with equal weightings therefore making the design of opportunities offered of crucial importance; see Benartzi and Thaler (2001). However, studies such as Kallberg and Ziemba (1981) show that out-of-sample, the 1/n strategy performs well compared to optimized portfolios. See Chapters 4 and 13 for more on investment classes and learning from the great investors.

Four countries Chile, Australia, England, Mexico—have begun some form of privatization; however, it is not a cure-all. Where implemented, privatization has been disappointing. While greeted with enthusiasm in Chile, the plan covers only about half the workers, and the investment accounts are not as large as expected due to high commissions and administrative costs. The returns have averaged only 5.1% instead of the 11% expected between 1982 and 1999 so that a regular savings account would have been had higher returns. This has meant that 41% of those eligible for pensions continue to work. Fully 28 to 33% of the contributions made by employees retiring in 2000 went toward fees. The military, which imposed mandatory private accounts, does not participate and continues to receive pensions under the old governmental system. Studies reveal high management fees, low participation rates, unexpectedly heavy dependence on an inadequate safety net, and prohibitively high costs to the government. This has led to largely disappointing results, leaving many Chilean workers with no reliable retirement plan. The UK has had some problems with fees and misselling that the UK pensions commission warns not to emulate them.

Investment firms stand to gain. Goolsbee (2004) calculated the costs of privately managed individual accounts would likely reduce the retirement value of the accounts by 20% and cost nearly $1 trillion over seventy five years. Since 1988 when UK workers have been able to open private accounts, management fees and marketing costs among financial intermediaries have taken an average of 43% of the return on investment.

Proposals that a portion of the SSTF assets be invested in equities raise the possibility that the fund's assets will fall below the level needed to pay currently mandated benefit levels. In such a scenario, existing taxpayers might have to become insurers of last resort. Constantinides, Donaldson, and Mehra (2005) calculate the cost of a put option that would guarantee to cover this shortfall. They calibrate a model using realistic equity premia. Their formulation accounts for the nonstationarity of security returns resulting from trust fund purchases and other phenomenon. If 20% of the fund's assets are in equities, the highest level in current discussions, the cost of the put is 1% of GDP or equivalently a temporary increase in social security taxation of at most 20%. If only 90% of the benefits are guaranteed, then the put only costs 0.03% of GDP. Since all such puts generally have negative expected value, see Tompkins, Ziemba, and Hodges (2008), this cost is expensive, so it is only one of the alternatives to consider. Other options include investment in the best hedge funds, stocks with superior records, and other assets projected to have superior returns such as oil and commodities in 2006; see Section 4.11, Ziemba (2005), and Ziemba and Ziemba (2007) for a study of such superior investors.

European governments face a dual problem in dealing with the future of social security pensions. They, like other governments, must deal with the rising cost of pensions resulting from increasing life expectancy. This is complicated by the free movement of labor within the EU. Feldstein (2001) and Holzmann (2003) investigate this significant problem. They each develop a solution based on a notational defined contribution as the core, combined with a fully funded second pillar. While Holzmann does not elaborate on the second pillar, Feldstein suggests individual investment accounts. Notational defined contribution plans are further discussed below.

Feldstein (2001) predicts a need for a 50% increase in the payroll tax rate and even more for funding health costs. He simulates the probability distribution of returns relative to the social security benchmark of saving 6% of earnings during a working life and investing the savings in a 60–40 bond-stock portfolio. On retirement, the accumulated savings would purchase a variable annuity also invested in the 60–40 mix. The median investment-based annuity at age 67 is more twice the benchmark, even though the savings rate is only one-third that which would be needed with the PAYG system. However, there is almost a 20% chance of receiving less and an equal probability of receiving at least four times the benchmark benefit.

While these studies show the feasibility of shifting to privatized accounts, there is no analysis of the impact of the shift of these funds to the market and the attendant increase in the government deficit. On the one hand, since the evidence is that index funds beat about 75% of the managers and it is hard to predict future currency moves, a well defined index of world wide assets might be wise. However, given the volume of assets required, it is not at all clear that they could all be invested in indexes without inflating the value beyond the real economic worth. There is a paradox here that indexes are only good investments on the margin. For example, if the volume in the S&P 500 index got into a level to take a substantial portion of the social funds, then its return distribution would be altered. It is clear that many places to invest are needed to absorb these funds and actually turn them into real capital investment and not just inflate asset values. But it is hard to beat equal weighting implemented through low cost exchange traded funds (ETF) using a fixed mix rebalancing scheme; see Mulvey (2010).

3.5 RETHINKING PENSION PROMISES: BREAKING THE FIXED LINK TO A MONETARY VALUE

There are several broad directions for redesigning social security systems to get both the benefits of market investment and some retirement income security. All break the link with a predetermined monetary guarantee at retirement and thus shift the risk to the retiree. Some use derivative securities to partially insure the assets, and there are a variety of ways to keep track of defined contributions without giving them market valuations so that the payout can be related to the economic output at the time of payout. As liabilities become relative, this eliminates the possibility of not being able to meet them. This class of programs is known as nonfinancial-defined contributions.

3.5.1 Feldstein's PRA with Guarantees

If social security contributions are invested in the equity markets, retirement income is exposed to all the attendant market risks. Feldstein (2005) presents a market-based approach to reducing the risk of investment-based social security that could be tailored to individual risk preferences. His plan substitutes an investment-based personal retirement account (PRA) for the traditional pure PAYG plan to achieve both significantly higher expected retirement income and a very high probability that the investment-based annuity would be at least as large as the PAYG benefit. The guarantee is purchased each year based on that year's PRA savings. The basic contract would guarantee the individual a *No Lose* investment, that the amount saved in each year would be guaranteed to retain at least its real value by age 66. Such a guarantee could be provided by the firm that manages the PRA product (i.e., the mutual fund, bank, insurance company, etc.).

Feldstein suggests that the simplest way to achieve a No Lose PRA account would be to combine TIPS (Treasury Inflation Protected Securities, which have a guaranteed real return) with equities. The ratio of these would depend on the age of the saver and the rate of return on the TIPS for the relevant maturity. For example, if the saver is 21 years old and the real return on TIPS is 2%, a $1000 PRA saving would be divided between $410 in TIPS and the remaining $590 in equities. At older working ages, there are fewer years for the TIPS to accumulate and therefore a larger fraction of the initial saving must be invested in TIPS. A 40-year-old would have to invest $598 out of each $1000 of new saving in TIPS.

When the individual reaches age 66, all of the annual PRA accounts would be combined to provide a single retirement fund and a conventional annuity would be purchased. The No Lose approach could be continued into this phase as well with the annuity provider offering a guarantee that the annual annuity payments would be at least as large as the individual's retirement fund could purchase with a zero real return. Other modifications could be made as desired.

Feldstein's study demonstrates how expensive the guarantees are. If society truly wanted to guarantee some minimal level of retirement security, then a grand societal type *self-insurance* like the PAYG system might well be the most cost effective. Also it is not at all clear that these guarantees could be purchased without even higher costs for small PRAs. In addition the increased demand for insurance would likely greatly increase the costs. In the end, those who most need the security would be least likely to benefit.

3.5.2 NDC: Notational or Nonfinancial Defined Contributions

Notational or nonfinancial-defined contribution (NDC) systems as opposed to financial-defined contributions (FDC), break the link between financial contributions and retirement payments. NDCs are designed to eliminate the monetary risk from the liability of PAYG systems. Some countries already have variants of this, see Table 3.2.

Over a working life individuals accumulate notational credits that are converted to monetary payments at retirement based on the contributions of the working cohort not the accumulated financial contributions over the working life. Values continue to accumulate as long as the participant works and makes contributions. There is no *full-benefit* age, but instead all new contributions add to the size of the individual's annuity when claimed. There is a minimum pension age but not a mandatory one. When cashed in the annuity is calculated by dividing the account balance with an estimate of life expectancy at retirement.

NDCs address the fiscal, political, social, and economic needs of reform while keeping the fiscal burden of low. Holzmann and Palmer (2003) review the experiences with these systems. Sweden (1994), Italy (1995), Lativa, and Poland were early adapters. NDC promises to address the issues confronting pension policy in the twenty-first century,

NDC is designed to balance liabilities and assets providing stability and sustainability. An NDC scheme is a defined contribution, pay-as-you-go (PAYG) pension scheme. Contributions are defined in terms of a fixed contribution rate on individual earnings that are noted on an individual account; however, they are not "funded." An NDC makes adjustments on the benefit side given the contributions, while a DB makes adjustment on the contribution side given the promised benefits. The payments reflect life expectancy improvements, productivity (and real wage) improvements, and changing demographics. The internal rate of return reflects these factors rather than a financial market rate of return. All in the same cohort are treated equally, but there is allowance for differential treatment across cohorts. When the total contributions fall because of a smaller working population (increased dependency ratio), the financial payout is lower. Thus, the NDC establishes a limit for the public pension commitment and thus encourages individual saving for retirement. Given the valuation of accumulated credits upon retirement, there is much scope for flexibility. If the demographics or productivity is unfavorable, the actual monetization of the NDC is lower.

The NDC benefit is a life annuity. It can be claimed at any time after the minimum retirement age. The annuities issued at each point in time reflect life expectancy, so in principle, an NDC is an actuarially fair pension system. It also distributes individual resources over the life cycle, as part of a national (universal) PAYG insurance scheme. It is an illiquid, individual cash balance scheme, while the annuity becomes an insurance plan by redistributing the capital to the survivors. It fulfills the function of insuring against the individual risk of outliving the average participant. However, it may not provide sufficient resources in old age. An NDC scheme must be supplemented with some form of low-income support, in the form of minimum income or minimum benefit guarantee.

How is NDC different from a funded DC plan? Most PAYG systems have some reserve fund: in Sweden, the reserve fund is about five years of expenditures, while the German system has only about a few days reserves. A crucial question is whether the accumulated balances are collateralized and which claims represent the collateral. NDC systems are *notional* in the sense that there is no collateral at all. Balances are claims against future taxpayers, and they are not backed by a financial instrument. Funded DC plans are usually understood as being collateralized against physical capital, mostly through financial instruments such as commercial bonds or stocks. We use the word *funded* only for these plans. Some authors also call those DC plans that are collateralized with government bonds *funded*. We think that this is a misuse of the word *funded*. Although benefit claims of such plans are marketable and yield a well-defined rate of interest, they do not represent claims on physical capital. NDC systems may permit a *natural* way to make the implicit debt of a PAYG system explicit by linking the NDC balances to government bonds, and the resulting insights about future benefits and contributions may create saving incentives on the microeconomic level. However, NDC systems and conventional DB systems share the crucial macroeconomic features of PAYG systems: NDC systems do not accumulate savings in real assets with the potential beneficial side effects on the national saving rate, capital market development, and growth. NDC systems are therefore no substitute for prefunding.

An NDC system does not change the basic PAYG mechanism in which the children pay for the pensions of their parents, and it does not create savings unless it generates a benefit cut, which in turn precipitates savings. However, an NDC system can be designed to automatically respond to changes in the demographic and macroeconomic environment because benefits are indexed to longevity (due to the annuitization mechanism), fertility, and employment (through the notional rate of interest, if indexed to the contribution bill). Moreover, an NDC system has potentially important microeconomic effects. It will create a sense of actuarial fairness (because annual benefits are in line with lifetime contributions) and actuarial neutrality (because the system creates automatic adjustments to retirement age). It exposes redistribution because any noncontributory credits appear clearly marked on the account statements. An NDC system changes the rhetoric of pension systems. It makes people think in terms of accounts rather than entitlements and thus may make the transition to partial funding psychologically easier. Moreover, by exposing the dwindling balance of first pillar pensions, it may actually create incentives to save in the second and third pillar. An NDC system makes workers and administrators think in terms of *pension wealth*, which may ease portability both within a country and between countries. It enables interpersonal transfers (for example, between husband and spouse) and eases replacement of survivor pensions by independent pension claims.

An NDC system takes some issues out of the political agenda. It minimizes the role of the *normal retirement age* and permits a more flexible choice between working longer and getting a lower replacement rate. The new format helps pension reform because it provides a framework to introduce actuarial adjustments (since they come *automatically*), a framework to diffuse the explosiveness of changes in the retirement age (since a flexible choice of retirement age minimizes opposition), and a framework to change intergenerational redistribution.

NDC plans deal well with longevity and handle slow changes in fertility. But sudden changes, like the baby boom/baby bust transition, still require prefunding as the older generation will not be able to pass the entire burden onto the next. NDC are still PAYG and do not change the basic macroeconomic characteristics such as growth, savings, or improvements in capital market. To change the growth path of an economy, these systems should be supported by an improvement of second and third pillar pensions.

As with any reform, the real key is in the implementation; there needs to be effective communication with the stakeholders and a high level of trained administrators. The strength of NDC is also a weakness if through a large economic shock it must respond dramatically with lowered payouts. The benefits can only accrue after the tax overhang of current DB systems are dealt with. Finally, NDC schemes must be seen as part of a multipillar pension system. Some attention should be paid to how the entire system functions, including occupational groups that are hard to handle: farmers or persons involved in the informal or semiformal agricultural setting in developing economies. Educating people to respond to the concept that benefits depend only on one's own contributions, with life expectancy determining the size of the life benefit, overall, that for any given contribution rate and retirement age the benefit level will be lower—perhaps markedly lower—than under the old NDB scheme. Individuals can adjust by choosing a later retirement age and increasing savings. It is important that individual choices do not undermine the system by creating more people who fall below the poverty level in old age.

3.5.2.1 Coordinated Europe-wide System

An issue confronting further integration of European labor and financial markets is pension schemes based on the individual nations. Holzmann (2003, p. 225) suggests a scheme with an "(NDC) system at its core and coordinated supplementary funded pensions and social pensions at its wings." This would balance harmonization and the preferences of individual countries for contributions, benefits, and eligibility. A big challenge would be the transition to such a system. We saw that transitions are difficult for an individual country, but for this harmonization to work NDC and quasi-NDC countries would need to be harmonized with unfunded and semifunded traditional systems—all with differing contributions, benefits, eligibility, and debt overhang from the past. In addition, the various social assistance programs would have to be clearly separated from the pension program. Perhaps before this is possible, more countries would need to transition to an NDC-type scheme and sort out past problems. It is interesting to consider this future challenge.

Henkel created the first cross-border notional pension scheme. It took two years to restructure the €2.4 billion funded pension assets navigating five sets of pension regulations IPE (2009).

3.5.3   The PAAW (Personal Annuitized Average Wage Security), a Variant of the NDC

The system designed by Geanakopolos and Zeldes (2005) is based on personal accounts (progressive personal accounts or PPA) and a derivative security based on the average wage (personal annuitized average wage security of PAAW). The PPA can be defined in a way to redistribute lifetime retirement credits through a variable matching of contributions by the government the higher the income, the lower the matching. This is done on an annual basis and depends on total lifetime contributions. A PAAW is a derivative that securitizes the contingent liability of the government. Each PAAW pays one inflation-corrected dollar for every year of life after a fixed date t-(retirement age) multiplied by the economy-wide average wage at t. Individuals would get PAAWs in exchange for social security contributions, and these would be held in the PPAs.

The PPA ensures intragenerational equity by creating risk sharing across generations. If young workers are doing well and receiving high wages, the old will get higher payoffs from their PAAWs, and conversely. Such a system maintains the core of the current system, but would increase transparency and enhance property rights as the accounts would be personal, and lower the political risk of legislation removing benefits.

Initially the PPAs could be required to hold all their wealth in PAAWs, without any opportunity to trade them in financial markets. If done this way, it is similar to the NDC. If the PAAW is tradeable, then a value true not notational value will be attached, and individuals would be better able to plan for retirement assets outside social security, knowing what they would get. To prevent people from selling off all their PAAWs, the authors propose limiting sales to 10% which they claim would be enough to get a fair value without destroying the risk-sharing aspects of the plan.

3.5.3.1 PAAWs vs. Notional Accounts Typically the money in notional accounts is legislated to grow at the rate of the growth of wages. By the year of retirement the money in the account is proportional to the wages of the next generation's workers. PAAWs are real securities and can be traded, so their market prices would convey useful information.

A number of papers have proposed the creation of related new financial securities. Geanakoplos and Zeldes suggest that this follows a number of papers that have proposed the creation of related financial securities: for example, Shiller (1993) proposes GDP-linked securities; Blake and Burrows (2001) propose longevity or survivor bonds; and Bohn (2002) and Goetzmann (2005) propose aggregate wage-related securities

3.6 INTERGENERATIONAL RISK-SHARING

Chauncey Starr, speaking at a 1999 conference at the Electric Power Research Institute, Palo Alto, California, in the honor of the late George Dantzig organized by the late Alan Manne and William Ziemba on Planning under Uncertainty referred to intergenerational planning as the ultimate uncertainty. Starr, the president emeritus of EPRI concluded that "neither science, nor technology, nor politics, nor religion, nor any ideology is likely by itself to provide the best roadmap" . . . to an intergenerational future. This recognizes the difficulty of the problem. In 2009 we have the added problem of trillions of borrowed money by the US, the UK, and other governments to try to deal with the 2007–2009 credit crisis leading to either inflation or some other way to eliminate off this debt—any method is likely to result in a redistribution of income, if held internally the redistribution will be within these economies, if held externally it will result in a redistribution among countries.

Starr feels that our recorded history shows mixed results to successfully plan the future with unforeseen events generally dominating outcomes. Nassim Taleb (2007) refers to these events as black swans. We in stochastic programming refer to them as extreme scenarios. It is clear though that the norm is greatly affected by these tail events. Starr does feel that societies do shape intergenerational outcomes, usually as a consequence of near-term decisions. There is a responsibility issue of the current generation trying to shape the status, boundaries, and priorities of succeeding generations. Economic growth is at the top of the societal priority list, and, sadly, the natural environment is at or near the bottom and especially so in the developing countries. In between there are national security through the military, personal security via the police, public health, education, and a quality-of-life melange merging into environment. So from this short-term politics withstanding, we can model the situation with objectives, constraints, and targets. But there are unpredictable, unexplainable, and uncontrollable events. Still Starr feels that despite the noisiness of future projections there is merit in intergenerational planning exercises and models. Generations are about 25 years, and new innovations and technologies can span 50 years, so a lot of this is planning for grandchildren. Perhaps the best we can do is *do no harm* and try to leave the capacity for growth and change in the system.

Gollier (2008) studies intergenerational risk-sharing and risk-taking for a DC pension fund using a series of related expected utility models. He concludes that better intergenerational risk-sharing does not reduce the risk each generation has, but it increases the expected return of the workers' contributions. Diamond (1977), Gordon and Varian (1988), Ball and Mankiw (2001), and Shiller (1999, 2003) have argued that in competitive capital markets, the inability of current generations to share their risk with those who are not born yet makes these markets inefficient. Gollier examines whether or not a prefunded system can resolve this inefficiency. Such a funded system makes intergenerational risk sharing possible if the trust funds can disconnect the generational contributin to generational pension benefits.

Gollier analyzes this by studying the rules to govern the intergenerational cross subsidization that determines the retirement benefit policy and what the asset management strategies should be. His model has a guaranteed minimum return from the pensions to all future generations. He assumes that the funding ratio is always at least one, so that the fund's assets are always larger than their liabilities. Each generation contributes yearly for 40 years, and each year a new generation appears and one leaves so the model has a rolling infinite horizon. The portfolio choice is endogenous and based on the fund's reserves. Using a Samuelson (1969) and Merton (1969) type model under the assumptions, a fixed mix myopic policy is optimal. So the policy is to rebalance to the fixed mix so one sells after high equity returns and buys after low equity returns. Equity returns 5.9% with 13.6% standard deviation and cash, 2%. He assumes that the utility is negative power with $\gamma = 5$, so

$$u(w) = \frac{w^{1-\gamma}}{1 - \gamma} = -0.25\,W^{-4},$$

which is a conservative utility function. To understand this, the workers certainty equivalent is that to avoid a 50–50 chance to gain or lose 10% of their wealth they would pay 2.4% of this wealth.

The trust fund is managed and controlled by shareholders who bring equity to the fund in exchange for future dividends. The optimization model determines for each year and for each contingency, the optimal portfolio of assets, the payment of benefits to the new pensioners, and the distribution of dividends to the shareholders of the insurance company.

The minimum guarantee constraint reduces the ability of the funded scheme to transfer risk to future generations. Better intergenerational risk sharing makes it socially efficient to raise the collective risk exposure to take advantage of the large assumed equity premium. The benefit distributed to new pensioners is increasing and concave in the market value of the fund's assets. For personal retirement accounts, it is optimal for workers to invest a decreasing share as they age of the pension balances.

With the minimum guarantee, the fund also must maintain in every period and every economic scenario a minimum capital, which is the guaranteed capital accumulated by the current contributing generations. The solvency is at the beginning of each year, after pensions and dividends have been paid but before contributions have been received. The minimum capital requirement is $820y$, y being the yearly contribution of the workers, and the minimum benefit is $40y$. At the time $t = 0$, the pension fund is created and funded with equity from shareholders and initial contributions $y_0 = 1638y$ from the n generations of workers living at the time of conversion.

Gollier calculates the sharing of risk between the workers' benefit, b, and the shareholders' dividend, $d = c - b$, where c is the total yearly payment of the fund. The solvency constraint reduced risk-taking at low wealth levels so it is more risk averse if the fund had decreasing absolute risk aversion which $-.25 W^{-4}$ has. At high-wealth levels, the fund takes more portfolio risk. The growth rate is always positive but declines to zero for high levels of reserves. This model accumulates reserves quickly because the distribution of benefits to retirees is not very generous and less because of the solvency constraint. The target share of the fund's assets to be invested in equity is 40–50% with this target reduced when the fund's wealth declines. The target share of the fund's reserves to be distributed as pension benefits is about 3.5% with the minimum guarantees.

3.7 CONCLUSIONS

Suggestions for pension reform point the way to the challenges for individual retirement planning:

- Increase retirement age over time as longevity increases
- Reduce benefits further for early retirement
- Link indexation to prices not earnings
- Cut earnings related public pensions and restore safety net aspects (min.)

The social security debate is an important arena in which market economics and social welfare vie. We must reflect back to the original insurance purpose of social security provision—that when people were too old, infirm, or disabled to work, there would be a safety net to protect them, funded by a general tax on earnings. This evolved into an expectation of an active retirement made possible by benefits earned from contributions to a social account. Looking at the data it is clear that for the most part it still is the poorer quintile of elderly that rely solely on social security, while other segments use social security as a supplement to other sources of income when they are no longer working. This aspect of the social security dilemma must be emphasized in any attempt to make the system sustainable.

Retirement income is complicated by the growing costs of health care in the final years of life and in all cases the overall increase in the dependency ratio—not narrowly seen as the social security dependency but overall as financial resources are turned into real demand for currently produced goods and services. So, while the social security crisis might be solved by manipulating contributions, benefits, and retirement age, the broader issues must be resolved through a new understanding of the intergenerational social contract. Furthermore, in the end, there is a fallacy of composition. Goods and services must be produced sufficient to meet the needs of all participants in society—the employed as well as the retired.

3.8   CASE STUDY: PUBLIC SECTOR VS. PRIVATE PENSIONS

Pierlot (2007) and Munnell and Soto (2008) show the gap between the pension coverage of public and private schemes. They also show what could be possible for all. Two key factors stand out, one the contribution rates are higher than private DC plans and both employer and employee contribute; and the administrative costs and access to plan advisors is superior.

3.8.1   Government Plans Are Different: US

Munnell and Soto (2007) find that state and local retirement plans (public) are usually far better than private plans, providing better benefits and relying on the contributions of employees to increase the assets available. In 2006, assets per worker totaled $185,900 in public plans more than double the $84,800 in private plans, and the coverage was 76% versus only 43%, respectively.

These plans total a significant part of retirement assets as shown in Table 3.8 where federal, state, and local governments total 30% of the retirement asset pool. See also Chapter 11. Munnell and Soto (2007) note that the public sector also offers DC plans as supplementary, and some are

TABLE 3.8 Retirement Plan Assets, 2006

Pension Type	Assets, $ tril.	% of total
State and local governments	3.0	22
Federal government	1.1	8
Private sector DB	2.2	16
Private sector DC	3.3	24
IRAs	4.2	30
Total	13.8	100

Source: Munnell and Soto (2007).

beginning to offer them as the primary plan. These account for another half trillion but are not included here.

The role of the DB plans is more significant in the total retirement assets of public sector employees. In the public sector, 80% have DB plans only, while in the private sector 64% have DC plans only (6% of public and 26% of private have both types of plans) (Munnell and Soto 2007). The public plans are often allowed to substitute for social security, so only 72% of public versus 98% of private are covered by social security. Contribution rates for employer and employee are shown in Table 3.9

Management fees for public plans are very low. Private 401(k) typically pay 1.7% for a global fund, 1.2% for a balanced fund and 0.6% for an S&P index fund while public plans average only 0.2% (Munnell and Soto 2007).

Munnell and Soto do not directly compare public and private sectors workers with equal tenure, but the example they give is striking: A public sector worker after 20 years service can typically retire with a benefit of $20,000. A private sector worker with final salary of $50,000 would need about $260,000 in a 401(k) to buy an annuity yielding $20,000 per year. And more striking, median 401(k) balances for household near retirement in 2004 were only $60,000. For more on annuities see Section 12.2.

TABLE 3.9 Employer and Employee Contributions, %, 2006

Plan	Employer	Employee
State and local	7	5
Private DB	8	0
Private DC	3	6

Source: Munnell and Soto (2007).

TABLE 3.10 Comparing Two Couples, Employment Pension Excluding
Government CPP

	Public Sector	Private Sector
Retire	Age 58 after 30-years	Age 62 after 34-years
Final salary	$50,000	$50,000
Value of retirement savings	$1,205,572 ($602,786 each)	$244,800 ($122,400 each)
Pension value	Age 58–65 $74,806 indexed from age 65, $50,622 indexed	Buy indexed annuities $11,652 indexed
Span	27 years	23 years

Source: Pierlot (2008).

3.8.2 Government Plans Are Different: Canada

Pierlot (2008) compares the retirement savings of two couples, one public
sector and one private. He uncovers both the great disparity in benefits
and the inequitable treatment regarding access to means to adequately save
for retirement depending on the source of income. If we are going to solve
the retirement problem, these inequities will need to be solved. Table 3.10
compares the retirement benefits of two couples. Clearly their retirement
positions are far apart.

As in the US, 80% of public sector workers participate in a DB plan
while private sector occupational pension plans cover only about 23% or
workers. The remaining private sector workers have only RRSPs (registered
retirement savings plans), home equity, and nonsheltered savings. The public
sector plans typically cover 60 to 70% of pre retirement salary and are
indexed. To get the *same* benefits, the private sector couple would need
to save twice as much as the public sector one. Private sector workers are
prohibited from participating in a plan not sponsored by their employer,
and typical employer sponsored plans have higher management fees. Tax
rules and incentives would need to be changed to make the field equal. His
study goes through all the issues.

Tax-sheltered income is limited to 18% of earned income—this is really only enforced on private plans and not DB plans by public sector or
employers.

Those with employer-sponsored DC plans face higher administrative
costs as well as lower employer contributions. For the self-employed, the
earned income makes it hard for small business and even professionals like
doctors to shelter much income. An example compares two workers earning

$60,000: the public sector worker has retirement *saving room* of $25,002, more than double the private worker without a plan (Pierlot, 2008). Also the path of income over the working span will affect the retirement savings limits.

3.8.3 What Do We Learn from These Comparisons?

Akin to the health care debate in which many would like to have the opportunity to join a public plan like that enjoyed by the members of congress, many are advocating opening up public pension plans to individuals as a way of improving preparation for retirement.

REFERENCES

Ball, L., and N. G. Mankiw. 2001. Intergenerational risk sharing in the spirit of Arrow, Debreu and Rawls, with applications to social security design. Harvard Institute of Economic Research DP 1921.

Bernartzi, S., and R. H. Thaler. 2001. Naive diversification in defined contribution savings plans. *American Economic Review* 91(1):79–98.

Blake, D., and W. Burrows. 2001. Survivor bonds: Helping to hedge mortality risk. *Journal of Risk and Insurance* 68(2) (June):339–348.

Bohn, H. 2002. Retirement savings in an aging society: A case for innovative government debt management. In *Aging, Financial Markets and Monetary Policy* Springer.

Chateau, J., and X. Chojnicki. 2008. Disparities in pension financing in Europe: Economic and financial consequences. CEPII technical report No. 2006–09 (May 9).

Constantinides, G. M., J. B. Donaldson, and R. Mehra. 2005. Junior must pay: pricing the implicit put in privatizing Social Security, *Annals of Finance* 1:1–34.

Diamond, P. 1977. A framework for social security analysis. *Journal of Public Economics* 8:275–298.

The Economist. 2006. Turning boomers into boomerangs. Feburary 16.

Feldstein, M. 2001. The future of social security pensions in Europe. NBER 8487.

———. 2005. Reducing the risk of investment-based social security. NBER 11084 (January).

Geanakoplos, J., O. S. Mitchell, and S. P. Zeldes. 1998. Would a privatized social security system really pay a higher rate of return? NBER WP No. 6713 (August).

Geanakoplos, J., and S. P. Zeldes. 2005. Reforming social security with progressive personal accounts. NBER 05–07.

Goetzmann, W. N. 2005. More social security, not less. Yale ICF Working Paper No. 05–05.

Gollier, C. 2008. Intergenerational risk-sharing and risk taking of a pension fund. *Journal of Public Economics* 92(5–6):1463–1485.

Goolsbee, A. 2004. The fees of private accounts and the impact of social security privatization on investment managers. Working paper. University of Chicago Graduate School of Business (September).

Gordon, R. H., and H. R. Varian. 1988. Intergenerational risk sharing. *Journal of Public Economics* 37:185–202.

Holzmann, R. 2003. *Toward a Coordinated Pension System in Europe: Rationale and Potential Structure.* In Holzmann, R., and E. Palmer eds. 2003. *Pension Reform: Issues and Prospects for Non-Financial Defined Contribution (NDC) Schemes,* Proceedings of the NDC Conference in Sandhamn, Sweden, September 28–30.

Holzmann, R., and E. Palmer, eds. 2003. *Pension Reform: Issues and Prospects for Non-Financial Defined Contribution (NDC) Schemes,* Proceedings of the NDC Conference in Sandhamn, Sweden, September 28–30.

IPE. 2009. Henkel creates global fiduciary pensions structure (27 April).

Kallberg, J. G., and W. T. Ziemba. 1981. Remarks on optimal portfolio selection. In *Methods of Operations Research,* eds. G. Bamberg and O. Opitz, 507–520. *Oelgeschlager* 44.

Martin, J. P., and E. Whitehouse. 2008. Reforming retirement-income systems: Lessons from the recent experiences of OECD countries. Institute for the Study of Labor DP. No. 3521 (May).

Merton, R. 1969. Lifetime portfolio selection under uncertainty: The continuous time case. *Review of Economics and Statistics* 51:247–257.

Mulvey, J. 2010. Rebalancing gains in ETFs. In *The Kelly Criterion: Theory and Practice,* eds. L. C. MacLean, E. O. Thorp, and W. T. Ziemba. World Scientific.

Munnell, A. H., and M. Soto. 2007. State and local pensions are different from private plans. CRR Number 1, (November).

OECD. 2005. Ageing and pension reform systems. Financial Market Trends Supplement 1.

OECD. 2005. Pensions at a glance: Public policies across OECD countries.

OECD. 2007. Pensions at a glance: Public policies across OECD countries.

Orszag, P. 1999. Individual accounts and Social Security: Does Social Security really provide a lower rate of return? Center on Budget and Policy Priorities, (March 9):1.

Pierlot, J. 2008. A pension in every pot: Better pensions for more Canadians. C. D. Howe Institute, No. 275, (November).

Queisser, M., E. Whitehouse, and P. Whiteford. 2007. The public-private pension mix in OECD countries. MPRA paper 10344.

Samuelson, P. A. 1958. An exact consumption loan model of interest with or without the social contrivance of money. *Journal of Political Economy.*

Samuelson, P. A. 1969. Lifetime portfolio selection by dynamic stochastic programming. *Review of Economics and Statistics* 51:239–246.

Schwartz, S. L., and W. T. Ziemba. 2007. ALM in Social Security. In *Handbook of Asset and Liability Modeling, Volume 2: Applications and Case Studies.* S. A. Zenios, W. T. Ziemba (eds.). Handbooks in Finance Series, North Holland: 1069–1117.

Shiller, R. J. 1993. *Macro Markets: Creating Institutions for Managing Society's Largest Economic Risks.* Oxford University Press.

———. 1999. Social security and institutions for intergenerational, intragenerational and international risk sharing. *Carnegie-Rochester Conference Series on Public Policy* 50:165–204.

———. 2003. *The New Financial Order: Risk in the 21st Century.* Princeton University Press.

Taleb, N. 2007. *The Black Swan.* Random House.

Tompkins, R. G., W. T. Ziemba, and S. H. Hodges. 2008. The favorite-longshot bias in S&P 500 futures options: The return to bets and the cost of insurance. In *Handbook of Sports and Lottery Markets*, eds. D. B. Hausch and W. T. Ziemba, 161–180. Handbooks in Finance, North Holland.

Ziemba, W. T. 2005. The symmetric downside risk Sharpe ratio and the evaluation of great investors and speculators. *Journal of Portfolio Management* (Fall):108–122.

CHAPTER 4

Asset Classes: Historical Performance and Risk

Historically, five asset classes were considered for retirement savings: stocks, bonds, real estate, and cash and commodities. Here we consider an expanded list that considers both domestic and foreign assets. Thus currency risk also becomes important. We also distinguish own-company stocks from the universe of stocks. The number of assets, asset classes, strategies, products, etc is immense. Here we discuss aspects of this literature and the possibilities and risks of various ways to combine asset classes. In Chapters 14–16 we discuss how one might put some of these assets together in individual and corporate asset-liability modeling, using scenarios of asset and liability return and other parameters in a dynamic optimization approach with investor goals.

4.1 EQUITIES

Figure 4.1 shows the changing relative sizes of world stock markets from the end of 1899 to the end of 2008. Japan peaked at about 44% of the world at the end of 1989 and in the twenty years since has lost about 80% of its value. Table 4.1 shows annual US stock market returns from 1802 to 2006 with mean reversion. The longer the horizon, the closer the mean returns are to the long run 8.3% nominal and 6.8% real returns per year. Observe that of the 8.3%, fully 5.1% is from dividends.

Figure 4.2 shows the real equity returns in three periods: 2000–2008, 1950–1999, and 1900–2008 for 18 countries plus the US.

Figure 4.3(a) shows the total nominal return from the US stocks including dividends, from 1802 to 2006. Long horizons have produced very high returns from stocks. However, in short periods, the stock market is very risky. Figure 4.3(b) shows the total real return indexes from 1802 to 2006.

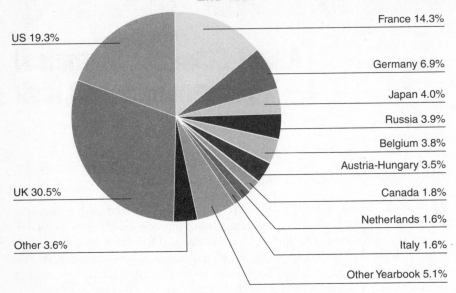

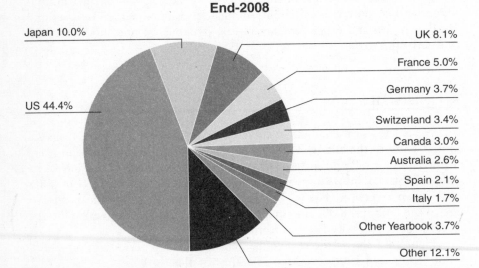

FIGURE 4.1 Changing Relative Size of Stock Market Around the World *Source:* Dimson, Marsh, Staunton (2009).

TABLE 4.1 Annual Stock Market Returns, 1802 to December 2006, percent

Comp = compound annual return
Arith = arithmetic average of annual returns
Risk = standard deviation of arithmetic returns
All Data in Percent (%)

		Total Nominal Return			Nominal Capital Appreciation			Div Yld	Total Real Return			Real Capital Appreciation			Real Gold Retn	Consumer Price Inflation
		Comp	Arith	Risk	Comp	Arith	Risk	Comp	Comp	Arith	Risk	Comp	Arith	Risk		
Periods	1802–2006	8.3	9.7	17.5	2.9	4.3	17.4	5.1	6.8	8.4	18.1	1.5	3.0	17.8	0.3	1.4
	1871–2006	8.9	10.5	18.5	4.2	5.8	18.3	4.5	6.7	8.4	18.8	2.1	3.9	18.5	0.4	2.0
Major Subperiods	I 1802–1870	7.1	8.1	15.5	0.3	1.3	15.4	6.4	7.0	8.3	16.9	0.1	1.4	16.4	0.2	0.1
	II 1871–1925	7.2	8.4	15.7	1.9	3.1	16.1	5.2	6.6	7.9	16.8	1.3	2.7	17.1	-0.8	0.6
	III 1926–2006	10.1	12.0	20.1	5.8	7.7	19.5	4.0	6.8	8.8	20.1	2.7	4.6	19.5	1.2	3.0
Postwar Periods	1946–2005	11.2	12.5	16.9	7.4	8.6	16.3	3.6	6.9	8.4	17.4	3.2	4.6	16.8	0.5	4.0
	1946–1965	13.1	14.3	19.5	8.2	9.2	18.7	4.6	10.0	11.4	18.7	5.2	6.5	18.1	-2.7	2.8
	1966–1981	6.6	8.3	17.2	2.6	4.3	16.6	3.9	-0.4	1.4	17.1	-4.1	-2.4	16.7	8.8	7.0
	1982–1999	17.3	18.0	12.5	13.8	14.5	12.4	3.1	13.6	14.3	12.6	10.2	10.9	12.6	-4.9	3.3
	1985–2006	12.4	13.6	15.6	9.8	11.0	15.1	2.4	8.4	10.3	15.4	6.6	7.7	14.9	0.3	3.0

Source: Siegel (2008).

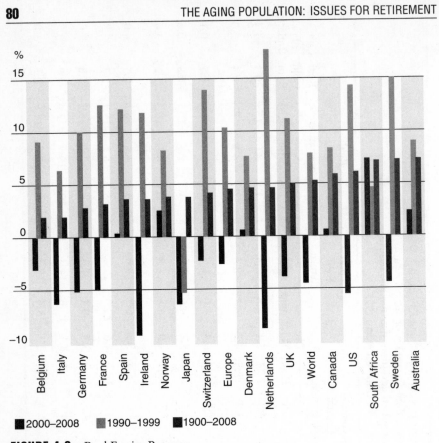

FIGURE 4.2 Real Equity Returns
Source: Dimson, Marsh, Staunton (2009).

These real returns from 1900 to 2008 are shown in Figure 4.4 and in Figure 4.5 from 1850 to 2008. US real equity returns during the latter period averaged 6.2% but with a very high standard deviation of 33.8%. The returns for equities, bond and bill averaged 6% plus 1.7% capital gains and dividends, 2.2% and 1.0%, respectively.

There have been four periods in the US markets where equities had essentially zero gains in nominal terms, not counting dividends, 1899 to 1919, 1929 to 1954, 1964 to 1981 and 1997 to 2009. Conversely, there have only been three periods were there were nominal gains not counting dividends: 1919–1929, 1954–1964, and 1981–1997.

Figure 4.6 shows the real returns without dividends for the 30-stock Dow Jones Average from 1885–2006 in 2006 dollars. Figure 4.7 shows the real returns from 1900–2008. One sees a quite violent but upward trending path. In the lower graph, one sees the DJIA in nominal terms. This provides a similar but still bumpy path. The effect of dividends tends to smooth this

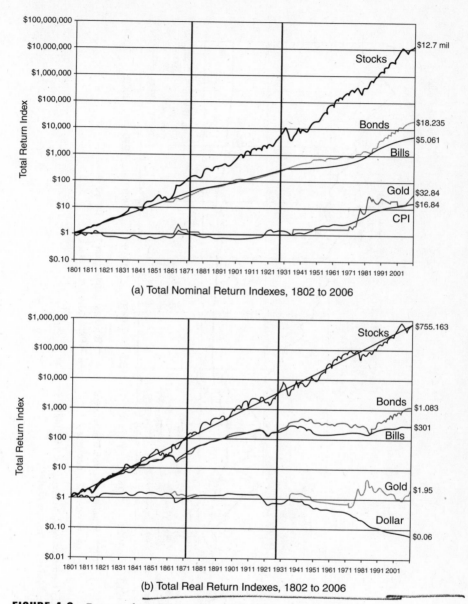

FIGURE 4.3 Returns from US Stocks and Other Assets, 1802–2006
Source: Siegel (2008).

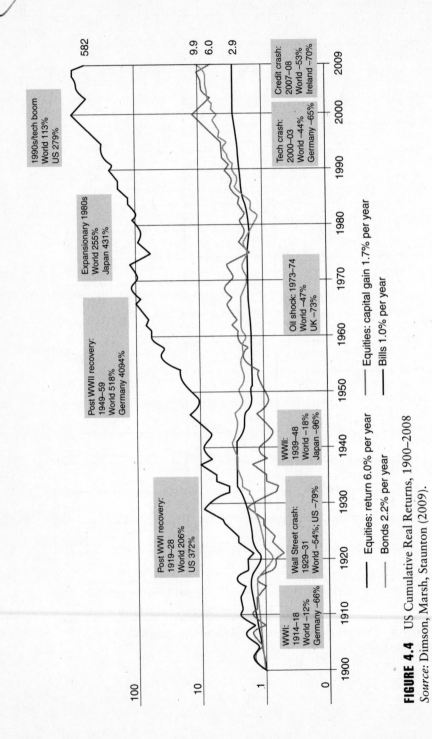

FIGURE 4.4 US Cumulative Real Returns, 1900–2008

Source: Dimson, Marsh, Staunton (2009).

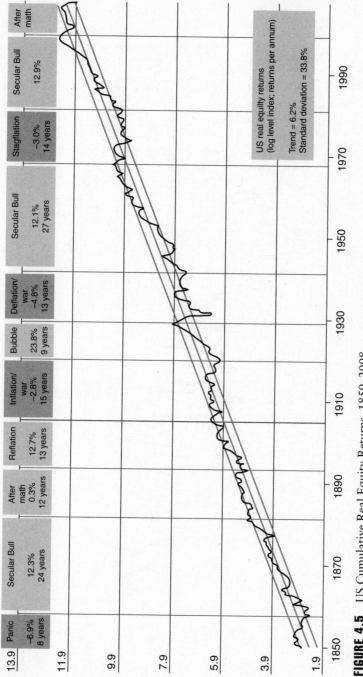

FIGURE 4.5 US Cumulative Real Equity Returns, 1850–2008
Source: Credit Suisse, Wilmot, J. (2009).

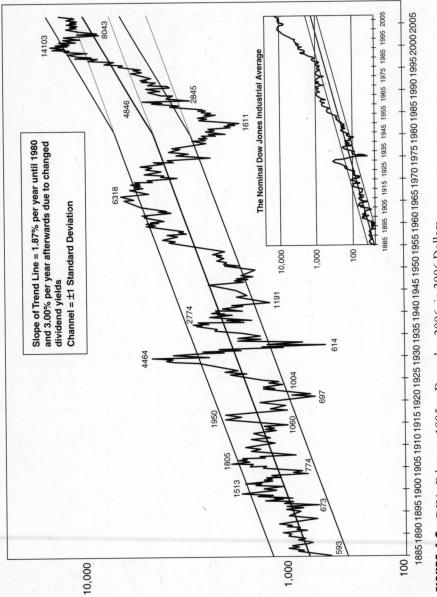

FIGURE 4.6 DJIA, February 1885 to December 2006, in 2006 Dollars
Source: Siegel (2008).

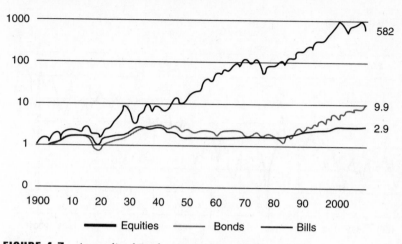

FIGURE 4.7   Annualized Performance from 1900 to 2008
Source: Dimson, Marsh, Staunton (2009).

path and provide a substantial part of the total returns. Indeed, despite long periods with losses in the indexes, the total returns can be positive. Siegel (2008) has shown that from 1900 to 2006 in every 30-year period, stocks have outperformed bonds; and in 10- and 20-year periods stocks have outperformed bonds most, but not all, of the times. Table 4.2 shows the dividend yields from 1871–2006.

Table 4.3 shows the total return of equities in the 73-year period from December 31, 1925 to December 31, 1998 and portfolio allocations based on risk aversion in Table 4.4. See Kallberg and Ziemba (1983) for the theory behind these calculations of the portfolios based on risk aversion. For those with long horizons, a high amount of equities is suggested. But what is the long run? We will return to this issue repeatedly in this book.

We know that, most of the time, stocks move with earnings. As earnings move, so will stock prices. Of course, the average PE ratio varies with time

TABLE 4.2   Summary Statistics for Dividends per Share, Earnings per Share, and Stock Returns for the US Economy, 1871 through December 2006

	Real GDP Growth	Real per Share Earnings Growth	Real per Share Dividend Growth	Dividend Yield*	Payout Ratio*
1871–2006	3.57%	1.88%	1.32%	4.58%	58.17%
1871–1945	3.97%	0.66%	0.74%	5.29%	66.78%
1946–2006	3.09%	3.40%	2.03%	3.53%	51.38%

*Denotes median.
Source: Siegel (2008).

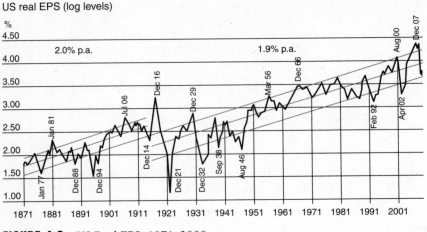

FIGURE 4.8 US Real EPS, 1871–2008
Source: Credit Suisse, Wilmot, J. (2009).

and market sentiment which can lead to oversold or overbought conditions for a long time. Figure 4.8 shows these real earnings from 1871 to 2008 in the US.

Figure 4.9 shows these real returns by country from 1900 to 2008. Australia, Sweden, and South Africa are at the top, just above the US and Canada; and various European countries like Belgium, Italy, Germany, France and Spain are at the bottom.

Figure 4.10a shows prices and earnings over time for the US just before the 2000–2003 stock market decline. Observe the slow climb in earnings and the steep climb in prices. This is shown in terms of PE ratios in Figure 4.10b and Figure 4.6. In contrast, Figure 4.11 shows the PERs from 1871 to 2006.

TABLE 4.3 Equities Have Generated Superior Returns in the Long Run, December 1925–December 1998

Asset Class	Multiple	
Inflation	9	times
Treasury bills	15	times
Treasury bonds	44	times
Corporate bonds	61	times
Large-capitalization stocks	2,351	times
Small-capitalization stocks	5,117	times

Source: Ibbotson (1999) in Swensen (2000).

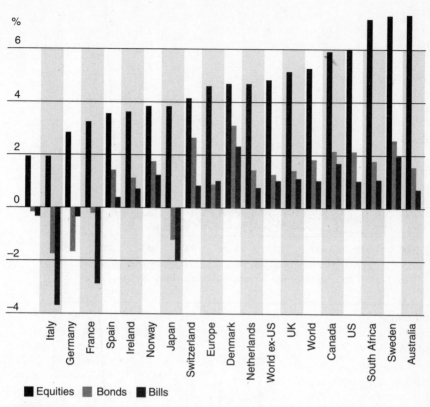

■ Equities ▨ Bonds ▮ Bills

FIGURE 4.9 Real Returns on Equities, Bonds, and Bills Internationally, 1900–2008
Source: Dimson, Marsh and Staunton (2009).

TABLE 4.4 Portfolio Allocation: Percentage of Portfolio Recommended in Stocks Based on All Historical Data (R_A = risk aversion index)

Risk Tolerance	R_A	Holding Period			
		1 year	5 years	10 years	30 years
Ultraconservative	10	9.0%	22.0%	39.3%	71.4%
Conservative	6	25.0%	38.7%	59.6%	89.5%
Moderate	4	50.0%	61.6%	88.0%	116.2%
Risk Taking	2	75.0%	78.5%	110.1%	139.1%

Source: Siegel (2008) using theory from Kallberg and Ziemba (1983).

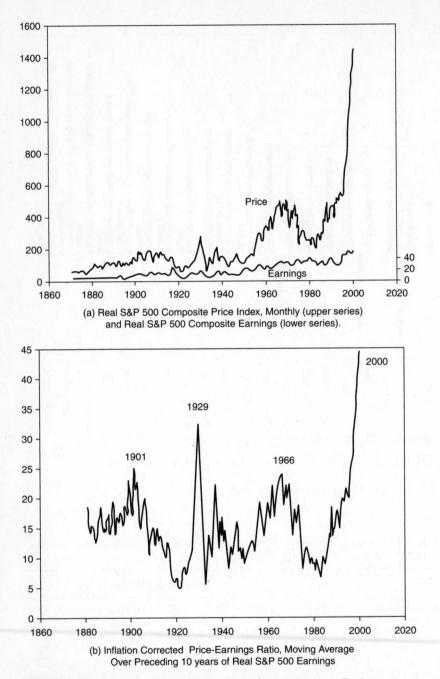

(a) Real S&P 500 Composite Price Index, Monthly (upper series)
and Real S&P 500 Composite Earnings (lower series).

(b) Inflation Corrected Price-Earnings Ratio, Moving Average
Over Preceding 10 years of Real S&P 500 Earnings

FIGURE 4.10   US Stock Prices, Earnings, and Price Earnings Ratios,
January 1871–January 2000
Source: Shiller (2000).

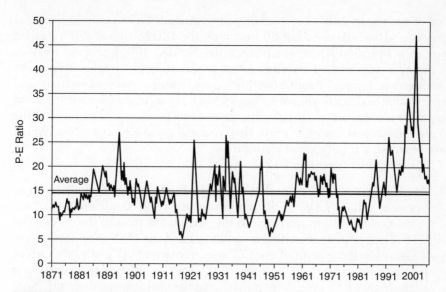

FIGURE 4.11   US Historical Price Earnings Ratios Based on the Last 12 Months of Reported Earnings, 1871 to December 2006
Source: Siegel (2008).

A new key issue then is could one know how to be in stocks when they are good and bonds or cash when stocks fall? In Section 4.3 we discuss the bond-stock measure approach for this purpose.

4.2   ETFs: EXCHANGE-TRADED FUNDS

ETFs are a special class of index funds. Index funds are very popular with institutional investors as an inexpensive way to hold the market. The theory is derived from the Sharpe (1994), Lintner (1965), Mossin (1966) capital asset pricing model and is the corner stone of efficient market theory. Around 1980, Rex Sinquefield and David Booth, students of University of Chicago Professor Gene Fama, founded the index fund company Dimension Fund Advisors.

Despite the competition and low fees, there is considerable profit in running an index fund. Witness, for example, the 2008 $300 million gift by Booth following a previous gift to the Graduate School of Business to form the Booth Graduate School of Business at the University of Chicago.

Historically, index funds started with the S&P 500 then moved to other indexes like the Russell 2000 and EAFE and now through ETFs can mimic a vast array of indexes and strategies. The latter can include shorting the S&P 500 or double shorting it. Those in regular long index funds lost a lot of money in 2007–2009 while others gained. ETFs trade like regular stocks and include the S&P 500 through the SPDRs (the old SPYs called spiders), and the QQQs which track the Nasdaq 100. The vast array of ETFs allows individual investors a simple way to hold complex investment positions including foreign investments, and various types of hedging and speculating and mimicking of strategies, such as the Yale endowment, at low cost. Of course, the usual risks apply, and just because you can mimic the Yale endowment does not mean that you will get their net returns, which are based on a lot of careful research.

Some points regarding ETFs:

1. The fund trades at a price that resembles but is not necessarily equal to net asset value (NAV). If the market price divergences from NAV there is the possibility for arbitrage so the price tends toward the NAV. The ETF is transparent regarding its holdings, and the NAV is updated every 15 seconds. If the price of the ETF rises above its NAV, APs (authorized participants) can buy up the underlying stocks and present them for shares at the higher ETF price. The purchase of the basket helps drive the NAV toward the price, and the AP pockets a gain. If the price falls below the NAV, the process works in reverse with the APs presenting shares for the basket. The ETF itself is not under an obligation to maintain the price at the NAV, and indeed the structure of the ETF is designed to avoid trading in the basket itself to avoid accumulating capital gains and losses within the fund. With market turbulence, this activity can fail because of lack of trades, liquidity, fast moving VIX, etc. An example was the eight trading days in October 2008 following the Lehman Brothers failure when the S&P 500 fell 23% from 1166 to 899. The dislocation then was most acute in the bond markets and bond ETFs. As Kay (2009) points out

    During the few days when panic sweeps over a market like it did in October 2008, net asset values mean very little due to the lack of fresh prices, and frequently traded ETFs provide a better estimate of their holdings true value then any estimate based on the old prices.

    In a crash, ETF holders likely cannot cash out except at a discount (and who can avoid that?).
    We can contrast this with a typical mutual fund that must redeem shares and issue new shares at the end of each trading day, thus accumulating losses and gains depending on the prices.

2. ETFs have lower expense ratios than most mutual funds. For example, the expense ratio for SPDRs, for the S&P 500, is at 0.12% per year versus Vanguard 500 index funds (VANX) 0.18%. Other ETFs are higher but are still low, under 1% per year for the buy and hold investor and not

much on a yearly basis for the trader who is trying to time sectors or the market.

Taxes are possibly lower with ETFs versus mutual funds. Both distribute capital gains, but mutual funds must buy and sell to cover purchases and redemptions in the fund. Some ETF redemptions are met by large index arbitragers, but they happen as exchange in kind rather than direct purchases of the basket in the fund.

3. There are many ETFs to choose among. Wisdom Tree, using research by Professor Jeremy Siegel has funds mimicking markets around the world and uses fundamental indexing bases on earnings or dividend yields, etc. The idea is that historically, these fundamental indexes have beaten the S&P 500; see Siegel (2008). The claim is that the earnings based S&P 500 outperforms the regular value weighted S&P 500 by 1.5–2.0% per year. Ziemba (2003), looking at the 2000–2003 decline, notes that while the value weighted S&P 500 fell about 50% from top to bottom, the equally weighted S&P 500 hardly fell, so this is consistent with Wisdom Tree results.

Finance theorists like UCLA Professor Richard Roll dispute this, arguing that these indexes are not mean-variance efficient; see Levy and Roll (2009). Another voice in this dispute is Rob Arnott, who was actually the originator of the idea. In fact, though, it is simply a factor model with basically one fundamental factor such as earnings. So, in theory, an actively managed portfolio using a full-fledged model with say 10–30 factors ought to do even better. See Jacobs and Levy (1988), who have a large firm using such ideas and Ziemba and Schwartz (2000), who made a similar model for Japan (see Section 4.12 for a brief description of this model).

MSCI country indexes form useful ETFs and RYDEX has many funds and encourages trading among them with low commissions. Ranking the countries involves currency consideration and local as well as global economic conditions. One simple model to rank countries is by Harvard Professor John Campbell and uses three variables; short-term (one year) momentum, long-term (ten year) mean reversion, and value measured by the dividend yield. Figure 4.12 shows some results for countries with Japan and the UK the best and the US the worst. Figure 4.13 shows some for industry sectors with Information Technology the best and Financials the worst. The Cambridge, Massachusetts institutional investor firm Arrowstreet Capital uses such ideas.

Merrill Lynch has HOLDRs that can be exchanged for the underlying stocks for a small $10 fee in lots of 100 shares. These are another way to invest in sectors such as biotechnology, semiconductors, broadband, etc.

Barclay's has also been active in the ETF arena with many equity and bond funds, which amount to over half of all the money invested in ETFs

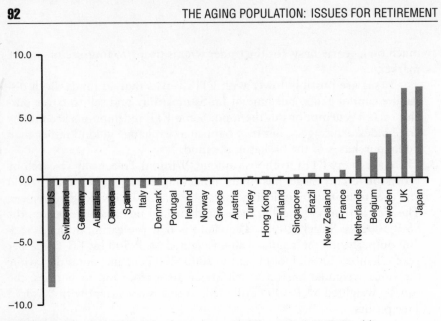

FIGURE 4.12   April 2009 Active Country Weights (%) (MSCI World)
Source: Arrowstreet Journal (2009).

globally. They, like others with bond funds, had some liquidity problems
in September and October 2008. In such cases, one might have to buy at a
premium. They have recently sold their iShare division.

Yale University Professor Robert Shiller, a perpetual bear, is behind
MacroShares, a way to play commodities and illiquid markets. The funds

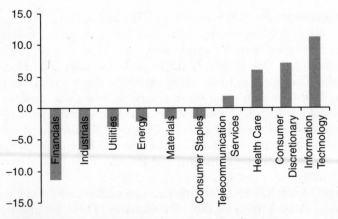

FIGURE 4.13   April 2009 Active Sector Weights (%)
(MSCI World)
Source: Arrowstreet Journal (2009).

are in pairs so the up fund will pay $2 to the down fund when the market falls 2% from a $100 base. Thus there is no hedging needed, but it is crucial that there be similar numbers of up and down investors.

As argued in Section 4.12 of this book, look out for September and October, the worst stock market months for the last 100 years across the world. Since all ETFs are passive investments, you will get the market return.

With 500 ETFs in the United States and more globally, there is a lot to choose among. The major players each have many of them; Wisdom Tree has 36 for example. So you can shop around or simply stay with one fund group.

4.2.1　Levered ETFs

First one must be careful here as, like Warren Buffett says, "Derivatives are instruments of mass destruction of wealth." That said, one should use care and not overbet; and stay diversified in all scenarios.

Covered call and buy/write strategies are reasonably safe and have the advantage of being equivalent to short putting, which, on average, has positive expectation. One goes long stock and short a call so at expiry, the premium is collected and buffers possible loss on the long stock. So one can lose if the stock falls more than the premium. Also the gain is capped at the premium for selling the call plus the stock price at the call less the buy price of the stock.

Funds that track the CBOE Buy Write Monthly (BXM), an index tracking buy write on the S&P 500, covered call fund (BEP) and Power Shares's S&P 500 BuyWritePortfolio (PBP).

Protective puts are equivalent to the old portfolio insurance buy not with futures which can fail as it did in October 1987 but rather with put options. You are long stock and long puts. You pay the premium so you gain all of the upside less the premium and if the stock falls, you only lose the premium. The stock can be the S&P 500, the SPY, bought through SPDRs. We know that on average, this is a losing strategy except if you can do this before market declines like September-October 2008. A third position is to simply buy the put to hedge.

4.3　BONDS AND FIXED INCOME

Bonds are very useful as a hedge against equity positions. When stocks fall, bonds tend to rise as shown in Figures 4.14 and 4.15. This was especially true in the 2000–2003 and 2007–2009 stock market declines. This is a major reason why 60–40 stock-bond portfolio mixes are often suggested for pension funds and other long-term investors.

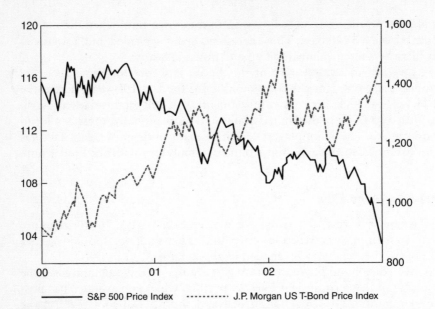

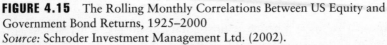

FIGURE 4.14   S&P 500 Index and US Government Bonds, 2000–2003
Source: Schroder Investment Management Ltd. (2002).

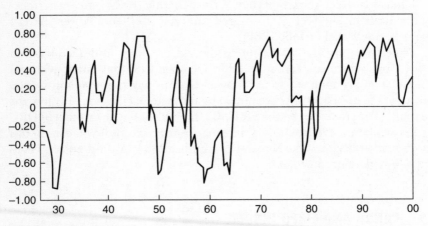

FIGURE 4.15   The Rolling Monthly Correlations Between US Equity and
Government Bond Returns, 1925–2000
Source: Schroder Investment Management Ltd. (2002).

Historically, as we have already seen, for example in Figure 4.3, b
as a long-term instrument have greatly underperformed equity positions
both in total nominal and real terms. Hence, once again one must be careful
about asset allocation across various investment categories.

Long-term bonds typically have higher returns than short-term bonds;
hence they are useful to "knock out liabilities" by lining them up agains
future liabilities. Then the short-term losses, due to higher interest rates than
the noted face interest, are not important since the purpose of the bonds is
to hold them and use them to pay off future liabilities as they come due.

Van Antwerpen et al. (2004) argue that long bonds can be preferable
to short bonds even when interest rates are low. The argument is that the
longer dates bonds pay a higher interest coupon and that a substantial
rise in interest rates may take a long time to occur. Their scenario analysis
shows that longer-dated bonds are superior (and have higher expected return
and lower risk) to short-dated bonds, especially when there are long-dated
liabilities. The evidence from 2004 to 2009 is that this conclusion has been
correct, so far.

Bodie (1995) argues that you can construct bond portfolios that are
superior to equity portfolios in the long run. Unfortunately, as Wilkie (1987)
shows, this is not true except in shorter horizons with specific return results.
See also Wilkie (1989, 1998). The real issue is to cover liabilities over time
so that models like those in Chapters 14–16 are usually needed to do these
calculations.

Table 4.5 shows fixed income returns from 1802 to 2006.

4.3.1 TIPS

TIPS (Treasury inflation protected securities) are a simple way to be in bonds
but not to risk them being hurt by high inflation. Coupon payments and the
underlying principal are increased by the CPI every six months. For example,
currently in June 2009, the rates are about 1.64% for 30 year TIPS, 1.06%
for 10-year and 0.0% for 5-year maturing 15 April 2032, 15 January 2018,
and 15 July 2012, respectively according to PIMCO. These rates are low
because TIPS are in a sense the safest investment as they have the safety of
ordinary treasuries but with the added inflation protection. In Canada they
are known as real return bonds.

4.4 THE BOND-STOCK MEASURE FOR
MEDIUM-TERM LARGE CRASH PREDICTION

The bond-stock measure called the 1987 US, the 1990 Japan, the 2000–
2001 US, and the 2002 US crashes. The idea is that when long bond interest

TABLE 4.5 US Fixed-Income Returns, 1802 through December 2006.

Comp = compound annual return
Arith = arithmetic average of annual returns
Risk = standard deviation of arithmetic returns
All Data in Percent (%)

| | | Long-Term Governments | | | | | | Short-Term Governments | | | |
| | | Nominal Return | | | Real Return | | | | Real Return | | |
	Coupon Rate	Comp	Arith	Risk	Comp	Arith	Risk	Nominal Rate	Comp	Arith	Risk
Major Periods											
1802–2006	4.8	5.0	5.1	6.2	3.5	3.9	8.8	4.3	2.8	3.0	6.0
1871–2006	4.7	5.0	5.3	7.4	2.9	3.3	8.9	3.8	1.7	1.8	4.5
Major Subperiods											
I 1802–1870	4.9	4.9	4.9	2.8	4.8	5.1	8.3	5.2	5.1	5.4	7.7
II 1871–1925	4.0	4.3	4.4	3.0	3.7	3.9	6.4	3.8	3.2	3.3	4.8
III 1926–2006	5.2	5.5	5.8	9.2	2.4	2.9	10.3	3.8	0.7	0.8	4.0
Postwar Periods											
1946–2006	6.0	5.7	6.2	10.2	1.6	2.2	10.9	4.7	0.6	0.6	3.2
1946–1965	3.1	1.6	1.7	7.1	-1.2	-1.0	8.1	2.0	-0.8	-0.7	2.1
1966–1981	7.2	2.5	2.8	12.0	-4.2	-3.9	12.9	6.9	-0.2	-0.1	2.4
1982–1999	8.5	12.1	12.9	13.8	8.5	9.3	13.6	6.3	2.9	2.9	1.8
1985–2006	7.0	10.4	11.0	12.3	7.2	7.7	12.0	4.9	1.7	1.8	2.1

Source: Siegel (2008).

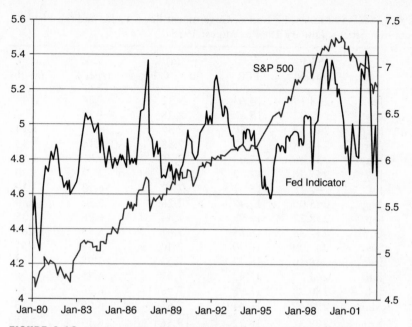

FIGURE 4.16 Fed Model, 1980–2002, Logs of Bond-Stock Yields
Source: Koivu, Pennanen, and Ziemba (2005).

rates get too high relative to stock returns as measured by the earnings over price yield method, then there almost always is a crash. That is, the bonds and stocks compete for the money in a strategic asset allocation. We used a difference method in Ziemba and Schwartz (1991), Ziemba (2003), Berge, Consiglio, and Ziemba (2007), and Ziemba and Ziemba (2007), which have various results.

Figure 4.16 uses a ratio or log approach and is equivalent to what is now called the Fed model; see Koivu, Pennanen and Ziemba (2005). It called the −22% fall in the S&P 500 in 2002.

Ziemba started using these measures in 1988 in a study group in Japan at the Yamaichi Research Institute. It predicted the 1987 crash; see Table 4.6 and Figure 4.17. Observe that all three danger zone violations led to 10%+ declines. It also predicted the 1990 Japan crash and, through one of his research team members, he told Yamaichi executives about this in late 1989. but they would not listen. Yamaichi went bankrupt in 1995; they would have survived if they had listened to Ziemba and his study group. They could have paid a million dollars for an hour's consulting and still made more than 1000 times profit from the advice. It was more important for them to be nice to his family, as they were, than to listen to the results of a *gaijin* professor. How could he possibly understand the Japanese stock

TABLE 4.6 S&P 500 Index, PE Ratios, Government Bond Yields and the Yield Premium over Stocks, January 1984 to August 1988

		S&P Index	PER	(a) 30 Yr G bd	(b) 1/pe,%	(a)–(b)
1986	Jan	208.19	14.63	9.32	6.84	2.48
	Feb	219.37	15.67	8.28	6.38	1.90
	Mar	232.33	16.50	7.59	6.06	1.53
	Apr	237.98	16.27	7.58	6.15	1.43
	May	238.46	17.03	7.76	5.87	1.89
	Jun	245.30	17.32	7.27	5.77	1.50
	Jul	240.18	16.31	7.42	6.13	1.29
	Aug	245.00	17.47	7.26	5.72	1.54
	Sep	238.27	15.98	7.64	6.26	1.38
	Oct	237.36	16.85	7.61	5.93	1.68
	Nov	245.09	16.99	7.40	5.89	1.51
	Dec	248.60	16.72	7.33	5.98	1.35
1987	Jan	264.51	15.42	7.47	6.49	0.98
	Feb	280.93	15.98	7.46	6.26	1.20
	Mar	292.47	16.41	7.65	6.09	1.56
	Apr	289.32	16.22	9.56	6.17	3.39
	May	289.12	16.32	8.63	6.13	2.50
	Jun	301.38	17.10	8.40	5.85	2.55
	Jul	310.09	17.92	8.89	5.58	3.31
	Aug	329.36	18.55	9.17	5.39	3.78
	Sep	318.66	18.10	9.66	5.52	4.14
	Oct	280.16	14.16	9.03	7.06	1.97
	Nov	245.01	13.78	8.90	7.26	1.64
	Dec	240.96	13.55	9.10	7.38	1.72
1988	Jan	250.48	12.81	8.40	7.81	0.59
	Feb	258.10	13.02	8.33	7.68	0.65
	Mar	265.74	13.42	8.74	7.45	1.29
	Apr	262.61	13.24	9.10	7.55	1.55
	May	256.20	12.92	9.24	7.74	1.50
	Jun	270.68	13.65	8.85	7.33	1.52
	Jul	269.44	13.59	9.18	7.36	1.82
	Aug	263.73	13.30	9.30	7.52	1.78

Source: Ziemba and Schwartz (1991).

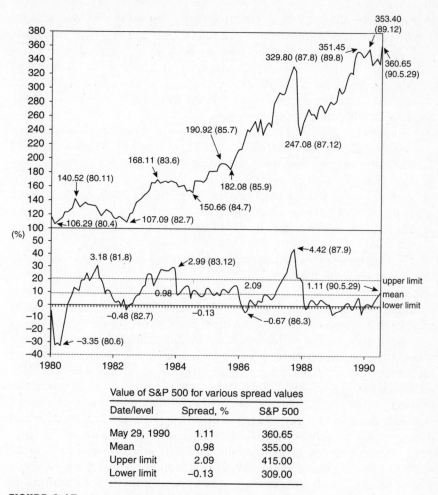

FIGURE 4.17 Bond and Stock Yield Differential Model for the S&P 500, 1980–1990
Source: Ziemba and Schwartz (1991).

market? In fact all the economics ideas were there; see Ziemba and Schwartz (1991). Ziemba did enjoy these lectures, dinners, and golf but being listened to dominates.

■ The great economist Paul Samuelson wrote Ziemba: the Japanese stock market is held together with chewing gum. He was right, sort of. But Ziemba did find that all the US research on anomalies, prediction models, and so on worked in Japan on 1948–1988 data; see Ziemba and Schwartz (1991).

- Ziemba found for 1948 to 1988 for Japan that every time the measure was in the danger zone there was a fall of 10% or more with no misses. This was 12/12 but 8 other 10% declines were not predicted. From 1948 to 1989, the Nikkei stock average rose 221 times in yen and 550 times in US dollars, yet there were 10%+ declines. In late 1989 the model had the highest reading ever in the danger zone and predicted the January 1990 start of the crash then.
- George Soros shorted Japan in 1988 before the bond-stock model went into the danger zone and lost millions. He also shorted too soon in 2000 and lost millions there, too. But do not worry, net he has made, and continues to make, billions most years.
- Had he waited till the model said to short, late fall 1989, he would have made millions with his deep pockets.
- The market peaked at the end of December 1989 with one more interest rate hike.
- Then in January 90 the market started to fall on the first trading day and the entire decline was −56%.

The boxes in Table 4.6 indicate that there is extreme danger in the stock market because 30-year government bond yields are very much higher than usual stock market yields measured by the reciprocal of the last year's reported price earnings ratio. These high interest rates invariably lead to a stock market crash. Here the danger indicator moved across a statistical 95% confidence line in April 1987 (S&P 500 = 289.32). In August and September it moved further into the danger zone. The market ignored this signal but did eventually crash in October 1987. The S&P 500 peak was 329.36 at the end of August which declined to 245.01 at the end of November 1987. These are the monthly values; the actual fall was 22% in the cash and 29% in the futures on the Monday October 19, 2007 crash. Studies of this measure in various countries over long periods of time suggest that stocks continue to rally in the danger zone, but once they get in the zone, it is quite certain they will eventually fall, that is, have a decline of 10% or more within one year. There was a similar signal ignored by most investors in the US S&P 500 in 1999 and then a crash that began in August 2000 and a weak stock market in 2001/02, which is discussed next. For a study of this measure from 1970 to 2000 in five major markets (US, Japan, Canada, Germany, and Hong Kong), see Berge, Consigli, and Ziemba (2007). They show that the simple rule:

> Be in the stock market when the bond-stock yield model is not in the danger zone and in cash when the model is in the danger zone.

Provides final wealth about double *buy and hold* with lower risk and higher Sharpe ratios.

So the measure was successful at predicting future crashes—but when and how deep there is no precise way to know. However, long-run mean reversion suggests that the longer the bull run is and the more overpriced the measure is, the longer and deeper the decline will probably be. Then one can use the measure as part of an econometric system to estimate future scenarios.

Each time the spread in Japan exceeded the 4.23 cutoff (which was higher than 95% confidence) there was a crash. The measure was way in the danger zone in late 1989, and the decline (the 21st crash) began on the first trading day of 1990 with the Nikkei stock average peaking at 38,916.

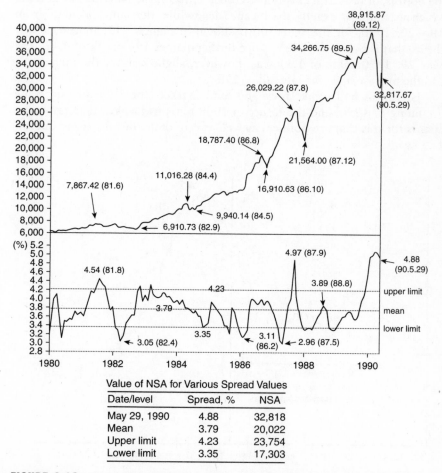

Value of NSA for Various Spread Values		
Date/level	Spread, %	NSA
May 29, 1990	4.88	32,818
Mean	3.79	20,022
Upper limit	4.23	23,754
Lower limit	3.35	17,303

FIGURE 4.18 Bond and Stock Yield Differential Model for NSA, 1980–1990
Source: Ziemba and Schwartz (1991).

See Figure 4.18. The 4.88 in May 1990 means that even after the drop from 39,816 to 32,818, the stock market was still way in the danger zone. The lower limit then was 17,303, and the upper limit was 23,754. So 32,818 was still way too high, and the market later fell way below this. In 2009 it is 80% below the 1989 peak in nominal prices, well below 10,000. It is too bad Yamaichi's top management did not listen to Iishi when Ziemba sent him up to explain our results in Japanese; there was much greater danger in the market then they thought in 1989. By 1995 Yamaichi Securities was bankrupt and ceased to exist.

The model also indicates that the valuation was still high as of May 29, 1990, at 4.88. Not much later, the 22nd crash began. Interestingly, at the bottom of the 22nd crash on October 1, 1990, the NSA was at 20,222, which was almost exactly the mean. Meanwhile, the same calculation on May 29, 1990, for the S&P 500 is shown in Figure 4.17. Indeed, it was cheap, that is below the mean, since the September 1987 peak of 4.42. The May 29, 1990 value of 1.11 was, however, slightly above the mean level and the highest since the late fall of 1987.

Japan has had weak stock and land markets for 20 years, since the beginning of 1990, and the future in 2009 remains bleak. There are many factors for this that are political as well as economic. But the rising interest

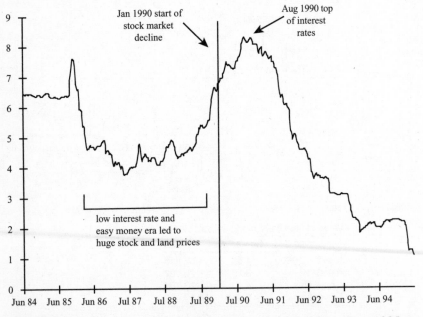

FIGURE 4.19   Short-Term Interest Rates in Japan, June 1984 to June 1995

rates for eight full months until August 1990, see Figure 4.19, is one of them. The vertical line shows the start of the decline on the first day of January 1990. This extreme tightening of an over-leveraged economy was too much. Cheap and easily available money, which caused the big run-up in asset prices in the 1980s turned into expensive and unavailable money in the 1990s. Since 1990, despite 20 years of declining and low interest rates, the economy and financial markets have never recovered.

4.4.1 The 2000–2003 Crash in the S&P 500

The S&P 500 was 470.42 at the end of January 1995. It was about 750 in late 1996 at the time of Alan Greenspan's famous speech on irrational exuberance in the US stock market. It peaked at 1,527.46 on March 24, 2000, fell to 1,356.56 on April 4th, and then came close to this peak reaching 1,520 on September 1st, the Friday before Labor Day. The bond-stock crash model was in the danger zone from April 1999, and it moved deeper in the danger zone as the year progressed as the S&P 500 rose from 1,229.23 at the end of December 1998 to 1,460.25 at the end of December 1999. The PE ratio was flat, increasing only from 32.34 to 33.29, while long bond yields rose from 5.47 to 6.69. The S&P 500 fell to 1,085 on September 7 prior to September 11, 2001.

Table 4.7 and Figure 4.20(a) detail this from January 1995 to December 1999. The spread reached three which was well in the 95% confidence danger band in April and rose to 3.69 in December 1999. The stage was set for a crash, which did occur as shown in Figure 4.21a. Long-term mean reversion indicates that the 1996–2000 S&P 500 values were too high relative to 1991–1995, and a linear interpolation of the latter period gives a value close to that in May 2003.

On March 24, 2000, the S&P 500 was 1,527.46, up from 1,460.25 at the end of December 1999 and 1,229.23 at the end of December 1998. It fell to 1,356.56 on April 4. It then recovered to 1,420 on September 1, a bit below the April 7 high of 1,516.35. The PE ratio was high and flat, moving from 32.34 to 33.29 as of the end of 1999 versus the end of 1998. What caused the market to move into the danger zone according to the bond-stock yield difference model was the increase in the long bond interest rate from 5.42 to 6.69 during 1999. The spread was in the danger zone as of April 1999 at 3.03, and it moved further into the danger zone during 1999, reaching 3.69 in December 1999.

Meanwhile Hong Kong, as shown in Figure 4.20(b), was also in the danger zone. Figure 4.22 shows the Nasdaq 100 index, which went even higher and fell more. But again, the mean reversion line shows that the 2002 value was consistent with the earnings gain from 1991–2002.

TABLE 4.7 Bond and Stock Yield Differential Model for the S&P 500, 1995–1999

		a	b	c = 1/a	b−c
Year	Month	S&P 500 Index	PER	30-yr Gov't Bond	Return on Stocks	Crash Signal
1995	Jan	470.42	17.10	8.02	5.85	2.17
	Feb	487.39	17.75	7.81	5.63	2.18
	Mar	500.71	16.42	7.68	6.09	1.59
	Apr	514.71	16.73	7.48	5.98	1.50
	May	533.40	16.39	7.29	6.10	1.19
	Jun	544.75	16.68	6.66	6.00	0.66
	Jul	562.06	17.23	6.90	5.80	1.10
	Aug	561.88	16.20	7.00	6.17	0.83
	Sep	584.41	16.88	6.74	5.92	0.82
	Oct	581.50	16.92	6.55	5.91	0.64
	Nov	605.37	17.29	6.36	5.78	0.58
	Dec	615.93	17.47	6.25	5.72	0.53
1996	Jan	636.02	18.09	6.18	5.53	0.65
	Feb	640.43	18.86	6.46	5.30	1.16
	Mar	645.50	19.09	6.82	5.24	1.58
	Apr	654.17	19.15	7.07	5.22	1.85
	May	669.12	19.62	7.21	5.10	2.11
	Jun	670.63	19.52	7.30	5.12	2.18
	Jul	639.96	18.80	7.23	5.32	1.91
	Aug	651.99	19.08	7.17	5.24	1.93
	Sep	687.31	19.65	7.26	5.09	2.17
	Oct	705.27	20.08	6.95	4.98	1.97
	Nov	757.02	20.92	6.79	4.78	2.01
	Dec	740.74	20.86	6.73	4.79	1.94
1997	Jan	786.16	21.46	6.95	4.66	2.29
	Feb	790.82	20.51	6.85	4.88	1.97
	Mar	757.12	20.45	7.11	4.89	2.22
	Apr	801.34	20.69	7.23	4.83	2.40
	May	848.28	21.25	7.08	4.71	2.37
	Jun	885.14	22.09	6.93	4.53	2.40
	Jul	954.29	23.67	6.78	4.22	2.56
	Aug	899.47	22.53	6.71	4.44	2.27
	Sep	947.28	23.29	6.70	4.29	2.41
	Oct	914.62	22.67	6.46	4.41	2.05
	Nov	955.40	23.45	6.27	4.26	2.01
	Dec	970.43	23.88	6.15	4.19	1.96
1998	Jan	980.28	24.05	6.01	4.16	1.85
	Feb	1,049.34	25.09	6.00	3.99	2.01
	Mar	1,101.75	27.71	6.11	3.61	2.50
	Apr	1,111.75	27.56	6.03	3.63	2.40

TABLE 4.7 (*Continued*)

Year	Month	S&P 500 Index	a PER	b 30-yr Gov't Bond	c = 1/a Return on Stocks	b−c Crash Signal
1998	May	1,090.82	27.62	6.10	3.62	2.48
	Jun	1,133.84	28.65	5.89	3.49	2.40
	Jul	1,120.67	28.46	5.83	3.51	2.32
	Aug	97.28	27.42	5.74	3.65	2.09
	Sep	1,017.01	26.10	5.47	3.83	1.64
	Oct	1,098.67	27.41	5.42	3.65	1.77
	Nov	1,163.63	31.15	5.54	3.21	2.33
	Dec	1,229.23	32.34	5.47	3.09	2.38
1999	Jan	1,279.64	32.64	5.49	3.06	2.43
	Feb	1,238.33	32.91	5.66	3.04	2.62
	Mar	1,286.37	34.11	5.87	2.93	2.94
	Apr	1,335.18	35.82	5.82	2.79	3.03
	May	1,301.84	34.60	6.08	2.89	3.19
	Jun	1,372.71	35.77	6.36	2.80	3.56
	Jul	1,328.72	35.58	6.34	2.81	3.53
	Aug	1,320.41	36.00	6.35	2.78	3.57
	Sep	1,282.70	30.92	6.50	3.23	3.27
	Oct	1,362.92	31.61	6.66	3.16	3.50
	Nov	1,388.91	32.24	6.48	3.10	3.38
	Dec	1,469.25	33.29	6.69	3.00	3.69

Source: Berge and Ziemba (2001).

The model for Japan was hard to interpret because there were high PE ratios, but interest rates were close to zero, so one had a close to 0–0 situation so the model did not seem to apply to Japan in 1999. The model was not in the danger zone with return differences close to zero; see Figure 4.20(c).

We witnessed a dramatic fall in the S&P 500 from its peak of 1,527 in March 2000 to its September 2000 low of 1,085. Further declines occurred in 2001 and 2002; see Figure 4.20(c). The lowest close to May 2003 was 768.63 on October 10, 2002. This decline was similar to previous crashes. There were other signals:

> History shows that a period of shrinking breadth is usually followed by a sharp decline in stock values of the small group of leaders. Then broader market takes a more modest tumble. (Paul Bagnell in late November 1999 in the *Globe and Mail*.)

Figure 4.23 shows the rise in Canada on the Toronto stock exchange (TSE 300) during 1999 and 2000, and the subsequent fall in 2001 and 2000.

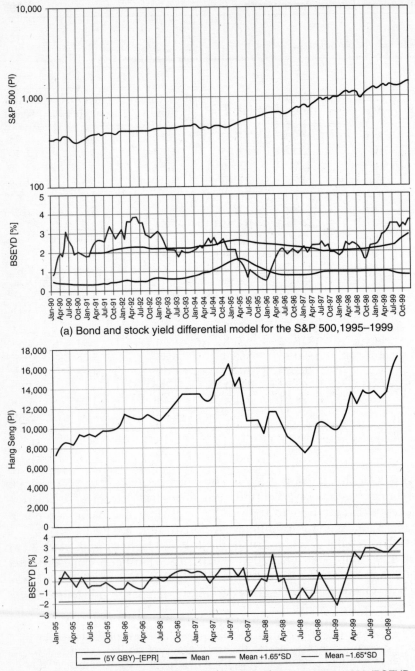

(a) Bond and stock yield differential model for the S&P 500, 1995–1999

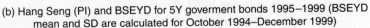

| (5Y GBY)–[EPR] | Mean | Mean +1.65*SD | Mean –1.65*SD |

(b) Hang Seng (PI) and BSEYD for 5Y goverment bonds 1995–1999 (BSEYD mean and SD are calculated for October 1994–December 1999)

FIGURE 4.20 (*Continued*)

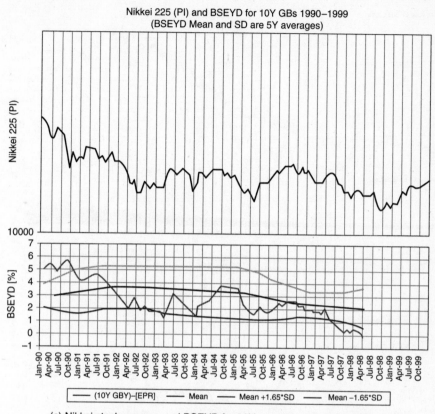

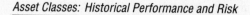

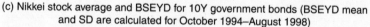

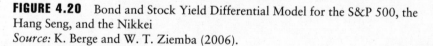

(c) Nikkei stock average and BSEYD for 10Y government bonds (BSEYD mean
and SD are calculated for October 1994–August 1998)

FIGURE 4.20   Bond and Stock Yield Differential Model for the S&P 500, the
Hang Seng, and the Nikkei
Source: K. Berge and W. T. Ziemba (2006).

During 1999, the TSE 300 gained 31% but the gain was only 3% without
three very high PE, high cap stocks. The largest gainer in market value,
Nortel Networks, peaked at US$120 and was about US$1.70 at the end of
2002 and about $3 at the end of May 2003 and under $1 in 2009.

The concentration of stock market gains into very few stocks with momentum and size being the key variables predicting performance was increasing before 1997 in Europe and North America. Table 4.8 for 1998 shows
that the largest cap stocks had the highest return in North American and
Europe, but small cap stocks outperformed in Asia and Japan. The situation
was similar from 1995 to 1999 with 1998 and 1999 the most exaggerated.

(a) 1991–2002

(b) Around Sept 11, 2001

FIGURE 4.21 The S&P 500
Source: Yahoo! Finance.

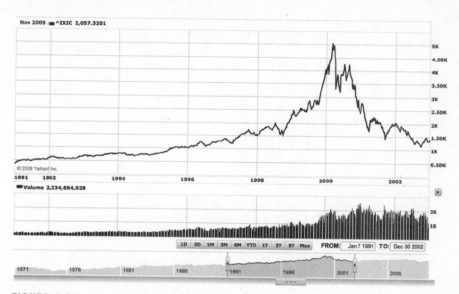

FIGURE 4.22 The Nasdaq, 1990–2002
Source: Yahoo! Finance.

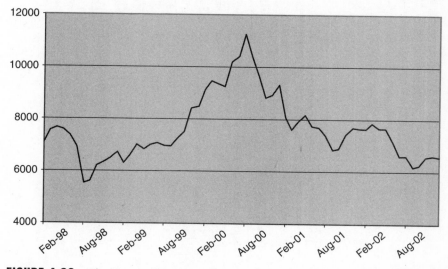

FIGURE 4.23 The Toronto Stock Exchange, February 1998 to January 2003

TABLE 4.8 MSCI Indexes Grouped into Quintiles by 12/31/97 P/E ratio, 12/31/98

Quintile	World All P/E	Equity MktCap	Total Return	North America P/E	Equity MktCap	Total Return	Europe – All P/E	Equity MktCap	Total Return	Latin America P/E	Equity MktCap	Total Return	Asia ex Japan P/E	Equity MktCap	Total Return	Japan P/E	Equity MktCap	Total Return
1 Highest	57	13%	48%	48	20%	63%	55	25%	53%	31	−38%	−31%	36	−6%	7%	134	8%	−5%
2	25	13%	45%	26	16%	43%	24	24%	25%	19	−32%	−21%	18	10%	10%	39	16%	16%
3	18	9%	30%	20	7%	24%	19	16%	32%	14	−38%	−28%	13	15%	11%	29	15%	12%
4	14	−1%	17%	17	1%	30%	15	−0.4%	35%	9	−34%	−37%	8	−2%	13%	22	28%	24%
5 lowest	8	3%	17%	13	−1%	11%	10	−3%	13%	5	−27%	−25%	5	19%	35%	14	38%	32%

The influential book *Irrational Exuberance* by Yale behavioral finance economist Robert Shiller (2000) hit the market in April 2000. It was a monumental success in market timing, with an especially bearish view that is consistent with our Figure 4.20 and Table 4.18. Shiller's Figures 4.10ab document very high PE ratios in relation to earnings in 2000 with most of the rise in the 1995–2000 period similar to our Table 4.7 for the S&P 500. His 100-plus year graphs are very convincing, in 1996–2000 that the stock market was over priced relative to historical norms.

1. We should be able to use measures like the bond-stock return difference and research like Shiller's graphs to create better scenarios. We argue in this book that the mean is by far the very most important aspect of return distributions, and that is clear here. Figure 4.14 for the S&P 500 in 2000–2002 reminds us of that. The bond-stock yield differential model post 2003 is discussed in Chapter 5

2. The extent of such danger measures also suggest that the entire distribution from which scenarios are drawn should be shifted left towards lower and more volatile returns. We know that volatility usually increases as markets decline. Koivu, Pennanan, and Ziemba (2005) show one way to create such *better* scenarios.

3. The evidence is high that, over long horizons, stocks outperform bonds, T-bills, and most other financial assets in the long run; see especially Siegel (2008) and Dimson, Marsh, and Staunton (2009) and Figures 4.3(a) and 4.3(b), and Table 4.3. Stocks generally outperform in times of inflation and bonds outperform in times of deflation; see, for instance, Smith (1924). Why do stocks generally outperform bonds? "A major reason is that businesses retain earnings, with these going onto create more earnings and dividends too" (from the review of Smith (1924) by J. M. Keynes in 1925 quoted in Buffett (2001)). In times of growth, firms borrow at fixed cost with the expectation of earning positive economic profit so in the long-term, equities as a reflection of this positive income creation should grow at the rate of productivity.

4. There are occasional long periods when stocks underperform alternative asset classes. Figure 4.3(b) from Siegel (2008) shows this for the real Dow Jones average from 1885 to 2006 in 2006 dollars, and Figure 4.14 shows the 2000–2002 period. When bonds outperform stocks, as in this latter period, they are usually negatively correlated with stocks as well; see Figure 4.15, which has rolling correlations. Between 1982 and 1999 the return of equities over bonds was more than 10% per year in EU countries. The question is whether we are moving back to a period where the two asset classes move against each other or whether this will just prove to be a temporary phenomenon.

Moreover, the historical evidence since 1802 for the United States and 1700 for the UK indicates that the longer the period the more likely is this dominance to occur. Siegel (2008) shows that over all 30- and most 20-year periods from 1926 to 2006 US equities outperformed bonds and that over 30-year horizons, it is optimal (with a mean-variance model) to be more than 100% in stocks and short bonds based on the past. Siegel uses a range of risk tolerance attitudes such as ultraconservative and risk taking. These are easy to devise using the Kallberg-Ziemba (1983) results by just assigning Arrow-Pratt risk aversion values as I have done in the second column of Siegel's Table 4.4. Over 100% means more than 100% stocks or a levered long position, which would be short bonds or cash.

4.5   HEDGE FUNDS

Hedge funds are pools of largely other people's money. The idea is to be independent of equity and other markets and to produce positive returns in all markets: up, down or sideways. They are lucrative to run with typical management fees of 2% of assets under management and 20% of the net new profits by the high watermark system so this incentive fee is only paid when it is earned. But previous fees are usually not returned if a hedge fund goes out of business or never again reaches its high watermark. Currently in June 2009 there are many hedge funds in this situation, and it is projected that about half of the hedge funds in existence in 2007 will no longer be in business by 2010. But recently the exodus of hedge funds has slowed. According to Hedge Fund Research and Eurekahedge, 376 funds closed in Q1:2009 versus 778 in Q4:2008, to about 9,050 funds; see Gangahar (2009). Still, ordinary hedge funds and funds of hedge funds, which typically charge an additional 1%+ plus 10%+ on top of the various fees for the individual hedge funds can be good investments. Indeed they are a favorite of wealthy investors, pension funds, university endowments, etc. There is pressure to reduce fees to secure new permanent capital. Many hedge funds are reducing the 2+20 to 1.5+10 for new money, which will greatly reduce fees; see Brewster (2009). A factor here is funds below their benchmarks are not providing incentive fees and the generally poor performance of many hedge funds. In some cases, such as Calpers, there is also a push toward a *clawback* of fees for funds that did well after a money-losing year. In addition, it is possible to attempt to clone hedge fund strategies using less expensive ETFs to replicate them such as shorting the market, double shorting the market, covered calls, Hasanhodzic and Lo (2007) studied how this cloning might be done and discuss some of the pitfalls of such ETFs.

In choosing a hedge fund or fund of hedge funds, there are many considerations. In particular, it is important to consider the risk-taking behavior of the management. Kowenberg and Ziemba (2007) have studied this behavior both in a theoretical continuous time model and in an empirical study.

In a continuous time model, they study how incentive fees and manager's own investment in the fund affect the investment strategy of hedge fund managers. The behavioral finance objective function penalizes losses more than it rewards gains with the breakpoint being the point where incentive fees are earned. Loss-averse managers increase the risk of the fund's investment strategy with higher incentive fees. However, risk taking is greatly reduced if a substantial amount of the manager's own money (at least 30%) is in the fund. Using the Zurich hedge fund universe, with data from 1977 to 2000, they test the relation between risk taking and incentive fees empirically. Hedge funds with incentive fees have significantly lower mean returns (net of fees), while downside risk is positively related to the incentive fee level. Funds of funds charging large incentive fees achieve relatively high mean returns, but with significantly higher risk as well.

Figure 4.24 displays the implicit level of loss aversion as a function of the incentive fee for three different levels of the manager's stake in the

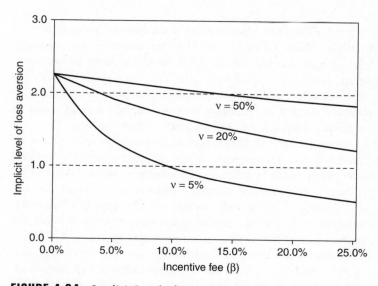

FIGURE 4.24 Implicit Level of Loss Aversion as a Function of Incentive Fee, with Fixed Fee of $\alpha = 1\%$, and with Separate Lines for Different Levels of the Manager's Stake in the Fund (v)
Source: Kouwenberg and Ziemba (2007).

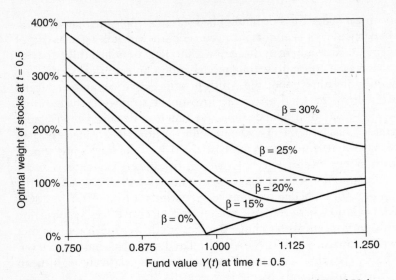

FIGURE 4.25 Optimal Weight of Stocks as a Function of Fund Value at Time t, with Manager's Stake in the Fund of $v = 20\%$, and with Separate Lines for Different Levels of Incentive Fee (β)
Source: Kouwenberg and Ziemba (2007).

fund (5%, 20% and 50%). The manager's implicit level of loss aversion is equal to 2.25 without incentive fees ($\beta = 0$). As the incentive fee increases, the implicit level of loss aversion of the fund manager starts to decrease, indicating that the manager should optimally care less about losses and more about gains due to the convex compensation structure assumed in the model. The negative impact of incentive fees on implicit loss aversion is mitigated if the manager owns a substantial part the fund.

Figure 4.25 shows that the fund manager takes more risk in response to an increasing incentive fee. The increase in risk is more pronounced when the fund value drops below the benchmark. Due to the structure of the value function of prospect theory, a fund manager without an incentive fee will increase risk at low fund values as well; incentive fees amplify this behavior. Figure 4.26 shows the effect on the optimal investment strategy of changing the manager's own stake in the fund v, given an incentive fee of $\beta = 20\%$. An increase of the manager's share in the fund can completely change risk taking. With a stake of 10% or less, the manager behaves extremely risk seeking as a result of the incentive fee. However, with a stake of 30% or more, the investment strategy is very similar to the base case of 100% ownership (without an incentive fee).

A typical hedge fund charges an incentive fee of 20%. For hedge fund investors it is important to know what the cost of such a fee arrangement is.

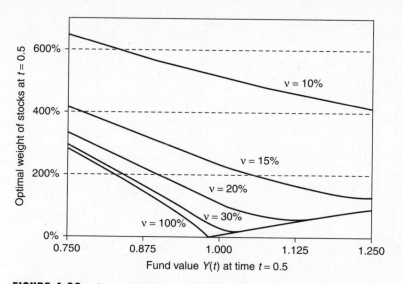

FIGURE 4.26 Optimal Weight of Stocks as a Function of Fund Value at Time t, with Incentive Fee of $\beta = 20\%$, and with Separate Lines for Different Levels of the Manager's Stake in the Fund (v)
Source: Kouwenberg and Ziemba (2007).

The incentive fee can be considered as a call option on fund value with exercise price $\beta(T)$, granted by the investors to the fund manager as additional management compensation.

Figure 4.27 plots the value of a 20% incentive fee as a function of the manager's stake in the fund. The value of the 20% incentive fee ranges from 0% to 17% of the initial fund value, depending on the manager's own stake in the fund. If the manager's stake in the fund is 100%, the manager does not care about the incentive fee and manages the fund conservatively since it is a personal account. However, as the manager's stake in the fund goes to zero, the manager starts to increase the riskiness of the investment strategy in order to reap more profits from the incentive fee contract, and the value of the option increases greatly.

Kouwenberg and Ziemba (2007) test empirically whether hedge fund managers with incentive fees take more risk in practice, using the Zurich Hedge Fund Universe (formerly known as the MAR database). They apply a cross-sectional regression of risk on the incentive fee level and four control variables. Apart from volatility, they employ alternative risk measures such as maximum drawdown and the first downside moment as the dependent variable. They correct for the highly nonnormal cross-sectional distribution of the risk measures by using log-transformations and a skewed Student-t error distribution.

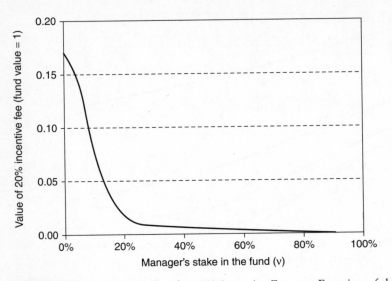

FIGURE 4.27   Option Value of a 20% Incentive Fee, as a Function of the
Manager's Stake in the Fund
Source: Kouwenberg and Ziemba (2007).

The cross-sectional analysis shows that hedge funds with incentive fees
have significantly lower mean returns (net of fees). The risk measures, maximum drawdown and first downside moment, are positively related to the
level of the incentive fee. There is no significant relation between volatility
and incentive fees. Among funds of funds there is a significantly positive
relation between incentive fees and all three risk measures at the 5% level.
Funds of funds with higher incentive fees also have higher average returns,
increased risk taking, and more upside return potential, while the impact on
the risk-adjusted performance measures is insignificant. A potential explanation for these results is that loss-averse fund of funds managers with incentive
fees opt for a more risky basket of hedge funds to increase the value of their
call option on fund value. Another explanation could be that funds of funds
with high incentive fees try to add value with an active hedge fund allocation
strategy, while low fee funds tend to focus on offering due diligence service
and diversification. It is difficult to disentangle the two explanations, as the
investment strategy might depend on the incentive fee level.

Based on their empirical results, investors should evaluate individual
hedge funds with incentive fee arrangements critically. The presence of a
20% incentive fee reduces a fund's average after-fee return by 2.93% (absolute reduction) and the Sharpe ratio by 0.16, compared to a fund without an
incentive fee, assuming other things are equal. Among funds of funds, the

impact of incentive fees appears to be a shift upward in both risk and return, without adverse consequences for risk-adjusted performance. The presence of a 20% incentive fee increases the average after-fee return by 2.87% and volatility by about 4.5%, while the fund's alpha and Sharpe ratio are not affected significantly.

An interesting unresolved question is why the relation between incentive fees and risk taking is relatively mild for individual hedge funds, but quite strong for funds of funds. A potential explanation fitting in the theoretical framework of this chapter is that managers of individual hedge funds tend to have a larger stake in their own fund than funds of fund managers. Alternative explanations might be that peer group pressure is stronger among managers of individual hedge funds, or differences in high-water mark provisions.

LeSourd (2009) has studied hedge fund performance in 2008 and for the past 12 years using EDHEC Alternative Asset indexes for different hedge fund strategies. Even including the difficult 2008, where most but not all strategies lost money, more than half of the strategies had cumulative net returns over 100% in the past 10 years (see Fig. 4.28). In 2008, funds of hedge funds lost 17%, the worst year since EDHEC began keeping these records in 1997. Of the hedge funds, only CTAs and short sellers had positive returns, while other strategies lost from −1.03 (merger arbitrage) to −30.30 (emerging markets). See Table 4.9 for these results as well as the results for 2007 and 3- and 10-year average and cumulative returns. Table 4.10 has the net returns for individual years from 1997 to 2008.

Five of the strategies (Convertible Arbitrage, Distressed Securities, Emerging Markets, Fixed Income Arbitrage, and Funds of Funds) had a negative average return during 2006–2008, and only four (CTA Global, Global Macro, Merger Arbitrage, and Short Selling) had an average return above 5% for this same period. The two positive strategies, CTA Global and Short Selling, had higher average performance for the recent 3 year period than for the last 10 years. All other strategies, except Merger Arbitrage, did considerably worse over the short-term (the past three years) than over the long-term (the past 10 years). The short-term performance of Merger Arbitrage is only slightly worse than its long-term performance.

After a return of 10.07% in 2007, the Funds of Funds strategy posted negative returns (−17.08%) in 2008, the first year that this strategy has posted a negative annual return. 2008 losses cause short-term performance (over the last three years) to fall into negative territory, at −0.41%. Over the long-term, this strategy posts an average return slightly above 6%, less than one basis point below the average return of the median strategy (LeSourd, 2009).

TABLE 4.3 Comparison of 2008, Short-Term, and Long-Term Hedge Fund Strategy Performance

	2008 Annual Return*	2007 Annual Return*	3-Year Average* Return (2006–2008)	3-Year Cumulative Return (2006–2008)	10-Year Average* Return (1999–2008)	10-Year Cumulative Returns (1999–2008)
Convertible Arbitrage	−26.48%	3.87%	−5.02%	−14.31%	4.75%	59.00%
CTA Global	12.78%	9.89%	10.40%	34.55%	7.39%	104.02%
Distressed Securities	−19.40%	7.16%	−0.93%	−2.76%	9.28%	142.93%
Emerging Markets	−30.30%	20.79%	−1.69%	−4.97%	10.71%	176.56%
Equity Market Neutral	−7.34%	8.34%	2.18%	6.69%	6.46%	87.06%
Event Driven	−16.20%	9.65%	1.06%	3.23%	8.06%	117.12%
Fixed Income Arbitrage	−16.80%	6.01%	−1.82%	−5.35%	4.65%	57.48%
Global Macro	−2.88%	12.93%	5.60%	17.76%	8.17%	119.24%
Long/Short Equity	−15.57%	10.53%	0.05%	0.14%	7.00%	96.79%
Merger Arbitrage	−1.03%	9.11%	6.63%	21.23%	7.46%	105.33%
Relative Value	−13.70%	9.43%	1.44%	4.39%	6.80%	93.07%
Short Selling	24.72%	7.38%	9.04%	29.66%	3.02%	34.64%
Funds of Funds	−17.08%	10.07%	−0.41%	−1.23%	6.22%	82.83%

*Annualized statistics are given.
Source: LeSourd (2009).

TABLE 4.10 Hedge Fund Strategies' Annual Performance from 1997 to 2008, %

	1997	1998	1999	2000	2001	2002	2003	2004	2005	2006	2007	2008
Convertible Arbitrage	14.80	3.13	16.08	17.77	13.78	8.60	10.79	1.10	-1.93	12.32	3.87	-26.48
CTA Global	12.27	14.29	1.80	7.31	3.52	14.58	11.64	5.18	-0.35	5.86	9.89	12.78%
Distressed Securities	16.67	-2.25	19.74	4.82	14.66	5.86	27.35	17.90	9.22	15.27	7.16	-19.40
Emerging Markets	22.56	-26.66	44.59	-3.81	12.52	5.76	31.27	14.31	17.20	18.85	20.79	-30.30
Equity Market Neutral	15.44	10.58	13.17	15.36	8.19	4.72	6.28	4.71	6.52	7.49	8.34	-7.34
Event Driven	21.01	0.99	22.74	9.02	9.31	-1.07	20.47	12.44	7.30	15.48	9.65	-16.20
Fixed Income Arbitrage	12.43	-8.04	12.62	5.72	7.81	7.58	8.37	6.27	4.63	7.43	6.01	-16.80
Global Macro	23.91	8.42	15.72	8.17	5.50	4.98	17.26	4.59	9.50	7.48	12.93	-2.88
Long/Short Equity	21.36	14.58	31.40	12.03	-1.20	-6.38	19.32	8.62	11.35	11.77	10.53	-15.57
Merger Arbitrage	17.44	7.77	17.98	18.11	2.87	-0.88	8.34	4.83	4.95	13.70	9.11	-1.03
Relative Value	16.53	5.28	17.17	13.36	8.61	2.78	12.13	5.72	5.23	11.84	9.43	-13.70
Short Selling	3.07	27.07	-22.55	22.79	10.19	27.27	-23.86	-4.66	7.26	-8.29	7.38	24.72
Funds of Funds	17.40	4.18	28.51	7.83	3.52	1.25	11.46	7.07	6.80	11.25	10.07	-17.08

Annualized statistics are given.
Source: LeSourd (2009).

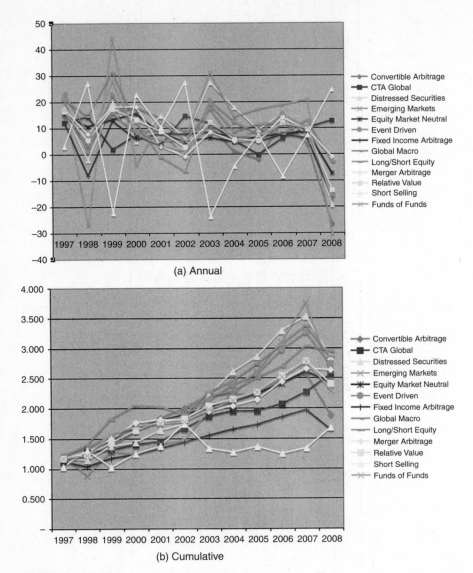

FIGURE 4.28   Performance of Hedge Funds
Source: LeSourd (2009).

During 2008, the S&P 500 fell 37% with major losses in the historically weak months of September (−9%) and October (−17%), but November, usually a strong month with the strongest turn of the month, also fell 9%. In 2007, the S&P 500 had a total return of 5.49%. The historical volatility was much higher in 2008 (21%) versus 2007 (9.66%) and 2006 (5.64%). This pales in comparison with the implied volatility of S&P 500 index puts and calls which reached 90% in October 2008.

4.6 REAL ASSETS

The Yale and Harvard endowments made real assets fashionable for university endowments and pension funds. Timber, oil leases, and various sorts of property were invested in successfully. Real assets tend to preserve value in inflationary times. Mohammed El-Erian, who ran the Harvard endowment and left before the returns turned sour, writes regarding real assets that they will be less potent in the future. For example, for timber, much of the gain from taking advantage of historically poor management has already been captured. The Harvard Management Company (HMC) improved this; then others followed, and HMC sold and capitalized the value. Thus competitive behavior and imitation will limit future gains.

4.6.1 REITs

A real estate investment trust (REIT) is a tax designation for a corporation investing in real estate that reduces or eliminates corporate income taxes. To do this REITs must distribute at least 90% of their income, which may be taxable, directly to the investors. REITs were designed to provide a structure for real estate similar to what mutual funds provide for stock investment. REITs can be publicly or privately held. Public REITs may be listed on stock exchanges similar to shares of common stock. REITs can be classified as equity, mortgage, or hybrid. Key data on a REIT are its NAV (net asset value), AFFO (adjusted funds from operations) and CAD (cash available for distribution). REITs face challenges from both a slowing economy and the global financial crisis, depressing share values by 40 to 70% in some cases.

A similar structure in Canada is the income trust, which is being phased out.

4.7 HOUSING AS AN ASSET CLASS

Surveys and ads for reverse mortgages have shown that many people expect that their homes will pay for their retirement. How accurate is this expectation?

From 2002–2006 there was a housing bubble so many speculators gained by buying extra houses on margin. In 2007–2009 the declines in the US hurt such speculators hard, and many went into receivership. Indeed over 10 million houses in the US in January 2009 were under water in the sense that their mortgages exceed their current market value.

The Standard and Poor's Case-Shiller US Home Price Index measures the index price of 10 and 20 metropolitan areas in the US. It gives an estimate of the change in home values across the US. Figure 4.29a shows the Case-Shiller US house price index year to date for each month, and Figure 4.29b shows the historical price index. Observe that in February 2009 housing prices had fallen to their third-quarter 2003 levels.

For the period December 1, 2007, to November 30, 2008, prices in the 20 areas fell a record 18.2% with November 2008 adding a 2.2% decline. The housing market continues to suffer from a large supply of unsold homes, tighter lending standards, and a record number of foreclosures. The 10 metro regions also fell 2.2% in November for a yearly drop of 19.1%. The composite 10 and 20 metro regions peaked in mid-2006 and since then (to February 2009) have fallen 32% and 30%, respectively.

Areas that had large increases had large falls. This includes many cities in California, Nevada, and Florida. From March 2008 to March 2009, for example, San Francisco fell 43%. There were similar drops in San Jose and other areas in California.

The lending organizations sold off the mortgages, and they were cut and diced and bundled into packages like CMOs and CDOs and sold to others who had trouble figuring out what is in them but had looked at the rating agency's stamp of approval. A triple-A rating was desirable for sales of these derivative securities.

Figure 4.30, starting in 1890, shows the buildup to overpriced areas in 2004–2005 that led to the drop now that is shown in Figure 4.29. There have been 12 consecutive months of negative returns. The 10-city, 20-city decline and 10-city composite all declined. Case-Shiller and others predict up to a 25–35% drop in prices from the peak in 2004–2005.

The housing price declines have left more than 20% of US homeowners owing more on their mortgages than their houses are worth by the end of Q1:2009. That represents 20.4 million households, up from 16.3 million in Q4:2008. That is 21.9% of all homeowners, up from 17.6% Q4:2008 and 14.3% Q3:2008. On the one hand, the falling home prices are making housing more affordable for first-time buyers and others who have had difficulty getting into the market. On the other hand, the fall in home equity has cut off the ability of homeowners to use their homes like an ATM as refinancing is harder so they cannot take advantage of the low interest rates. The regions with the highest percentage of homes under water are shown in Table 4.11

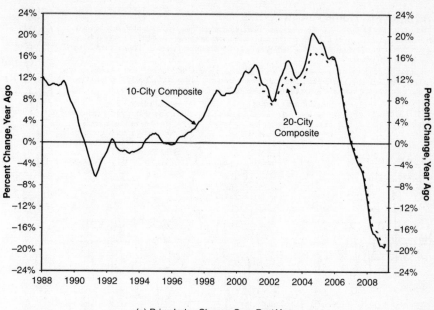

(a) Price Index Change Over Past Year

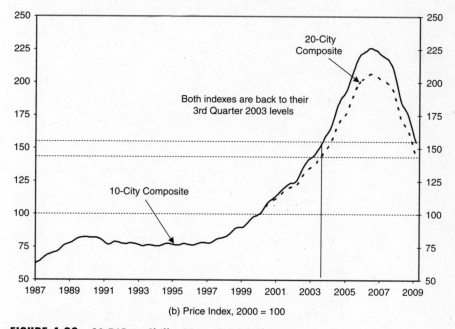

(b) Price Index, 2000 = 100

FIGURE 4.29 S&P/Case-Shiller Home Price Indexes
Source: S&P Press Release, April 28, 2009; Standard & Poor's & Fiserv.

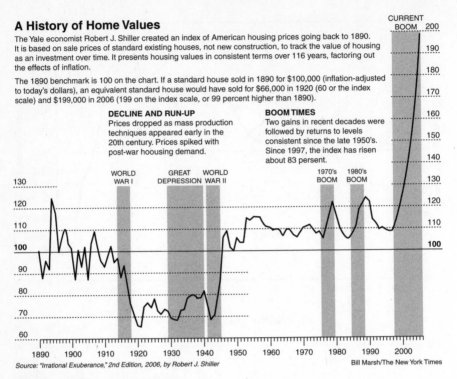

A History of Home Values

The Yale economist Robert J. Shiller created an index of American housing prices going back to 1890. It is based on sale prices of standard existing houses, not new construction, to track the value of housing as an investment over time. It presents housing values in consistent terms over 116 years, factoring out the effects of inflation.

The 1890 benchmark is 100 on the chart. If a standard house sold in 1890 for $100,000 (inflation-adjusted to today's dollars), an equivalent standard house would have sold for $66,000 in 1920 (60 or the index scale) and $199,000 in 2006 (199 on the index scale, or 99 percent higher than 1890).

DECLINE AND RUN-UP
Prices dropped as mass production techniques appeared early in the 20th century. Prices spiked with post-war hoousing demand.

BOOM TIMES
Two gains in recent decades were followed by returns to levels consistent since the late 1950's. Since 1997, the index has risen about 83 percent.

Source: "Irrational Exuberance," 2nd Edition, 2006, by Robert J. Shiller   Bill Marsh/The New York Times

FIGURE 4.30   A History of Home Values
Source: Nouriel Roubini (2006).

TABLE 4.11 Metropolitan Regions with the Highest Percentage of Homes with Negative Equity in Q1:2009

Region	% Underwater
Las Vegas, NV	67.2
Stockton, CA	51.1
Modesta, CA	50.8
Reno, NV	48.5
Vallejo-Fairfield, CA	46.5
Merced, CA	44.4
Port St Lucie, FL	43.5
Riverside, CA	42.8
Phoenix, AZ	41.7
Orlando, FL	41.7
US average	21.9

Source: Simon and Hagerty (2009).

With such a large number of households under water, it will be hard to get a consumer-led recovery. In the UK, the declines are similar, with the year on year values down about 20% for high-end properties in London during 2008–2009.

4.8   GOLD AND OTHER COMMODITIES

Gold is very hard to predict short-term with many ups and downs for reasons that are hard to explain based on rational models. Gordon Brown sold much of the UK gold supply when it was about $200/ounce during the 2000–2003 stock market decline. Other central banks are selling gold. But the Chinese are accumulating large amounts especially from domestic sources. Yet many advocate holding gold long-term as a store of value in both inflationary and deflationary times. This can be seen in the popular culture where TV ads remind us that gold has been a store of value for thousands of years—some periods it does better than others. In fact, gold peaked in real terms in 1980 and Figure 4.3 shows that $1 invested in gold in 1802 was only worth $14 in 2002. Figure 4.31 shows gold's price behavior from July 1, 2007, to June 30, 2009, using the ETF GLD which has the price of 1/10th of an ounce of gold. Still it and other precious metals are valid asset classes. Silver, using the ETF SLV, is shown in Figure 4.32 for the two years up to June 30, 2009. Platinum has real uses in catalytic converters and gold and silver are prized for jewelry. The world's supply of gold is not large and would fill the area under the base of the Eiffel Tower in Paris.

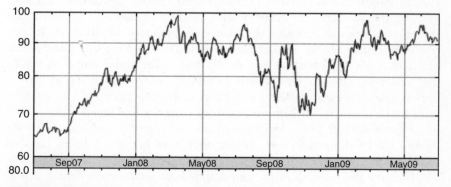

FIGURE 4.31   SPDR Gold Shares (GLD), June 30, 2009
Source: Yahoo!

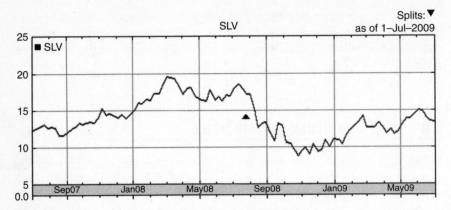

FIGURE 4.32   iShares Silver Trust (SLV), June 30, 2009
Source: Yahoo!

4.9   PRIVATE EQUITY AND RELATED ASSETS

Private equity is discussed in the context of its use by the university endowments such as Yale and Harvard in Sections 13.1 and 13.1.1. One sees very good results up to June 2008 and dismal results since then.

4.10   CURRENCIES

Currency values fluctuate quickly with over $3 trillion traded in the forex market each day plus more in over-the-counter forwards and exchange-traded futures. The relative values of currencies are related to interest rates: current, nominal and real and forecasted and various fundamentals. However, sentiment shifts can occur quickly, and the speculative nature of the traders can lead to overshooting of currency declines and advances. Examples of the latter are the euro at 1.60 in June 2008 and the Canadian dollar at 1.10 in early 2008 both against the US dollar. Yen and dollar carry trades are used from time to time where monies are borrowed in the low yield currency and invested in high yield assets in another country. The strategy works well unless the low interest country currency like Japan falls.

Figures 4.33(a) and 4.33(b) shows the movement of various currencies against the US dollar and euro, respectively from January 2000 to January 2009.

Observe the strength of the yen despite high government debt and low interest rates. But there was a break in the yen based on poor fundamentals in April 2009.

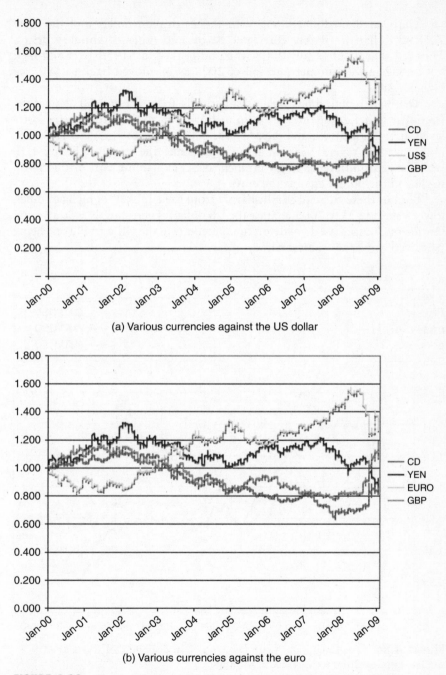

(a) Various currencies against the US dollar

(b) Various currencies against the euro

FIGURE 4.33 Currency Movements from January 2000 to January 2009.
Note: January 2000 = 100.

The Canadian dollar along with the Australian dollar and the New Zealand dollar are highly correlated to oil and other commodity prices. They fell sharply after July 2008 when oil peaked at $147/barrel and then fell to $32 in the summer and fall of 2008 as oil moved back to $80 (see Figure 4.34).

The British pound has fallen dramatically from about 2.00 against the US dollar and 1.25 against the euro in July 2008 to the late January 2009 levels at 1.40 and 1.09, and the May 18, 2009, levels of 1.53 and 1.13. The pound was for several years at about 1.40 versus the euro (see Figure 4.3), with the great difference in government debts explaining part of this sharp decline in the pound against the euro.

Both of these currencies fell sharply from their July 2008 highs to much lower values in May 2009 against the US dollar. There simply was a strong sentiment change based partly on fundamentals in the UK and Europe being perceived as weaker than the US.

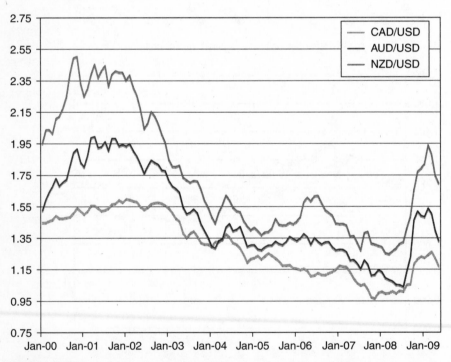

FIGURE 4.34 The Canadian, Australian, and New Zealand Dollars vs. the US Dollar, January 2000 to May 2009, Monthly
Source: Pacific Exchange Rate Service, UBC.

4.11   EVALUATION OF GREAT INVESTORS

In the search for where to invest, the identification of great investors and investing with them is very valuable. Many of these investors are not accepting funds or have had good returns in the distant past but not recently. Here we discuss how we might evaluate them fairly.

Using the ordinary Sharpe ratio does not work well to evaluate great investors, but a modification that does not penalize gains does. The ordinary Sharpe ratio is

$$S = \frac{\mu_p - r_f}{\sigma_p}$$

where μ_p = portfolio mean return, r_f = risk free return, σ_p = portfolio standard deviation, all based on yearly data or less frequent data aggregated S is based on normal distribution theory and is not accurate for distributions like those great investors with large gains and few losses.

Eling (2008) and Eling and Schulmacher (2007) show that the Sharpe ratio is accurate for most mutual funds since they are likely close to normally distributed and the relative rankings of most funds remain about the same in a large sample of nonnormally distributed hedge funds. But we will see here that this is not the case for the greatest investors with mostly gains and few losses.

Figure 4.35 shows some great investors returns from 1985 to 2000. Table 4.12 shows how often they had monthly, quarterly, and yearly losses. We find that there are monthly or quarterly losses about 25–35% of the time. The idea of the DSSR, the downside symmetric Sharpe ratio, as presented in Ziemba (2005) and earlier in Ziemba and Schwartz (1991), is shown in Table 4.13.

Among other things, we want to determine if Warren Buffett through Berkshire Hathaway really is a better investor than the rather good but lesser funds considered here, especially the Ford Foundation and the Harvard endowment, in some fair way.

The idea is presented in Figure 4.36. In Figure 4.37 we have plotted the Berkshire Hathaway and Ford Foundation monthly returns as a histogram and show the losing months and the winning months in a smooth curve. We want to penalize Buffett for losing but not for winning. So define the downside risk as

$$\sigma_{x_-}^2 = \frac{\sum_{i=1}^{n}(x_i - \bar{x})_-^2}{n - 1}.$$

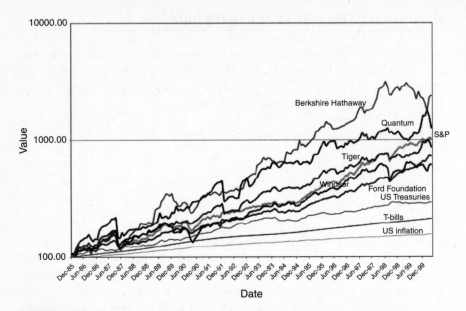

FIGURE 4.35   The Wealth Levels from December 1985 to April 2000 for the Windsor Fund of George Neff, the Ford Foundation, the Tiger Fund of Julian Robertson, the Quantum Fund of George Soros, and Berkshire Hathaway (32% pa 1977–2000), the Fund Run by Warren Buffett, and the S&P 500 Total Return Index

This is the downside variance measured from $\bar{x} = 0$, not the mean, so it is more precisely the downside risk. To get the total variance we use twice the downside variance.

Berkshire is the only fund that improves, but it still does not beat the Ford Foundation—and Harvard is also better than Berkshire, but not Ford, with the quarterly data.

TABLE 4.12   Summary over Funds of Negative Observations and Arithmetic and Geometric Means

	Windsor	BH	Quantum	Tiger	Ford Fd	Harvard	S&P	US Treas
Neg months out of 172	61	58	53	56	44	na	56	54
Neg qtrs out of 57	14	15	16	11	10	11	10	15
Neg years out of 14	2	2	1	0	1	1	1	2

TABLE 4.13 Comparison of Ordinary and Symmetric Downside Sharpe Yearly Performance Measures, 1985 to 2000

	Ordinary	Downside
Ford Foundation	0.970	0.920
Tiger Fund	0.879	0.865
S&P 500	0.797	0.696
Berkshire Hathaway	0.773	0.917
Quantum	0.622	0.458
Windsor	0.543	0.495

Why is this when Berkshire's geometric mean was so much higher than Ford's or Harvard's in this period? The answer as shown in Figure 4.37a,b is that the Berkshire tail returns are too fat.

We now show two outstanding funds. Unfortunately neither is available for investment now. The first with DDSR=13.8 reflecting only three monthly losses in 20 years and no quarterly or yearly losses is Princeton Newport. The fund ran from 1968 to 1988, directed by Dr. Edward O. Thorp. Figure 4.38a and Table 4.14 show the results. Figure 4.38b shows a fund of hedge funds

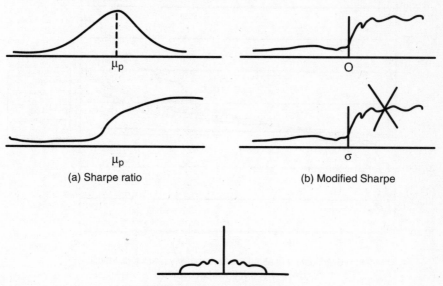

(a) Sharpe ratio (b) Modified Sharpe

(c) Modified Sharpe, symmetric

FIGURE 4.36 Modifying the Sharpe Ratio to Evaluate the Great Investors

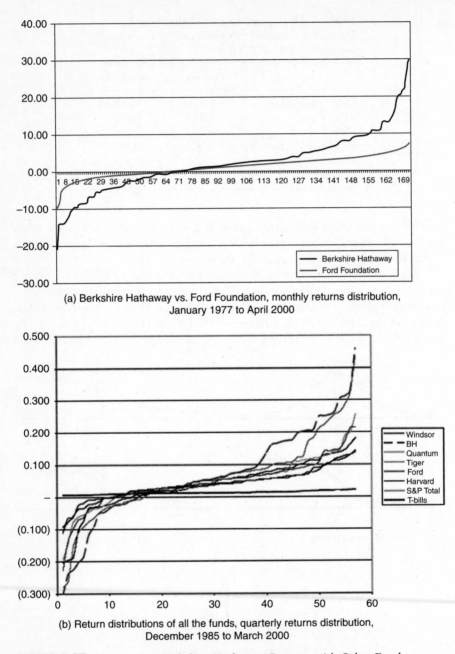

(a) Berkshire Hathaway vs. Ford Foundation, monthly returns distribution,
January 1977 to April 2000

(b) Return distributions of all the funds, quarterly returns distribution,
December 1985 to March 2000

FIGURE 4.37   Comparing Berkshire Hathaway Returns with Other Funds

Price (US dollars)

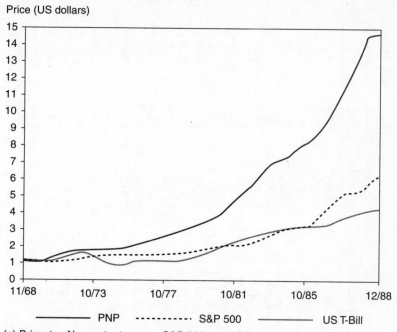

(a) Princeton Newport returns vs. S&P 500 and US T-bills, 1968–1988.
Source: Ziemba (2003).

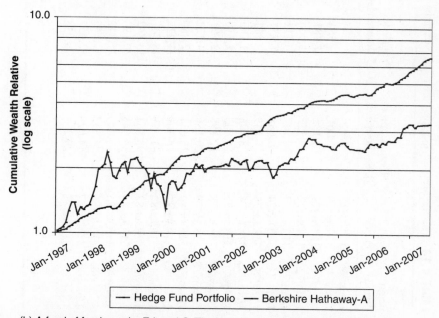

(b) A fund of funds run by Edward O. Thorp vs. Berkshire Hathaway, 1997–2007.
Source: E. O. Thorp private communication (2009).

FIGURE 4.38 Comparing Two Funds Managed by Edward O. Thorp

TABLE 4.14 The Record of Princeton-Newport, November 1, 1969 to December 31, 1988

Begin Period	End Period	Begin Capital (US$ thousands)	Profit/Loss (US$ thousands)	End Capital (US$ thousands)	Added Capital (US$ thousands)	PNP Return (%)	S&P 500 Return (%)	3-Month T-Bill Return (%)
1/Nov/69	31/Dec/69	1,400	57	1,457	544	4.1	4.7	3.0
1/Jan/70	31/Dec/70	2,001	364	2,365	737	18.2	4.0	6.2
1/Jan/71	31/Dec/71	3,102	1,281	4,383	1,944	41.3	14.3	4.4
1/Jan/72	31/Dec/72	6,327	1,046	7,373	1,134	16.5	19.0	4.6
1/Jan/73	31/Dec/73	8,507	711	9,218	(2,550)	8.4	−14.7	7.5
1/Jan/74	31/Dec/74	6,668	751	7,419	(70)	11.3	−26.5	7.9
1/Jan/75	31/Oct/75	7,349	961	8,310	596	13.1	34.3	5.1
1/Nov/75	31/Oct/76	8,906	1,793	10,699	1,106	20.1	20.1	5.2
1/Nov/76	31/Oct/77	11,805	2,350	14,155	3,843	19.9	−6.2	5.5
1/Nov/77	31/Oct/78	17,998	2,797	20,795	(635)	15.5	6.4	7.4
1/Nov/78	31/Oct/79	20,160	4,122	24,282	4,349	20.4	15.3	10.9
1/Nov/79	31/Oct/80	28,631	7,950	36,581	9,728	27.8	21.4	12.0
1/Nov/80	31/Oct/81	46,309	13,227	59,536	2,343	28.6	22.8	16.0
1/Nov/81	31/Oct/82	61,879	18,747	80,626	18,235	30.3	21.8	12.1
1/Nov/82	31/Oct/83	98,861	13,842	112,703	26,342	14.0	10.5	9.1
1/Nov/83	31/Oct/84	139,045	20,193	159,238	(6,195)	14.5	11.6	10.4
1/Nov/84	31/Oct/85	153,043	21,813	174,856	(40,244)	14.3	11.4	8.0
1/Nov/85	31/Oct/86	134,612	41,143	175,755	(21,727)	30.6	24.5	6.3
1/Nov/86	31/Dec/87	154,028	52,451	206,479	17,722	34.1	26.7	7.1
1/Jan/88	31/Dec/88	224,201	8,918	233,119	(232,118)	4.0	3.2	7.4
						1,382.0	545.5	345.0
						15.10	10.2	8.1

run by Thorp from 1997 to 2007 versus Berkshire Hathaway. We see that the funds of funds had a smoother path with higher returns.

Finally we discuss what is arguably the top hedge fund in the world, Renaissance Medallion. Dr. James Simons, a former mathematics professor, hires technical people to devise and implement various proprietary strategies involving some very short-term trading strategies that are in and out in seconds. From a slow start in 1988, Dr. Elwyn Berylkamp, UC Berkeley professor, was instrumental in getting it winning as a smooth path. Now they have about 90 employees, and charge very high fees: 5+44% which is effectively about 50% of the gains. They have very few outside investors (only about six are still in the fund) plus the employees.

Renaissance Medallion's outstanding yearly DSSR of 26.4 is the best we have seen. The yearly Sharpe of 1.68 is decent but not outstanding. The DSSR is needed to capture the true brilliance of this hedge fund. Figures 4.39a,b show the histogram of monthly returns and the monthly rates of return in increasing order for January 1993 to April 2005. The latter shows very few losses and these are small, see Table 4.15 for the monthly, quarterly and yearly returns. Their returns continue strong as shown in the difficult 2008 year; see Table 4.16.

4.12 FUNDAMENTAL AND SEASONAL ANOMALIES OF ASSET RETURNS

The search for excess alpha returns in equity and other markets takes many shapes. One way is to look for anomalies: that is, predictable returns that deviate from the strict random walk model of efficient market theory. One can have fundamental anomalies when the returns are predicted from a series of independent or nearly independent predictive variables such as price earnings ratios, earnings surprise, mean reversion, and so on. The book by Keim and Ziemba (2000) discusses many of these seasonal and fundamental anomalies in various countries across the world. Hirsch (2009) provides a daily commentary on various seasonality effects in US markets throughout the year.

Figure 4.40 shows such a model, which Ziemba and Schwartz (2000) devised for Japan with out-of-sample results in Figure 4.41 for the best 50, 100, 500 stocks rotated monthly versus the market indexes of the price weighting Nikkei 225 and the value weighted Topix index of about 1,000 stocks. Their approach follows that of Jacobs and Levy (1988) who made similar models for the US.

Mean reversion, which has grown in popularity especially since Poterba and Summers (1988), shows up as the second and third best variables. They

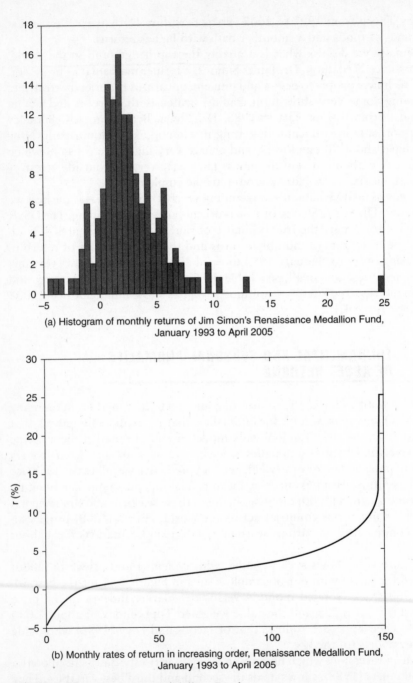

(a) Histogram of monthly returns of Jim Simon's Renaissance Medallion Fund, January 1993 to April 2005

(b) Monthly rates of return in increasing order, Renaissance Medallion Fund, January 1993 to April 2005

FIGURE 4.39 Renaissance Medallion Fund
Source: Ziemba and Ziemba (2007).

TABLE 4.15 Net Returns in Percent of the Medallion Fund, January 1993 to April 2005, Yearly, Quarterly, Monthly

	1993	1994	1995	1996	1997	1998	1999	2000	2001	2002	2003	2004	2005
Annual	39.06	70.69	38.33	31.49	21.21	41.50	24.54	98.53	31.12	29.14	25.28	27.77	
Quarterly													
Q1	7.81	14.69	22.06	7.88	3.51	7.30	(0.25)	25.44	12.62	5.90	4.29	9.03	8.30
Q2	25.06	35.48	4.84	1.40	6.60	7.60	6.70	20.51	5.64	7.20	6.59	3.88	
Q3	4.04	11.19	3.62	10.82	8.37	9.69	6.88	8.58	7.60	8.91	8.77	5.71	
Q4	(0.86)	(1.20)	4.31	8.44	1.41	11.73	9.48	20.93	2.42	4.44	3.62	6.72	
Monthly													
January	1.27	4.68	7.4	3.25	1.16	5.02	3.79	10.5	4.67	1.65	2.07	3.76	2.26
February	3.08	5.16	7.54	1.67	2.03	1.96	−2.44	9.37	2.13	3.03	2.53	1.97	2.86
March	3.28	4.19	5.68	2.77	0.29	0.21	−1.49	3.8	5.36	1.12	−0.35	3.05	2.96
April	6.89	2.42	4.1	0.44	1.01	0.61	3.22	9.78	2.97	3.81	1.78	0.86	0.95
May	3.74	5.66	5.53	0.22	4.08	4.56	1.64	7.24	2.44	1.11	3.44	2.61	
June	12.78	25.19	−4.57	0.73	1.36	2.28	1.71	2.37	0.15	2.13	1.24	0.37	
July	3.15	6.59	−1.28	4.24	5.45	−1.1	4.39	5.97	1	5.92	1.98	2.2	
August	−0.67	7.96	5.91	2.97	1.9	4.31	1.22	3.52	3.05	1.68	2.38	2.08	
September	1.54	−3.38	−0.89	3.25	0.85	6.33	1.15	−1.02	3.38	1.13	4.18	1.33	
October	1.88	−2.05	0.3	6.37	−1.11	5.33	2.76	6.71	1.89	1.15	0.35	2.39	
November	−1.51	−0.74	2.45	5.93	−0.22	2.26	5.42	8.66	0.17	1.42	1.42	3.03	
December	−1.2	1.62	1.52	−3.74	2.77	3.73	1.06	4.3	0.35	1.81	1.81	1.16	

Source: Ziemba and Ziemba (2007).

TABLE 4.16 Hedge Funds, January to September 2008

World's Best-Performing Hedge Funds

Fund	Management Firm	Strategy	Return
Medallion	Jim Simons, Renaissance Technologies	Quantitative	58.0%
Paulson Advantage Plus	John Paulson, Paulson & Co	Event driven	24.6%
Cive	Christian Levett, Clive Capital	Commodities	19.4%
Comac Global Macro	Colm O'Shea, CormacInternational	Macro	19.2%
Clarium	Peter Thiel, Clarium Capital Mgmt	Macro	18.9%
Paulson Credit Opportunities	John Paulson, Paulson & Co	Credit	18.9%
Hoseman European Select	Stephen Roberts, Horseman Capital Mgt	Long/short	18.0%
Horseman Global	John Horseman, Horseman Capital Mgt	Long/short	17.4%
Paulson Credit Opportunities II	John Paulson, Paulson & Co	Credit	15.8%
BlueTrend	Michael Platt, Leda Braga, Blue Crest Capital Mgt	Managed futures	15.7%

World's Most-Profitable Hedge Funds

Fund	Management Firm	Strategy	Profit, $mil
Medallion	Jim Simons, Renaissance Technologies	Quantitative	1,427.7
Paulson Advantage Plus	John Paulson, Paulson & Co	Event driven	617.4
Brevan Howard	Alan Howard, Brevan Howard Asset Mgt	Macro	489.3
BlueTrend	Michael Platt, Leda Braga, Blue Crest Capital Mgt	Managed futures	193.8
Paulson Credit Opportunities	John Paulson, Paulson & Co	Credit	188.2
Clarium	Peter Thiel, Clarium Capital Mgmt	Macro	185.2
Quantitative Global Program	Jeffrey Woodriff Quantitative Investment Mgt	Managed futures	148.5
Winton Futures	David Harding, Winton Capital Mgt.	Managed futures	146.6
Horseman Global	John Horseman, Horseman Capital Mgt	Long/short	123.5

Source: Bloomberg.

Multivariate (Pure) Effects of Thirty Factors on the TSE-I, Ranked by t-Statistics, June 1979 to August 1989

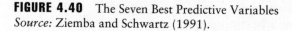

	Factor	Monthly Mean Return from Factor, %	t-Statistic	p-Significance, 2 sided test
1	EST-LACT	0.00788	7.85	0.000
2	EPS	−0.00693	−3.65	0.000
3	RELSTR	−0.00645	−3.42	0.001
4	PDBR	−0.00397	−2.87	0.005
5	R-MAX24	0.00363	2.86	0.005
6	PER	0.00385	2.69	0.008
7	TMVLOG	−0.00429	−2.21	0.029

future earnings relative to current price

mean reversion of monthly prices, measured by monthly residual and by lagged monthly returns

price to book ratio changes

current price relative to previous 24-month high

price earnings ratio

small cap effect

FIGURE 4.40   The Seven Best Predictive Variables
Source: Ziemba and Schwartz (1991).

looked at indexes. We found these mean reversions in 1989 for individual Japanese stocks. For similar results in US stocks, see Jegadeesh and Titman (1993). The fifth-best variable, R-MAX24, suggests that if a stock has fallen too much from its 24-month high, then it will have poor subsequent performance. The other 23 variables add to the predictive power of the model, but

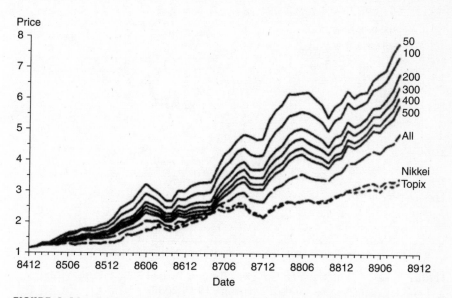

FIGURE 4.41   The 30 Variable Factor Model Predictions Out of Sample, 1984–1989
Source: Ziemba and Schwartz (1991).

these seven are very useful. Beta was not among the seven best predictive variables in Japan but was the eleventh best of the 30 variables.

Portfolios of the top 50, 100, 200, ..., 500 stocks are determined with monthly rebalancing assuming 1% transactions costs. These portfolios beat the Topix (value weighted average of all 1000 plus stocks on Tokyo's first section) and the Nikkei (price weighted average of 225 major stocks) by a good measure. The small firm effect is shown by the difference between these indexes and *All*, an equally weighted measure of all 1,000+ stocks on the first section.

Many firms devise such models, and they frequently are called statistical arbitrage. A second major type of anomaly is based on seasonality. Typical results are that the small stocks have had high returns in January, stocks rise before options expiry and before holidays, and so on. September and October tend to be the worst months with many large declines and crashes.

Figures 4.42 and 4.43 show the strategy *sell in May and go away* from 1993 to 2008 for the S&P 500 large cap index and the Russell 2000 small cap index. Observe that most of the 2007 and 2008 large declines in the stock market were avoided with this strategy. A detailed study of anomalies

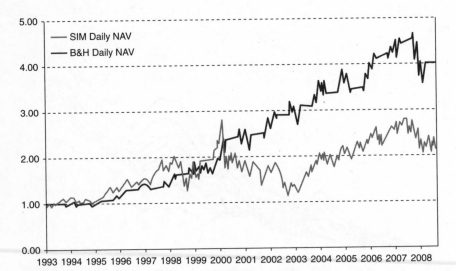

FIGURE 4.42 Sell in May and Go Away Results, Russell 2000 Futures vs. Buy and Hold, Cumulative Sectoral Comparison, 1993–2008
Source: Dzahabrov and Ziemba (2009).
Note: Entry at Close on 6th Day before End of October. Exit 1st Day of May.

Schwartz, S. L., and W. T. Ziemba. 2000. Predicting Returns on the Tokyo Stock Exchange. In D. B. Keim, and W. T. Ziemba (eds.). *Security Market Imperfections in World Wide Equity Markets*, Cambridge University Press, pp. 492–511

Sharpe, W. F. 1994. The Sharpe ratio. *Journal of Portfolio Management* 21, No. 1:49–58.

Shiller, R. 2000. *Irrational Exuberance*. Princeton University Press.

Siegel, J. 2008. *Stocks for the Long Run*, 4th ed. McGraw-Hill.

Simon, R., and H. R. Hagerty. 2009. House price drops leave more underwater. *Wall Street Journal*, May 6.

Smith, E. L. 1924. Common Stocks as Long-Term Investments. Kila, MT: Kessinger Publishing Company.

Swensen, D. W. 2000. Pioneering portfolio management: an unconventional approach to institutional investments. The Free Press.

van Antwerpen, V. A., J. P. Engel, H. M. Kat, and T. P. Kocken. 2004. Why investors should hold long-dated bonds, even when interest rates are low. Working Paper #0020, Alternative Investment Research Centre, Cass University.

Wilkie, A. D. 1987. An option pricing approach to bonus policy. *Journal of the Institute of Actuaries* 114:2190.

———. 1995. On the risk of stocks in the long run: a response to Zvi Bodie, mimeo.

———. 1998. Why the long-term reduces the risk of investing in shares. *Proceedings of the 8th International AFSR Colloquium*, Cambridge, 16–17 (September):525–538.

Wilmott, J. 2009. Possible futures. In *Credit Suisse Global Investment Returns Yearbook*.

Ziemba, W. T. 2003. *The Stochastic Programming Approach to Asset Liability and Wealth Management*, AIMR.

———. 2005. The symmetric downside risk Sharpe ratio and the evaluation of great investors and speculators. *Journal of Portfolio Management* (Fall):108–122.

———, and S. L. Schwartz. 1991. *Invest Japan*. Probus.

Ziemba, R. E. S., and W. T. Ziemba. 2007. *Scenarios for Risk Management and Global Investment Strategies*. John Wiley & Sons.

CHAPTER 5

The Current Economic Crisis and Its Impact on Retirement Decisions

There is a time bomb for boomers: How to restore value to their pension savings? Retirement is only ever out of current production. The March to September 2009 equity market rally has restored some of the losses.

5.1   HOUSEHOLD AND GOVERNMENT DEBT

While house prices surged from 2000 to 2005–2007, household debt was also surging. Household debt went from 60% of disposable income (after tax) in 1985 to 80% in the early 1990s and soared to 120% in 2007. In the years from 2001 to 2004 about 40% rewrote their mortgages, 25% extracted equity in the process. The under 30s and the over 63s extracted lower rates of equity (15% and 18%, respectively). The funds were used for consumption (10.5%), payment of other debt (23.5%), home improvement (32.2%), and investment including the stock market (33.8%). In sum, the value of primary residences increased $4,164 billion, and $783 billion was extracted from equity, and $267 billion went into consumption. House values increased another $6.4 trillion from 2004 to 2006, if the same ratios held then, about $410 billion went into consumption. For the households that extracted equity and then consumed it, their net worth did not increase, but when the bubble burst they lost net worth as their assets have declined in value while their debt has increased. Up to 2008 those workers near retirement that remortgaged and extracted wealth had lost 14% of net worth just from this shift, in addition they likely lost a lot on their retirement savings. They will have the hardest time recovering retirement savings (Munnell and Soto 2008).

TABLE 5.1 G7 Debt to GDP Ratios, 2008

Canada	22%
Britain	33%
France	36%
Germany	43%
US	46%
Italy	87%
Japan	88%

Source: Globe and Mail, January 22, 2009.

The US and UK households have very high debt compared to disposable income which has been steadily rising from 1990 to 2008. This is at the heart of the housing declines in both countries. Canada and the euro zone have much less debt, which is partly a result of much tighter standards for mortgages and other lending. Banks in the US and the UK basically would lend money to anyone for real estate transactions given their false forecast that prices would continue to rise. Then the decline in real estate values had a much bigger effect in these countries. Table 5.1 shows the government debt as a percentage of GDP in 2008. Japan and Italy have the highest debt ratios. But the citizens of Japan have large savings, which tempers the risk there. Italy like the UK is in serious financial trouble. The US has one big advantage with its government debt in very high demand around the world so their constant printing of money, while dangerous, is less so than other countries who have debt in other currencies and thus must earn foreign currency to repay it. Japanese and UK debt is also primarily in their own currencies.

Some 44% of US households were participating in the equity markets in 2007, up from 29% in 1994 representing 88 million individual investors.

More than half of these investors are 45 years old or older, and a third of this group (approximately 17.6 million people) are older than 65, so they have limited opportunities to earn back their retirement savings, given the 2007 to 2009 declines of about 50% in equity markets.

5.2 WERE THE CRASH MODELS HELPFUL IN SIGNALING THE US AND WORLDWIDE 2007–2009 CRASH?

Unfortunately not!

Well, they did call the Chinese and Iceland crashes in 2008 as interest rates crept up enough for the measure, which was close to the danger

TABLE 5.2 Bond-Stock Yield Model Calculations for the US Leading Up to the Current Crisis

Date	Long Bond (10 yrs), %	Trailing PE	1/PE, %	$B - Y_{PE}$
February 2006	4.49	20	5	−0.56
June 2007	5.15	17	5.98	−0.74
June 2008	4.14	18	5.55	−1.41
May 2009	3.70	33.3	3.00	0.70

zone in 2007 in the analyses of these countries in Ziemba and Ziemba (2007). But they did not call the US and worldwide 2007–2009 crash as we shall see.

Table 5.2 shows the bond-stock yield model calculations for February 2006, June 2007, June 2008, and May 2009. In all cases the measure did not signal the coming crash. You need to be about +3 to be in the danger zone. That would take a huge increase in the 10-year bond rate plus a big PE expansion (higher stock prices and/or greatly lower earnings). Neither seems likely. Even now with earnings dropping dramatically the measure is still not in the danger zone.

Finally in late 2008 and the first few months of 2009, S&P 500 earnings and forecasts for 2008 and 2009 were continually dropping. Table 5.3 from Mauldin (2009) shows this dramatic drop. Even with these low earnings, the model is not in the danger zone. Interest rates have dropped dramatically with short-term rates near zero—however access to these low posted rates is not readily available. It is the liquidity crisis that has created a real interest rate that is dramatically high and approaching infinity as credit for many is totally unavailable, credit card companies are denying previous credit limits and recalling credit cards.

The 10-year bond rate in June 2009, when we went to press, was about 3.7%. So the bond-stock earnings yield model failed to call the large equity declines even with a trailing PE ratio of 33.3!

What went wrong? It was simply another type of crash. The 2007–2009 crash was not caused by high interest rates relative to earnings. Indeed we have been in a period of declining interest rates. The decades before the crash and the crash itself were transitional economic times. While consumption spending is normally a large part of GDP, it had become even more significant as people withdrew equity from their homes, treating them as ATMs. This both fueled the economy and at the same time planted the seeds for the crash, since clearly this level of spending was unsustainable especially once housing prices began to soften. During the same period, there was a rapid

TABLE 5.3 Earnings Revisions for 2008 and 2009, Analysts Estimates of S&P 500 Earnings in Dollars

Date	Earnings
2008	
March 2007	92.00
December 2007	84.00
February 2008	71.20
June 1, 2008	68.93
July 25, 2008	72.01
September 30, 2008	60.00
October 15, 2008	54.82
February 20, 2009	26.23
April 10, 2009	14.88
2009	
March 20, 2008	81.52
April 9, 2008	72.60
June 25, 2008	70.13
August 29, 2008	64.66
September 10, 2008	58.87
October 14, 2008	48.52
February 1, 2009	42.00
February 20, 2009	32.41
April 10, 2009	28.51

Source: Mauldin (2009).

growth in derivative products that created a huge pool of liquidity, again, unsustainable. The way out of this crisis will be a return to more normal debt instruments that sustain the real economy. Let's look at the history of this crisis.

5.3 THE SUBPRIME CRISIS AND HOW IT EVOLVED[1]

Let's hope we are all wealthy and retired by the time this house of cards falters.—Internal e-mail, Wall Street, December 15, 2006

---

[1]This section utilizes the CNBC program hosted by David Faber called "A House of Cards" for much information on this episode.

In 2004 an estimated $900 billion dollars was withdrawn from home equity through refinancing.

In the days following September 11, 2001, with the attacks on US soil and the markets very weak, Fed chairman Alan Greenspan said he was extremely worried about the after effects on the US economy. So five day later, when the stock market reopened, the first of a number of interest rate cuts was made. In 2002 President George W. Bush said, "The goal is, everybody who wants to own a home has got a shot at doing so." He also referred to the homeownership gap that "three-quarters of Anglos own their homes, and yet less than 50% of African Americans and Hispanics own homes" (at a speech at HUD, June 18, 2002, reshown in Faber (2009)). At the same time he linked home ownership to national security.

Freddie Mac and Fanny Mae created the secondary mortgage market and between them insured about half the mortgages. Originally these had been made under strict qualifying procedures, but they came under pressure by the industry and government policy to loosen their standards. Orange County entrepreneurs wanted a way to circumvent these rules and create a profitable business that was unregulated. They invented the concept of sub-prime mortgages where anyone could get a loan at a time when Freddie and Fanny were in some trouble. Actual incomes and assets were not checked and largely inflated. Bad credit and no assets (or a lot of debt and liabilities) did not matter. What made this work was a great interest from Wall Street firms to package these mortgages and have them AAA rated so they were investment grade. Then the Wall Street firms could sell these CMOs (collateralized mortgage obligations) around the world. The rating agencies were paid by the firms selling the CMOs not the purchasers. The rating agencies were eager to have the business and the repeat business. Since it was assumed that house prices could not fall—(they had not fallen in since 1991–1992)—this seemed safe. Around the world, investors, a bit greedy to get higher returns were sucked into buying these securities. One example is Narvik, Norway, a small town 150 miles above the Arctic circle. They bought enough of these assets from a representative of Citi Bank through an Oslo representative to lose 25% of the town's assets.

Meanwhile, house prices roared higher and higher around the world, far outstripping income growth. Buyers with no money were able to buy houses and then refinance them and cash out the gains to upgrade their homes or just to spend the money. Indeed a huge percent of US consumption in 2003–2007 came from this source. Houses were assumed to rise in value by 6–8% forever. But a bubble was forming, and house prices in the US peaked in 2005–2006.

The packaging of the mortgages into AAA rated CMOs and later CDO (collateralized debt obligations, which include any asset with a future income stream) continued.

Recall the history of housing prices as seen in Figures 4.29 and 4.30.

Business was good. Even pizza deliverers became, with no training, mortgage brokers. There was no license, so no training, involved. Once they started arranging the mortgages, they quickly began earning $20,000/ month, and they soon were buying expensive cars. One Southern California Lebanese immigrant with a third-grade education had a firm selling Mercedes to his loan officers. At the peak in 2005–2006, he was making $5 million/month. When prices of houses and real estate stocks fell starting in late 2005, the defaults multiplied, and the CMOs and CDOs dropped sharply in value. One hedge fund trader in Texas saw this coming and made 600% on his investment, some $1 billion, by buying insurance on these instruments, which rose sharply in value, and was paid off as the house prices fell.

Another factor fueling this in 2004 was Greenspan saying that the market needs "new products for mortgage loans." These included adjustable rate mortgages with low or no interest payable in the first year or two with the interest added to the loan value. Then with higher interest, higher loans and declining house values, the situation became more difficult and led to millions of mortgage defaults. This destroyed the American dream of owning a home with other people's money.

Greenspan still insists that such bubbles are just a part of human behavior and will happen again and again and there was nothing the Fed could have done to prevent it. And it would be bad politics to stop home ownership. He admits now that he was shocked when he learned that 20% of all US mortgages were subprime and that he, with some math and economic training and a staff of 200 with many PhDs could not understand many of the CDO products which made use of option experts trained at leading math finance and other departments. Wow!!

Yet the issue was that there was a gap in regulations and application of prudence in lending. In Canada and many other countries, you cannot get these extreme subprime mortgages, and consequently there have not been such a fall in house prices nor as many defaults. Also in Canada unlike the US non-recourse loans, borrowers are at risk on all their assets not just the property that's being mortgaged.

5.3.1 Favoring the Financial Sector: Evaluating the Policy Responses

In the last 25 years or so, the deregulated finance sector grew as the real production sector was in the decline in the US and in the UK. Profits came to be concentrated in this sector, and indeed it was very innovate with securitization, interest-rate swaps, and credit default swaps among other instruments. The effect of this can be seen for the growth in the share of corporate profits going to the financial sector. From 1973 to 1985, this sector earned about 16% of the corporate profits; in the 1990s profit share ranged from 21% to 31% and in the most recent decade this escalated to 41% of all corporate profits. Concomitant with this increase in profits came rising incomes. From 1948 to 1982 average compensation in this sector was about average for the economy between 99% and 108% of the average for all domestic private industry. By 2007 it reached 181% (Johnson 2009).

In the global economic crisis there have been several phases and various responses by the US Federal Reserve, the US Treasury Department, and the Federal government and similar bodies in the UK and elsewhere. To June 2009, these policy responses of monetary easing (open market operations now referred to as quantitative easing) and fiscal spending have had some success, but that has been limited. Unfortunately, the policy response has to a large part been to continue to favor finance over real production. Instead of nationalizing the banks and cleaning them up, money has been allocated to them to shore them up.

In part this is a reflection of the structure of the Fed, the US central bank. The seven-member board of governors is appointed by the president with the approval of the Senate. The boards of the 12 independently incorporated regional banks are composed of three members appointed by the Fed board and 6 elected by the member banks. So the chairman of, say, the N.Y. Fed owes the position to the banks in the region and routinely consults with them. In May 2007 in a speech to the Atlanta Fed, Geithner said that "the financial innovations had improved the capacity to measure and manage risk" and that "the larger global financial institutions are generally stronger in terms of capital relative to risk" (quoted in Becker and Morgenson 2009). At this point, New Century Financial had already filed for bankruptcy due to subprime losses, and by July Fed chair Ben Bernanke warned that the US subprime crisis could cost up to $100 billion.

Geithner, encouraged by Citigroup and JPMorgan Chase, was proposing new looser standards for the banks. The problem, according to Callum McCarthy, a former British regulator, was that "banks overestimated their ability to manage risk, and we believed them" (Becker and Morgenson 2009).

Nobel Laureate and Columbia University Professor Joseph Stiglitz among other economists has expressed the concern that this relationship has led to a regulatory philosophy shaped by and shared with the industry itself. This led a bailout that was designed to get a lot of money into the banks to shore them up without necessarily considering the risks to the public at large (Becker and Morgenson 2009).

A variety of regulatory changes have been proposed by economists, politicians, journalists, and business leaders to minimize the impact of the current crisis and prevent recurrence. However, as of April 2009, many of the proposed solutions had not yet been implemented. Some, like Simon Johnson, want to limit growth of institutions to manageable size so they do not become too big to fail. It is hard determine the criteria for this, though of course market efficiency requires ease of entry and exit. Joseph Stiglitz would restrict leverage, while Alan Greenspan suggests that progressively increasing capital requirements with bank size will discourage them from too much growth and offset their competitive advantage.

The shadow banking system was a problem as it fell outside regulations, and solutions encompass a variety of modes of regulation. Paul Krugman wants to regulate institutions that *act like banks* similarly to banks, and, related to this, Ben Bernanke wants procedures for closing troubled financial institutions in the shadow banking system, such as investment banks and hedge funds. Joseph Stiglitz would reinstate the separation of commercial (depository) and investment banking established by the Glass-Steagall Act in 1933 and repealed in 1999 by the Gramm-Leach-Bliley Act. He would also like to see executive compensation related to long-term performance rather than quarter by quarter. In dealing with the current crisis Niall Ferguson and Jeffrey Sachs would have liked haircuts on bondholders and counterparties prior to bailouts while Nouriel Roubini would have nationalized the insolvent banks, clean them up of toxic loans, and sell them. Other proposals include regulating credit derivatives and ensuring they are traded on well-capitalized exchanges to limit counterparty risk (Eric Dinallo); requiring financial institutions to pay insurance to the government during boom periods, in exchange for payments during a downturn (Raghuram Rajan); requiring a minimum down payment for home mortgages of at least 10% and income verification (Warren Buffett). Michael Spence and Gordon Brown want to establish an early-warning system to help detect systemic risk. This would require a better model than VAR (see Chapter 14).

The U.N. Commission of Experts, chaired by Professor Stiglitz, was given the task by the General Assembly to suggest a cure for the gobal economic crisis. They diagnosed the problem and reached agreement on 10 key issues:

1. There was excess deregulation of the financial sector.
2. Self-regulation is inadequate.
3. Regulation is essential due to the externalities of the financial system on the economy at large.
4. The complexity of derivatives and other instruments requires more transparency and full disclosure of risk.
5. Perverse incentives encouraged excessive risk taking and short-sighted behavior led to bad banking practices.

6. Corporate governance contributed to poor incentives.
7. Banks had grown *too big to fail* so if they gambled and won they profited, and if they lost they were bailed out.
8. Comprehensive regulation is necessary, or there will be a *race to the bottom* with countries with lax regulations attracting the financial services.
9. In turn, those countries with poor regulations would need to protect their economies.
10. Regulation must be comprehensive across all bank-like institutions to avoid the race to the bottom.

As this is a global crisis, the first in the age of globalization, global strategies are needed, but policies have only been undertaken on a national level. They suggest that the developed economies should set aside 1% of their stimulus packages to help the poor developing economies. This should come in the form of grants not loans and should be distributed through international and regions channels. In addition, the spin-offs of the stimulus packages should not blocked by protectionism from benefiting these trading partners. International cooperation is needed to establish regulations of the global financial system. Finally there is a need to reform the dollar-based reserve system (Stiglitz, 2009).

5.4   IMPACT ON RETIREMENT EXPECTATIONS

Unfortunately some pensions got saddled with some of the most toxic assets. Evans (2007) warned that banks were selling the riskiest CDOs to public pensions and state trust funds. Up to this time returns to alternative investments had been high and the need for funds were enticed to join in by sale pitches from Bear Stearns, Merrill Lynch, Wachovia, Citigroup, and Morgan Stanley. They were told that the bottom level of a CDO can provide a 20% annual return, but this is the first loss portion, known as the equity tranch of CDOs, and the entire investment can also easily be lost (they are unrated). For example, Calpers had bought $140 million from Citigroup. The difficulty in tracking the returns in these CDOs is compounded by the fact that CDO managers can change their contents after they have been sold. Table 5.4 compares the investment holders of equity-grade and toxic-grade tranches of CDO. The banks who know what's in them have mostly off loaded them to hedge funds (who should understand the risk) and pension funds (who probably don't understand the risk). It is not unusual for the pension boards to rely on the advice of the bankers, thinking that they are managing risk by choosing who manages their money.

TABLE 5.4 Buyers of CDOs, Investment-Grade and
Equity- or Toxic-Grade, in Percent

Investor	Investment Grade	Equity Grade
Banks, private banks	55	32
Asset managers	19	22
Insurance	18	19
Pension funds	4	18
Hedge funds	3	19
Other	1	–

Source: Evans (2007).

Public pension funds had bought over $500 million of these equity CDOs.

In the race to sell the toxic assets to public investors that are forbidden to buy junk rated assets, they were dressed up to look like investment grade. An example from Bear Stearns is called principal protection:

[A] pension fund wants to buy $100 of CDO equity. Instead of buying it directly, the fund buys a zero-coupon government bond for $46 that will be redeemed for $100 in 12 years. That bond is paired with a $54 investment in CDO equity. Zero-coupon bonds pay no interest: the investor is paid the full face amount . . . when the bond matures.

So principal protection is guaranteed to be repaid so it is AAA. If the CDO does not default the return would be more than 9% annually. However, if the entire money went into zero-coupon bonds, the money would double in 12 years.

Five years of pension gains were wiped out in one year. These losses, under recently enacted funding rules, will force plans to "suck cash from salaries and jobs just when suffering companies need scarce resources to survive" (Millard 2009). Watson Wyatt estimated that there is a $20 to 100 billion gap that will need to be closed within seven years while firms will also need to continue with new contributions. No wonder plans are being frozen. The problem is not underfunding per se but underfunding in firms that go bankrupt. Millard suggests that a system like that in the UK be established. There the Pensions Regulator can regulate deals so that they do not force the firms into bankruptcy. See Table 5.5 for the one year (October 2007 to October 2008) equity declines in retirement plans.

TABLE 5.5   Equity Declines from October 9, 2007 to April 9, 2009 in Retirement Plans, Trillions of Dollars

Type of holding	10/9/07	4/9/09	Decline	% decline
Defined contribution plans	$4.90	$2.70	$2.20	44.90%
IRAs	2	1.1	0.9	45.00%
Private defined contribution plans	2.8	1.5	1.2	42.86%
Federal government plans	0.2	0.1	0.1	50.00%
Defined benefit plans	4.2	2.3	1.9	45.24%
Private defined benefit plans	1.8	1	0.8	44.44%
State and local plans	2.4	1.3	1.1	45.83%
Household non-pension assets	12.2	6.8	5.4	44.26%
Other	5.9	3.3	2.6	44.07%
Total	27.2	15.1	12.1	44.49%

Source: Munnell et al. (2009).

Munnell et al. (2009a) also note the numbers of corporations that have suspended matching contributions to DC plans. These include Sears Holding Corp. (305,08), FedEx (115,330), UPS (100,368), Sprint (79,321), Chrysler LLC (32,900), General Motors (32,000), Motorola (30,076), Ford Motor Companies (22,600).

In addition pensionpulse.blogspot reports a growing number of pension problems; one day in May the following global pension tensions were listed:

- AbitibiBowater Inc. tried to unilaterally rescind pension benefit improvements that had been negotiated in a collective agreement prior entering bankruptcy protection.
- Air Canada sought support from its unions for "a moratorium and other conditions on funding" its pension deficit, which is more than C$3 billion ($2.5 billion).
- A teacher pension tsunami is expected in Pennsylvania where the Pennsylvania Public School Employees' Retirement System (PSERS) lost 30%, and they are faced with record retirements in the next decade requiring districts to contribute more assets.
- Minnesota teachers are asking for a $223 million bailout for their pension fund.
- Ohio's five public pension plans lost nearly a quarter of their value.
- Rhode Island cities and towns are struggling with the increasing burden of pension costs where pension contributions have risen 50% in the last five years to $149 million a year.

- New York City is proposing a Tier 5 pension plan for city employees that would result in an immediate savings of $200 million for the city in the coming year and save $7 billion by 2030.
- The governor of Massachusetts wants to rescind the special pensions given to 10 former legislators because it appeared that those pensions were improperly awarded.
- In Australia, the rich will have their superannuation tax breaks slashed in half to fund the pension increase.
- The deficit in the UK's largest company pension plans almost doubled to £61 billion (91 billion) in the first quarter of 2009.
- Longer life expectancy means UK taxpayers will have to find billions of pounds more to fund public sector pensions.
- The Hungarian parliament Monday voted to cut pension benefits and gradually raise the compulsory retirement age from 62 to 65.

Source: http://pensionpulse.blogspot.com/2009/05/global-pension-tension.html.

5.4.1 Plan Sponsors in Trouble

The impact of the crisis has returned the plan sponsors to a lower level of funding: down to 85% at the end of 2008 (Figure 5.1). However, plans

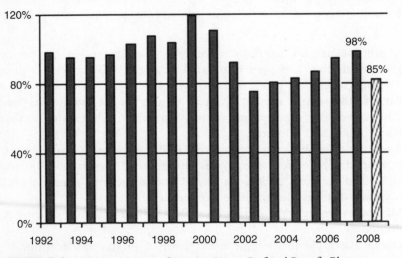

FIGURE 5.1 Funding Status of Private Sector Defined Benefit Plans, 1992–October 9, 2008
Source: Munnell and colleagues (2008).

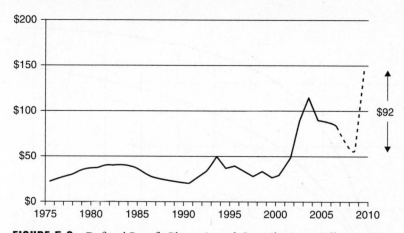

FIGURE 5.2 Defined Benefit Plans, Actual Contributions, Billions, 1975 to 2006 and Projections for 2007 to 2009
Source: Munnell et al. (2008).

can meet immediate commitments and could catch up again as the equity markets improve. However, if markets stay depressed, they will have to increase their contributions as unfunded liabilities need to be made up over a seven-year period. Figure 5.2 dramatically shows the impact of the accruals plus the amortized amount of the shortfall.

If firms are unable to make up the shortfalls, there are a number of options as we covered previously: cutting jobs to both lower current costs and avoid future liabilities for pensions, bankruptcy and turning over the underfunded pension fund to the PBGC, freezing plans, and shifting to DC.

While 401(k) plans were starting to do better, the crisis has been a real setback just as employees were beginning to see these as the main supplement to social security. In addition, they were not intended to play that role, and they suggest that a new tier to replace employee plans be established.

The IMF (2009) undertook study of recessions, their causes, and time to recovery. They found that recessions caused by financial problems that are widespread take a longer time for recovery. During the precrisis, bubbles develop in goods and labor markets and housing prices. When the crisis comes, the debt overhang takes a long time to deleverage, and generally people have to rebuild savings so consumption lags; also there is usually by that time overcapacity in capital goods, so investment will not restart the economy, therefore monetary policy will not work; in addition, since the recession is widespread, there will no relief from increased exports. The only policy that will help accelerate recovery is fiscal policy.

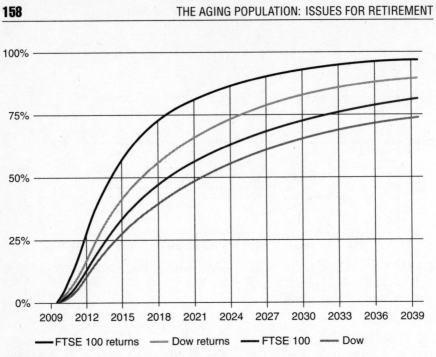

FIGURE 5.3 Cumulative Probability of Regaining Index Highs
(as of January 23, 2009)
Source: Dimson, March, and Staunton (2009).

Figure 5.3 shows the cumulative probability of recovery of the FTSE 100 and Dow indexes. There is a 50% probability that the FSTE will recover between 2015 and 2019; for the Dow will take to 2017 to 2020. This shows how dramatic has been the loss; see Table 5.6. These calculations are based on historical data following crashes.

While the indexes have gone up over 50% since March, as of early November 2009 this only makes up about half of the loss in these indexes. Also many funds have missed this rally by being out of equities. Indeed, one

TABLE 5.6 Relative Losses,
First 10 Months 2008

Australia	$200 billion
UK	$300 billion
US	$2.2 trillion

Source: OECD (2008).

thing that has pushed the rally higher is the buying by many funds trying to catch up. The rally seems to be a result of:

1. the marked overshot to the downside in March so that part of the rally is adjusting this;
2. anticipation of better economic news ahead as the stock market is known to forecast six or more months ahead;
3. a second derivative effect where the bad economic news is less bad, and
4. interest rates of essentially zero so stocks seem a better alternative than many markets with almost no returns or bonds which seem risky at thee low interest rates.

Brock (2009) investigates the subprime bailout and its long-term effect. He finds that it is very important that stimulus money go into infrastructure and investments to improve productivity that has a natural closure. In this way GDP growth over time will outpace the debt and return the debtto-GDP ratio to a sustainable level. He suggests that it is very important that the federal budget (and likely all government budgets) be separated into two separate parts: one part would clearly represent investment and be recognized as such and amortized over an appropriate time horizon; the other part would be transfer payments and consumption type expenditures. Table 5.7 shows the impact of various scenarios of growth of debt and GDP on the debt/GDP ratio.

TABLE 5.7 Impact of Various Scenarios of Growth of GDP and Debt on the Debt/GDP Ratio

		GDP growth			
	Debt	−1%	1%	2%	4%
2010	2%	0.9	0.9	0.9	0.9
2015		1.0	0.9	0.9	0.8
2025		1.0	1.0	0.9	0.8
2035		1.8	1.1	0.9	0.5
2045		2.4	1.2	0.9	0.4
2010	5%	0.9	0.9	0.9	0.9
2015		1.2	1.0	1.0	0.9
2025		2.1	1.5	1.4	1.0
2035		3.7	2.3	1.8	1.1
2045		6.7	3.3	2.4	1.2

Source: Brock (2009).

5.5 PENSIONS IN TROUBLE

Australia's pension system was restructured about 20 years ago to require people to manage their own pension savings. It has three pillars: compulsory savings by employers who contribute about 9% of wages into individual pension accounts, voluntary contributions by workers, and the income from state pensions. In 2008, the UK legislated a new pension scheme from 2012 similar to the Australian with compulsory employer contributions into workers' pension funds with the workers bearing the investment risk. See Bendeich (2009).

About 25% of the value of pension savings has been lost (total nearly US$1 trillion) according to the OECD in 2008. See Table 5.6 for the countries with the largest pension savings losses. See Figure 5.4 for a comparison of normal and real pension return.

Individuals have lost as much as 40 to 50% from 2007 to 2009. This is forcing Australians to apply for the state pension (the rate of applications has increased 50% in the final quarter of 2008). The old-age guarantee is about A$1,100 per month which is about 20% of a worker's average salary.

The OECD estimated that pension funds had lost US$3.3 trillion or 20%. These losses were moderated relative to all equity markets, and pension funds tend to be diversified, holding a significant share in bonds. They estimate that as of December 2007, 13 of 22 OECD countries, held over

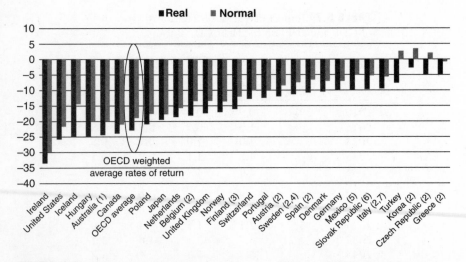

FIGURE 5.4 Nominal and Real Pension Returns, Various OECD Countries, January to October, 2008
Source: OECD (2008).

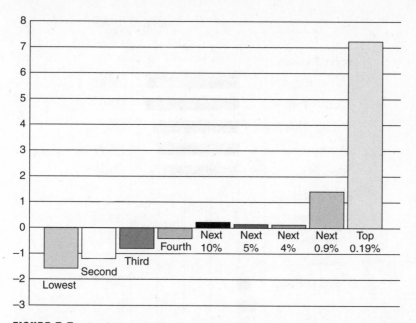

FIGURE 5.5   Real Income Gains 2002 to 2003 with Emphasis on the Highest Quintile
Source: Morris (2006). Internal Revenue Service/New York Times, October 5, 2005.
Note: Inflation for the period was 2.3 percent.

50% of their assets in bonds, and around 60% of these investments were in government bonds. Funds with a high share of equities like Australia and Ireland were hardest hit. The rally in equities since the low in March 2009 had enabled some of the losses to be made up but the crash has led some funds to cut their exposure to equities.

5.6   STATE PENSIONS

State and local government pensions play an important role in retirement assets. Indeed, 80% of state and local workers are covered by pensions compared to only 45% in the private sector. A large share of these are DB, 80% versus 40% the private sector. These public sector plans also have greater protection than private ones, as they are backed by the various governments, while PSGB, which insures private pensions has set limits on the maximum insured amount.

By 2004, the average state pension fund had assets only 84% of liabilities, which is a gap of about $284 billion, see Figure 5.6. While West

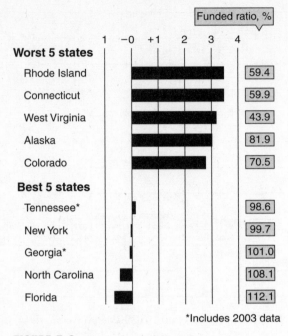

FIGURE 5.6   Underfunded State Pension
Liabilities, FY 2004, $'000 per Resident
Source: The Economist (2006).

Virginia has the highest percent gap, Rhode Island and Connecticut have the largest total liability gaps. Cities also have a similar gaps, Philadelphia has the largest shortfall, with assets of only 53% of its pension liabilities. The gaps in health care liabilities are even greater (*The Economist* 2006). By November 2009, the state and local pension gap was estimated to be about $1 trillion after losing about 20% or $0.6 trillion year on year. This large gap is now making it difficult for some governments to raise money in the bond market. Even an aggressive investment strategy would make it difficult to close this gap (McNichol, 2009).

5.7   FUTURE ERP

CIEBA (2004) raised the question as to whether the US pension system should rely on long-term ERP, use worst case planning, or use a more central scenario. Goldman Sachs predicted that the equity risk premium (ERP) in the next 10 years would be lower. Both Morgan Stanley and Goldman Sachs cited a report that indicated that the pension system has distorted the equity bubble. GS and Robert Shiller estimated that if one assumes a 2% ERP (low) then the odds of equities beating bonds are 2:1 in 10 years, 4:1 in 20 and 95% in 30.

During the 2000 bubble, private pensions were net sellers, as their plans were increasing in value and they sold stocks to bring them down to the required levels. Meanwhile, public pension plans were net buyers. MS estimated that the mark-to-market rule would have decreased earnings by 67% in 2002.

Figure 5.7 shows the ownership breakdown of equities. DB and DC plans together account for about 12% of the market. However, as shown in Figure 5.8, equities represent a large share of plan assets.

MS suggested that the 2000 bubble actually hurt plans in the long term as it made them look overfunded but did not provide any information about the actual risks they were taking.

Figure 5.9 shows the impact of marketing to market on the reported net income of pension plans. MS projected that in response to this potential, plans would reduce the risk taken in their portfolios to lessen the impact of the increased volatility.

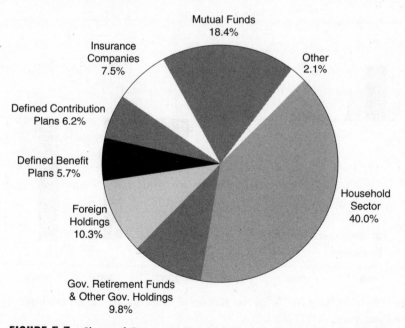

FIGURE 5.7 Share of Corporate Equities Outstanding by Sector, 2002, Q4
Source: CIEBA (2004).

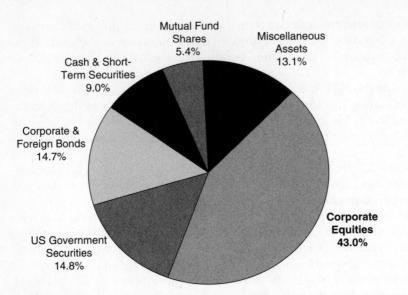

FIGURE 5.8 Composition of Corporate DB Pension Fund Assets, 2002, Q4
Source: CIEBA (2004).

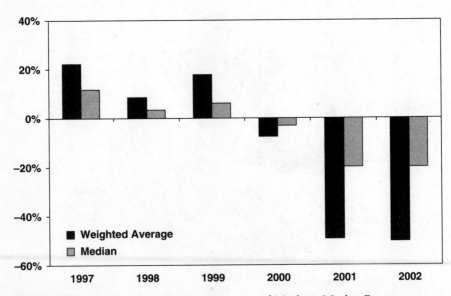

FIGURE 5.9 Estimated Impact of Net Income of Mark-to-Market Returns on
Pension Plan Assets, 1997–2002
Source: CIEBA (2004).

5.7.1 Companies Freezing Pension Plans

In 2008 up to May 11, at least 16 companies announced they were freezing their traditional DB plans. This is compared with 18 for all of 2008. One of the latest was Wells Fargo, which announced that its plan would stop accruing benefits as of July 1 (Block 2009). This means that long-time employees will not get the various bonuses that are typically calculated in the final year after sufficient work time. One part of the reason is the requirement to bring plans up to proper funding. However, in addition, companies have begun to see the DB pension plan as a huge liability.

5.7.2 The Ultimate Strategy: Bankruptcy

The burden of future pension commitments has pushed some companies toward bankruptcy. With bankruptcy they can renege on pension and health care promises.

In the US, DB plans of 44 million workers are insured by a quasi-governmental agency, Pension Benefit Guaranty Corporation (PBGC), which itself is in the red.

The Canadian Province of Ontario pension-plan safety net makes payments when companies go bankrupt, but it is itself in danger should a large corporation fail. In existence since 1980, it has paid pensions of $1,000 per month in the case of corporate pension shortfalls. And shortfalls are increasing. They have in the past been challenged by Algoma Steel, Massey Combines, and Stelco, but now there is a reported deficit of $102 million, and the government faces problems of companies like Nortel, and the auto makers, manufacturers, and the pulp and paper sector.

5.8 FUTURE INFLATION AND PENSIONS

An important issue is protecting retirement wealth and income from inflation. A growing economy with increased productivity is surely necessary, but this is beyond the control of the individual. This is why we emphasize that it is necessary that retirement savings be effectively invested in the real economy; otherwise as the pool of retirees grows, their demand, unbalanced by productive work, will likely produce inflation. A growing pool of goods and services is required to support retirement.

Government statistics report that inflation for seniors rose a average of 3.3% from December 1982 to December 2007 (this calculates to 2.25 times). The economy-wide CPI averaged 3% in this time period. So $1 in 1983 was worth only $0.44 in contrast to the average $0.47. Housing and health care are the two major sources. Social security is tied to the cost-of-living adjustment (COLA) but not at the full rate, so while benefits increased 31%, actual cost of living increased more than 58%.

Beyond that there are strategies that can be taken to ameliorate the impact of inflation. One recommendation is TIPS, which we have already mentioned in section 4.3.1. This is of limited value as the real return on TIPS is still low. We finished this book in June 2009. Since then there has been a substantial rally in world wide equity markets led by the US stock market. For example, the S&P 500 bottomed in early March in the 666 area. So the total fall was well in excess of 50% just like the 2000–2003 decline. In that decline, the recovery was V-shaped and by 2007 the markets were at the 2000 highs with the S&P 500 over 1500. In this 2007–2009 decline, there is much discussion about whether the recover will be a V-shape (most think it will not), a U-shape with recovery dragged out over a number of years (the highest probability scenario) or a W-shape where there is a second decline just like in the early 1930s. While there continued to be layoffs, drops in housing prices and commercial real estate and much other bad economic news, the March low combined with very low interest rates was seen as a buying opportunity. Less bad news, much cash on the sidelines and a momentum effect of those who did not want to miss out on the recovery were involved. By late September, the S&P 500 had recovered to the 1,070 area, a greater than 50% recovery. Many other countries had even large recoveries in their currencies and more so in the declining US dollar. This recovery has helped some retirees depending on their circumstances. Buy and hold portfolios are thus down only about 25%. But those who cashed out at the bottom or levered had substantial losses. While this recovery has lowered the level of the losses, the retirement situation is still fragile.

REFERENCES

Becker, J., and G. Morgenson. 2009. Geithner, member and overseer of finance club. *New York Times*, April 27.

Bendeich, M. 2009. Pension system reels from meltdown. *G&M*, February 1.

Block, S. 2009. More companies freeze pension. *USA Today*, May 11.

Brock, H. 2009. The end game draws nigh—The future evolution of the debt-to-GDP ratio. In *Outside the Box*, ed. J. Mauldin, May 18.

Committee on Investment of Employee Benefit Assets (CIEBA). 2004. The US pension crisis: Evaluation and analysis of emerging defined benefit pension issues. Association for Financial Professionals, March.

Dimson, E., P. Marsh, and M. Staunton. 2009. *Global Investment Returns Yearbook*. ABNAmbro, London.

The Economist. 2006. Public-sector pensions: The known unknowns. November 16.

Evans, D. 2007. The poison in your pension. *Bloomberg Market*, July.

IMF. 2009. *World Economic Outlook.*

Johnson, S. 2009. The quiet coup. *The Atlantic*, May.

Mauldin, J. 2009. Is that recovery we see? John Mauldin's Weekly E-Letter, April 10.

McNichol, D. 2009. State and local pension gap may be $1 trillion, Kramer says. Bloomberg.com, November 5.

Millard, C. 2009. Vampire pensions could be a corporate nightmare. *Financial Times*, April 18.

Morris, C. R. 2006. Apart at the Seams: The collapse of private pension and health care protections. Century Foundation Press available at www.socsec.org/publications.asp?pubid=553.

Munnell, A. H., J.-P. Aubry, and D. Muldoon. 2008. The financial crisis and private defined benefit plans. CRR Number 8–18.

Munnell, A. H., F. Golub-Sass, and D. Muldoon. 2009a. An update on 401(k) plans: insights from the 2007 SCF, CRR Number 95.

Munnell, A. H., and M. Soto. 2008. The housing bubble and retirement security. CRR IB#8-12, August.

OECD. 2008. Pension markets in focus. December.

Stiglitz, J. E. 2009. A real cure for the global economic crackup. *The Nation*, July 13, 12–14.

Ziemba, R. E. S., and W. T. Ziemba. 2007. *Scenarios for Risk Management and Global Investment Strategies*, John Wiley & Sons.

PART

Two

Special Issues and Models

CHAPTER 6

The Impact of Population Aging on Household Portfolios and Asset Returns

Costanza Torricelli
Universitá di Modena e Reggio Emilia, Cefin

Marianna Brunetti
Universitá di Roma Tor Vergata, Cefin, Child

6.1 INTRODUCTION

The objective of this chapter is to present the evolution of the literature on household portfolios and its research perspectives. In doing this, the viewpoint assumed is not that of an institution, such as a pension fund, but that of an individual household decision-maker who has to make consumption and portfolio decisions throughout her life.[1] In this specific connection, the chapter highlights the modeling requirements necessary to analyze the impact of population aging on household portfolios, and ultimately on asset returns, with special focus on the financial segment of the portfolios. Recent demographic trends have given impetus to the literature with contributions that are diversified according to the approach (theoretical and/or empirical) and the perspective taken (micro vs. macro).

We thank Bill Ziemba and Enrico Biffis for helpful comments and suggestions on a previous version of this chapter. The authors acknowledge financial support from MIUR—PRIN 2007. The usual caveat applies.
[1]In other chapters of this book the institutional viewpoint is taken and asset-liability management models are illustrated: see Chapters 7, 9, 10, and 14–16.

The possible impacts of aging on household portfolios rest on the observed heterogeneity in portfolio allocations, which, beside other factors (e.g., income, wealth, education, family size, etc.), is determined by the age of the household making the financial decisions. Such portfolio heterogeneity, which is apparent both in terms of stock market participation and asset allocations, has been studied both in empirical literature, providing detailed evidence on the issue, and in theoretical literature, aiming to find an explanation for it.

We believe that a useful approach to the understanding of the whole issue is first to look at the empirical regularities emerging from the data and then to review theories of portfolio choices developed to account for the observed portfolio features. In fact, most recent theoretical models have been progressively extending the seminal Merton-Samuelson model with the aim of explaining empirical regularities that are at odds with model predictions as stressed by many (e.g., Curcuru et al. (2009) and Gomes and Michaelides (2005)).

This evolution of the literature suggests the structure of this chapter. In Section 6.2 we review the empirical studies: we first take a microeconomic perspective and look at the evidence on household portfolio allocations and then briefly recall the literature that takes a macroeconomic perspective and looks at the possible impact of aging on financial markets and hence on asset returns. In Section 6.3 we overview theoretical models that provide a microeconomic foundation and normative implications for the household portfolio decisions. The last section concludes and points out some open research questions.

6.2   THE EMPIRICAL EVIDENCE

Since the mid-1990s, the nexus between age and finance has inspired a lively debate, which has given rise to an increasing number of empirical studies highly diversified in terms of methodology, data, and results.

In this section we review this literature distinguishing two streams, microeconomic and macroeconomic. The studies with a microeconomic perspective, that is, those assessing the link between age and financial portfolio choices[2] are our main focus and are reviewed first and more extensively (Section 6.2.1). The evidence reported by most of these studies, if considered at an aggregate level, is the foundation for what financial markets fear the most for the aging population, that is, the asset meltdown hypothesis (AMH): a

---

[2]Attention has also been given to the life-cycle pattern in savings and wealth accumulation, which goes beyond the scope of this chapter. For reviews of this literature, see, for example, Bosworth et al. (1991) and Browning and Lusardi (1996).

larger working-age cohort, such as that of *baby boomers*, first drives up the demand for financial assets (accumulated to finance retirement), thereby exerting an upward pressure on asset prices, and then, upon the arrival of the following smaller cohort of working-aged to sell their assets to, puts downward pressure on asset prices. Hence, in Section 6.2.2 we will review some of the studies that, taking a macroeconomic perspective, look at the possible impact of aging on financial markets and hence on asset returns.

6.2.1   The Empirical Evidence in a Micro-Perspective

In this section we discuss some empirical studies aimed at assessing the impact of age on household financial portfolio choices. When estimating the average portfolio allocation as a function of age, an important identification problem is faced, because financial choices are simultaneously affected by three different but related effects, namely age, time, and cohort. The time effect refers to the particular moment in which the decision is taken. As an example, a favorable (negative) period for stock market returns not only increases (decreases) the average financial wealth of households, but may also modify its average allocation. The cohort effect concerns those consequences that the date of birth may have on individual financial choices. As Poterba (2001) puts it:

> Individuals born prior to the Great Depression may have a greater desire to save than those born later, reflecting their greater experience with economic hardship and the loss of financial wealth.

Finally, the age effect captures the life-cycle effect on financial wealth allocation. The identification problem can be thus summarized as follows: at any time t a person born in year c is a_t years old, where $a_t = t - c$. Being age (a_t), time (t), and cohort effect (c) a linear combination of each other, they cannot be separately identified.[3] The solution is to rule out one of these three effects and try to assess the two remaining, recalling that time-series or single cross-section data allows depicting only one of them at time, while panel data or repeated cross-sections allow the separate estimation of any two out of three of these effects.[4]

---

[3] For an investigation of this issue, see Ameriks and Zeldes (2004).
[4] In studies investigating the role of age on household portfolio choices (micro level), such as those described in this section, panel data are collected across time and across different households. While in data used to investigate the effect of the aging population on financial market (aggregate level, Section 6.2.2), the additional dimension besides time generally refers to different countries.

We now review the contributions considering the intensive margin of portfolio decisions, that is, how much of financial wealth to allocate to risky assets (allocation decision), and then those studies considering also the extensive margin, that is, whether to hold or not hold risky assets at all (participation decision).

All of these contributions are basically framed into the life-cycle theory, stating that the optimal allocation of financial portfolio should vary with age, and share the following features: (1) they are quite recent, as the availability of the data on which they are based (mainly survey) has recently increased; (2) to some extent, they all find evidence of a relevant effect of age on household portfolio decisions.

Yoo (1994a) is one of the first investigating the role of age in portfolio selection and uses to this end data from the 1962 Survey of the Financial Characteristics of Consumers and from the 1983 and 1986 Surveys of Consumer Finances (SCF). He finds that the percentage of individuals seeking riskier (safe) assets progressively diminishes (increases) along with age and the average portfolio allocation in cash, bonds and stocks is different across the 5 different age classes analyzed (25–34, 35–44, 45–54, 55–64, 65+): the share held in cash diminishes throughout the working life and increases thereafter, while those of bonds and stocks display an inverse pattern, increasing until retirement and decreasing thereafter. To isolate the effect of age from that of other household characteristics, the following tobit regression is estimated.

$$\alpha_i = \beta_0 + \beta_1 Pop_i^{25-34} + \beta_2 Pop_i^{35-44} + \beta_3 Pop_i^{45-54} + \beta_4 Pop_i^{55-64}$$
$$+ \beta_5 Pop_i^{65+} + \beta_6 Kids_i + \beta_7 Adults_i + \beta_8 Male_i + \beta_9 White_i \quad (6.1)$$
$$+ \beta_{10} Married_i + \beta_{11} HS_i + \beta_{12} Col_i + \beta_{13} Y_i + \beta_{14} W_i + \epsilon_i$$

where α_i is the portfolio share held in each of three assets (cash, bonds, and equities) and ϵ_i represents the error term. Explanatory variables include dummies for age-class ($Pop_i^{25-34}, \ldots, Pop_i^{65+}$), gender (Male), marriage status (Married), High School (HS) and College (Col) education, as well as the number of children (Kids) and adults (Adult) in the household, income (Y) and wealth (W). The results suggest that age is a significant factor in determining portfolio composition and that, consistent with the life-cycle model, the share held in equities increases while working and decreases after retirement.

Bodie and Crane (1997) use a different dataset, namely the 1996 Teachers Insurance and Annuity Association-College Retirement Equities Fund (TIAA-CREF), which allows the analyses to be performed at an individual rather than at a household level. The authors create four net worth and four age categories, for a total of 16 groups, and observe the pattern of four kinds of assets (cash, tax-exempt bonds, taxable bonds, and equity). They find that the fraction of equities varies systematically and inversely with age. This result is further supported by an OLS multiple regression in which the fraction held in equity is regressed on a set of variables, including age, net worth, home ownership, job category, education, gender, and marital status. The results suggest that, at a 95% level of significance, for each additional year of age, the share held in risky assets reduces by 0.6%, which is consistent with generally accepted investment principles according to which the equity fraction should decline by 1% for each year of age (see, e.g., Malkiel, 1996).

Tin (1998) also uses US data, taken from the 1991 Survey of Income and Program Participation (SIPP), to investigate the household demand for financial assets in a life-cycle framework. The author estimates via OLS the following regression

$$\log m_i = \beta_0 + \beta_1 \log w_i + \beta_2 \log \pi_i + \sum_{n=1}^{N} \delta_n \log \pi_{ni} + \alpha S_i + \epsilon_i \qquad (6.2)$$

where m_i is the quantity of asset demanded by household i; w_i is either labor income, wealth, or net worth of the household; π_i is the opportunity cost of holding the asset; similarly π_{ni} is the price or user cost of the nth asset other than m_i; S_i is a set of socio-demographic control variables; and ϵ is the error term. The regressions are run for several assets (including noninterest- and interest-earning checking accounts, money market deposits, certificates of deposits, municipal or corporate bonds, stocks and mutual funds) and for three households categories: young (under 35); middle-age (35 to 59); and elderly (60 and over). As the author puts it:

> the results show that the propensities to hold financial assets differ substantially among young, middle-age, and old householders. . . . The life-cycle hypothesis generally holds as far as the relation between labor income and asset demand is concerned.

The contributions by James Poterba are among the most influential in the age-finance literature. In Poterba (2001), the author analyzes the implications of a simplified OLG model describing the link between demographic variables and capital price. In this framework, he examines the age-profile of corporate stock holdings, net financial assets, and net-worth for individuals in different age classes, as from the US 1995 SCF. It emerges that the asset holdings reach their apogee in the age classes between 30 and 60 and then slightly decrease, although "there is only a limited downturn in average asset holdings at older ages." Next, the analysis is moved from single to repeated cross-section data (1983, 1986, 1989, 1992 and 1995 SCF) to estimate the following regression

$$y_{it} = \sum_{j=1}^{13} \alpha_j Age_{ijt} + \sum_{c=1}^{12} \gamma_c Cohort_{ict} + \epsilon_{it} \qquad (6.3)$$

where the dependent variable is the level of either common stocks, net financial assets or net worth held by investor i at time t; Age_{ijt} is a dummy for j different 5-year age groups (from 15–19 to 75 and over); and $Cohort_{ict}$ is specific for 5-year birth cohorts (from 1971–1975 to before 1925). In this way the author focuses on age and cohort effects and implicitly assumes no time effect. For the α_j coefficients, Poterba (2001) reports that they have "a surprisingly small impact on the estimated age structure of asset holdings." In fact, the values for late middle-aged and retired are not that different: around \$32,500 for the former against around \$28,000 to 25,000 for the latter. Furthermore, for net financial assets "there is virtually no decline in old age."

By contrast, Bellante and Green (2004) find age to be a significant determinant of portfolio allocation. The authors test the life-cycle risk-aversion hypothesis specifically for elderly. Using a single cross-section dataset on a subset of US households whose one or more members are 70 or over in 1993 to 1994, the authors estimate several OLS regressions including:

$$\alpha_i = \beta_0 + \beta_1 \ln(NW)_i + \beta_2 [\ln(NW)]^2 + \beta_3 Age_i \ln(W)_i + \beta_4 Female_i$$
$$+ \beta_5 Male_i + \beta_6 Health_i + \beta_7 Non\text{-}White_i + \beta_8 HS_i \qquad (6.4)$$
$$+ \beta_9 College_i + \beta_{10} Kids_i + \epsilon_i$$

where α is the share of risky assets in the financial portfolio of household i; $\ln(NW)$ the log of net wealth; Age the age of the head-of-the-household minus 65; $Kids$ the number of children; $Female$ and $Male$ are dummies for single-female or single-male households; and $Health$, $Non\text{-}White$, HS and $College$ are dummies respectively for poor health status, nonwhite race, and highest education level. Overall, all coefficients but β_5 and β_{10} are significant and display the expected signs. In particular, the age coefficient is negatively signed and highly significant, suggesting that the share held in risky assets tends to decline with age: that is, aging is typically associated with a stronger relative risk aversion.

The studies reported so far focus mainly on the allocation decision. Some studies however distinguish the intensive margin of portfolio decision (i.e., the decision concerning how much of financial (or total) asset to hold in risky assets) from the extensive margin (i.e., the decision to hold or not risky assets at all (participation decision)).

One example is Poterba and Samwick (2001) who, focusing on age and cohort effects, investigate the relationship between age and portfolio structure for US households, analyzing both the decisions of holding risky assets as well as on the fraction of net worth allocated to risky assets. They use data from the 1983, 1989, and 1992 SCF to estimate the regression

$$y_{ij} = \alpha + \sum \beta_n Age_{in} + \sum \gamma_m Cohort_{im} + \epsilon_{ij} \qquad (6.5)$$

where Age_{in} is a dummy variable for whether the household head is in the relevant age class, $Cohort_{im}$ is a dummy variable for the relevant cohort the household head belongs to, and y_{ij} denotes the holdings by household i of asset j (taxable equity, all equities, tax-exempt bonds, taxable bonds, tax-deferred accounts, bank accounts, other financial assets), being either a dummy for whether the household has positive amounts of the asset category (probit estimate) or the share of the household's total financial assets held in each category j (tobit estimate). For directly-held equities, the authors find statistically significant age effects and cohort effects: as for the former, both the probability of holding and the share held in risky assets evolve according to a hump-shaped pattern along the life cycle; as for the latter, older cohorts seem to be more likely to hold stocks, so that all in all, both the participation and the allocation decision seem to point towards and increasing risk attitude of elderly with respect to young people.

Ameriks and Zeldes (2004) carry out a further distinction, by analyzing separately: (i) equity ownership; (ii) equity portfolio share; and (iii) equity portfolio share conditional of equity ownership. For each of these portfolio decisions, the authors perform an analysis of the age-cohort-time effect identification problem based on US data from SCF (1989, 1992, 1995, and 1998) and TIAA-CREF (1987 to 1999), by means of a set of regressions (probit for i and OLS for ii and iii) in which either no cohort effect is assumed (i.e., explanatory variables include only time and age dummies), or no time effect is assumed (i.e., only age and cohort dummies are included as independent variables). Their result is summarized as follows. Assuming no time effect, basically all of the three decisions that were considered display an increasing pattern along with age (whereby the extensive margin decision is increasing only up to 58 and flat after retirement), which is at variance with the typical view of financial advisors. By contrast, if no cohort effect is assumed, the decision whether or not to hold risky assets as well as the unconditional equity portfolio shares display hump-shaped patterns along with age, while the age effect seems to disappear only if equity portfolio shares conditional on equity holding are considered. As a result, the evidence in terms of age effect on portfolio allocation depends on the identifying assumptions. Nevertheless, based on parsimony and plausibility arguments, the authors conclude that time effects should always be considered in this kind of analyses, suggesting therefore that cohort effect should be excluded instead. The conclusion reached is that age strongly affects portfolio decisions at the extensive margin, but, once the decision to hold risky assets has been taken, age does not really matter in determining how much of financial wealth to allocate to these assets.

The analysis by Coile and Milligan (2006) further contributes to the investigation of US household average portfolios by specifically focusing on its evolution after retirement, once again distinguishing between participation and allocation decision. Five asset categories are considered: (i) principal residence; (ii) vehicles; (iii) financial risky assets, including bonds, Individual Retirement Accounts (IRAs), and stocks; (iv) bank accounts; and (v) business and other real estate. The authors use six waves of the US Health and Retirement Study (HRS) spanning the period 1992–2002 and estimate the panel regression

$$\alpha_{it} = \beta_0 + \beta_1 Age_{it} + \beta_2 X_{it} + \gamma_t + \epsilon_{it} \tag{6.6}$$

where the dependent variable is either a dummy for the household holding the asset class (participation decision), the share of total assets held in each asset class or the dollar amount held in each asset category (allocation decision). Explanatory variables include the wave dummies (γ_t), the age of the older member of the household (Age_{it}), and a set of control variables (X_{it}), including marital status, region of residence, religion, race, being US born, and educational category. The age coefficients are overall significant and negatively signed for all assets but bank accounts: that is, older households have generally lower ownership probability and hold lower shares/dollar amounts of all assets but bank accounts. Coile and Milligan (2006) note that

> Bank accounts are dominated by other assets on a risk-return basis, yet there is an increasing proportion of household assets devoted to them with age. . . . It may be a transitory result as windfalls of insurance money, pension lump sums, or proceeds from the sales of housing pass through bank accounts on their way to other asset classes. Alternatively, it may be that the complexity of financial arrangements leads seniors, particularly those with diminished mental or physical capacity, to select portfolios that are easier to manage.

Based on this evidence, the authors conclude in favor of sizable effects of age on asset allocation over the long term.

The impact of age on household portfolio choices has been recently studied also for countries other than the US.

Guiso et al. (2002) collect a number of relevant papers referred to several countries, namely Alessie et al. (2002) for the Netherlands, Banks and Tanner (2002) for the UK, Bertaut and Starr-McCluer (2002) for the US, Eymann and Börsch-Supan (2002) for Germany, and Guiso and Jappelli (2002) for Italy. All empirical studies basically follow the same methodology. First, financial assets are grouped into three broad risk categories: "safe" (e.g., bank accounts), "fairly safe" (e.g., government bonds), and "risky" (e.g., stocks), whereby the definitions may slightly change from country to country. Then, for both extensive and intensive margin portfolio decisions, the authors carry out both explorative and econometric analyses. As for the former, the authors examine the average household portfolios across different age classes. Except for the Dutch and the German cases, a clear hump-shaped age profile is observed, at least with regards to the participation decision. For instance, for the US case Bertaut and Starr-McCluer (2002) report that the average share invested in risky assets peaks for households aged between 45 and 64, while it declines moving towards younger or older investors. Similarly, Guiso and Jappelli (2002) observe that the share of Italian households investing in risky assets increases from around 15% of those 30 years of age or lower to almost 20% of the middle-aged and then falls once again to around 10% for the 60 to 69 cohort, and to less than 7% for those over 70. By contrast, Eymann and Börsch-Supan (2002) for Germany and Alessie et al. (2002) for the Netherlands report that the elderly seem more willing to hold risky assets. For the econometric analyses, national survey data are used to estimate either cross sectional and/or panel regressions in which the dependent variable is either a binary variable (participation decision) and/or the share of financial wealth invested in some assets (allocation decision). Explicative variables include all other household features that could play a role in shaping portfolio choices, including age, net wealth, income, gender, and level of education, although the exact specification varies across countries. For instance, Guiso and Jappelli (2002), for the Italian case, estimate (with both cross-section and panel data)

$$\alpha_i = \beta_0 + \beta_1 A_i + \beta_2 \frac{A_i^2}{1000} + \beta_3 Y_i + \beta_4 \frac{Y_i^2}{1000} + \beta_5 W_i + \beta_6 \frac{W_i^2}{1000}$$
$$+ \beta_7 Size_i + \beta_8 Kids_i + \beta_9 Married_i + \beta_{10} Male_i + \beta_{11} South_i \quad (6.7)$$
$$+ \beta_{12} Edu_i + \beta_{13} u_i + \beta_{14} Bank_i + T + \epsilon_i$$

where the dependent variable is in turn the dummy variable or the share invested in risky assets and explanatory variables include the age of the family head (A), household income (Y), and wealth (W), both in linear and quadratic terms, the family size (*Size*) and the number of children (*Kids*), dummy variables for the marital status (*Married*), gender (*Male*), geographic zone of residence (*South*), level of education of the family head (*Edu*), as well as the average unemployment rate (u) and the index of bank diffusion (*Bank*) in the province of residence together with year dummies (T). Bertaut and Starr-McCluer (2002) for the US case estimate

$$\alpha_i = \beta_0 + \beta_1 A_i^{<35} + \beta_2 A_i^{55-64} + \beta_3 A_i^{65+} + \beta_4 \ln(Y_i) + \beta_5 ln(W_i)$$

$$+ \beta_6 NonWhite_i + \beta_7 HS_i + \beta_8 Col_i + \beta_9 Married_i + \beta_{10} Female_i$$

$$+ \beta_{11} Self_i + \beta_{12} DBPens_i + \beta_{13} RET_i + \beta_{14} u_i + T + \epsilon \tag{6.8}$$

where the dependent variable is again either a dummy for the participation decision or the share invested in risky assets for the allocation one and explanatory variables include dummies variables for age-class ($A^{<35}$, A^{55-64}, A^{65+}), log income ($\ln(Y)$) and wealth ($\ln(W)$), and dummies for being nonwhite (*NonWhite*), for the highest level of education (*HS* for High School and *Col* for College), for the marital status and the gender (*Married* and *Female*), for being self-employed (*Self*), retired (*RET*), or owner of a defined benefit pension fund (*DBPens*), as well as the average unemployment rate (u) in the state of residence. In all studies but the Dutch, the results confirm that age plays a significant role in determining whether or not to hold risky assets, although once this decision is taken this factor only slightly affects the final portfolio allocation. For instance, Guiso and Jappelli (2002) in the probit regression for participation report that age coefficients are statistically different from zero and quite high in magnitude (probability of holding risky assets increasing by 4% between ages 25 and 40 and declining by 8% between age 40 and 70) while in the allocation-decision regression, despite being still significant, they are discernibly smaller in magnitude. Banks and Tanner (2002) report similar results for the UK since the probability of holding risky assets progressively increases with age classes up to the 60–69 age class and then falls.

Cerny et al. (2005) structure an OLG model in which rational and forward-looking households optimize the allocation between risky and safe financial assets and housing. After having calibrated the model on the UK economy, the authors perform simulations under different scenarios and find in all cases that the optimal portfolio composition substantially varies with age: portfolios of older households should generally show decreasing portion of real assets and increasing importance of financial ones, whereby within the latter safe assets should tend to progressively increase with respect to risky ones along with the age of the household.

Brunetti and Torricelli (2007) examine the Italian household portfolios using data taken from the Bank of Italy Survey of Household Income and Wealth (SHIW) for 1995 to 2004. The authors first group financial assets into comparable credit and market risk categories and then examine the average portfolio by dividing households first by age classes, in order to depict a possible age effect on allocation choices, and then by both age classes and NW quartiles, in order to test whether the age effect persists even under different economic conditions. In addition, the 5% richest households are separately studied. The results show that, despite the several changes occurred over the decade from 1995 to 2004, the average Italian household portfolios are allocated consistently with the life-cycle theory: the middle-aged hold riskier portfolios, while older ones tend to disinvest risky financial instruments and turn to safer assets. As the age effect is depicted also across all NW quartiles, with the sole exception of the 5% richest households, the authors conclude that the age effect on financial choices is robust to both economic conditions and to the market changes that occurred during the decade under analysis. Clear hump-shaped age effects for central quartiles are reported in Brunetti and Torricelli (2009), where the period under analysis is extended to 1995–2006.

Frijns et al. (2008) introduce a model that links various behavioral finance concepts to individual investor's portfolio choice and collect survey data (on university students and employees) to test, inter alia, how socio demographic factors such as age and gender affect portfolio choices. Both market conditions (e.g., risk-return tradeoff) and individual factors play a significant role in portfolio choices, whereby specifically for the latter they find evidence that older investors tend to invest more in risky assets.

To sum up, with very few exceptions (e.g., Poterba, 2001), age is found to be among the most relevant determinants of portfolio decisions, although the shape of portfolio decision along the life cycle arising by data might slightly differ (i.e., hump-shaped rather than linear) depending on the decision on which the study is focused (participation vs. allocation decision) as well as the dataset used.

6.2.2   The Empirical Evidence in a Macro-Perspective

Provided that age affects portfolio choices, which is what many studies reviewed in the previous section suggest, a change in the age structure of the population might translate into different aggregate demand for certain financial assets with direct consequences on their prices and returns. This fear, which is referred to as the asset meltdown hypothesis (AMH), implies that financial markets might be significantly affected by the ongoing population "greying."

From an empirical point of view, this issue has been mainly addressed by means of regression analyses aimed at assessing the degree of correlation between some measures of financial asset prices, or returns, and a set of demographic measures. Financial variables however, are generally quite volatile, while demographic ones are typically slow moving: as a result, the statistical power of the analyses is reduced, and the observations required for reliable estimates need to be increased.[5] Some contributions face this problem by using time series as long as possible (accordingly to data availability). Others instead turn for their analyses to panel datasets, by pooling observations from different countries.

The studies are highly diversified, not only in terms of datasets, and hence estimation techniques used, but also in terms of model specifications: the dependent variable used might be either asset prices, asset returns, or equity risk premium; the explanatory variables might include only demographic variables or both demographic and economic and financial measures; finally, the demographic measures chosen can also differ, with some studies employing the average age of working population or old-dependency ratios, while others preferring the proportion of different age classes over the total population. The empirical evidence reported is not conclusive: some contributions, which will be reviewed at first, find only weak, if any, relationship between population aging and financial asset returns, while others report evidence which substantiates the concerns for the AMH.

James Poterba has extensively investigated the link between population aging and financial asset returns. In Poterba (2001), the author examines the age-wealth profiles in the US based on several waves of SCF (1983, 1986, 1989, 1992, and 1995) merging them with the projected evolution of the US population over the period 2000–2050 to forecast the future aggregate asset demand of financial assets. He concludes that "the aging of the baby boom cohort does not result in a significant decline in asset demand" thereby disproving the AMH. Poterba (2001) also examines the historical relationship between population age structure and asset prices and returns, by estimating the regression

$$r_t = \beta_0 + \beta_1 Demo_t + \epsilon_t \tag{6.9}$$

where the dependent variable is the real return on either T-bills, long-term government bonds or stocks and *Demo* represents several demographic

---

[5]For the econometric problems entailed by low frequency financial data see, for example, Campbell et al. (1997).

measures, namely median age, average age of adult population (i.e., aged 20 or over) and the ratios of those aged between 40 and 64 over total, adult and retired (i.e., aged 65 or over). The regressions are estimated using data for three countries and spanning over different time periods: the US (full sample, 1926–1999, and the postwar period, 1947–1999), Canada (1961–1997 for stocks and 1950–1997 for fixed-income instruments), and the UK (1961–1996 for equities and 1950–1996 for fixed-income assets). For the US, the author finds weak evidence of a link between asset returns and demographic structure, whereby the best results are obtained for fixed-income markets and using the ratio of those aged 40–64 over the total population as demographic measure. The estimated coefficients suggest that

> An increase in the fraction of the population in the key asset-accumulating years . . . lowers observed returns.

Although with implausibly large effects, possibly due to an omitted-variable problem. For Canada, the coefficients are statistically significant only for fixed-income assets and point towards a positive relation between real returns and middle-aged. By contrast, the results for UK show negatively signed and generally non-significant coefficients, which "further weaken the claim that demographic structure and asset returns exhibit systematic linkages." For the US, Poterba (2001) also studies the relationship between demographic variables (*Demo*) and stock prices normalized by corporate dividend (*P/D*), by estimating the following regression both in levels and in first differences

$$\left(\frac{P}{D}\right)_t = \beta_0 + \beta_1 Demo_t + \epsilon_t \tag{6.10}$$

In levels, several demographic variables are significant, although the possibility of "spurious regression" cannot be excluded. By contrast, the analysis in first differences originates statistically significant coefficients in only two out of five cases.

Poterba (2004) presents new findings on the historical correlation between population age structure and asset prices and returns, by estimating different specifications of equation 6.10 using US data spanning over the period 1926–2003. As in the previous study, the results are provided both over the whole sample period and over the post-war period (i.e., 1947–2003), but the demographic measures considered are (i) the share of the total population between ages 40 and 64; (ii) the share of the total population over age 65; (iii) the share of the adult population between the ages of 40 and 64; and (iv) the share of the adult population over the age of 65. Most of the estimated coefficients turn out to be non-significant, providing evidence against the relationship between asset returns and population age structure, at least over the last 70-year period. However, results are slightly different when the estimated model is

$$\left(\frac{P}{D}\right)_t = \beta_0 + \beta_1 Demo_t + \beta_2 Z_t + \epsilon_t \qquad (6.11)$$

where Z_t represents a set of additional variables included as control variables (i.e., the real interest rate and the economic growth rates). The coefficients of demographic variables are generally found significant and correctly signed, but when the same regression is run in first differences the coefficients become non-significant again, casting serious doubts on the robustness of previous results.

Bellante and Green (2004) report a significant effect of age on portfolio decisions (see previous section); as for AMH they agree with Poterba (2001, 2004) and are skeptical about the eventual consequences that might occur at an aggregate level. In their words,

> The concern for a securities market "meltdown" may be grossly exaggerated, since as retirees age, they do not seem greatly inclined to sell off their risky assets.

[and]

> Concerns for a dramatic shift in the market returns to risky assets may be unwarranted.

Basically the same conclusion is reached in GAO (2006), in which the possible impact of aging on financial market prices is examined by means of a twofold analysis. First, the plausibility of dramatic dis-savings by retirees is checked, based on data from both SCF (over the period 1992–2004) and HRS (1994–2004). Inter alia, the explorative analyses show that retirees do not really liquidate their assets and, if any thing, asset dis-saving occurs quite gradually due to bequest motive and the need to hedge longevity risk. Furthermore, almost two-thirds of the baby boomers' financial assets are concentrated in the portfolios of the 10% richest households, which are traditionally less sensitive to age affect on asset allocations (see, e.g., Guiso et al. (2002) or Brunetti and Torricelli (2007)). Based on this evidence the authors conclude that the AMH is not likely valid. Then, the historical link between financial and demographic dynamics is further tested by estimating the regression

$$r_t = \beta_0 + \beta_1 DY_{t-1} + \beta_2 TS_{t-1}$$
$$+ \beta_3 DefSpread_t + \beta_4 \Delta IP_{t+1} + \beta_5 Demo_t + \epsilon_t \tag{6.12}$$

where r_t is the real annual return on stocks while explanatory variables include the dividend yield (DY_{t-1}), the term spread (TS_{t-1}), the default spread shock ($DefSpread_t$), the change in industrial production (ΔIP_{t+1}), and a demographic variable ($Demo$) defined either as the proportion of the population age 40–64 or as the "middle-aged-to-young" or "MY" ratio, that is, the ratio of people aged 40–49 to those aged 20–29. The demographic coefficients are overall positively signed and statistically significant: yet, non-demographic variables can explain more variation in historical stock returns with respect to demographic ones, leading the authors to conclude that baby boomers' retirement is unlikely to have such a dramatic impact on financial asset prices.

Basically the same conclusion is reached by Börsch-Supan (2004), Oliveira Martins et al. (2005), and Saarenheimo (2005), who simulate the long-run effects of population aging by means of simulations on OLG models. Despite different calibrations and different scenarios that are considered, all contributions provide little support for the AMH.

If one strand of the literature provides reassuring evidence against the concrete realization of the AMH, other contributions, some of which are reviewed hereafter, find dissimilar results, pointing towards substantial and significant effects of population aging on financial markets.

Yoo (1994b) empirically tests the relationship between the population age structure and asset returns in the US over the period 1926–1988. His results suggest that a 1% increase in the relative size of the 45-year-old group can reduce the asset returns up to around 2%. The robustness of the result is further tested by estimating

$$R_t = \beta_0 + \beta_1 Pop_t^{25-34} + \beta_2 Pop_t^{35-44} + \beta_3 Pop_t^{45-54}$$
$$+ \beta_4 Pop_t^{55-64} + \beta_5 Pop_t^{65+} + \epsilon_t \tag{6.13}$$

where the dependent variable (R_t) is the total return on either equities, bonds, and T-bills, while the explanatory ones represent the share of the US population in several age classes. Once again, the evidence reported is of a statistically significant relationship between age distribution and the returns for several types of financial assets, especially in the postwar era.

Bakshi and Chen (1994) also perform several analyses on US data, referring to the period 1900–1990 and preferring the average age of adult population (aged 20 or over) as a demographic measure. The rationale is twofold: first, people younger than 20 generally do not play a determinant role in economic decision making; second, in the authors' words,

> The fraction of persons 65 and older can increase, but this does not necessarily mean that population is ageing, because the fraction of young persons may increase at the same time.

So that they believe the average age measures more correctly the real aging process. The authors observe a strong coevolution of the demographic variable with stocks markets prices, especially between 1946 and 1966 and 1981 and 1990. This result is further confirmed by a forecasting exercise aimed to assess whether and to what extent demographic variables might predict future risk premiums (RP_{t+1}), that is,

$$RP_{t+1} = \beta_0 + \beta_1 \Delta \bar{A}_t^{20+} + \beta_2 \Delta C_t + \beta_3 DivY_t + \beta_4 Term_t + \epsilon_t \qquad (6.14)$$

where explanatory variables include the percentage change in average age and in real per capita consumption, as well as the dividend yield on S&P 500 and the term premium. Several specifications of equation 6.14 are estimated by means of OLS and results over the postwar period imply that a progressively older population might substantially affect capital markets by increasing the equity risk premium.

Erb et al. (1997) utilize panel data to empirically assess the relationship between real equity returns and average age. They use data spanning the period 1970–1995 and referring to 18 countries.[6] First time-series and cross-section regressions are run. As for the former, the authors report a positive relationship between the proportion of middle-aged and equity returns. As for the latter, a positive relationship is detected between real equity returns and demographics across all countries. Then, data are pooled, and the same forecast exercise as in Bakshi and Chen (1994) is implemented, that is,

$$r_{it+k} = \beta_0 + \beta_1 \Delta \bar{A}_{it} + \beta_2 LE_{it} + \beta_3 \Delta Pop_{it} + \epsilon_{it} \qquad (6.15)$$

Where the expected rate of return over the next K periods is regressed on three demographic measures: change in average age, current life expectancy, and current population growth. Either considering one- or five-year horizons, only $\bar{A}_{it}$ displays significant (and positive) coefficients. The authors

---

[6]Australia, Austria, Belgium, Canada, Denmark, France, Germany, Hong Kong, Italy, Japan, Netherlands, Norway, Singapore, Spain, Sweden, Switzerland, UK, and US.

find consistent results including in the sample 27 additional emerging countries[7] and provide further evidence of the forecast power of demographic variables on long-run expected returns.

Brooks's contributions (2000, 2002) are among the most representative simulation-based studies aimed to assess the implications of aging on financial market. Both papers are based on a closed-economy OLG model with rational and forward-looking agents, but they substantially differ for the demographic changes simulation. Brooks (2000) explores the effects that aging might have on the rates of return of both safe and risky assets. He assumes no bequest motive and studies the effects of two demographic shocks, namely a baby boom and a following baby bust. The results point toward significant impact of these demographic changes, whereby the baby boom exerts a downward pressure on asset prices while the opposite occurs during the baby bust. Accordingly, the equity premium first decreases and then increases, making the author conclude that, even accounting for rationality and forward-looking behavior, demographic changes may affect financial markets. The same experiment is repeated in Brooks (2002), using US real demographic data (1870–2020), so that the following demographic changes are considered: (i) the prewar baby bust in the 1940s; (ii) the postwar baby boom in the 1960s; and (iii) the postwar baby bust in the 1980s. In fact, the rate of return changes in response to each of these demographic changes. More specifically, the first baby bust leads to a reduction of both risk-free and risky rates of return, while during the baby boom risk-free returns increase as well as risky assets return, although the latter are projected to increase less than the former, so that the baby boom translates into a lower equity risk premium. Hence, results are consistent with Brooks (2000) and point towards relevant repercussions of demographic dynamics on financial markets.

Davis and Li (2003) use data from 1950 to 1999 for 7 OECD countries (US, UK, Japan, Germany, France, Italy, and Spain) to empirically test the relationship between demographics and equities, which is at first investigated by means of the panel regression.

$$\Delta \ln(P^e)_{it} = \beta_0 + \beta_1 Pop_{it}^{20-39} + \beta_2 Pop_{it}^{40-64} + \beta_3 \Delta GDP_{it}^{HP}$$
$$+ \beta_4 \Delta (GDP - GDP^{HP})_{it} + \beta_5 LR_{it} \qquad (6.16)$$
$$+ \beta_6 Vol(P^e)_{it} + \beta_7 DY_{it-1} + \epsilon_{it}$$

---

[7]Argentina, Brazil, Chile, China, Colombia, Finland, Greece, Hungary, India, Indonesia, Ireland, Jordan, Malaysia, Mexico, New Zealand, Nigeria, Pakistan, the Philippines, Poland, Portugal, South Africa, South Korea, Sri Lanka, Thailand, Turkey, Venezuela, and Zimbabwe.

where the dependent variable is the log difference of real equity prices. Explanatory variables include the shares of population aged from 20 to 39 and from 40 to 64, the trend GDP growth rate, the output gap, the long-term real interest rate, the average equity prices volatility, and the lagged dividend yield. In all the specifications tested, both demographic variables are strongly significant and positively signed, although the coefficient for Pop_{it}^{20-39} is lower in magnitude with respect to Pop_{it}^{40-64} Cross-country data are then aggregated (using annual GDP as weights) and a time-series regression is run (which differs from equation 6.16 only for the absence of country-subscripts i). Here quite different results are obtained since most nondemographic variables are not significant, and among demographic ones only Pop_{it}^{40-64} has a (positive) significant coefficient. Yet, nondemographic and demographic variables together can explain overall up to 30 to 50% of the real equity prices variation, which is much more than what other studies report (e.g., Yoo (1994b) reports a maximum of 15%). Davis and Li (2003) also study the link between demographics and long-term government bond yields, that is,

$$LR_{it} = \beta_0 + \beta_1 Pop_{it}^{20-39} + \beta_2 Pop_{it}^{40-64} + \beta_3 \Delta SR_{it} + \beta_4 (LR - SR)_{it-1}$$
$$+ \beta_5 \Delta \ln(CPI)_{it-1} + \beta_6 \Delta\Delta \ln(CPI)_{it} + \beta_7 \Delta GDP_{it}^{HP} \qquad (6.17)$$
$$+ \beta_8 \Delta (GDP - GDP^{HP})_{it} + \epsilon_{it}$$

where the dependent variable is the bond yield, and explanatory variables include, besides the ones defined above, the first difference of the short rate, the lag of the term structure differential, and both lag and acceleration of inflation. Once again, the authors find that both demographic variables are significant, and results suggest a positive (negative) relation between young (middle-aged) generation size and bond yields. Davis and Li (2003) thus conclude that demographic changes (especially those concerning the most financially active part of the population, that is, those aged 40–64) can have a significant impact on both stock prices and bond yields, even in the presence of additional nondemographic explanatory variables.

Like Yoo (1994b) and Poterba (2001, 2004), Goyal (2004) studies the link between age structure and stock market returns in an OLG framework and empirically tests its implications by means of econometric techniques. US data spanning almost all the twentieth century are used to estimate, both in levels and in first differences

$$RP_{t+1} = \beta_0 + \beta_1 \bar{A}_t^{25+} + \beta_2 Pop_t^{25-44} + \beta_3 Pop_t^{45-64} + \beta_4 Pop_t^{65+}$$
$$+ \beta_5 DY_t + \beta_6 Flows_t + \epsilon_t \qquad (6.18)$$

where RP_{t+1} is the next-year excess stock returns, and explanatory variables include several current demographic variables, namely the average age of the population above 25 and the proportions of people aged between 25–44, 45–64, and 65+ as well as two control variables, that is, the dividend yield and net outflows from the stock market. In both levels and first differences regressions, estimated coefficients are significantly different from zero and point toward a positive (negative) relationship between the proportion of middle-aged (retired) people and stock prices. Overall demographic variables show a strong explanatory power, particularly if used in first differences. Next, the analysis is extended to a multiyear forecast framework by estimating

$$\sum_{i=1}^{K} RP_{t+i} = \beta_0 + \beta_1 \Delta Pop_{tk}^{25-44} + \beta_2 \Delta Pop_{tk}^{45-64} + \beta_3 Pop_{tk}^{65+}$$
$$+ \beta_4 DY_{tk} + \epsilon_{t+K}$$

(6.19)

where the dependent variable is the sum of next K-periods excess returns while explanatory variables include the dividend yield and the projected percentage change in the proportions of population of aged 25–44, 45–64 and 65+ between now and K-periods ahead. Results are presented for three- and five-year horizons. In both cases the demographic variables are jointly highly significant, and their signs suggest an inverse (direct) relation between the proportion of middle-aged (retired) people and stock returns.

Most recent works agree on the fact that the evidence of a relationship between aging population and financial markets might be substantially different across countries.

Geanakoplos et al. (2004) develop two versions of a closed-economy OLG model: one "stochastic," including business cycle shocks, and one "deterministic," in which the size of the generations, dividends, and wages are set in accordance with historical data for the US. Assuming either myopic or forward-looking agents, the model predicts that stock prices vary in response to the ratio of middle-aged to young people. The issue is further investigated by linear regression analyses. First, the regression is run

$$y_t = \beta_0 + \beta_1 \Delta \left(\frac{N_{MA}}{N_Y} \right)_t + \epsilon_t$$

(6.20)

where y_t is either the S&P 500 rate of return or the real short-term interest rate and the independent variable is the ratio between the number of middle-aged (N_{MA}) and the young people (N_Y). While the link with the short-term interest rate seems weak, the ratio of middle-aged to young people can explain up to 14% of the variability of stock market returns. Consistent results are obtained regressing the price-earnings ratio of the S&P 500 firms on the ratio of middle-aged to young people, since a positive and highly significant coefficient is found. Some international evidence is also provided, using data for Germany, France, Japan, and UK spanning over the period 1950–2001, by estimating:

$$P_t = \beta_0 + \beta_1 Demo_t + \epsilon_t \tag{6.21}$$

where P_t is the real stock price index and $Demo_t$ is either (N_{MA}/N_Y) or the size of the 35-to-59 cohort of the country under analysis. They find mixed results: no relationship at all in the UK, a weak relationship in Germany, a relatively significant relationship in France and quite strong relationship in Japan, which thus turns out to be one of the countries for which the demographic changes might more soundly affect financial markets.

Consistent results are found in Ang and Maddaloni (2005), where the predictive power of demographic changes on future equity risk premium is examined using use two distinct datasets. The first spans over the whole twentieth century and refers to France, Germany, Japan, the US, and the UK. The second includes monthly data over a smaller sample period (1970–2000) for 15 developed countries.[8] For the econometric analysis, the authors first study the predictability of the excess return k-periods ahead RP_{t+k} over three different forecast horizons (k = 1, 2 and 5 years) estimating the following regression with GMM for each country separately

$$RP_{t+K} = \beta_0 + \beta Z_t + \epsilon_{t+K} \tag{6.22}$$

where Z_t represents the set of explanatory variables including both demographic and control variables. For the latter, the authors choose delayed consumption growth and term spread, since both are recognized predictors of equity returns and have data available over quite long sample periods. For the demographic measures, the authors use the average age of the adult population, the proportion of adults over 65, and the proportion of the population of working age, that is, between 20 and 40, all used in first differences rather than in levels. The results are sensibly different by country. The US has only a weak positive relationship between demographics and excess returns. The same holds for the UK, for which the only demographic measure robust to control variables across all forecast horizons is Pop^{65+}. In France and Germany all demographic variables are significant, although

---

[8]Australia, Austria, Belgium, Canada, Denmark, France, Germany, Italy, Japan, Netherlands, Spain, Sweden, Switzerland, the UK, and the US.

only at the 10% level and over short time horizons, displaying in addition negative signs in contrast to the US and UK cases. Finally, in Japan all demographic variables show strongly significant and negative coefficients, at least at the 1-year horizon. Next, the authors pool the data and estimate equation 6.22 across all five countries simultaneously. The results for the panel analysis confirm that Pop^{65+} is the only demographic variable that maintains significant predictive power across all forecast horizons, also when control variables are included. Finally, the authors extend the analyses to the 15 countries and reestimate (6.22) using the monthly dataset. Also in this case results confirm the significant and negative correlation between Pop^{65+} and excess returns across all forecast horizons. Ang and Maddaloni (2005) thus conclude that, despite some cross-countries differences,[9] demographics play an important role in predicting excess returns.

Country differences also matter in Brooks (2006), where the author constructs a long-run (1900–2005) panel dataset referred to 16 developed countries[10] and estimates the linear regression

$$y_{it} = \lambda_i + \beta_t + \gamma_1 Z_{1it} + \gamma_2 Z_{2it} + \gamma_3 Z_{3it} + \epsilon_{it} \tag{6.23}$$

with

$$Z_{Nit} = \sum_{j=1}^{J} j^N p_{ijt} - \frac{1}{J} \sum_{j=1}^{J} j^N, \quad N = 1, 2, 3$$

where y_{it} is either the price or the total return on stocks, stock indexes, bonds, and T-bills, while the explanatory variables include two dummies, λ_i for the country and β_t for the year, and indirectly $p_{1it}, p_{2it}, \ldots, p_{Jit}$, that is, the shares over the entire population of people in the J age group. The econometric specification proposed by Brooks (2006), as in Yoo (1994a), includes the entire age distribution in the regression, thereby avoiding an arbitrary partition of the population. Nonetheless, the demographic variables are not explicitly included into the model, so that the coefficients $\gamma_1, \gamma_2, \gamma_3$ are not directly interpretable: yet, the implicit age coefficients, capturing the sensitivity of asset price and returns to age distribution, can easily be recovered. The results are presented for both financial asset prices and returns. Indeed

---

[9] In particular, the authors observe more significant and higher coefficients for countries with more generous social security systems and less developed financial markets.

[10] Australia, Belgium, Canada, Denmark, Finland, France, Germany, Italy, Japan, Netherlands, New Zealand, Norway, Sweden, Switzerland, the UK, and the US.

different pictures arise: with asset prices, a significant effect of age is reported whereby the older the population, the lower the price of stock relative to the T-bill. On the other hand, when using real financial asset returns only little evidence of a link between demographics and financial markets is found and only with regards to fixed-income market, consistently with Poterba (2001, 2004) and opposite to Davis and Li (2003) and Brunetti and Torricelli (2008), as described in what follows. Furthermore, when equation 6.23 is estimated, allowing the coefficients $\gamma_1, \gamma_2, \gamma_3$ to vary across countries, the results point toward a substantial heterogeneity across countries. In particular, Brooks (2006) observes that "English-speaking economies ... do not conform well the life-cycle hypothesis," thereby confirming the little evidence of decumulation during retirement already reported by other studies (e.g., Poterba (2001) and GAO (2006)). By contrast, countries such as Italy, Finland, Sweden, Norway, and Japan exhibit the more familiar life-cycle pattern, which the author brings back to the limited household participation to the equity markets that characterizes these countries. Hence, also in this case, the conclusion strongly depends on the country considered.

The evidence reported in Brunetti and Torricelli (2008) implicitly supports the same argument. In this contribution, the empirical connection between financial asset returns and population aging dynamics is investigated using annual data over from 1958 to 2004 referred to Italy, taken as a case study based on its pronounced aging, which is much steeper than the US one. The authors first follow Poterba (2001, 2004) and estimate regressions such as

$$r_t = \alpha + \beta D_t + \epsilon_t \tag{6.24}$$

where r_t is the real return on either stocks, long-term government bonds, or short-term government bonds (*Buoni Ordinari del Tesoro*, BOT), D_t is the vector of demographic variables, basically represented by the shares of different age classes (20–40, 40–64, over 65) over total or adult population. Consistently with Poterba (2004), the results are not robust across the variants examined, leading to the conclusion that demographic variables alone cannot satisfactorily explain the dynamics of financial asset returns. Next, observing that the purely demographic specification might be affected by omitted-variable problems, the authors follow Davis and Li (2003) and estimate

$$r_t = \alpha + \beta D_t + \gamma F_t + \epsilon_t \tag{6.25}$$

where F_t represents a vector of financial variables, differently defined depending on the dependent variable (e.g., dividend-yield, stock prices volatility for stocks, and term spread, inflation, GDP grow rate and output gap for bonds). From the extended specification a different picture emerges: the results are largely consistent across variants and point toward a significant role of demographic variables in affecting financial returns, especially in the stock market, for which it appears that a higher share of early (late) working-aged is associated with an increase (decrease) of real returns on stocks. Hence, based on a comparative analysis of the evidence obtained for Italy and that reported by Poterba (2001, 2004) and Davis and Li (2003) for the US, the authors notice that the evidence for Italy, experiencing a stronger population dynamics, is more clear-cut, providing evidence in support the importance of the country-specific age dynamics in explaining the impact of demographics on financial markets.

6.3 MODELS FOR PORTFOLIO CHOICES AND LIFE-CYCLE ASSET ALLOCATIONS

Portfolio selection models for the household are based on classical portfolio theory and have closely followed its evolution which, as for the application to the household, has also been fostered by the empirical evidence surveyed in Section 6.2.1. The present section cannot, and by no means aspires to, provide an exhaustive survey of a theory which is vast, manifold, and still growing. Rather, by concentrating on models that analyse both consumption/saving and asset allocation decisions, the purpose here is twofold:

1. To recall the evolution of the household portfolio theory from the early models to the more realistic ones highlighting how the basic assumptions have been progressively, and often alternatively, released, in order to capture empirical facts and life-time effects (see Sections 6.3.1 and 6.3.2);
2. To focus on lifetime asset allocation models that account for the effect of age and attain consistency with the empirical findings; in this connection preference is accorded to models which rest on assumptions that better depict two relevant sources of risk for households: labor income and the length of life. In order to better illustrate the state of the art, two main models will be taken as representative and illustrated in more detail (see Sections 6.3.3 and 6.3.4).

In other words, preference is given here to models where the causes of heterogeneity are not so much related to external factors (e.g., returns distribution, tax frictions) as rather to household-specific features (e.g., objectives and/or human capital).

6.3.1   The Seminal Models

The basic model for the optimal portfolio selection is the static one-period model based on the maximization of a concave Von Neumann-Morgenstern utility function of end-of-period wealth. Under specific assumptions on absolute risk tolerance or risk aversion (one measure being the reciprocal of the other) and/or the asset return distribution, this model produces a fundamental result in the theory of finance known as the two-fund separation theorem. The theorem essentially states that all agents choose a portfolio made of two funds: the risk-free asset and a fund comprising all other risky assets. The Markowitz (1952) mean-variance formulation is by far the most well-known one. Its main implications, that is, the risk-return tradeoff and portfolio diversification, hinge on either a quadratic expected utility or normally distributed returns.

More generally, the basic static model mainly suffers from two major drawbacks that are particularly apparent in connection with household portfolios: empirically it is not supported by the data since real portfolios do not appear to be as diversified as predicted by the model, and, theoretically, being a static model, it is not appropriate for the analysis of the life-cycle asset allocations. If the first limitation could be overcome also within the static framework by making the model setup more realistic (e.g., including a form of background risk such as uninsurable labor income), the second one calls for an extension of the model to a multiperiod setting.[11]

In the late 1960s, multiperiod versions of the basic model were proposed in the pioneering papers by Mossin (1968), Merton (1969, 1971), and Samuelson (1969). As for the modeling setup, the common feature of these papers is to solve a dynamic optimization problem for a risk-averse household, which maximizes expected utility subject to a budget constraint. The models can differ for the setup (discrete vs. continuous), for the specification of the utility function, and the assumption about the asset return process, whereby explicit solutions can be in some cases derived, depending on the utility function and the asset return process assumed.

Additionally, the models differ according to their main focus. In fact, the multiperiod setup immediately calls for consideration of optimal decision

---

[11] Gollier (2002) provides an excellent survey on the classical theory of household portfolios, where also the static problem is discussed in detail. In particular, the author highlights the dual interpretation of the very same as either a static portfolio selection problem under uncertainty (Arrow-Debreu portfolio problem) or a lifetime consumption-saving problem under certainty and clearly illustrates the condition for the validity of the two-fund separation theorem (i.e., all agents must have linear absolute risk tolerance with the same slope).

rules not only for portfolio selection, but also for consumption. However, some models (e.g., Mossin 1968) abstract from the consumption/saving problem and aim to find the optimal portfolio that is specific to retirement (i.e., there is no consumption from portfolio before retirement). As summarized by Brandt (2009) both in the discrete and in the continuous time case, it can be shown that the optimal multiperiod portfolio consists of two components: a myopic portfolio, which is equal to the sequence of one-period optimal portfolios and a hedging portfolio, which serves to hedge against changes in investment opportunities. It follows that the optimality of the myopic strategy depends on assumed features for the household objectives (i.e., the utility function) and returns process (i.e., the investment opportunities). Specifically, the myopic strategy is optimal with constant relative risk aversion (CRRA) utility, under which the optimization problem is nonrecursive and utility is homothetic in wealth, if excess returns are independent of the innovations in the state variables.[12]

However, by considering that, intermediate consumption results change since the decision maker can attain smoothing in wealth shocks by means of variations in consumption. In this connection, it is useful to follow Gollier (2002) and stress three effects that play a role in determining the optimal consumption and portfolio rules. The first is the time diversification effect: it means that, ceteris paribus, longer horizons allow to better smooth shocks and hence younger household should take up more risk. The second one is the wealth effect and accounts for the role of wealth in connection with the time horizon: if the wealth level in each period changes with the horizon, so does consumption per period (e.g., lower for younger households that face longer horizons) and the overall effect on risk taking depends on the relationship between risk tolerance and consumption.[13] Finally, the repeated risk effect captures the idea that, in a multiperiod setting, taking risk today can affect risk taking in the future: this again depends on risk tolerance.

In sum, in a multiperiod model, while the time-diversification effect is quite clear-cut, the latter two effects depend on the utility function taken to represent household preferences. An interesting benchmark to illustrate

---

[12] Hakansson (1971) discussed Mossin's (1968) results and provided weaker conditions for the optimality of myopic strategies. Specifically, log utility for general asset return distributions. In Mossin, with power utility, the assets must be independent to have the myopic property. Brandt (2009) summarizes and argues three cases where the myopic investment strategy is optimal. Constant investment opportunity set, stochastic but unhedgable investment opportunities, and logarithmic utility.

[13] Specifically, it is the risk-tolerance degree of homogeneity with respect to consumption that determines whether the time diversification effect prevails on the wealth effect (see Gollier 2002).

the joint working of these three effects is that of CRRA utility, which is a special case of hyperbolic absolute risk aversion (HARA) utility displaying linear risk tolerance: in this case, the time diversification effect offsets the wealth effect, while taking risk today does not influence risk taking in subsequent period. It follows that the myopic strategy is the optimal one,[14] a result that prevails in the early models. In fact, Merton (1969) confirms in continuous time an important result proved by Samuelson (1969) in discrete time: for isoelastic marginal utility (i.e., CRRA) and a geometric Brownian motion for returns, the portfolio-selection decision is independent of the consumption decision, and, for Bernoulli logarithmic utility, the separation goes both ways. Moreover, under the assumption of log-normally distributed asset prices (implied by the geometric Brownian motion hypothesis for the returns), a mutual-fund theorem result holds, and Merton (1971) extends these results to more general utility functions and asset price assumptions thus showing that the classical Markowitz mean-variance rules hold without the hypotheses of the static case (i.e., quadratic utility and normal prices).

Therefore, overall seminal portfolio models provide portfolio rules that are independent of wealth, but more importantly of age so that life-cycle implications cannot be analysed. It is thus not surprising that the predictions of the classical models are markedly at odds with the empirical evidence presented in Section 6.2.

To make a step towards more suitable models for household portfolios, it is necessary to consider a setup which is more household-specific.

6.3.2 More Realistic Portfolio Models

The review in Section 6.2.1 has highlighted some empirical regularities in household portfolios, which although different in magnitude, characterize household portfolios in most countries over the world. Specifically, three main stylized facts are apparent: low stock market participation, scarce diversification, and a life-cycle pattern in household portfolio choices (either participation or allocation) that in most cases displays a hump shape, whereby the investment in stocks peaks at middle age.

The predictions of the models recalled in the previous section are not consistent with these empirical facts, and, as a consequence, a body of literature has been growing since the 1990s to reconcile theory with evidence.

---

[14] Watcher (2002) shows that, assuming CRRA preferences, the possibility of intermediate consumption affects the hedging component of a portfolio only and not the myopic one, with the overall effect of shortening the time horizon of the investor.

In doing so, the more recent models, while departing from some classical assumptions, have extended and added more realistic features to the model setup.

To summarize, three are the main routes the literature has taken to attain life-cycle patterns in household portfolios:

- The modeling of household preferences different from CRRA
- The predictability in asset returns
- The consideration of trading frictions and market incompleteness

By contrast to the classical papers where the primary assumptions (i.e., stationarity of returns and CRRA preferences) allowed for closed form solutions, most realistic models are not so easily tractable, requiring numerical and approximate solution methods.

A fundamental issue in portfolio models is modeling of household risk preferences via the utility function. In the previous section, the role of the CRRA utility assumption clearly emerged in determining both desirable results (e.g., analytic tractability, asset demands independent of wealth) and undesirable ones, such as the independence of asset allocations from the time horizon. It follows that an important generalization has concerned preferences: some authors (e.g., Campbell and Viceira 1999) use Epstein-Zin-Weil preferences (Epstein and Zin 1989) which are a generalization of CRRA preferences based on recursive utility. They retain the wealth scale independence of power utility, but in contrast to CRRA, make it possible to distinguish risk aversion from the elasticity of intertemporal substitution in consumption:[15] an important feature given that these parameters have different effects on optimal consumption and portfolio choice.

A different departure from the CRRA preference structure consists in assuming that past consumption choices affect current consumption, as in the so-called habit formation (or habit persistence) proposed by Costantinides (1990), who shows that this assumption helps in explaining the equity premium puzzle (Mehra and Prescott 1985) and variation in returns.

Based on some empirical evidence, a strand of literature (e.g., Barberis (2000), Campbell and Viceira (1999) have assumed the predictability of asset returns. Brandt et al. (2005) also consider the case of an investor that is uncertain about the parameters of the data-generating process and learns

---

[15] For CRRA utility functions, the elasticity of intertemporal substitution is the inverse of the coefficient of absolute risk aversion. This implies an unrealistic connection between two distinct feature of household preferences: the willingness to substitute consumption intertemporally and the willingness to take up risk.

from realized returns and dividend yields: in this setting he observes that learning reduces the allocation to stocks due to parameter uncertainty.[16]

Early models generally neglected trading frictions, whose consideration in the dynamic framework makes the analysis quite complex. In particular the absence of transaction costs, and specifically of fixed costs, has been demonstrated to be a possible explanation for the low levels of stock market participation (e.g., Basak and Cuoco 1998). By contrast, the effect of proportional transaction costs is less clearcut: for instance, Constantinides (1986) concludes they do not discourage stock holding, while Heaton and Lucas (1997) find that they shift portfolios towards assets with lower transaction costs. Some kind of taxes play a role similar to proportional transaction costs in that they may prevent investors from portfolio rebalancing (e.g., Dammon et al. 2004).

The consideration of market incompleteness is often based on liquidity constraints or short selling restrictions, which in fact impede intertemporal smoothing of consumption and portfolio return and can provide an alternative explanation for nonparticipation. Frictions are also behind models that consider the role of uninsurable labor income in explaining life-cycle asset allocations.

In sum, there are three main issues in long-term portfolio choices: the stochastic opportunity set, the consideration of illiquid assets (and particularly labor), and the uncertainty in the length of life. As for the former issue, many papers have contributed, especially from the late 1990s, by considering interest rate or inflation risk and time-varying risk premia, an issue that is more tractable for an institution than for a household decision maker.[17] Given the focus of this chapter on individual household decisions, the attention is restricted to the inclusion into life-cycle models of the latter two issues, which are more household-specific and increasingly necessary to attain features of realism in the decision scenario of most households. For these reasons in the next sections we will concentrate on the role of labor income risk and uncertainty in the length of life.

6.3.3 Life-Cycle Asset Allocation Models with Uninsurable Labor Risk

A crucial element in setting up a model for life-cycle asset allocation is to account for the main reasons that motivate wealth accumulation: that is,

---

[16] See the *Review of Financial Studies* 21, no. 4 (2008), where several articles are centered on the return predictability debate, which is far from being resolved.

[17] Examples are: Campebell and Viceira (1999, 2001) and Watcher (2002). More references are in the survey by Brandt (2009). See also the models presented in Part III of this book.

the precautionary savings motive connected with background risks and the bequest motive.

The most important background risk for household is possibly labor risk, which has been in fact considered in connection with portfolio choices by a strand of literature starting with the Merton (1971). The author analyzes the issue in a framework where labor income can be capitalized and hence the risk insured.

By contrast, in order to see the effect of labor risk on portfolio choices it is fundamental to assume incompleteness so that labor income risk has to be considered, more realistically, uninsurable. In this connection Cocco et al. (2005) provide a model for consumption and portfolio choices in the presence of uninsurable labor income risk, which is becoming a milestone in the analysis of this issue.[18] The article provides life-cycle consumption and portfolio rules for a realistically calibrated model with nontradable labor income and borrowing constraints.[19] Although in other and subsequent papers, the model has been extended, the main feature and implications are already present in Cocco et al. (2005).[20] For this reason, we believe it is worth illustrating the major model assumptions and their implications in order to highlight what are the modeling characteristics that make it possible to capture features of realism of portfolio rules such as the dependence of asset allocations on age.

Intuitively, the main departure of Cocco et al. (2005) from classical models is the inclusion of uninsurable labor risk (i.e., markets are incomplete). Specifically, the authors maintain that moral hazard problems, via borrowing constraints, prevent households from capitalizing future labor income, and thus labor income is a risky asset in household portfolios. However, labor income risk has no or very low correlation with the other financial assets: it is thus a substitute of the risk-free asset and plays a role in terms of portfolio diversification: for instance, young households, who already own a sort of risk-free asset in the form of labor income, tend to hold more risky assets than older households, who by contrast have lower "risk-free" labor

---

[18] Also Heaton and Lucas (1997) and Viceira (2001) analyze the effect of uninsurable income risk on portfolio composition, but they do it in a infinite-horizon setting and hence in a stationary setup, which is less appropriate for the analysis of life-cycle pattern. More related to Cocco et al. (2005) is Bertaut and Haliassos (1997), who also assume a finite horizon.

[19] On these issues see also Guiso et al. (1996).

[20] In Gomes et al. (2008) the authors allow for flexible labor supply but results remain overall qualitatively similar to Cocco et al. (2005) although the ability to increase labor supply represents an alternative to an increase in savings against future income uncertainty so that the portfolio pattern can be less conservative with respect to the case of fixed labor supply.

holdings. Overall, as the authors conclude, "the share invested in equities is roughly decreasing with age. This is driven by the fact that the labor income profile itself is downward sloping," and the result is attained with no need to rest on the predictability of asset returns.

To get more insight into the model, its limitations and extensions it is worth illustrating the benchmark model proposed in Cocco et al. (2005) where, beside the standard ingredients of an optimal portfolio choice problem (i.e., preferences, asset returns processes, and various constraints), the modeling labor income risk plays an important role.

Let K be a deterministic and exogenous working age, T the uncertain length of life, and p_t the probability that the household-investor is alive at date $t + 1$. The household i is assumed to have time-separable CRRA preferences of the following type

$$E_t \sum_{t=1}^{T} \delta^{t-1} \left(\prod_{J=0}^{t-2} p_j \right) \left\{ p_{t-1} \frac{C_{it}^{1-\gamma}}{1-\gamma} + b(1 - p_{t-1}) \frac{D_{it}^{1-\gamma}}{1-\gamma} \right\} \tag{6.26}$$

where: $\delta < 1$ is the discount factor, $\gamma > 0$ is the coefficient of relative risk aversion, C_t and D_t are, respectively, the consumption level and the amount of bequest at time t.

The exogenous labor income process, for $t < K$, is assumed to be the sum of a deterministic component that can capture the hump shape of earnings over the life-cycle and a stochastic one, which is made of a persistent part v_{it} and a transitory shock ϵ_{it}

$$\log Y_{it} = f(t, Z_{it}) + v_{it} + \epsilon_{it} \tag{6.27}$$

with
   Z_{it} = vector of individual characteristics
   ϵ_{it} distributed as $N(0, \sigma_\epsilon^2)$

$$v_{it} = v_{it-1} + u_{it} \tag{6.28}$$

u_{it} is uncorrelated with ϵ_{it} and distributed as $N(0, \sigma_u^2)$.

While the transitory component ϵ_{it} is uncorrelated across households, the permanent shock u_{it} can be decomposed in an aggregate component ξ_t and a transitory one w_{it}, both normally distributed with zero mean and constant variance

$$u_{it} = \xi_t + w_{it} \tag{6.29}$$

The *retirement income*, for $t > K$, is assumed to be a constant fraction λ in the last working year

$$\log Y_{it} = \log(\lambda) + f(t, Z_{ik}) + v_{it} \qquad (6.30)$$

In the financial markets, two assets exist: a risk-free asset and a risky one whose gross real *excess return* over the risk-free is

$$R_{t+1} - \bar{R}_f = \mu + \eta_{t+1} \qquad (6.31)$$

where $\bar{R}_f$ is the risk-free return and the innovation η_{t+1} is assumed to be normally i.i.d. with constant variance, but correlated with the aggregate component of labor income with a coefficient ρ.

A crucial assumption is the borrowing constraint, since it impedes the household from capitalizing or borrowing against future labor income or retirement wealth

$$B_{it} \geq 0. \qquad (6.32)$$

It is justified by moral hazard/adverse selection arguments, which as the authors stress are particularly stringent in the early years of the household adult life.

The *short-selling constraint*

$$S_{it} \geq 0. \qquad (6.33)$$

implies nonnegative allocation in equities at all dates. Borrowing and short-selling constraints imply that the proportion invested in equities is $\alpha_{it} \in [0, 1]$ and wealth is nonnegative.

Against this setup, the household i in period t starts with a wealth W_{it} and maximizes equation 6.26 subject to constraints 6.27–6.33 in order to obtain optimal consumption and portfolio rules

$$C_{it}(X_{it}, v_{it})$$

and

$$\alpha_{it}(X_{it}, v_{it})$$

which are a function of the state variables: time t, cash-on-hand ($X_{it} = W_{it} + Y_{it}$) and the stochastic persistent component of labor income, v_{it}.

Although the dimensionality of the problem can be reduced,[21] the model cannot be solved analytically, and the authors obtain numerical solutions by backward induction, after appropriate calibration of the model to real data. Given the role of labor income in the model, particular attention is devoted to the calibration of the corresponding process which is done on PSID data (a longitudinal US Panel Study on Income Dynamics) and in line with the literature on the subject (e.g., Attanasio (1995), Hubbard et al. (1994)).

Simulation results are presented for the benchmark case of the second education group (i.e., high school) but are shown to remain qualitatively unaltered for the other income groups: this is due to the fact that in this model the different groups are solely characterized by the age at which working age begins. A stronger characterization of the benchmark case lies in the correlation between labor income risk and the stock market, which is assumed to be absent (i.e. $\rho = 0$).

As for the life-cycle pattern of portfolio choices, the result is quite clear: the investment in stocks is roughly decreasing with age. To understand this result, recall that in the paper labor is essentially characterized as a bond-like assets, and portfolio decisions are determined by the household labor income profile also in relation to wealth. Thus young households, who have a very steep labor income profile, display a rapidly increasing implicit riskless holding (represented by labor income) and diversify by investing in stocks. Later in life the labor income profile is not so steep, and the portfolio rule is evaluated at higher wealth levels so that the portfolio moves away from stocks. This overall result rationalizes and supports professional advice suggesting to shift portfolio towards relatively riskless assets as the household ages,[22] but, as discussed below, this is in contrast to most empirical evidence on the issue (see Section 6.2.1).

However, some extensions considered in the paper attain results that are closer to the empirical evidence. For example, an empirically calibrated small probability of disastrous labor income draw lowers stock holding and produces heterogeneity in young household portfolio choices, while endogenous borrowing can explain nonparticipation decisions of young households. Moreover, the sensitivity analyses performed in many directions pave the way to many subsequent literature contributions. Worth mentioning is the sensitivity analysis with respect to labor income risk and in particular to its correlation with stock returns: a positive correlation has significant portfolio effects, indicating a lower level of stock for young and a higher level

---

[21] The value function is homogeneous with respect to v_{it} which can be normalized to one.

[22] The typical reference here is the rule suggesting to place (100-age)% of wealth in a well-diversified stock portfolio (see Malkiel (1996)).

for middle-aged households. This line of research is taken up by Benzoni et al. (2007) as described below.

A related paper is Gomes and Michaelides (2005) where the labor income process is calibrated as in Cocco et al. (2005), but preferences are Epstein-Zin and a fixed entry cost is assumed. The objective is to provide theoretical support for empirical findings on participation rates and asset allocations conditional on participation: heterogeneity in risk aversion seems to explain both. In fact, on the one hand households with small risk aversion and small elasticity of intertemporal substitution can smooth earning shocks with little buffer wealth, and this explain low participation; on the other hand, more risk-averse household accumulate more wealth and hence participate in the stock market, since they are young, but they do not invest the whole portfolio in it.

As for the role of labor income risk, Cocco et al. (2005) and related extensions highlight that the assumption of null correlation with stock market risk impedes obtaining realistic portfolio rules. Based on previous evidence on the correlation between human capital and market returns, Benzoni et al. (2007) study, in a continuous time model, the optimal portfolio choice over life-cycle in a setup that is essentially the same[23] as the one just described for Cocco et al. (2005), but for the correlation assumption. Specifically, the authors assume that the aggregate component of labor income (the equivalent of ξ_t in equation 6.29) is cointegrated with aggregate dividends and hence with the stock returns. The cointegration assumption makes labor income more of a stock-like asset (than a bond-like one as in Cocco et al. 2005). The cointegration is modeled as a mean reverting process with k being the coefficient of mean reversion, whereby if $k = 0$ there is no cointegration. Its inverse $1/k$ provides the time necessary for cointegration to act. If the residual working life is long (i.e., young households), the return on the household's human capital is highly exposed to stock market returns and labor income resembles more a risky asset than a risk-free one so that young households, who are already overexposed to stock market risk, find it optimal to go short in stocks or, in the presence of borrowing constraint, to invest the entire wealth in the risk-free bond. For the middle-aged the cointegration has no time to act, labor income has bond-like features, and the opposite is true. This is still true in the years before retirement, but for a sufficiently short time before retirement a second effect prevails: due to lower future labor income, the value of the bond position implicit in human

---

[23] Benzoni et al. (2007) do not explicitly model retirement income, but calibrate the bequest function so as to capture the saving necessary for consumption in the retirement years. This is equivalent to assuming that the household receives an annuity in retirement years.

capital decreases and the household starts reducing stocks in favor of risk-free assets. This is the hump-shape profile that Benzoni et al. (2007) obtain in the simulations of their model, which, in line with the literature is solved numerically by backward induction, using standard difference method. Beyond robustness exercises, the authors also prove that the result still holds in the presence of return predictability.

In sum, by contrast to similar models (even micro data calibrated ones) and conventional professional wisdom, Benzoni et al. (2007) attain a hump-shaped pattern for lifetime portfolio that is consistent with most empirical evidence on the topic. The result provides an explanation to limited stock market participation that the authors stress to be different but complementary to those typically put forward in the literature:

> In particular, our paper emphasizes that long-run cointegration between aggregate labor income and aggregate dividends has a first-order effect on the optimal portfolio decisions of an agent over the life cycle.

However, it has to be stressed that the fundamental assumption for this result is questionable in that it is difficult to test. Evidence on the cointegration between human capital and market return is disparate if not weak, due to the well-known lack of power of cointegration tests. Moreover the results are very sensitive not only to the very same existence of a cointregation but also to the specific level.[24]

6.3.4 Life-Cycle Asset Allocation Models in the Presence of Annuities

The stochastic nature of a household investment horizon calls for the consideration of a further source of risk, which is known as longevity risk; that is, the risk for the investor of living longer than predicted and hence running out of savings. To account for this issue, household portfolio models have to consider uncertainty in the length of life in connection with the role played by a particular type of assets, annuities, which in fact permit transferring longevity risk to the insurer but are an illiquid instrument.[25]

---

[24] In fact, as the authors stress, it is econometrically very difficult even to distinguish between $k = 0$ and $k = 0.05$, and the peak of the hump shape of the portfolio pattern depends on the value of the coefficient governing the cointegration k.

[25] An overview on the treatment of longevity risk from the viewpoint of annuity providers and pension plans is provided by Biffis and Blake in Chapter 10 of this book.

The question in a portfolio framework becomes the optimal investment in annuities. The seminal paper to answer this question is Yaari (1965), which ignores other sources of risks other than mortality and provides conditions for full annuitization, that is, market completeness and no bequest motive, otherwise partial annuitization becomes optimal. Later on, portfolio models have analyzed the case of constant life annuities (that is, annuities providing a fixed payout), but they have often simplified the problem by either imposing full annuitization (e.g. Cairns et al. (2006)) or disregarding other important features of the decision problem, such as the irreversibility of the annuities purchase, other sources of risks (e.g., Richard (1975)) or the impact of annuity markets during working life (e.g., Milevsky and Young (2007) consider the case of a retiree).

However, in their recent work Horneff et al. (2008)[26] overcome some limitations of the previous literature and study the optimal consumption and saving strategy in the presence of constant life annuities, bonds, and stocks in an incomplete market setting. The model allows for gradual purchase of annuities and considers the three main sources of risks faced by an household: risky stocks, untradable labor income during working life, and stochastic time to death. In connection with the latter two features their model can be seen as extending those presented in the previous section. In particular, the model shares many features of Cocco et al. (2005), and some of the parameters taken for the numerical solution of the optimization problem are borrowed from the former.

More precisely, the problem differs from the one represented by equations 6.26–6.33 in the following:

1. Since Epstein-Zin preferences are assumed, equation 6.26 is replaced by the recursive formulation of intertemporal utility that makes it possible to disentangle risk aversion γ from the elasticity of intertemporal substitution ψ.
2. An incomplete annuity market is considered. Against the payment of an actuarial premium A_t, the annuitant receives a constant payment L until death

$$A_t = Lh_t \tag{6.34}$$

with

$$h_t = (1 + \delta) \sum_{s=1}^{T-t} \left(\prod_{u=t}^{t+s} p_u^a \right) R_f^{-s}$$

---

[26] Cocco and Gomes (2008) also consider longevity risk and the role of longevity bonds in the optimal consumption/saving problem, but they do not study the optimal asset allocation.

where $\delta =$ loading factor and $p_u^a =$ survival probability used by the annuity provider, which is higher than the average survival probabilities p_u^s. The annuity provider hedges the guaranteed annuity payments by pooling mortality risks of annuitants: the funds of those who die are allocated among the living member of a cohort, and this represents the source of the so-called mortality credit: that is, the excess annuity return over a bond. The market is incomplete because only life-long payouts are available and funds from annuity are invested in bonds only.

3. Mortality is modelled by means of Gompertz's law. The force of mortality used by the provider and the subjective one are specified as the following function of the parameters m^i and b^i

$$\lambda_i^t = \frac{1}{b^i} \exp\left(\frac{t - m^i}{b^i}\right) \tag{6.35}$$

with

$$i = a, s$$

and the survival probability is

$$p_t^i = \exp\left(-\int_0^1 \lambda_{t+s}^i ds\right). \tag{6.36}$$

Additionally the subjective force of mortality is taken to be a linear transformation of the one derived from average mortality tables.

It follows that wealth accumulation is determined by annuities as well, and a borrowing constraint is placed on the annuities too ($A_t \geq 0$). In this setup, beyond demand for stocks, bonds, and consumption, there is one more choice variable that has to be determined: the optimal level of annuities in each period. Moreover all policy rules are a function of the same state variables as in Cocco et al. (2005) plus the annuity payouts from previously purchased annuities.

There is a tradeoff between liquid financial savings and illiquid annuities, which provide the mortality credit. The introduction of annuities thus poses a central question: is the mortality credit high enough to compensate for the illiquidity of the annuity? The irreversibility of the annuity purchase makes the consideration of labor income risk even more important, given the need for liquidity that income shocks normally bring with them. Moreover extreme income shocks can also be interpreted as reflecting health care and nursing costs, and hence the analysis in relation to annuities becomes even more important.

The model is first solved for the baseline case (no loads, no asymmetries between insurer's and anunuitant's beliefs, no bequest) so as to isolate the role of the annuities in the portfolio problem. As for investment in stocks and bonds results are qualitatively very similar to Cocco et al. (2005) given that the setup implies the same interpretation of labor income, which is more a bond-like asset than a stock-like one (as in Benzoni et al. (2007)). However, the presence of annuities in most cases crowds out bonds thus indicating that mortality credit compensates for illiquidity of annuities. Moreover the optimal annuity holding increases over time in contrast to stock holdings and the explanation, as in Cocco et al. (2005) rests on the characterization of labor as a bond-like asset, whose holding decreases with age.

Sensitivity analyses make it possible to highlight important determinants of optimal annuities holdings. As expected, the correlation between human capital and market risk increases the purchase of annuities at least until the retirement period (since retirement income is assumed to be uncorrelated with the market), while during retirement the purchase of annuities depends positively on the retirement income replacement ratio but does not vanish even if the latter were set to one, a result that can help in the debate over the pension system.

6.4 CONCLUSIONS

In this chapter the literature on household portfolio choices was analyzed in view of population aging by taking both a positive and a normative approach. The analysis starts with a recognition of the most important stylized facts emerging from the empirical literature surveyed in Section 6.2 and then shifts to models that can account for these facts or provide suggestions for optimal asset allocations. Since the literature has been extending in many directions in recent years, the objective here is not to provide an exhaustive survey, and many issues had to be left out. Rather, by focusing on financial portfolio choices over both the working and the retirement period, the aim is to conclude with some research implications.

Since the mid-1990s, the nexus between age and finance has inspired a lively debate, which has given rise to an increasing number of empirical studies highly diversified in terms of approach, methodology, data, and results. According to the approach taken by the studies, we have distinguished two main streams in this literature: one assuming a micro-perspective and basically aimed at assessing the role of age as a determinant of the household portfolio decisions, and the other assuming instead a macro-perspective and basically aimed at investigating the possible implications, in terms of direction and magnitude, of aging population on asset returns and ultimately on financial markets. The two strands of literature differ for the overall evidence reported: the works assuming a micro-perspective on the whole agree on age being an important determinant of portfolio decisions, although the specific pattern along the life cycle is humped rather than linear depending primarily on whether participation or allocation decision is analyzed. At a macro-perspective, the evidence on the link between demographics and financial asset prices/returns is less uniform: some studies find only a weak, if any, relationship between demographic dynamics and financial variables, while others report significant effects of age and aging on financial markets. The most recent contributions in this literature seem to agree that a role in explaining these differences might rely on the country analyzed, and more specifically on its peculiarities in terms of both demographic dynamics and institutional settings, thereby encouraging further investigation on these issues.

Overall, three facts most strikingly emerge from the empirical literature: low stock market participation, scarce diversification, and a life cycle of household portfolios that display a hump shape, whereby the investment in stocks peaks at middle age. This evidence contradicts popular financial advice suggesting investment in stocks decreasing with age and most portfolio models. The survey over the theoretical literature highlights that, in order to capture real portfolio patterns, the dynamic nature of most recent models has to be coupled with an appropriate modeling of household-specific assets, which share the feature of being illiquid. The most important among these is surely human capital, which materializes in the portfolio framework via labor income. This is why particular emphasis was devoted to Cocco et al. (2005) where the inclusion of labor income risk is made in an incomplete market setting so that labor income risk is uninsurable, an assumption that well represents real market conditions. However, an important source of background risk such as labor income risk alone is not sufficient to explain the hump-shaped pattern of observed portfolio choices, but a long-run cointegration between human capital and the stock market, as in Benzoni et al. (2007), can account for it.

We believe this is the direction that future research should take. More specifically, models for household portfolio decisions should account for three main features affecting household decisions in a specific way: finite horizon together with longevity risk, borrowing constraints, and nonfinancial assets. As for the latter, it has to be highlighted that nonfinancial wealth represents the major part of an household portfolio so that its features in terms of tradability, insurability, and correlation with the stock market are of uttermost importance in determining financial choices.

The two most important component of nonfinancial wealth are labor income and housing. A literature that addresses housing choices in connection with portfolio choices has been growing (e.g., Cocco (2004), Flavin and Yamashita (2002), Yao and Zhang (2005)). However, the different nature of housing with respect to other assets (consumption and investment) and its often leveraged status requires a specific focus and deserves a separate chapter, but its consideration is in some cases essential to explain some portfolio puzzles (e.g., in Cocco (2004) housing crowds out stock holding). As for the link between labor income and financial markets, Benzoni et al. (2007) show how the correlation between human capital and market returns can change the optimal household portfolio and suggests the inclusion of housing in their setup. This is interesting especially if evidence on the cointegration between the housing and the stock market is strong. However, since results under the cointegration assumption are very sensitive, not only to the very same existence of a cointegration (which is also hard to test), but also to the specific level, very high on the research agenda is still the modeling of the link between labor income and financial markets. In particular, the long-run cointegration assumption essentially focuses on the time dimension of the link between human capital and financial markets, whereby the idea is that in the long run only young people will be alive and thus be hit by the long-run cointegration. However, we believe that another important dimension to be considered in this connection is the type of human capital as captured, for instance, by the different education groups, which might deserve more differentiation in term of labor income risk (e.g., recall that in Cocco et al. (2005) education groups are solely characterized by the age at which working age begins). Also the modeling of the postretirement period leaves room for further investigation: if in Cocco et al. (2005) retirement income is simply a constant fraction of labor income, in Benzoni et al. (2007) the postretirement consumption and investment decisions are not explicitly modelled. Moreover there is a further element that differentiates the household in terms of income risk beside age: it is the connection between gender and marital status, which has been rarely considered in the portfolio setting (e.g., Bertocchi et al. (2009) and Love (2009)) and yet not in relation to life-cycle choices.

To conclude, two main challenges of household finance emerge from this chapter overview, which, along with Campbell (2006), can be summarized as follows: empirical analyses that highlight how households do invest (i.e., positive household finance) have important measurement problems, while suggestions about how investments should be made (i.e., normative household finance) encounter modeling problems, which naturally bring about numerical solutions and calibration issues.

As far as measurement problems are concerned, most of the studies aimed at investigating household portfolio choices base their empirical analyses on micro-datasets, which could either be drawn from surveys (e.g., SCF for US, SHIW for Italy, etc.) or from (usually not publicly available) financial-institution datasets (e.g., bank or insurances data). Both sources however suffer from measurement problems. Survey data offer the advantages of being designed based on representative samples and providing a comprehensive picture of household portfolios, including information about housing property, labor income, and financial assets owned; by contrast, they are generally associated with low response rates and with generally unrealistic levels of diversification and riskiness of household portfolios due to the well-known problems of nonreporting (i.e., the interviewee does not want to reveal the ownership of a certain financial asset) or under-reporting (i.e., the interviewee reports the presence of a certain asset in his or her portfolio, but does not know or reveal its amount). On the other hand, institutional datasets are more reliable, as they do not suffer from these reporting issues, but besides being typically confidential, they have the relevant drawback of offering only a partial view of the portfolios (e.g., only financial assets held in that bank or insurance company), thereby being not really suitable for a comprehensive investigation of the whole allocation choices implemented by the households.

As for some modeling problems (e.g., numerical solutions and calibration issues) implied by more realistic models, the household finance theory can benefit from a large and useful literature developed in connection with institutional portfolio choices (see, e.g., Geyer and Ziemba (2008), Rudolf and Ziemba (2004), Zenios and Ziemba (2007), and contributions presented in other chapters in this book). In addition, as we have stressed previously pointing out some research directions, more research on modeling is also needed to provide a source of financial advice and for economic policy considerations in view of current and perspective socio economic scenarios increasingly characterized by more volatile labor income, important changes in the family structure, population aging and less generous public pension systems. A further source of worry comes from recent financial market downturns (two in a decade) that cast doubts over the possibility of pension funds and annuity providers to cover, by relying on the market only, demographic risks typical of an aging society.

REFERENCES

Alessie R., S. Hochguertel, and A. Van Soest. 2002. Household portfolios in the Netherlands. In *Household Portfolios*, ed. L. Guiso, M. Haliassos, and T. Jappelli, 341–388. Cambridge: MIT Press.

Ameriks, J., and S. P., Zeldes. 2004. How do household portfolio shares vary with age? Working Paper, Columbia Business School.

Ang, A., and A. Maddaloni. 2005. Do demographic changes affect risk premiums? Evidence from international data. *Journal of Business* 78, no. 1:341–380.

Attanasio, O. 1995. The intertemporal allocation of consumption: Theory and evidence. *Carnegie-Rochester Conference Series on Public Policy* 42:39–89.

Bakshi G., and Z. Chen. 1994. Baby boom, population aging, and capital markets. *Journal of Business* 67:165–202.

Banks J., and S. Tanner. 2002. Household portfolios in the United Kingdom. In *Household Portfolios*, ed. L. Guiso, M. Haliassos, and T. Jappelli, 219–250. Cambridge: MIT Press.

Barberis, N. 2000. Investing for the long run when returns are predictable. *Journal of Finance* 55:225–264.

Basak, S., and D. Cuoco. 1998. An equilibrium model with restricted stock market participation. *Review of Financial Studies* 11:309–341.

Bellante D., and C. A. Green. 2004. Relative risk aversion among the elderly. *Review of Financial Economics* 13:269–281.

Benzoni, L., and P. Collin-Dufresne, and R. S. Goldstein. 2007. Portfolio choice over the lifecycle when stock and labour markets are cointegrated. *Journal of Finance* 62:2123–2167.

Bertaut, C. C., and M. Haliassos. 1997. Precautionary portfolio behaviour from a lifecycle perspective. *Journal of Economic Dynamics and Control* 21:1511–1542.

Bertaut C. C., and M. Starr-McCluer. 2002. Household portfolios in the United States. In *Household Portfolios*, ed. L. Guiso, M. Haliassos, and T. Jappelli, 181–217. Cambridge: MIT Press.

Bertocchi G., M. Brunetti, and C. Torricelli. 2009. Marriage and other risky assets: A portfolio approach. CEPR Discussion Paper No. 7162 and IZA Discussion Paper No. 3975.

Bodie Z., and D. B. Crane. 1997. Personal investing: Advice, Theory, and Evidence from a survey of TIAA-CREF participants. *Financial Analysts Journal* 53, no. 6:1323.

Börsch-Supan, A. 2004. Global aging: Issues, answers, more questions. University of Michigan, Retirement Research Centre, Working Paper 84.

Bosworth B., G. Burtless, and J. Sabelhaus. 1991. The decline in saving: Evidence from household surveys. *Brookings Papers on Economic Activities I*: 183–241.

Brandt, M. W. 2009. Portfolio choice problems. In *Handbook of Financial Econometrics*, ed. Y. Ait-Sahalia and L. P. Hansen. Amsterdam: North Holland, 269–336.

———, A. Goyal, P. Santa-Clara, and J. R. Stroud. 2005. A simulation approach to dynamic portfolio choice with an application to learning about return predictability. *Review of Financial Studies* 18:831.

Brooks R. 2000. What will happen to financial markets when the baby boomers retire? IMF Working Paper 18. www.imf.org/external/pubs/ft/wp/2000/wp0018.pdf.

———. 2002. Asset-market effects of the baby boom and Social Security reform. *American Economic Review* 92:402–406.

———. 2006. Demographic change and asset prices. In *Demography and Financial Markets*, ed. C. Kent, A. Park, and D. Rees. Reserve Bank of Australia.

Browning, M., and A. Lusardi. 1996. Household saving: micro theories and micro facts. *Journal of Economic Literature* 34:1797–1855.

Brunetti M., and C. Torricelli. 2007. The population ageing in Italy: Facts and impact on household portfolios. In *Money, Finance and Demography: The Consequences of Ageing*, ed. Morten Balling, Ernest Gnan, and Frank Lierman. Vienna.

Brunetti M., and C. Torricelli. 2008. Demographics and asset returns: Does the dynamics of population ageing matter? *Annals of Finance,* forthcoming.

Brunetti M., and C. Torricelli. 2009. Population age structure and household portfolio choices in Italy. *European Journal of Finance*, forthcoming.

Cairns, A., D. Blake, and K. Dowd. 2006. Stochastic lifestyling: Optimal dynamic asset allocation for defined-contribution pension plans. *Journal of Economic Dynamics and Control* 30:843–877.

Campbell, J. 2006. Household finance. *Journal of Finance* 61:1553–1604.

Campbell J., and L. Viceira. 1999. Consumption and portfolio decisions when expected returns are time varying. *Quarterly Journal of Economics* 114:433–495.

Campbell J., and L. Viceira. 2001. Who should buy long term bonds? *American Economic Review* 87:181–191.

Campbell J., and L. Viceira. 2002. *Strategic Asset Allocation*. New York: Oxford University Press.

Campbell, J. Y., A. W. Lo, and A. C. MacKinlay. 1997. *The Econometrics of Financial Markets*. Princeton, NJ.

Cerny A., D. K. Miles, L. Schmidt. 2005. The impact of changing demographics and pensions on the demand for housing and financial assets. Centre for Economic Policy Research (CEPR). Discussion Paper 5143. http://ideas.repec.org/p/cpr/ceprdp/5143.html.

Cocco, J. F. 2004. Portfolio choice the presence of housing. *Review of Financial Studies* 18:535–567.

———, and F. J. Gomes. 2008. *Longevity Risk and Retirement Savings*. London Business School, Mimeo, January.

———, F. J. Gomes, and P. J. Maenhout. 2005. Consumption and portfolio choice over the life-cycle. *Review of Financial Studies* 18:491–533.

Coile C., and K. Milligan. 2006. How household portfolios evolve after retirement: The effect of aging and health shocks. NBER Working Paper 12391. National Bureau of Economic Research. Cambridge, MA.

Constantinides, G. M. 1986. Capital market equilibrium with transaction costs. *Journal of Political Economy* 94:864–862.

———. 1990. Habit formation: A resolution of the equity premium puzzle. *Journal of Political Economy* 98:519–543.

———, J. B. Donaldson, and R. Mehra. 2002. Junior can't borrow: A new perspective on the equity premium puzzle. *Quarterly Journal of Economics* 117:269–296.

Curcuru S., J. Heaton, and D. Lucas. 2009. Heterogeneity and portfolio choice: Theory and evidence. In *Handbook of Financial Econometrics*, ed. Y. Ait-Sahalia and L. P. Hansen. Amsterdam: Elsevier Science, in press.

Dammon, R., C. Spatt, and H. Zhang. 2004. Optimal asset allocation with taxable and tax-deferred investing. *Journal of Finance* 59:999–1037.

Davis E. P., Li C. 2003. Demographics and financial asset prices in the major industrial economies. Brunel University–West London Working Paper. www.ephilipdavis.com/.

Epstein, L., and S. Zin. 1989. Substitution, risk aversion and the temporal behaviour of consumption and asset returns: A theoretical framework. *Econometrica* 57:937–969.

Erb, C. B., C. R. Harvey, and T. E. Viskanta. 1997. Demographics and international investment. *Financial Analysts Journal* 53:14–28.

Eymann, A., A. Börsch-Supan. 2002. Household portfolios in Germany. In *Household Portfolios*, ed. L. Guiso, M. Haliassos M., and T. Jappelli, 291–340. Cambridge: MIT Press.

Faig, M., and P. Shum. 2002. Portfolio choice in the presence of personal illiquid projects. *Journal of Finance* 57:303–328.

Flavin, M., and T. Yamashita. 2002. Owner-occupied housing and the composition of the household portfolio over the life cycle. *American Economic Review* 92:345–362.

Frijns B., E. Koellen, T. Lehnert. 2008. On the determinants of portfolio choice. *Journal of Economic Behavior & Organization* 66:373–386.

GAO. 2006. Retirement of baby boomers is unlikely to precipitate dramatic decline in market returns, but broader risks threaten retirement security. United States Government Accountability Office. www.gao.gov/new.items/d06718.pdf.

Geanakoplos J., M. Magill, and M. Quinzii. 2004. Demography and the long-run predictability of the stock market. *Brookings Papers on Economic Activities* 1:241–325.

Geyer A., and W. T. Ziemba. 2008. The Innovest Austrian pension fund financial planning model InnoALM. *Operations Research* 56:797–810.

Gollier C. 2002. What does classical theory have to say about household portfolios? In *Household Portfolios*, ed. L. Guiso, M. Haliassos, and T. Jappelli. Cambridge: MIT Press.

Gomes, F., and A. Michaelides. 2005. Optimal life-cycle asset allocation: Understanding the empirical evidence. *Journal of Finance* 60:869–904.

Gomes, F., L. K. Kotlikoff, and L. M. Viceira. 2008. Optimal life-cycle investing with flexible labour supply: A welfare analysis of life-cycle funds. *American Economic Review: Papers and Proceedings* 98:297–303.

Goyal A. 2004. Demographics, stock market flows, and stock returns. *Journal of Financial and Quantitative Analysis* 39:115–142.

Guiso L., M. Haliassos, and T. Jappelli. 2002. *Household portfolios.* Cambridge: MIT Press.

Guiso L., and T. Jappelli. 2002. Household portfolios in Italy. In *Household Portfolios*, ed. L. Guiso, M. Haliassos, and T. Jappelli, 251–289. Cambridge: MIT Press.

Guiso, L., T. Jappelli, and D. Terlizzese. 1996. Income risk, borrowing constraints and portfolio choice. *American Economic Review* 86:158–172.

Hakansson, N. H. 1971. On optimal myopic portfolio policies, with and without serial correlation of yields. *Journal of Business* 44:324–334.

Heaton, J., and D. J. Lucas. 1997. Market frictions, saving behavior and portfolio choice. *Macroeconomic Dynamics* 1:76–101.

Horneff, W. J., R. H. Maurer, and M. Z. Stamos. 2008. Life-cycle asset allocation with annuity markets. *Journal of Economic Dynamics and Control* 32:3590–3812.

Hubbard, G., J. S. Skinner, and S. Zeldes. 1994. The importance of precautionary motives for explaining individual and aggregate saving. In Carnegie-Rochester Conference Series on Public Policy 40, ed. Allan H. Meltzer and Charles I. Plosser, 59–125.

Love, D. 2008. The effects of martial status and children on savings and portfolio choice. *Review of Financial Studies*, forthcoming.

Malkiel, B. G. 1996. *A Random Walk Down Wall Street, Including a Life-Cycle Guide to Personal Investing*. New York: W. W. Norton & Company.

Markowitz, H. M. 1952. Portfolio selection. *Journal of Finance* 7:77–91.

Mehra, R., and E. Prescott. 1985. The equity premium puzzle. *Journal of Monetary Economics* 15:145–161.

Merton, R. 1969. Lifetime portfolio selection under uncertainty: The continuous-time case. *Review of Economics and Statistics* 51:247–257.

———. 1971. Optimum consumption and portfolio rules in a continuous-time model. *Journal of Economic Theory* 3:373–413.

Milevsky M. A., and V. R. Young. 2007. Annuitization and asset allocation, *Journal of Economic Dynamics and Control* 31:3138–3177.

Mossin, J. 1968 Optimal multiperiod portfolio policies. *Journal of Business* 41:215–229.

Oliveira-Martins J., F. Gonand, P. Antolin, C. De la Maisonneuve, and K. Y. Yoo. 2005. The Impact of Ageing on Demand, Factor Markets and Growth. OECD Economics Department Working Paper No. 420.

Poterba, J. M. 1991 House price dynamics: The role of tax policy and demography. *Brookings Papers on Economic Activity* 2:143–183.

———. 2001. Demographic structure and asset returns. *Review of Economics and Statistics* 83:565–584.

———. 2004. The impact of population aging on financial markets. NBER Working Paper 10851. National Bureau of Economic Research, Cambridge, MA.

———, and A. A. Samwick. 1997. Household Portfolio Allocation over the Life Cycle. NBER Working Paper. 6185. National Bureau of Economic Research, Cambridge, MA.

———, and A. A. Samwick. 2001. Portfolio allocations over the life-cycle. In *Aging Issues in the United States and Japan*, ed. S. Ogura, T. Tachibanaki, and A. D. Wise, 65–103. Chicago: University of Chicago Press.

Richard S. 1975. Optimal consumption, portfolio and life insurance rules for an uncertain lived individual in a continuous time model. *Journal of Financial Economics* 2:187–203.

Rudolf M., and W. T. Ziemba. 2004. Intertemporal surplus management *Journal of Economic Dynamics Control* 28:975–990.

Saarenheimo, T. 2005. Ageing, interest rates, and financial flows. Bank of Finland Research Discussion Paper 2/2005. http://ideas.repec.org/p/wpa/wuwpla/0508015.html.

Samuelson, P. A. 1969. Lifetime portfolio selection by dynamic stochastic programming. *Review of Economics and Statistics* 51:239–246.

Tin, J. 1998. Household demand for financial assets: A lifecycle analysis. *Quarterly Review of Economics and Income* 38, no. 4:875–897.

Viceira, L. M. 2001. Optimal portfolio choice for long-horizon investors with nontradable labor income. *Journal of Finance* 56:433–470.

Watcher, J. A. 2002. Consumption and portfolio decisions under mean-reverting returns: Exact solutions for complete markets. *Journal of Financial and Quantitative Analysis* 37:63–91.

Yaari, M. 1965. Uncertain lifetime, life insurance, and the theory of the consumer. *Review of Economic Studies* 32:137–150.

Yao, R., and H. Zhang. 2005. Optimal consumption and portfolio choices with risky housing and borrowing constraints. *Review of Financial Studies* 18:197–239.

Yoo P. S. 1994a. Age dependent portfolio selection. Federal Reserve Bank of St. Louis Working Paper 3. http://research.stlouisfed.org/wp/1994/94003.pdf.

———. 1994b. Age distributions and returns of financial assets. Federal Reserve Bank of St. Louis Working Paper 2. http://research.stlouisfed.org/wp/1994/94002.pdf.

Zenios S., and W. T. Ziemba (eds.). 2007. *Handbook of Asset and Liability Management*, vol. 2, *Applications and Case Studies*. Amsterdam: North Holland.

CHAPTER 7

A Continuous Time Approach to Asset-Liability Surplus Management

Rudolf and Ziemba (2004) present a continuous time model for pension or insurance company surplus management over time. Such lifetime intertemporal portfolio investment models date to Samuelson (1969) in discrete time and Merton (1969) in continuous time. Rudolf and Ziemba use an extension of the Merton (1973, 1990) model that maximizes the intertemporal expected utility of the surplus of assets net of liabilities using liabilities as a new variable. They assume that both the asset and the liability return follow Itô processes as functions of a risky state variable. The optimum occurs for investors holding four funds: the market portfolio, the hedge portfolio for the state variable, the hedge portfolio for the liabilities, and the riskless asset. This is a four-fund CAPM while Merton has a three-fund CAPM and the ordinary Sharpe-Lintner-Mossin CAPM has two funds. The hedge portfolio provides maximum correlation to the state variable: that is, it provides the best possible hedge against the variance of the state variable. In contrast to Merton's result in the assets-only case, the liability hedge is independent of preferences and depends only on the funding ratio. With hyperabsolute risk-aversion utility, which includes negative exponential, power and log, the investments in the state variable hedge portfolio are also preference-independent, and with log utility, the market portfolio investment depends only on the current funding ratio.

Having surplus over time is what life and other insurance companies, pension funds, and other organizations try to achieve. In both life insurance companies and pension funds, parts of the surplus are distributed to the clients usually once every year. Hence, optimizing their investment strategy is well represented by maximizing the expected lifetime utility of the surplus.

Section 7.1 describes the model, and then Section 7.2 provides a summary of the main points using a case study.

7.1 THE RUDOLF-ZIEMBA (2004) INTERGENERATIONAL SURPLUS MANAGEMENT MODEL

The model is summarized as follows: For $t \geq 0$ the stochastic processes $A(t)$, $L(t)$, $Y(t)$, represents assets, liabilities, and a state variable Y such as purchasing power parity, respectively.

The surplus $S(t) = A(t) - L(t)$ and the funding ratio $F(t) = A(t)/L(t)$.

According to Merton (1973), the state variable Y follows a geometric Brownian motion (i.e., it is log-normally distributed) where μ_Y and σ_Y are constants representing the drift and volatility and $Z_Y(t)$ is a standard Wiener process. The return processes $R_Y(t)$, $R_A(t)$, $R_L(t)$ for the state variable, assets and liabilities are $R_Y(t) = dY(t)/Y(t)$, $R_A(t) = dA(t)/A(t)$, and $R_L(t) = dL(t)/L(t)$.

Following Sharpe and Tint (1990), the surplus return process is

$$R_S(t) = \frac{dS(t)}{A(t)} = R_A(t) - \frac{R_L(t)}{F(t)} = \left[\mu_A - \frac{\mu_L}{F(t)}\right]dt + \sigma_A dZ_A(t) - \frac{\sigma_L}{F(t)}dZ_L(t)$$

The objective is to maximize the expected lifetime utility of surplus. To avoid underfunding in particular periods, a steady state is assumed implying that the dollar value of employees (insurance policies) entering equals those leaving the pension fund (insurance company) dollar value. The expected utility is positively related to the surplus in each period because positive surpluses improve the wealth position, even if the yearly benefits are over funded by the surplus. The insurants are like shareholders of the fund.

The fund's optimization problem, where U is an additively separable, twice differentiable, concave utility function and T is the end of the fund's existence is

$$J(S, Y, t) = \max_w E_t \left(\int_t^T U(S, Y, \tau)d\tau\right)$$

$$= \max_w E_t \left(\int_t^{t+dt} U(S, Y, \tau)d\tau + \int_{t+dt}^T U(S, Y, \tau)d\tau\right)$$

where E_t denotes expectation with respect to the information set at time t and the J-function is the maximum of expected lifetime utility. The maximum is taken with respect to w, the vector of portfolio weights of the risky assets, where n is the number of portfolio assets and $\omega_i (1 \le i \le n)$ is the portfolio fraction of asset i.

Applying the Bellman principal of optimality yields ($J xy$ means the cross derivative of J with respect to x and y)

$$w = -a \frac{J_S}{A(t)J_{SS}} w_M - b \frac{Y(t)J_{SY}}{A(t)J_{SS}} w_Y + \frac{c}{F(t)} w_L$$

where

$$w_M = \frac{V^{-1}(m_A - re)}{e'V^{-1}(m_A - re)}, w_Y = \frac{V^{-1}v_{AY}}{e'V^{-1}v_{AY}}, w_L = \frac{V^{-1}v_{AL}}{e'V^{-1}v_{AL}}$$

$$a = e'V^{-1}(m_A - re), b = e'V^{-1}v_{AY}, c = e'V^{-1}v_{AL}$$

The vectors w_M, w_Y, and w_L, are of dimension n with elements that sum to 1, and a, b, and c are constants. The optimum portfolio consists of a weighted average of four portfolios: the market portfolio w_M, the hedge portfolio for the state variable w_Y, which is Merton's (1973) state variable hedge portfolio, the hedge portfolio for the liabilities w_L, and the riskless asset. A perfect hedge for the state variable could be achieved if the universe of n risky assets contains forward contracts on the state variable. Then the state variable hedge portfolio consists of a single asset, the forward contract. The third liability hedge portfolio w_L is interesting. For the liabilities there exist no hedging opportunities in the financial markets (i.e., a portfolio that hedges wage increases or inflation rates). This is related to the problem addressed by Ezra (1991) and Black (1989), and solves it in continuous time. Life insurance and pension funds invest in the following four funds:

1. The market portfolio w_M with level $-a \frac{J_S}{A(t)J_{SS}}$
2. The state variable hedge portfolio w_Y with level $-b \frac{Y(t)J_{SY}}{A(t)J_{SS}}$
3. The riskless asset with level $1 + a \frac{J_S}{A(t)J_{SS}} + b \frac{Y(t)J_{SY}}{A(t)J_{SS}} - \frac{c}{F(t)}$
4. The liability hedge portfolio w_L with level $\frac{c}{F(t)}$

The holdings of the liability hedge portfolio are independent of preferences. The liability hedge portfolio holdings depend only on the current funding ratio and not on the form of the utility function. To maximize its lifetime expected utility, the fund should hedge the liabilities according to the financial endowment.

The percentages of each of the three other funds differ according to the risk preferences of the fund. For example, $-a\frac{J_S}{A(t)J_{SS}}$ is the percentage invested in the market portfolio. Since J is a *derived* utility function, this ratio is a times the Arrow-Pratt relative risk tolerance (the reciprocal of the Arrow-Pratt relative risk aversion index) with respect to changes in the surplus. Hence, the higher the risk tolerance toward market risk is, the higher the fraction of the market portfolio holdings. The percentage of the state variable hedge portfolio is $-b\frac{Y(t)J_{SY}}{A(t)J_{SS}}$. Merton (1973) showed that this ratio is b times the Arrow/Pratt relative risk tolerance with respect to changes in the state variable. The percentage of the liability hedge portfolio is $\frac{c}{F(t)}$. In contrast to Merton's results, this portfolio does not depend on preferences nor on a specific utility function, but only on the funding ratio of the pension fund. The lower the funding ratio, the higher is the percentage of the liability hedge portfolio.

This allows for a simple technique to monitor funds, which extends Merton's (1973) approach. In most funding systems, funds are legally obliged to invest subject to a deterministic threshold return. Since payments of life insurance or pension funds depend on the growth and the volatility of wage rates, this is not appropriate. For instance, if the threshold return is 4% per year and wages grow by more than this, the liabilities cannot be covered by the assets. This model suggests instead that a portfolio manager of a pension fund should invest in a portfolio that smoothes the fluctuation of the surplus returns caused by wage volatility: that is, in a liability hedge portfolio. Since the liability hedge portfolio depends only on the funding ratio, preferences of the insurants need not be specified.

The utility function is assumed to be from the linear risk tolerance HARA or hyper absolute risk-aversion class. This means that $\frac{u'}{u''} = a + bw$, the reciprocal of the Arrow-Pratt absolute risk aversion, namely the risk tolerance is linear in wealth. Merton (1971, 1990, p. 140) shows that this is equivalent to assuming that the J function belongs to the HARA class as well. If $\alpha < 1$ is the risk tolerance coefficient then

$$J(S, Y, t) = J[S(A(Y)), t] = \frac{1-\alpha}{e^{\rho t}\alpha}\left(\frac{\kappa S}{1-\alpha} + \eta\right)^{\alpha}$$

where κ and $\eta > 0$ are constants and r is the utility deflator. This implies linear absolute risk tolerance since $-J_S/J_{SS} = S/(1-a) + \eta/\kappa$. The HARA class of utility functions contains the negative exponential utility functions $J = -e^{-aS}$ for $\alpha \to -\infty, \eta = 1$, and $\rho = 0$, isoelastic power utility (see Ingersoll 1987, p. 39), $J = S^{\alpha}/\alpha$ for $\eta = 0, \rho = 0$, and $\kappa = (1-\alpha)^{(\frac{\alpha-1}{\alpha})}$, and log utility when $\alpha \to 0(\eta = \rho = 0)$.

Under the HARA utility function assumption the percentage holdings of the market portfolio equal

$$\frac{1}{1-\alpha} \left(1 - \frac{1}{F}\right) + \frac{\eta}{A\kappa}$$

The market portfolio holdings thus depend on the funding ratio and on the risk aversion. The higher F, the higher the investment in the market portfolio will be, and the higher α, the lower the market portfolio investment will be for funding ratios smaller than 1. If a sufficient funding is observed (i.e., $F > 1$), then there is a positive relationship between α and F. If $\alpha \to 0$ (log utility case), the coefficient for the market portfolio investment becomes $1 - 1/F$ plus the constant $\eta/(A\kappa)$. Thus, for log utility funds, risk aversion does not matter.[1] Only the funding ratio matters to determine the market portfolio investment. For either case of utility functions, if the funding ratio is 100%, there will be no investment in the risky market portfolio. The funding ratio of a fund does not only determine the capability to bear risk but also the willingness to take risk.

Consider the percentage holding of the state variable hedge portfolio. Suppose the state variable Y is an exchange rate fluctuation, which affects the surplus of a fund. Then

$$-\frac{YJ_{SY}}{AJ_{SS}} = -\frac{\frac{dA}{A}}{\frac{dY}{Y}} = -\frac{R_A}{R_Y}$$

Hence, the weight of the state variable hedge portfolio is preference independent with HARA utility $R_A = \beta(R_A, R_Y)R_Y$. If asset returns are linear functions of currency returns, then, R_A/R_Y is the negative beta of the portfolio with respect to the state variable, and

$$-\frac{YJ_{SY}}{AJ_{SS}} = -\beta(R_A, R_Y)$$

If Y is an exchange rate, then $-\beta$ equals the minimum variance hedge ratio for the foreign currency position. The holdings of the state variable hedge portfolio are independent of preferences; they only depend on the foreign currency exposure of the portfolio. The higher the exchange rate risk in the portfolio is, the higher the currency hedging will be. Hence, for the HARA utility case, only the investment in the market portfolio depends on the risk aversion α. The investments in all other funds are preference independent.

---

[1]Log's risk aversion of $1/w$ is virtually zero anyway. Ziemba argues that log is the most risky utility function one should ever consider. The results below are consistent with that notion.

They depend only on the funding ratio and on the exposure of the asset portfolio to the state variable.

When there are k foreign currencies contained in the fund's portfolio, let $Y_1, \ldots, Y_k$ be the exchange rates in terms of the domestic currency, and the exchange rate returns of the k currencies. Then

$$-\frac{Y_1 J_{SY_1}}{A J_{SS}} = -\beta(R_A, R_{Y_1}), \ldots, -\frac{Y_k J_{SY_k}}{A J_{SS}} = -\beta(R_A, R_{Y_k})$$

which are the Arrow/Pratt relative risk tolerances with respect to changes in the exchange rates for the HARA case. Let $v_{AY_1}, \ldots, v_{AY_k}$ be the covariance vectors of the returns of the asset portfolio with the k exchange rate returns

$$w_{Y_1} = \frac{V^{-1} v_{AY_1}}{e V^{-1} v_{AY_1}}, \ldots, w_{Y_k} = \frac{V^{-1} v_{AY_k}}{e V^{-1} v_{AY_k}}$$

which are the state variable hedge portfolios 1 to k, and $b_1 = e V^{-1} v_{AY_1}, \ldots, b_k = e V^{-1} v_{AY_k}$ are the coefficients of the state variable hedge portfolios. A fund with a HARA utility function facing k state variables has the following investment strategy $R_l = d A_l / A_l$ return on risky asset $l = 1, \ldots, n$

$$w = \left[\frac{a}{1-\alpha} \left(1 - \frac{1}{F(t)} \right) + \frac{a\eta}{A\kappa} \right] w_M - \sum_{i=1}^{k} b_i \beta(R_A, R_{Y_l}) w_{Y_l} + \frac{c}{F(t)} w_L$$

where

$$\beta(R_a, R_{Y_l}) = \sum_{i=1}^{n} \omega_l \beta(R_l, R_Y)$$

Since the right-hand side depends on the portfolio allocation w, it is not possible to solve analytically for w and numerical solutions must be used. For k state variables a $k + 3$ fund theorem follows.

7.2 A CASE STUDY APPLICATION OF THE RUDOLF-ZIEMBA MODEL

Rudolf and Ziemba (2004) provide a case study that illustrates the reasons why, in practice, discrete time-constrained stochastic programming models are preferred to unconstrained continuous time models. We will also see why these continuous time models are so popular with finance academics: they have a simple elegance that yields direct answers to economic questions.

Consider a US dollar-based surplus optimizer investing in the stock and bond markets of the US, UK, Japan, the EMU countries, Canada, and Switzerland. Monthly MSCI data between January 1987 and July 2000 (163 observations) are used for the stock markets. The monthly JP Morgan indexes are used for the bond markets in this period (Salomon Brothers for Switzerland). The stochastic benchmark is the quarterly Thomson Financial Datastream index for US wages and salaries. Quarterly data is linearly interpolated in order to obtain monthly wages and salaries data. The average growth rate of wages and salaries in the US between January 1987 and July 2000 was 5.7% per year with annualized volatility of 4.0%, see Table 7.1.

TABLE 7.1 Basic Data in Dollars

	Mean Return	Volatility	Beta GBP	Beta JPY	Beta EUR	Beta CAD	Beta CHF
Stocks							
US	13.47	14.74	0.18	0.05	0.35	−0.59	0.35
UK	9.97	17.96	−0.47	−0.36	−0.29	−0.48	−0.14
Japan	3.42	25.99	−0.61	−1.11	−0.45	−0.44	−0.43
EMU*	10.48	15.80	−0.32	−0.27	−0.26	−0.45	−0.11
Canada	5.52	18.07	0.05	−0.02	0.27	−1.44	0.34
Switzerland	11.56	18.17	−0.14	−0.32	−0.26	0.13	−0.32
Bonds							
US	5.04	4.50	−0.03	0.00	−0.06	−0.04	−0.06
UK	6.86	12.51	−0.92	−0.44	−0.80	−0.39	−0.59
Japan	3.77	14.46	−0.53	−1.04	−0.75	0.09	−0.72
EMU	7.78	10.57	−0.69	−0.42	−0.93	−0.06	−0.74
Canada	5.16	8.44	−0.09	0.03	−0.02	−1.14	0.02
Switzerland	3.56	12.09	−0.67	−0.53	−1.03	0.19	−0.99
Exchange rates in USD							
GBP	0.11	11.13	1	0.37	0.86	0.42	0.64
JPY	−2.75	12.54	0.48	1	0.65	0.04	0.61
EUR*	1.13	10.08	0.7	0.42	1	0.1	0.79
CAD	0.79	4.73	0.08	0	0.02	1	−0.02
CHF	0.32	11.57	0.69	0.52	1.04	−0.13	1
Wages and salaries	5.71	4.0	0	0.01	0	−0.01	0

The stock market data is based on MSC indexes and the bond data on JP Morgan indexes (Switzerland on Salomon Brothers data). The wage and salary growth rate is from Datastream. Monthly data, January 1987 to July 2000 (163 observations). The mean returns and volatilities are in percent per annum.
*ECU before January 1999.
Source: Rudolf and Ziemba (2004).

This table also contains the stock and bond market descriptive statistics in USD, and the currency betas of the indexes.

All foreign currencies except CAD, that is, GBP, JPY, EUR, and CHF, have volatility of about 12% p.a., and all currencies except JPY depreciated against the USD by a little more than 0% to 1.13% per year. From a USD viewpoint, the GBP-beta is especially high (absolute value) for the UK bond market. The Japanese stock and bond market reveal a JPY-beta of -1.11 and -1.04, respectively, and the EMU bond market has a EUR-beta of -0.93. Furthermore, the CAD-beta of the Canadian bond market is -1.14, the CHF-beta of the Swiss bond market is -0.99. All other countries have substantially lower currency betas. Since the betas are close to zero, the wages and salaries do not depend on currency movements.

The investor faces an exposure against five foreign currencies (GBP, JPY, EUR, CAD, CHF), and has to invest into eight funds. Five of them are hedge portfolios for the state variables, which are assumed to be currency returns, and the others by portfolio separation are the market portfolios, the riskless asset, and the liability hedge portfolio. The compositions of the eight mutual funds appear in Table 7.2.

The holdings of the six fund situations shown in Table 7.3 depend only on the funding ratio and on the currency betas of the distinct markets. For a

TABLE 7.2 Optimal Portfolio Weights in Percent, Assuming a Riskless Interest Rate of 2%

	Market Portfolio	Hedge Portfolios					
		Liability	GBP	JPY	EUR	CAD	CHF
Stocks							
USA	83.9	−30.4	3.9	−4.5	−7.5	60.9	−5.1
UK	−14.8	60.6	−31.0	−1.1	−8.6	−85.3	1.9
Japan	−6.7	2.7	6.1	8.9	−2.4	−4.0	−0.7
EMU	−19.2	−68.3	35.3	12.8	23.5	138.3	−3.8
Canada	−39.2	5.1	14.6	13.6	5.5	−2.6	−0.9
Switzerland	21.6	1.5	−24.8	−14.6	−14.7	−100.7	1.0
Bonds							
USA	14.8	126.0	−126.4	−28.6	−41.2	−627.3	−35.9
UK	−9.7	−56.8	189.7	7.9	−3.4	97.5	−8.5
Japan	0.6	39.1	−31.2	133.9	−3.6	−30.1	6.4
EMU	138.5	9.6	−16.4	−38.0	97.3	−170.1	34.0
Canada	7.9	5.0	−11.8	−32.6	−7.9	679.6	0.9
Switzerland	77.7	5.9	91.9	42.4	62.9	143.8	110.7

Source: Rudolf and Ziemba (2004).

TABLE 7.3 Optimal Portfolio Weights with Log Utility and Differing Funding Ratios

Funding ratio	0.9	1	1.1	1.2	1.3	1.5
Market portfolio	−11.5%	0.0%	6.3%	12.3%	18.2%	24.6%
Liability hedge portfolio	14.8%	13.3%	12.1%	11.1%	10.2%	8.9%
Hedge portfolio GBP	−0.6%	−0.5%	−0.5%	−0.5%	−0.4%	−0.4%
Hedge portfolio JPY	1.2%	1.1%	1.0%	0.9%	0.9%	0.8%
Hedge portfolio EUR	0.3%	0.2%	0.1%	0.0%	0.0%	−0.1%
Hedge portfolio CAD	−0.1%	−0.1%	−0.1%	−0.1%	−0.1%	−0.1%
Hedge portfolio CHF	1.1%	1.0%	0.9%	0.8%	0.8%	0.7%
Riskless assets	94.9%	85.1%	80.2%	75.3%	70.4%	65.6%
Portfolio beta vs. GBP	−0.01	−0.01	−0.01	−0.01	−0.01	−0.01
Portfolio beta vs. JPY	0.02	0.02	0.02	0.02	0.02	0.02
Portfolio beta vs. EUR	0.01	0.00	0.00	0.00	0.00	0.00
Portfolio beta vs. CAD	−0.02	−0.02	−0.01	−0.01	−0.01	−0.01
Portfolio beta vs. CHF	0.02	0.01	0.01	0.01	0.01	0.01

Source: Rudolf and Ziemba (2004).

funding ratio of one, there is no investment in the market portfolio and only diminishing investments in the currency hedge portfolios. The portfolio betas against the five currencies are close to zero for all funding ratios. The higher the funding ratio is, the higher is the investment in the market portfolio, the lower are the investments in the liability and the state variable hedge portfolios, and the lower is the investment in the riskless fund. Negative currency hedge portfolios imply an increase of the currency exposure instead of a hedge against it. The increase of the market portfolio holdings and the reduction of the hedge portfolio holdings and the riskless fund for increasing funding ratios show that the funding ratio is directly related to the ability to bear risk. Rather than risk-aversion coefficients, the funding ratio provides an objective measure to quantify attitudes toward risk.

Good features of the study and approach are that the portfolio is able to hedge out all five currency risks. The strategy is very conservative with high investments in riskless assets. There are 85.1% riskless assets with a funding ratio of one, when assets match liabilities. This ratio drops monotonically to 65.6% with F a funding ratio of 1.5. Small changes in funding ratios change the asset weights significantly but in a reasonable way. Market weights range from 0% at $F = 1$ to 12.3% at $F = 1.2$ to 24.6% at $F = 1.5$. The equity component of these values still are low compared to typical insurance and pension fund weightings, since the market portfolio is composed of stocks and bonds. Compare with the InnoALM model calculations in Tables 14.4 and 14.5. The sensitivity of the continuous time model is less dramatic here than in many applications. More dramatic are the weights in the market and hedge portfolios; see Tables 7.2 and 7.3.

The equity portfolio is short 39.2% Canadian, and 14.8% UK stocks and long 83.9% US and 21.6% Swiss stocks and long 138.5% euro bonds and short 77.7% Swiss bonds. While optimal in the model, these weightings are more like a hedge fund rather than a pension or insurance portfolio. The hedge portfolios have similar huge long and short positions, namely long 679.6% Canadian and 97.5% UK bonds and short 627.3% US and 170.1% EMU bonds.

Hence in practice one must view these results with caution. In addition in a continuous time model, the portfolio is being constantly revised and this and most other continuous time models omit transactions costs. The recommendation is to understand such models and look at their calculations, but given that investment decisions have transactions costs, are made at intervals of one quarter or year, and have many other complications, the discrete time scenario based constrained SP models are usually more practical.

REFERENCES

Merton, R. C. 1969. Lifetime portfolio selection under uncertainty: the continuous time case. *Review of Economics and Statistics* 51:247–59.

———. 1973. An intertemporal capital asset pricing model. *Econometrica* 41:867–887.

———. 1990. *Continuous-Time Finance*. Cambridge, MA: Blackwell Publishers.

Rudolf, M., and W. T. Ziemba. 2003. Intertemporal surplus management. *Journal of Economic Dynamics and Control* 28:975–990.

Samuelson, P. A. 1969. Lifetime portfolio selection by dynamic stochastic programming. *Review of Economics and Statistics* 51:239–246.

CHAPTER 8

Should Defined Benefit Pension Schemes Be Career Average or Final Salary?

Charles Sutcliffe

The ICMA Centre, University of Reading, UK

There is widespread dissatisfaction amongst employers with defined benefit pension schemes, and many are switching to defined contribution schemes. Career average is a form of defined benefit scheme that has some important advantages over final salary schemes. The comparison of career average and final salary schemes is a neglected area, and this paper offers one of the first in-depth analyses of this topic. This is done within the UK context. It considers the advantages and disadvantages of a cost-neutral switch to a career average revalued earnings (CARE) scheme.

8.1   INTRODUCTION

There is widespread dissatisfaction in the UK and elsewhere among employers with defined benefit pension schemes, and many are switching to defined contribution schemes. In 1997 34% of UK workers were in a defined benefit scheme, but by 2005 this had fallen to just 19% (PPF and TPR 2006). However, a form of defined benefit scheme exists with a number of important

The author wishes to thank John Board, Maureen Merrison, and particularly Bill Trythall for their comments on an earlier draft of this paper, as well as participants in the Governance and Regulation of Risk Management for Defined Benefit Pension Funds Conference at Oxford University.

advantages over final salary schemes. This offers an attractive alternative to switching away from defined benefit. Interest in switching to a career average scheme has recently increased, as they offer a viable alternative to final salary schemes, while maintaining the defined benefit structure. Within the context of the UK, this paper sets out the advantages and disadvantages of a cost-neutral switch from a final salary to a career average revalued earnings (CARE) scheme.

If markets are complete, pension scheme design is irrelevant (McCarthy 2005). In such a world, whatever the type of pension scheme, employers and scheme members can always rearrange their portfolio of assets and liabilities and the division of compensation between wages and pension to give them the same desired outcome. Therefore markets can be used to reconfigure any initial allocation into the desired allocation, and the design of the pension scheme is irrelevant. However, the real world does not offer complete markets because there are transaction costs, constraints, missing markets, moral hazard, and so forth: and so pension scheme design, such as the choice between career average and final salary schemes, does matter. An important aspect of the design of a pension scheme is the way the various inherent risks are shared between the employer and members, and career average schemes share salary risk in a different way to final salary schemes. They also distribute pension scheme benefits between members differently from final salary schemes.

Section 8.2 summarizes the design of career average schemes, while Section 8.3 investigates some possible meanings of the term "cost neutral" in the context of switching to a career average scheme. Section 8.4 sets out the alternative choices that are available when selecting the revaluation rate, and Section 8.5 provides evidence on the recent adoption of career average schemes. Sections 8.6 and 8.7 summarize the advantages and disadvantages for both employers and members of career average schemes, relative to final salary schemes. Section 8.8 analyzes the redistributive effects of a cost-neutral move to a career average scheme, along with a numerical example; and the conclusions appear in Section 8.9.

8.2 CAREER AVERAGE DEFINED BENEFIT SCHEMES

A career average scheme is still a defined benefit scheme, but with an important difference in how the pension is calculated. In a final salary 80ths scheme each accrued year earns an additional pension of the final salary, divided by 80. This can be re-expressed as the salary for that year uprated to retirement using that person's actual rate of salary increase (including promotional increases), divided by 80. For a career average revalued earnings 80ths scheme each accrued year earns an additional pension of the salary for that year uprated to retirement, using a specified revaluation rate, divided by 80.

The usual revaluation rate used in UK career average schemes is the retail price index (RPI), although some alternatives will be considered in Section 8.4. The same rate is often applied to the accrued benefits of both active and deferred members. Actuaries argue that salaries generally increase faster than RPI, and so ceteris paribus, a career average scheme revalued using RPI, gives lower pensions than a final salary scheme. This lower cost of a career average scheme can be offset by increasing the benefits, for instance, moving from an 80ths scheme to say a 60ths scheme, so that total expected cost is unaltered: that is, the switch is cost neutral. Blome, Fachinger, Franzen, Scheuenstuhl, and Yermo (2007) found that using FRS 17 (or IAS 19), a switch from final salary to career average (both with price indexation) but with no change in the accrual rate leads to a reduction of over 40% in pension liabilities.[1] Therefore whether or not a switch to career average is cost neutral can have major implications for the benefits.

8.3 COST NEUTRALITY

A number of recent proposals to switch from final salary to career average have been "cost neutral." However, cost neutrality is ambiguous, as it could mean cost neutral to: (a) the scheme, (b) the employer, or (c) the scheme members. In each case the time period covered in the calculation of the change in costs is generally the long term. All other aspects of the scheme are assumed to be unchanged.

In order that the proposal to switch to a career average scheme can be properly evaluated, it is important to have a clear definition of what is meant by cost neutrality. As argued in Section 8.6, a switch to career average can reduce the volatility of the contribution rate. This benefit from the switch will be ignored when defining cost neutrality, which will just use the expected values of the costs and benefits.

(a) Scheme. Cost neutrality to the scheme is probably the most obvious definition and covers benefit payments by the scheme. This is the cost number that the actuary is likely to compute.
(b) Employer. Cost neutrality to the employer covers employer contributions, and any changes in wages to offset alterations in pension benefits.

---

[1] They assumed five categories of active member; with 1% earning €200,000, 4% earning €100,000, 15% earning €80,000, 20% earning €60,000 and 60% earning €40,000; and that members' salaries increased each year due to three factors: salary rates (1.7%), promotions (2.5%) and last year's inflation.

It also includes the value of any nonpecuniary effects that stem from the switch, such as changes in staff turnover, early and late retirement patterns, the productivity of workers recruited and retained, and the risks of scheme funding (see Section 8.7.1). If the government is also the employer, cost neutrality can include the additional tax effects of the switch, as well as any effects on state pensions and benefits. For example, a career average scheme leads to a reduction in the pensions received by high flyers, and a matching increase in the pensions of low flyers (see Section 8.8). Due to the progressive nature of the tax system, this results in a decrease in the tax revenue received when these pensions are paid. The national insurance and income tax effects are considered further in Section 8.8.1.

(c) Members. Cost neutrality to the members covers their contributions to the scheme, and any changes in wage rates to offset alternations in pensions, as well as the value of non-pecuniary items, such as the removal of the pension capital loss (see Section 8.6.1) on becoming a deferred pensioner, and the ability to accrue pension on fluctuating emoluments (see Section 8.6.2).

Once cost neutrality has been defined, its computation depends crucially on a number of forecasts. These include the extent to which salary rises will exceed the chosen revaluation rate, the effect of removing the pension capital loss, the influence of the switch on wage rises, which are now less costly, and the consequences of changing pensions on the wage-pension tradeoff (see Section 8.7.1). Therefore the extent to which a switch is cost neutral is always a matter for legitimate debate. For the remainder of this paper "cost neutrality" refers to the scheme.

8.4 CHOOSING THE REVALUATION RATE

A key decision for any career average scheme is the choice of revaluation rate used to uprate accrued benefits. Viewing pensions as deferred wages,[2]

---

[2]About two thirds of contributions to defined benefit pension schemes are usually paid by the employer, and the present analysis of deferred wages is directly relevant to employer contributions. Member contributions, forming about one third of total contributions, are paid out of the member's wages; and represent an investment in the pension scheme. The money's worth for one year's investment by members in career average pension schemes has been studied by Hári, Koijen, and Nijman (2006). Money's worth is the expected present value of annuity payments per pound

the revaluation (or dynamization) rate can be set to meet various definitions of maintaining the value of the wages whose payment has been deferred.

- RPI. The most popular revaluation rate is RPI, which maintains the purchasing power of the deferred wages.
- LPI. In the UK there is a legal obligation to revalue deferred benefits by at least limited price inflation (LPI), and this can also be applied to revaluing the benefits of active members.
- NAE. Another possibility is to maintain the rate for the job: that is, if the work had been performed today, what would be the wage rate (Cooper 1998). Such revaluation of deferred wages is often proxied by the increase in national average earnings (NAE). Alternatively, wages could be revalued using the average rate of wage increases for the employer concerned. Provided the member is not promoted, such revalued wages may end up close to the members's final salary.
- Final Salary. Wages may be revalued at the member's actual wage rate: that is, a final salary (FS) scheme. In some final salary schemes, the salary used in the benefit calculation is not the final year, but the (revalued) average over the final 5 or 10 years. Such a modification moves a final salary scheme towards a career average scheme.
- Riskless Rate. A fifth possibility is to view deferred wages as a risk free loan by the member to the company, and so wages are revalued using the riskless rate of interest (r).
- Investment Return. Since the deferred wages have been invested by the pension scheme, wages can be revalued by the rate of return achieved by the fund on its assets (R). In this case the scheme becomes essentially a defined contribution scheme, with the investment risk passed to the members (Disney 1995; Thornton 1986).
- Zero. Finally, the revaluation rate may be zero: that is, no revaluation, and only the nominal value of the deferred wages is preserved.

The likely ordering of these alternative revaluation rates over the long run is $R > FS > r > NAE > RPI > LPI > 0$. Farr (2007) has proposed a new type of career average scheme where the revaluation rate is conditional on the funding status of the scheme, thereby sharing the revaluation risk with the members. A similar approach is taken by Dutch pension schemes.

---

spent to purchase an annuity or pension. Hári, Koijen, and Nijman (2006) show that young uneducated males have an incentive not to join career average pension schemes. A money's worth analysis of a final salary scheme would probably produce an even clearer case for not joining. The money's worth of member contributions is not covered in this paper.

The choice of revaluation rate depends on a range of factors, which include:

- The year to year volatility of the revaluation rates
- The ease of making accurate long-term forecasts of the revaluation rates
- The availability of financial instruments to hedge revaluation rate risk
- The extent to which the employer has control of the revaluation rates

These factors are discussed below in Sections 8.6 and 8.7.

8.5   THE ADOPTION OF CAREER AVERAGE PENSION SCHEMES

In 1963 29% of the members of UK occupational pension schemes were in career average schemes (Wesbroom and Reay 2005). However, as inflation increased, career average schemes declined in popularity because the absence of revaluation rendered the resulting benefits inadequate (Thornton 1986). By 1987 less than 1% of members of UK occupational schemes were in career average schemes; and this remained the case until 2000. The introduction of career average revalued earnings (CARE) schemes overcame this shortcoming, and in recent years there has been an increasing interest in career average schemes. In 2007 about 8% of active members of UK defined benefit schemes were in CARE schemes (Levy 2008).[3]

In addition, the UK government has shown a strong interest in career average schemes. The State Second Pension (S2P) is a career average scheme, as were its predecessors, the State Earnings Related Pension Scheme (SERPS) (1975–2002), and the Graduated Retirement Benefit (1961–1975).[4] In addition, local councillors, general practitioners, and dentists have career

---

[3]UK companies switching their final salary schemes to career average or offering a career average scheme along side another type of scheme include the Automobile Association, the Bank of England, the British Broadcasting Corporation, British Telecom, Clydesdale Bank, the Co-operative Group, DSG International, E.ON, First Group, Morgan Crucible, Morrisons, Mothercare, the Nationwide Building Society, Network Rail, Royal and Sun Alliance, Royal Mail, Sainsbury's, Scottish & Newcastle, Social Housing Pension Scheme, Standard Life, Students' Union Superannuation Scheme, Tesco, Union Bank of Switzerland, Unilever, United Biscuits, Watson Wyatt, and the Yorkshire Bank.

[4]The use of career average is common practice in the state earnings related pension schemes offered by many developed countries—Austria, Cyprus, Czech Republic, Finland, Germany, Hungary, Italy, Latvia, Lithuania, Luxembourg, Norway, Poland, Slovakia, Slovenia, Sweden, Switzerland, United Kingdom, and the US.

average schemes. In 2005 and 2006 the UK government proposed that the pension schemes for staff in the National Health Service (NHS), Civil Service, and local government should switch from final salary to career average.

Civil Service. In December 2004 the government issued proposals for reform of the Civil Service final salary scheme, which included a cost neutral switch to career average (Cabinet Office, 2004). The reaction of the Civil Service trade unions to the career average proposal was mixed. Mark Serwotka, general secretary of the Public and Commercial Services (PCS) union with 330,000 mainly lower paid Civil Service members, said that a move to career average pensions would create "great uncertainty, suspicion and anxiety" (*The Financial Times* December 9, 2004). However, 15 months later his views had mellowed, and he said that the

> PCS does not have a policy of support for career average pension schemes. The jury is still out on the benefits of such schemes and the union is yet to be convinced about the need to move to a career averaging scheme. Talks are continuing between the Civil Service trade unions and the government with a deal of the detail yet to be worked through. Only then can a view be taken on the merits of career averaging over a final salary pension scheme. (*Socialist Worker*, March 11, 2006)

Prospect, the trade union representing 60,000 scientists, engineers, and other specialist Civil Service workers, said that career average was an opportunity rather than a threat, and would be superior to the present arrangements (*Financial Times* December 10, 2004). The First Division Association (FDA), which represents top civil servants, opposed the introduction of a career average scheme and voted for strike action over this and the proposed increase in the retirement age (*Financial Times* March 15, 2005). In its consultation, 94% of FDA members were opposed to moving to a career average scheme (FDA 2005).

The collective response of the Civil Service unions (CCSU 2005) did not reject the concept of a career average scheme, but criticized the way it had been presented in the consultation. The career average aspect of the proposal was not understood by many staff, and insufficient evidence was provided that it would be fairer for those working part time or taking career breaks. There was also scepticism about the employer's motives, since other employers have introduced career average schemes to cut costs. The outcome was that from August 1, 2007, entrants to the Civil Service were offered a new career average pension scheme in place of the existing final salary scheme.

National Health Service. In January 2005 the government consulted on a cost neutral switch of the National Health Service (NHS) pension scheme for England and Wales, which has 1.26 million active members, to career average (NHS Employers 2005). A move to career average was strongly opposed by the Royal College of Nursing (RCN 2005), in part because the new NHS pay system, Agenda for Change, supported greater career progression for nurses, making a final salary scheme more attractive than a career average scheme (see Section 8.8). The British Medical Association (BMA) saw the possible switch to a career average scheme for all doctors as one of the greatest threats in the proposals. James Johnson, chairman of the BMA, said that "over 95% of consultants and 93% of junior doctors in the BMA survey want to stick with their current final salary scheme" (BMA 2006). Modeling by the BMA showed that full-time consultants with an NHS career from graduation to retirement age could have their pensions reduced by 25%. Amicus, which has 100,000 NHS members, came out against the career average scheme, mainly because they estimated that there would be many more losers than winners among their members (Amicus 2005). Amicus also made the point that some of the benefits of a career average scheme can be obtained with a final salary scheme.

General practitioners and dentists in the NHS have always had a career average scheme. This is because they are self-employed, which allows them to manipulate their final salary; and because their earnings tend to peak in midcareer (NHS Employers 2005). In the BMA consultation, 75% of general practitioners and dentists wished to continue with their career average scheme (BMA 2006). A summary of the consultation responses on retaining a career average scheme for general practitioners and dentists appears in Tables 8.1 and 8.2 (NHS Employers 2006a). These tables show a clear preference for the retention of the career average scheme. As a result of the consultation (which also included employers), the NHS decided to stick with a career average scheme for general practitioners and dentists, and to keep a final salary scheme for all other staff.

TABLE 8.1 Responses by General Practitioners and Dentists to the Choice between Final Salary and Career Average Schemes

	Individuals	NHS Organizations (Trusts, PCT)	Local Staff Groups	Others
For Career Average	6.0%	10.5%	5.0%	8.5%
For Final Salary	63.5%	46.5%	76.0%	50.0%
Do Not Know	30.5%	43.0%	19.0%	41.5%
Total Responses	5433	172	115	24

Source: NHS Employers (2006a).

TABLE 8.2 Responses Agreeing with the Retention of a Career Average Scheme for General Practitioners and Dentists

	Individuals	NHS Organizations (Trusts, PCT)	Local Staff Groups	Others
Agree	84%	98%	89%	100%
Disagree	16%	2%	11%	0%
Total Responses	678	47	18	4

Source: NHS Employers (2006a).

Local Government. In June 2006 the UK government proposed four options for the local government pension scheme for England and Wales, of which two were final salary, one was a switch to career average, and the fourth was a combination of career average and final salary (DCLG 2006). The overwhelming response from members of Unison was for a final salary scheme. Unison (2006a) believed that, to compensate members for the risk that the revaluation rate may be less than actual salary rises, a more generous accrual rate was required, along with changing the revaluation rate from RPI to NAE. Unison (2006b) reported that 84% of the employers also preferred a final salary scheme. So the final decision was in favor of one of the final salary schemes, and this came into operation in April 2008.

In these three government consultations, a number of common reasons were given by respondents for opposing a switch to a career average scheme:

- Career average is an unfamiliar concept, and is more difficult to explain and understand than final salary.
- An unwillingness to move away from final salary, which is seen as the gold standard pension scheme design that is widely trusted.
- Doubts about the ability of pension administrators to cope with the new career average design.
- Fears that a career average scheme will cause problems with the public sector transfer club.
- A fear that, while the proposal is meant to be cost neutral, it is actually a cost-reduction measure.
- Women, who have taken less demanding jobs when young to allow them to raise a family, did so expecting their final salary (and hence pension) to be unaffected. A shift to career average would thwart such plans.
- Staff who experience above-average salary growth lose out from a switch to a career average scheme.

Career average schemes have recently increased in popularity in the Netherlands. The two largest Dutch pension schemes: ABP, whose members are 2.4 million civil servants and teachers; and PGGM, which has 1.9 million healthcare and social worker members; have recently switched to career average. In 1998 25.0% of the active members of Dutch pension schemes were in career average schemes. By 2005 this figure had risen to 74.3%. This switch to career average in the Netherlands was particularly strong among industry-wide schemes; with 27.9% of their active members in career average in 1998, rising to 84.6% in 2005 (Ponds and Van Riel 2007). Swinkels (2006) reports that the following Dutch companies offer career average schemes: ABN Amro, Aegon, Ahold, AKZO Nobel, Hagemeyer, Heineken, KPN, Phillips, Reed Elsevier, TNT, and Wolters Kluwer (AVH has also switched to career average). In 2003 about 7% of the schemes run by large US companies were career average (Watson Wyatt 2005).

8.6 ADVANTAGES OF A SWITCH TO A CAREER AVERAGE SCHEME

This section sets out the benefits of switching to a career average scheme, within the UK context. The advantages of a career average scheme, relative to a final salary scheme, are split into those that accrue chiefly to the employer, and those received by scheme members. This classification is somewhat arbitrary, as a benefit to the employer may be a disbenefit to the members. For the purposes of this comparison, final salary schemes are assumed to base the pension on salary for the last 12 months of employment, and to use a single contribution rate for all members; as do career average schemes.

8.6.1 Employer

A career average scheme reduces the risks and costs to the employer of a large pay rise for all members. A large pay rise represents a double blow for an employer with a final salary scheme because it results in a large one-off increase in the past service liability, together with a smaller continuing increase in current salaries (and associated pension obligations). With a career average scheme a big pay rise does not lead to an uprating of past service liabilities, unless the employer's wage rates are used for revaluation.

For example, suppose an employer has a £10 million pension liability (computed using the projected unit method) for the past service of active members, and an annual wage bill of £1 million. This employer now grants an unexpected wage rise of 10%, which is 7% above inflation. With a final salary scheme the cost in the first year to the employer is the revaluation of past service (£10m × 0.10), plus the increase in annual salary costs (£1m × 0.10), or £1.1 million, ignoring the extra pension cost of the higher wages in the current year.[5] Under a career average scheme with RPI revaluation, the extra cost to the employer is the increase in salary cost for the current year of £0.1 million (and associated pension obligations), plus the revaluation of the past service liability using RPI of £0.3 m., giving a total additional cost of only £0.4 m. In general, for every extra 1% granted as a pay rise, the extra cost for a final salary scheme is (0.01 × Liabilities) higher than for a career average scheme. In this example, the marginal cost for a final salary scheme of an extra 1% pay rise is £110,000, not the £10,000 for a career average scheme. Even if changes in the revaluation rate are just as volatile as changes in the firm's average wage, the effect of wage rises on the past service liability of a final salary scheme means that the resulting surplus or deficit for a career average scheme reported in the accounts will probably be more stable than for the corresponding final salary scheme. This may result in the contribution rate for a career average scheme also being more stable.

Because a wage rise does not cause an uprating of the past service liability, members with a career average scheme have less incentive to engage in industrial action for higher wages; and career average schemes provide less incentive for members to seek large pay rises close to retirement. Career average schemes also reduce the cost to the employer of awarding favoured individuals large pay rises close to retirement.

If RPI is used as the revaluation rate, a career average scheme replaces final salary risk with RPI risk. This makes it much easier for the employer to hedge this risk if desired, such as by holding index linked bonds. There are no suitable instruments for hedging final salary risk (Sutcliffe 2005). If the riskless rate is used as the revaluation rate, fixed interest securities can hedge this risk. If the investment return is used to uprate past service, the investment portfolio of the pension fund will exactly hedge this risk.

If the same revaluation rate is used for deferred and active members in a career average scheme, staff turnover risk (i.e., the risk that an unknown proportion of the workers will cease to be active members of the scheme) is removed when valuing the liabilities of the scheme. This is because the cost to the scheme is the same whether the member stays or leaves. Removal of this risk allows the current deficit or surplus to be measured with greater accuracy, and one source of error disappears when forecasting future liabilities.

---

[5]It is assumed that the large wage rise does not cause the actuary to revise his or her expectations of future rates of wage increase used when valuing the past service liabilities.

A final salary scheme using the projected unit method to value the liabilities requires forecasts of future salary increases, while a career average scheme using the projected unit method requires forecasts of the revaluation rate. It may be easier to forecast the chosen revaluation rate, making the valuation of the liabilities more reliable. For example, actuaries already make use of the market forecasts of the long-term inflation rate implicit in the price of index linked gilts, and this can be used to forecast an RPI revaluation rate, while the riskless rate can be forecast using the yield curve for government bonds.

A career average scheme reduces the incentive in a final salary scheme for members to stay on to improve their pension (Cabinet Office 2004). In a final salary scheme this incentive is provided by the potential for a substantial pay rise, which then revalues all previously accrued benefits.

When designing a pension scheme, employers must ensure it complies with current legislation concerning discrimination on the grounds of age, race, sex, disability, sexual orientation, and belief. They may also wish to anticipate future changes in antidiscrimination requirements. The DCLG (2006) wanted the new local government scheme to be equality proof, and concluded that career average schemes are superior in this respect. They are fairer as between long and short service workers, and between high and low flyers (see Section 8.8). The Cabinet Office (2004) also wanted a career average scheme for the Civil Service in order to provide an equality-proof scheme.

Despite these government worries about equality, the NHS and local government schemes chose to continue with final salary; although the Civil Service scheme did not. This implies that the government thinks any discrimination inherent in these two final salary schemes will continue to be objectively justifiable. The advantages of final salary discussed in Section 8.7.1 might be used in such a justification. However, there is always the risk that circumstances change, and such a defense is unsuccessful.

To qualify for favorable tax treatment, US schemes must comply with highly complex nondiscrimination rules. These rules require scheme benefits and contributions not to favor highly compensated current and former employees, and this generally requires the uniform treatment of all current and former members (McGill, Brown, Haley, and Schieber 1996). However, final salary schemes can meet these nondiscrimination requirements.

Because they are more equitable as between members, career average schemes are preferable as the basis for multiemployer schemes (Thornton 1986; Cooper 2003). In a final salary multiemployer scheme with a common contribution rate differential employer behavior creates cross-subsidies. For example, the pensions cost of large wage increases by one employer is spread across all employers. For a career average multiemployer scheme, large wage increases do not revalue past service, and so do not result in a cross-subsidy.

When scheme membership is voluntary, a final salary scheme is subject to adverse selection: potential high flyers join, while those who expect a flat age-earnings profile do not. Since career average schemes do not favor high flyers, this adverse selection is removed. Cocco and Lopes (2004) conducted an empirical investigation into the presence of such adverse selection. UK workers have a choice between three types of pension scheme (a) SERPS/S2P, which is career average; (b) personal pensions, which are defined contribution; and (c) final salary occupational schemes. They studied the pension scheme choices made by 46,000 workers from 1999 to 2001, after controlling for the lower transfer value of occupational pensions and the lack of tax relief on SERPS contributions. They found that workers with a job offering high earnings growth tended to choose a final salary scheme, while workers facing low earnings growth tended to choose the career average scheme. This evidence suggests that final salary pension schemes are subject to adverse selection, which can be avoided by a switch to career average.

The use of career average offers the flexibility to change the revaluation rate and the definition of pensionable pay from time to time, without creating the administrative problem of tranches of past service that are necessary with a final salary scheme (Thornton 1986; Wesbroom and Reay 2005). This flexibility in the revaluation rate offers the possibility that (for future service) a career average scheme can become a final salary scheme, or change to something similar to a defined contribution scheme.

Final salary schemes generate a pension capital loss when a member becomes a deferred pensioner (Ippolito 1991) as the revaluation rate for past service drops from the member's actual pay rise to the RPI (or LPI). The presence of this pension capital loss depends on taking an "implicit contract" view of pensions, rather than a legal or spot interpretation (Ippolito, 1985). Under the implicit contract view, a pension is valued now using the forecast salary as at the normal retirement age (NRA), while the legal view uses the current salary. The empirical evidence clearly supports the implicit contract view, for instance, Ippolito (1985). Some members of a final salary scheme will require compensation for accepting this penalty for prematurely quitting. Since a switch to a career average scheme with the same revaluation rate for active and deferred members removes this penalty, it could lead to a corresponding reduction in wages (Ippolito 1997).

There is little difference in the administration costs of final salary and career average schemes (Cooper 1997). Only the total revalued salary to date, weighted by the appropriate accrual rate, need be recorded by a career average scheme.

8.6.2 Members

By reducing the effect of pay rises on pension costs, a career average scheme makes it easier for trade unions to negotiate larger pay rises; although workers have less incentive to seek such rises.

Career average schemes make it easier for members to predict their pension. This is because their pension forecast depends on the salary-weighted average of the revaluation rates across their remaining years of service, and this may be easier to forecast than their own final salary, which is based on their aggregate wage increase across the years to retirement.[6] Based on a Monte Carlo simulation using data from the Labor Force Survey, McCarthy (2005) concluded that career average schemes are preferable to final salary schemes, which he attributes to the size of the career average pension being less risky.

A career average scheme is more attractive than a final salary scheme to workers who are risk averse because revaluation rate risk is usually less than final salary risk.

Career average schemes using RPI as the revaluation rate give a pension that is guaranteed in real terms, rather than being uprated by the final salary (and so subject to final salary risk).

A cost-neutral switch to using career average makes joining a pension scheme more attractive to lower-paid staff, particularly staff without good career prospects, and/or those with short service (see Section 8.8). This should increase the uptake of pensions by disadvantaged groups.

Final salary schemes often exclude from pensionable earnings any fluctuating emoluments such as overtime, special payments, variable time employment, and so forth, because they are difficult to deal with in the benefit calculation. In addition, treating overtime and so forth, as pensionable pay for final salary schemes opens up the possibility of members pushing up pay in their final year by working excessive overtime and so on. Career average schemes can easily include fluctuating payments in the benefit calculation (Cabinet Office 2004; Cooper 1997; Thornton 1986); while members' deliberately increasing their final year's pay has much less effect in a career average scheme. Therefore career average schemes tend to include all earnings. Cooper (2003) pointed out that career average schemes are popular in the retail sector, which has many variable time workers.

---

[6]Assume that the variance of the revaluation rates is the same as that of the salary increases, and that changes in the revaluation rate and salaries are both independent over time. Then pensions based on the career average will be less risky than those based on the final salary.

The treatment of overtime and so on as pensionable pay by career average schemes increases the pensions of workers who receive such payments, unless there is some offsetting change.

Career average schemes are beneficial for members whose peak earnings are in midcareer: for instance, some manual workers (Thornton, 1986). Career average also allows members to step down to lower paid, less demanding, possibly part-time jobs as they approach retirement (Cabinet Office 2004) without suffering a substantial pension reduction.

Since the revaluation rate does not depend on the member remaining in employment, the same rate can be applied to deferred benefits, so ensuring equal treatment of active and deferred members. Such equal treatment removes the pension capital loss suffered by staff when they become deferred pensioners (Ippolito 1991).

Because all past benefits in a final salary scheme are revalued by subsequent salary increases, the employer has an incentive to dismiss members, particularly long-standing members, of a final salary scheme just before a large rise in salaries. Using data on US workers from 1966 to 1981, Cornwell, Dorsey, and Mehrzad (1991) found evidence supporting such opportunistic behavior by employers. A career average scheme that uses the same rate for revaluing the benefits of deferred and active members does not create this incentive for the employer.

8.7   DISADVANTAGES OF A SWITCH TO A CAREER AVERAGE SCHEME

The disadvantages of career average schemes, relative to final salary schemes, for the UK are now presented separately for the employer and the members. In points 3 to 6 in the following, the changes in productivity, staff turnover, training, and salaries are only relevant to the measurement of cost neutrality if it is defined with respect to the employer or members. In this paper, cost neutrality is taken to relate to just the scheme, making such costs and benefits irrelevant to quantifying cost neutrality. However, these effects still need to be taken into account in assessing the costs and benefits of a switch to career average.

8.7.1   Employer

The employer has control over each member's final salary and over the average rate of wage increase for their workforce. However, the employer does not control RPI, the riskless rate, NAE or the rate of return on the fund's assets. Therefore, if any of these variables is chosen as the revaluation rate for a career average scheme, the employer has lost control of this aspect of pensions costs. However, since wages are usually set in the context of a competitive labor market; the employer may not have meaningful long-run control of final salaries and average wage rates.

It is common practice to use the same revaluation rate for active members and deferred pensioners of a career average scheme. If RPI is used as the common revaluation rate, the cost of deferred pensioners is unchanged, but other choices of revaluation rate increase or decrease this cost in the absence of any change in the accrual rate. For example, the choice of NAE increases the cost of deferred pensions. If the switch to career average is cost neutral (irrespective of the common revaluation rate chosen), this implies a redistribution of pensions from active to deferred members because FS > RPI.

Lazear (1979, 1981) has argued that it may be in the interests of both the employer and the workers for there to be a penalty for workers who shirk or quit prematurely; with an incentive for workers to stay and work hard. Such an outcome increases staff productivity, which can then be shared between the workers and the company as higher wages and profits. Dorsey, Cornwell, and MacPherson (1998) found that offering a defined benefit, rather than a defined contribution scheme, is linked with higher labor productivity. Ippolito (1991) suggests that workers can be incentivized to stay and avoid being sacked for shirking by the introduction of a final salary scheme, which generates a pension capital loss for quitters and those sacked for shirking. Therefore the introduction of a career average scheme may lead to a reduction in productivity because members are not subject to the threat of a pension capital loss if sacked for shirking, leading to a reduction in wages. To avoid such a reduction in productivity, the employer could introduce a wage tilt, that is, initial low wages and high final wages (Lazear 1979, 1981), although this may result in some additional tax payments.

If the same rate is used for revaluing the benefits of active and deferred members, those who leave the firm cease to suffer a pension capital loss (i.e., there is no reduction in the revaluation rate on quitting). This may result in an increase in labor turnover and in the costs of recruiting and training replacement staff. Using US data, Allen, Clark, and McDermed (1993) found that being a member of a final salary scheme clearly reduces staff turnover. This is due to both the sorting effect of attracting workers who want to stay, and the presence of the pension capital loss suffered by leavers, which discourages quitting. An increase in staff turnover reduces the willingness of the employer to invest in staff training because the firm may get less benefit from the training, and less well trained staff will be less productive. Dorsey, Cornwell, and MacPherson (1998) found that offering a defined benefit pension scheme is associated with greater staff training.

A shift to a career average scheme may alter the type of staff who want to work for the firm: that is, there is a sorting effect (Ippolito 1997). Pensions attract staff with personal attributes that result in them placing a high value on the type of scheme on offer, and these attributes may be those desired by the employer, leading to higher productivity. A final salary scheme favours high flyers, who are more willing to take a risk with the size of their pension, and are low discounters who do not intend to quit. Low discounters attach a high value to long-term consequences, and so engage in less shirking, have a stronger desire for promotion, and appreciate the long-term consequences of their actions (Ippolito 1997). Such staff are less willing to work for a firm with a career average scheme, which tends to attract staff who are more risk averse low flyers with a higher personal discount rate who intend to quit earlier. These staff may have lower productivity and wages.

A cost-neutral switch to a career average scheme increases the total compensation (pension plus salary, net of any member pension contribution) of low flyers, and lowers the total compensation of high flyers (see Section 8.8). This raises the question of the extent to which members (and employers) take account of the deferred wages provided by the pension scheme when negotiating employment contracts.

If markets are complete and participants are fully rational, the wage-pension tradeoff will be a one-for-one negative relationship.[7] Salaries will change to offset any change in pension, and a switch to a career average scheme will not produce any income redistribution. But in the incomplete real world, the size of this tradeoff is an empirical question.

Labor economists have studied compensating wage differentials: that is, the extent to which wages adjust to allow for the other costs and benefits of employment, such as danger, unpleasantness, long holidays, free samples, security, fringe benefits, and so on. Researchers have tried to quantify the wage-pension tradeoff[8] when the member's own pension contributions are ignored, but they have faced formidable data and econometric problems

---

[7]Each member's salary is net of any contributions they make to the pension scheme.
[8]The following studies have estimated the size of the tradeoff between pension benefits and wages: Clark and McDermed (1986); Ehrenberg (1980); Ehrenberg and Smith (1981); Freeman (1985); Gerakos (2008); Gunderson, Hyatt, and Pesando (1992); Inkmann (2006); Montgomery and Shaw (1997); Montgomery, Shaw, and Benedict (1992); Moore (1987); Schiller and Weiss (1980); Smith (1981); and Smith and Ehrenberg (1983). In addition, Bulow and Landsman (1985); Dorsey, Cornwell, and MacPherson (1998); Even and MacPherson (1990); and Gustman and Steinmeier (1995) have estimated the effect on wages of being covered by a pension scheme.

(Allen and Clark 1987). The available evidence is very mixed, but suggests that the relationship between wages and pensions is usually negative, with no strong evidence that it is as large as one-for-one. This may partly be because pensions bring the benefits of reduced turnover and greater staff productivity. There is also the possibility that members, and perhaps employers, suffer from pensions illusion: that is, not require an offsetting increase in wages when their pension benefits are reducing, or not reduce wages when pension benefits are increased.

Building the compensating effects of switching to a career average scheme into the wage structure means that salaries at the top end will tend to rise, while those at the bottom end will tend to fall. However, a final salary scheme rewards those who experience a substantial increase in salary during their career, irrespective of where they start and finish on the salary scale. Therefore compensation for a switch to a career average scheme cannot simply take the form of increasing the salaries of the highly paid, and lowering the salaries of the lowly paid; it needs to reflect career progression. In a risky world, the extent to which a particular member gains or loses from a switch to career average is not known at the time he enters into a labor contract. Therefore such contracts can either reflect expected gains or losses from a switch to career average, or incorporate some retrospective element. In addition, there may be delays and rigidities in adjusting wages for existing workers.

Using the same revaluation rate for leavers and stayers does not allow the employer to penalize those members who quit before the NRA because the pension capital loss imposed on early leavers has disappeared. Therefore early retirement is not discouraged. A cost-neutral switch to career average will probably increase the incentive for low flyers and some high flyers to accrue additional years, rather than retire early. This is because the accrual rate has increased, while the difference between the expected revaluation rate and salary increases over the final few years will be small. Whether a switch to career average has increased or decreased the incentive for high flyers to retire early depends on the relative magnitude of the increase in the accrual rate and the decrease in the revaluation rate.[9]

Implementing the switch from final salary to career average will involve a range of administrative and legal issues, e.g., changing the rules of the scheme and the contracts of employment of the employees (Tsang 2007).

---

[9]The effects of a switch from final salary to career average are likely to be small compared with the effects of any actuarial reduction for early retirement, or actuarial enhancement for late retirement.

8.7.2   Members

Final salary schemes promise members with a specified number of accrued years a pension that is a specified proportion of their final salary: that is, the replacement ratio is fixed. This means that members can plan for any change in their standard of living as they move from employment to retirement. With a career average scheme, the relationship between their final salary and pension is uncertain (chiefly because their final salary is uncertain).

Without an increase in the accrual rate to make the switch from final salary to career average cost neutral, the introduction of a career average scheme will very probably decrease pensions, particularly those received by high flyers.

8.8   REDISTRIBUTION EFFECTS OF A SWITCH TO CAREER AVERAGE PENSIONS

A final salary scheme amplifies lifetime income inequality between members. Not only do high flyers receive a large salary, but they also receive a pension that is a higher proportion of the pension contributions made by themselves and their employer in respect of their employment than do low flyers. In addition, high flyers usually receive greater tax relief than low flyers on their pension contributions, and probably draw their higher pensions for longer due to their greater life expectancy. These effects further increase the inequality of lifetime incomes (salary plus pension).

A cost-neutral switch from a final salary to a career average scheme has a powerful effect on the size of pension received by different groups of members (Cooper 1997, 1998, 1999). Members with a flat age-earnings profile (low flyers) are gainers, while members who display considerable salary progression (high flyers) are losers. Being a high or low flyer tends to be correlated with other characteristics of the member, and this suggests that the losers from final salary schemes tend to be uneducated nonwhite women who experience career breaks, work part time or variable hours, or leave early. For example, a study of the NHS found that men receive about 10% more initial pension from the pension contributions made on their behalf by themselves and their employer than women as a result of higher career progression (NHS Employers 2005). Any changes in pension benefits caused by a switch from final salary to career average may be compensated for by a change in wages, but there is a strong possibility that any such adjustment is less than one-for-one.

Pensions are deferred pay, and the concept of equal pay for equal work leads to the principle of an equal pension for equal work. Career average schemes (where some common revaluation rate is used, rather than final salary) give pension equality between active members of the same age, who both perform the same work in the same year, and make the same pension contributions. Thus career average schemes meet the objective of delivering equal pension for equal work. A final salary scheme revalues accrued pension benefits by the rate of increase required to reach the member's final salary. This greatly favors members who experience rapid salary increases, particularly if these increases are near the end of their service. These winners from a final salary scheme tend to be educated white men who do not have career breaks, work full time with fixed hours, and do not leave early.

As well as equity between high and low flying active members, there is also the issue of equity between deferred pensioners and active members. If two members of the same age perform the same work in the same year for the same pay, the concept of equal pay for equal work implies that they should also receive the same pension for this work; regardless of whether one of them subsequently leaves the company. In a typical final salary scheme leavers have their benefits revalued by RPI, while stayers have their benefits revalued by their final salary. This usually means that leavers receive markedly less pension than stayers for identical deferred pay. If a career average scheme uses the same revaluation rate for actives and deferreds, this inequity is removed. However, some early leavers may choose to take a transfer value, rather than become a deferred pensioner. Typical transfer values are substantially less than the economic value of the accrued pension rights; and the issue of equity for leavers who choose to take a transfer value, rather than a deferred pension, remains.

The redistribution by final salary schemes from low to high flyers is not due to unequal incomes, but to unequal rates of change in incomes. If initial incomes are highly unequal, but every member receives the same percentage pay rises throughout their career, there is no redistribution of pension benefits. This means that members who experience a large promotion when young, and then remain on the same grade until retirement, may gain from a switch to career average. It also means that members who enter on a low salary, and are subsequently promoted to a middle-level salary late in their career, may lose from a switch to career average.

Den Hertog (1999) called the redistribution of pensions by final salary schemes from low to high flyers "reversed solidarity," and investigated why workers have negotiated such arrangements. He attributes this reversed solidarity to the standardized nonnegotiable pension deal offered to individual workers, the substantial costs that workers must incur to understand the pension (or to employ an advisor), the membership of the scheme by senior managers, and the lack of importance that workers tend to give to distant events, such as retirement.

Trade unions should be exempt from these problems when negotiating a pension scheme. However, democratic organizations, such as trade unions, represent the preferences of the median member, who tends to be older, more senior, and closer to retirement than young members. Trade union leaders tend to be even older than the median voter. Freeman (1985) argues that this should lead to pension schemes in unionized firms favoring seniority (long service) for calculating benefits. His empirical analysis of US data found that unionized firms are more likely to have flat rate benefits, where benefits depend on the number of years of service, not salary. However, flat rate benefits are uncommon in the UK, and there is no evidence that unionized firms have pension schemes that favor long service, rather than high final salaries.

A possible explanation for the presence of reverse solidarity in the UK is that trade unions tend not to represent the interests of deferred pensioners, who have probably ceased employment with the sponsor. By removing the pensions capital loss, a cost-neutral switch to career average represents a redistribution of pensions away from active members and toward deferred pensioners, which damages the interests of the trade union's current membership.

8.8.1 Compensatory Salary Changes, Pension Contributions, NIC, and Income Tax

The redistributive effects of a switch to career average may be offset by compensatory changes in gross salary. In the UK such a change in gross salary causes changes in pension contributions, national insurance contributions (NIC), and income tax paid by the member. Members' pension contributions (which are tax deductible) are assumed to be a fixed proportion of gross salary, members' NIC (which is not tax deductible) is a regressive proportion of gross salary, and income tax is a progressive proportion of the member's gross salary after deducting their pension contributions.

Consider the extreme case of a change in pension accrual that is fully offset by a change in gross salary. For low flyers the rise in the value of their pension accrual is exactly matched by a fall in their gross salary, so that they experience no change in their gross compensation. However, the salary reduction causes a fall in their pension contributions, NIC, and income tax.[10]

---

[10] Their income tax falls due to the drop in gross salary. However, the fall in their pension contributions, which are tax deductible, leads to a fall in their tax deductions.

This leads to a rise in their net compensation (ignoring any subsequent tax effects flowing from the increase in pension accrual). The opposite outcome applies to high flyers. Therefore, low flyers gain, and high flyers lose, from a fully compensated switch to career average due to pension contribution, NIC, and income tax effects.

As well as redistributing net compensation from high to low flyers, even in the extreme case of full compensation via changes in gross salary, there is probably a change in the aggregate net compensation of members due to changes in aggregate pension contributions, NIC, and income tax paid by members. Since NIC for members is regressive (although flat for employers), and income taxation is progressive, even after allowing for the effect of changes in pension contributions on tax deductions, the aggregate effect of a fully compensated switch to career average on net compensation summed across all members is unclear.[11] Since, in absolute terms, the degree of progression in income tax is greater than the regression in NIC, it is likely that the net effect of a switch to career average is an overall reduction in members' net compensation, and an increase in NIC and income tax payments to the government.

At the other extreme, if the switch to career average does not result in any compensating change in gross salary, there is no change in net salary, pension contributions, NIC or income tax for any member, again ignoring any subsequent tax effects flowing from the change in pension accrual.

8.8.2   Model of the Redistributive Effects of a Switch to Career Average

On the basis of her stochastic simulations of various types of pension scheme, Cooper (2005) concludes that the redistribution effect of moving from a final salary scheme to a career average scheme is overstated due to simplistic salary growth assumptions. She argues that most employees cannot manipulate their pay or career to maximize their advantage.

To explore this issue further, a basic model is developed to examine the redistributive effects of a cost neutral switch from final salary to career average. Assume for simplicity that there are no benefits other than members' pensions, there is no risk, deferred pensioners have their final salary uprated by RPI, the career average salary for active and deferred pensioners is uprated

---

Since the members' pension contribution rate is usually much less than 100%, the drop in gross salary is much larger than the drop in tax deductions; and the overall effect is a reduction in their income tax.

[11] It is assumed that the aggregate change in pension contributions is zero, which is consistent with a cost neutral switch.

by the revaluation rate (RPI) and pensions can only be brought into payment at the NRA. In which case the annual real pension for a member of a career average scheme is

$$A_{CA} = Sx_{CA} \sum_{i=0}^{n-1} (1 + w)^i (1 + d)^{m-i-1} \qquad (8.1)$$

where S is the salary for the first year of service (e.g., 25-year-olds), x_{CA} is the career average accrual rate (e.g., 0.01666 or 60ths), w is the annual real rate of increase in wages, d is the revaluation rate per year, n is the number of years until the NRA, where years of service run from 1 to n.

For a member of a final salary scheme, the annual real pension is

$$A_{FS} = Sx_{FS} n (1 + w)^{n-1} (1 + RPI)^{n-1} \qquad (8.2)$$

where x_{FS} is the final salary accrual rate. The value of the fixed-term annuity for the jth type of scheme (final salary or career average) of A_j per year for m years at the NRA are given by

$$PV_j = A_j \left(\frac{1}{r} - \frac{1}{r(1 + r)^m} \right) \qquad (8.3)$$

where r is the real discount rate, and m is the number of years in retirement.[12] The value of the contributions relating to a member at the time the pension starts being paid (TV_j) for the jth type of scheme (final salary or career average) is

$$TV_j = SCR_j \sum_{i=0}^{n-1} (1 + w)^i (1 + v)^{n-i-1} \qquad (8.4)$$

where CR_j is the total contribution rate for the jth type of scheme (final salary or career average) and is the same fixed proportion of salary for all members of the scheme, and v is the annual real rate of return on the invested contributions.

The required contribution rate for the final salary scheme is that value of CR_{FS} which equates the aggregate values of TV_{FS} and PV_{FS} (the value of final salary contributions at the NRA equals the present value of the final salary pension at the NRA) across all scheme members. The equivalent cost-neutral career average scheme requires that the aggregate cost of the career

---

[12] For simplicity an annuity certain, rather than a life annuity, is assumed.

average scheme be the same as the aggregate cost of the final salary scheme. This is achieved by setting the career average accrual rate (x_{CA}) so that, in aggregate, $A_{FS} = A_{CA}$, which implies that, in aggregate, $PV_{FS} = PV_{CA}$, and $TV_{FS} = TV_{CA}$.

8.8.3 Numerical Example of the Redistributive Effects of a Switch to Career Average

Some representative numbers are used in the simple model presented above to give an idea of the possible magnitude of the redistributive effects of a switch from final salary to career average. Consider a company that operates a final salary pension scheme with an accrual rate of 60ths and full price indexation. The company employs two types of full-time worker (L and H), both of whom can start work at 25 or later, retire at 65, and live for 20 years after retirement.[13] All workers join the pension scheme. The number of type L members is four times larger than the number of type H members, and each type of member starts with an annual salary of £20,000 at the age of 25. Type L members experience no real pay rise throughout their career, while type H members receive a 3.5% real pay rise every year, retiring at 65 on a real salary of £76,507 (i.e., 3.8 times larger than for type L members). The company operates an age-for-wage policy, and so late joiners start on a salary corresponding to their age. The real interest rate is assumed to be 1% per year, and the real rate of return on the fund's assets is assumed to be 3%.

Final Salary. If every member joins the final salary scheme at 25 and retires at 65, the resulting payments to, and contributions for, each member are set out in Table 8.3; along with the contribution and accrual rates. For type L members a contribution of £1,000 today generates a real pension of £94.18 per year at the NRA; while for type H members it generates a real pension of £178.24: that is, 89% more for type H members. This shows that the use of a final salary pension scheme amplifies the inequality in salaries. The lifetime salary (and pension contributions) of type H members are twice those of type L members. However, the annual pension of type H members is almost four times larger than that of type L members.

If the type L and H members had been in separate final salary schemes, with each scheme delivering the same pension as under the combined scheme, the resulting contribution rates and pension contributions are shown in Table 8.4. This reveals greater equality in the relationship between contributions and pensions, with type H members now getting slightly worse value

---

[13] The inequality that type H members will very probably draw their pensions for a longer period than type L members is ignored.

TABLE 8.3 Final Salary Scheme Combining Type L and H Members, 40 Years Accrued

	L	H	Ratio
Total contribution rates	21.3%	21.3%	1
Accrual rate	60ths	60ths	1
Present value of lifetime pensionable salary	£663,261	£1,340,673	2.02
Present value of lifetime pension contributions	£141,573	£286,167	2.02
Annual real pension	£13,333	£51,005	3.83
Real pension at 65 for a £1,000 contribution now	£94.18	£178.24	1.89

for money than type L members. A contribution of £1,000 now buys a real pension of £125.99 per year for type L members, and £115.28 per year for type H members: that is, 9% less for type H members.

This analysis of the separate final salary schemes indicates that in the combined final salary scheme 5.3% of the type L members' contribution rate represents a cross-subsidy to type H members, with each type H member receiving a reduction of 11.7% in their contribution rate. The contributions made on behalf of each type H member have a present value of £156,293 (or £3,907 per year of service) less than would be the case in the absence of type L members. The contributions made on behalf of each type L member have a present value of £35,749 (or £894 per service year) more than would be the case if there were no type H members. This cross-subsidy from type L to type H members represents what Den Hertog (1999) called reversed solidarity. It increases the inequality in pensions, which further increases the inequality in the distribution of lifetime incomes (salary plus pension).

TABLE 8.4 Separate Final Salary Schemes for Type L and Type H Members, 40 Years Accrued

	L	H	Ratio
Total contribution rates	16.0%	33.0%	2.06
Accrual rate	60ths	60ths	1
Present value of lifetime pensionable salary	£663,261	£1,340,673	2.02
Present value of lifetime pension contributions	£105,824	£442,460	4.18
Annual real pension	£13,333	£51,005	3.83
Real pension at 65 for a £1,000 contribution now	£125.99	£115.28	0.91

TABLE 8.5 Career Average Scheme Combining Type L and H Members, 40 Years Accrued

	L	H	Ratio
Total contribution rates	21.3%	21.3%	1
Accrual rate	47ths	47ths	1
Present value of lifetime pensionable salary	£663,261	£1,340,673	2.02
Present value of lifetime pension contributions	£141,573	£286,167	2.02
Annual real pension	£17,066	£36,074	2.11
Real pension at 65 for a £1,000 contribution now	£120.55	£126.06	1.05

Career Average. A cost-neutral switch from a final salary to a career average scheme (with no compensating adjustment in wages), means that the accrual rate must rise from 1.66667% (or 60ths) to 2.1333% (or 47ths). Table 8.5 shows that a contribution of £1,000 on behalf of type L members buys a real pension of £120.55, while the corresponding figure for type H members is £126.06: that is, 5% higher. The switch to career average has almost eliminated the large pension cross-subsidy from type L to H type members that was present in the final salary scheme.

Short Service. If a type L member joins a final salary scheme at 25 and becomes a deferred pensioner after 10 years, for each £1,000 of contributions she receives a real pension at the NRA of £81.62. The corresponding number for a type H member is £95.10: that is, 17% more for type H members. These amounts (shown in Table 8.6 are markedly less than the corresponding numbers for full-service members in Table 8.3. Relative to full service, short-service type L members of a final salary scheme suffer a reduction of 13% in real pension per £1,000 of contributions, while for type H members there is a reduction of 47%. This indicates that, while both types

TABLE 8.6 Combined Final Salary Scheme for Type L and H Members, 10 Years Accrued

	L	H	Ratio
Total contribution rates	21.3%	21.3%	1
Accrual rate	60ths	60ths	1
Present value of lifetime pensionable salary	£191,320	£223,813	1.17
Present value of lifetime pension contributions	£40,837	£47,773	1.17
Annual real pension	£3,333	£4,543	1.36
Real pension at 65 for a £1,000 contribution now	£81.62	£95.10	1.17

TABLE 8.7 Career Average Scheme Combining Type L and H Members, 10 Years Accrued

	L	H	Ratio
Total contribution rates	21.3%	21.3%	1
Accrual rate	47ths	47ths	1
Present value of lifetime pensionable salary	£191,320	£223,813	1.17
Present value of lifetime pension contributions	£40,837	£47,773	1.17
Annual real pension	£4,267	£5,005	1.17
Real pension at 65 for a £1,000 contribution now	£104.49	£104.77	1

of member suffer if they leave a final salary scheme early, type H members suffer much more.

Table 8.7 shows the consequences for short-service members if their employer switches to a career average scheme. For both type L and H members the real pension per £1,000 of contributions is approximately £104.50, and the inequality between types of member has been removed. Short-service members are markedly better off from being in a career average, rather than a final salary scheme because the real pension per £1,000 of contributions for type L members has risen by 28%, and for type H members it has risen by 10%. Therefore short-service members, both type L and type H, are better off being in a career average scheme.

This numerical example shows that a cost neutral switch from final salary to career average produces a substantial redistribution of pensions from high flyers to low flyers. At the moment members who have a low and flat salary path subsidize those with a rapidly rising salary path, particularly those with a large pay rise near retirement. A switch to career average would be a big step in removing such cross-subsidies from the poor to the rich. It has also been demonstrated that career average substantially reduces the penalty from leaving early. Indeed, for type L members, early leavers from the career average scheme get a better deal than full-service members of the final salary scheme

8.9 CONCLUSIONS

Many employers are considering changing their pension provision, and one type of scheme that deserves serious consideration is career average revalued earnings (CARE). This paper offers an in-depth cost neutral comparison of the advantages and disadvantages of these two alternative pension scheme designs, in a UK context.

Cost neutrality can be defined with respect to the scheme, the employer, or the members. In this paper cost neutrality is measured with respect to the scheme, removing the need to quantify some hard-to-measure behavioral responses (e.g., staff turnover, the wage-pension tradeoff, training and productivity) from this problem; although these factors still remain when assessing the costs and benefits to the employer and members.

Career average has increased in popularity in recent years, and the UK government has proposed the use of career average for some very large public sector schemes. Career average retains the advantages of a defined benefit scheme, while offering a much fairer distribution of pensions between high and low flyers, and between early leavers and full-service members. It also offers an extensive range of other benefits for both the employer and members, with only a few minor disadvantages. A switch to career average involves some risks, relative to staying with a final salary scheme. Although the switch is designed to be cost neutral to the scheme, the actual outcome may generate a deficit or surplus because the forecasts of movements in salaries and the chosen revaluation rate are incorrect. In addition, the behavioral responses to the switch may be better or worse than expected.

A wide choice of revaluation rates is available for use by career average schemes, and by an appropriate choice of the revaluation rate, final salary and defined contribution schemes can be viewed as special cases of a career average scheme. In consequence, career average schemes have the flexibility to move towards either of these other types of scheme design, if desired.

Numerical examples illustrate the substantial redistribution of pension that can accompany a cost neutral switch from final salary to career average, moving the scheme much closer to "equal pension for equal work." In view of their substantial attractions, career average schemes deserve to be considered more seriously by those redesigning pension provision.

REFERENCES

Allen, S. G., and R. L. Clark. 1987. Pensions and firm performance. In *Human Resources and the Performance of the Firm*, ed. M. M. Kleiner, R. N. Block, M. Roomkin, and S. W. Salsburg. Industrial Relations Research Association, 195–242.

Allen, S. G., R. L. Clark, and A. A. McDermed. 1993. Pensions, bonding and lifetime jobs. *Journal of Human Resources* 28, no. 3 (Summer):463–481.

Amicus. 2005. NHS pension scheme review consultation: Response from Amicus, Amicus, London.

Blome, S., K. Fachinger, D. Franzen, G. Scheuenstuhl, and J. Yermo. 2007. Pension fund regulations and risk management: Results from an ALM Optimization Exercise. OECD.

BMA. 2006. Proposed changes to the NHS pension scheme (UKWide). British Medical Association (March).

Bulow, J., and W. Landsman. 1985. The relationship between wages and benefits. In *Pensions, Labor and Individual Choice*, ed. D.A. Wise, 379–397. Chicago: University of Chicago Press.

Cabinet Office. 2004. Building a sustainable future: Proposals for changes to the civil service pension scheme. Civil Service Pensions (December). www.civilservice-pensions.gov.uk/consultation

Clark, R. L., and A. A. McDermed. 1986. Earnings and pension compensation: The effect of eligibility, *Quarterly Journal of Economics* 101, no. 2 (May) 341–361.

Cocco, J. F., and P. Lopes. 2004. Defined benefit or defined contribution? An empirical study of pensions choices. FMG Discussion Papers. UBS Pension Series, DP 505 (July).

Cooper, D. R. 1997. Providing Pensions for UK Employees with Varied Working Lives, Journal of Actuarial Practice 5, no. 1:547.

———. 1998. A reappraisal of the revalued career average benefit design for occupational pension schemes. *Journal of Pensions Management* 4, no. 2:123–132.

———. 1999. Occupational pensions for all employees. *Employee Relations*. 21, no. 2 (May):145–158.

———. 2003. Career average pension schemes. Mercer Human Resources, Technical Information Sheet TIS 27/2003 (October 13).

———. 2005. Comparing pension outcomes from hybrid schemes, Department of Work and Pensions. Research Report 269.

Cornwell, C., S. Dorsey, and N. Mehrzad. 1991. Opportunistic behaviour by firms in implicit pension contracts. *Journal of Human Resources* 26, no. 4 (Autumn):704–725.

CCSU. 2005. CCSU Response to building a sustainable future. Council of Civil Service Unions.

DCLG. 2006. Where next? Options for a new look local government pension scheme in England and Wales. Department for Communities and Local Government (June).

Den Hertog, J. 1999. Reversed solidarity in pension plans. *European Journal of Law and Economics* 7, no. 3 (May):241–260.

Disney, R. 1995. Occupational pension schemes: Prospects and reforms in the UK. *Fiscal Studies* 16, no. 3 (August):19–39.

Dorsey, S., C. M. Cornwell, and D. A. MacPherson. 1998. Pensions and Productivity. W.E. Upjohn Institute, Michigan.

Ehrenberg, R. G. 1980. Retirement system characteristics and compensating wage differentials in the public sector. *Industrial and Labour Relations Review* 33, no. 4 (July):470–483.

Ehrenberg, R. G., and R. S. Smith. 1981. A framework for evaluating state and local government pension reform. In *Public Sector Labour Markets*, ed. P. Mieszkowski and G. E. Peterson, 103–128. Washington, D.C. The Urban Institute Press.

Even, W. E., and D. A. MacPherson. 1990. The gender gap in pensions and wages. *Review of Economics and Statistics* 72, no. 2 (May):259–265.

Farr, I. A. 2007. A new breed of shared risk schemes to re-energise the provision of employer sponsored occupational pension schemes in the UK. London. Association of Consulting Actuaries (March).

FDA. 2005. Building a sustainable future proposals for changes to the civil service pension scheme: Analysis of pension questionnaires returned by FDA members. London. First Division Association.

Freeman, R. B. 1985. Unions, pensions and union pension funds. In *Pensions, Labor and Individual Choice*, ed. D. A. Wise, 89–121. Chicago: University of Chicago Press.

Gerakos, J. 2008. Chief executive officers and the pay-pension tradeoff. Working Paper, Graduate School of Business, University of Chicago (July).

Gunderson, M., D. Hyatt, and J. E. Pesando. 1992. Wage-pension trade-offs in collective agreements. *Industrial and Labour Relations Review* 46, no. 1 (October):146–160.

Gustman, A. L., and T. L. Steinmeier. 1995. Pension incentives and job mobility. Kalamazoo, MI: W. E. Upjohn Institute for Employment Research.

Hèri, N., R. Koijen, and T. E. Nijman. 2006. The determinants of the money's worth of participation in collective pension schemes. Working Paper, Tilburg University, (November).

Inkmann, J. 2006. Compensating wage differentials for defined benefit and defined contribution occupational pension scheme benefits. Working Paper, Department of Finance, Tilburg University.

Ippolito, R. A. 1985. The labour contract and true economic pension liabilities. *American Economic Review* 75, no. 5 (December):1031–1043.

———. 1991. Encouraging long-term tenure: Wage tilt or pensions? *Industrial and Labour Relations Review* 44, no. 3 (April):520–535.

———. 1997. *Pension Plans and Employee Performance: Evidence, Analysis and Policy*. Chicago: University of Chicago Press.

Lazear, E. P. 1979. Why is there mandatory retirement? *Journal of Political Economy* 87, no. 6 (December):1261–1284.

———. 1981. Agency, earnings profiles, productivity and hours restrictions. *American Economic Review* 71, no. 4 (September):606–620.

Levy, S. 2008. Occupational pension schemes annual report, No. 15, 2007 ed. London: Office for National Statistics.

McCarthy, D. 2005. The optimal allocation of pension risks in employment contracts. Department of Work and Pensions, Research Report 272.

McGill, D. M., K. N. Brown, J. J. Haley, and S. J. Schieber. 1996. *Fundamentals of Private Pensions*, 7th ed. Philadelphia: University of Pennsylvania Press, chapter 5.

Montgomery, E., and K. Shaw. 1997. Pensions and Wage Premia, *Economic Inquiry* 35, no. 3 (July):510–521.

Montgomery, E., K. Shaw, and M. E. Benedict. 1992. Pensions and wages: An hedonic price theory approach. *International Economic Review* 33, no. 1 (February):111–128.

Moore, R. L. 1987. Are male-female earnings differentials related to life-expectancy-caused pension cost differences? *Economic Inquiry* 25, no. 3, (July):389–401.

NHS Employers. 2005. The NHS pension scheme review consultation. Technical Document. NHS Employers (January).

———. 2006a. Moving to a 21st century pension scheme: A factual report on the results of the NHS pension scheme review consultation. NHS Employers.

———. 2006b. Joint Proposals from NHS Employers and the NHS trade unions. NHS Employers.

Ponds, E. H. M., and B. Van Riel. 2007. The recent evolution of pension funds in the Netherlands: The Trend to hybrid DBDC plans and beyond. Working Paper, Centre for Retirement Research. Boston College (February).

PPF and TPR. 2006. *The Purple Book*, Pension Protection Fund and The Pensions Regulator, Croydon and London.

RCN. 2005. NHS pension review members lobbying brief. Royal College of Nursing (May).

Schiller, B. R., and R. D. Weiss. 1980. Pensions and wages: A test for equalizing differences. *Review of Economics and Statistics* 62, no. 4 (November):529–538.

Smith, R. S. 1981. Compensating differentials for pensions and underfunding in the public sector. *Review of Economics and Statistics* 63, no. 3 (August):463–468.

Smith, R. S., and R. G. Ehrenberg. 1983. Estimating wage-fringe trade-offs: Some data problems. In *The Measurement of Labor Cost*, ed. J. E. Triplett, 347–369, Chicago: University of Chicago Press.

Sutcliffe, C. M. S. 2005.The cult of the equity for pension funds: Should it get the boot? *Journal of Pension Economics and Finance* 4, no. 1 (March):57–85.

Swinkels, L. 2006. Have pension plans changed after the introduction of IFRS? Working Paper, Erasmus University Rotterdam, Department of Finance.

Thornton, P. N. 1986. Some thoughts on pension scheme design. Presented to the Institute of Actuaries Students' Society (November 18th).

Tsang, D. 2007. Career average revalued earnings and other alternatives to final salary. In *Pension Scheme Deficits*, ed. S. Hull, 45–53. London: Globe Law & Business.

Unison. 2006a. Options for a new-look local government pension scheme in England and Wales. Unison's Response. Unison (October).

———. 2006b. Options for a new-look local government pension scheme (LGPS) in England and Wales: LGA/LGE. Response to the DCLG Consultation Paper. Unison (October).

Watson-Wyatt. 2005. The changing nature of defined benefit plans. *Insider* (February).

Wesbroom, K., and T. Reay. 2005. Hybrid Pension Plans: UK and international experience. Department of Work and Pensions. Research Report 271.

Wilkie, A. D. 1985. Some experiments with pensions accrual. *Journal of the Institute of Actuaries* 112:205–219.

CHAPTER 9

Applying Stochastic Programming to the US Defined Benefit Pension System

John M. Mulvey
Bendheim Center for Finance, Princeton University

Zhuojuan Zhang
BlackRock, Inc.

Abstract: *The defined benefit (DB) pension system in the US may not survive as a viable option for paying retirement benefits absent changes in the current regulations. We present a multi-stage stochastic programming model for assisting the US DB pension system. The model integrates an industry with its pension system, since their financial status may have considerable impact on each other. The stochastic program conducts a full global optimization of corporate and pension plan decisions. We show that there is a great deal of concentration in the DB problem areas. Industries potentially in danger in the S&P 500 are identified by employing Monte Carlo simulation in a forward-looking analysis. Stochastic programming is then combined with the policy simulations to refine rules for industries in trouble.*

Index terms: *defined benefit pension plan, Monte Carlo simulation, stochastic programming.*

The research in this paper is based in part of the project "Analysis of DB Pension Funding and Investment Decisions" jointly supported by the US Department of Labor, Employee Benefits Security Administration, Office of Policy and Research and Simulation Group. The work was also supported by National Science Foundation under Grant Number DMI-0323410.

9.1 INTRODUCTION

The defined benefit (DB) pension system in the US is in serious financial distress. For companies in the S&P 500, the aggregate deficit of their pension plans is estimated to be over $400 billion in 2009. Meanwhile, as the result of the terminations of a number of large DB pension plans in recent years, the net position of the Pension Benefit Guaranty Corporation (PBGC) has declined to over $50 billion in early 2009.

The roots of the pension crisis stem from a number of factors. Besides the poor performance of the equity markets relating to the 2000 to 2003 and 2008 to 2009 recessions and the commensurate decrease in interest rates, an important cause is the serious structural defects in current regulations of the defined benefit pension system. See Department of Labor (2005) for a detailed discussion of the structural problems in the DB system and the proposal for change.

Within S&P 500 companies, we define a number of sponsor classes that characterize variation in the financial situation of sponsoring companies and variation in the economic condition of sponsored plans. There is a great deal of concentration in the DB problem areas. Some industries are more able to weather their current deficits. For instance, the health care industry has a small deficit and substantial assets to support future contributions. Such industries are considered "secure." In contrast, other industries are deeply in the red. For example, our analysis shows that the auto industry faces severe difficulties and may become insolvent in future due to its heavy pension underfunding burden. For such industries it is an extremely tough task to try to find sound policy rules that will be effective enough to save the industry and its pension system. For these industries we will have to be prepared for the worst and hope for the best. Such industries are put on the watch list. There are also a number of industries that are on the border line. Either they are facing great challenges to reduce the pension deficits, or they may have potential financial difficulty in the future. Poor regulations and policy decisions could result in unfortunate outcomes of these industries; however, careful corporate planning and sound policy rules may be able to restore the industries to financial health. We call these industries and their DB systems "potentially in danger." Industries falling in different categories need to be regulated separately. For example, we may apply reasonable restrictions on new benefit promises for industries on the watch list. Moreover, the policy rules should be tailored to the characteristics of different industries. The optimal policy rule for one industry might not work well for another industry. Figure 9.1 illustrates the idea of classifying the defined benefit system.

We present a multi stage stochastic programming model for assisting the DB system. The stochastic program framework appeals on several fronts.

FIGURE 9.1 Concentration
in the DB Problem Areas

The integrated corporate/pension planning model can be readily posed as a stochastic program. The objective function can take a wide variety of forms. Stochastic programs can address realistic considerations such as transaction costs and borrowing. A grand optimization can be carried out without cluttering with too many details.

However, it is unrealistic and unnecessary to solve the stochastic program for each individual industry due to the expensive computational cost of solving a very large-scale stochastic program. Therefore we first identify the industries potentially in danger by employing simulations to project a range of outcomes using a wide range of assumptions for each industry.

Next, for those industries that are (potentially) in danger, we design a multi stage stochastic program for optimizing the joint entity of the industry and its DB system. In particular, the stochastic program can be used to discover sound policy rules that could help those industries. We propose that a policy rule is close to optimal if the policy solution lies near that of the stochastic program in terms of the objective function values. As an example, we compare two investment strategies for telecommunication services. We show that one successfully reduces the amount of large contributions needed as compared with the other.

9.2   INTEGRATED CORPORATE/PENSION PLANNING MODEL

We build a planning model to link the industry with its DB system. This is a variant of the corporate/pension planning model in Mulvey et al. (2008). The financial status of the DB system could have considerable impact on the financial health of an industry, and vice versa. This linkage is especially useful for aiding the regulations. When they propose a change in the regulation trying to strength the DB system, it is also important to see how it will affect the financial condition of the sponsoring industry. Our integrated model serves as a perfect framework for this purpose.

9.2.1 Multiperiod Stochastic Programming Model

The basic model is a variant of Mulvey et al. (2008). However, instead of modeling a single pension trust, we model the defined benefit pension system of an industry as a whole. Companies within the same industry are assumed to have similar characteristics such as volatility and the correlation with the market.

The target planning period is $T = 0, 1, \ldots, \tau, \tau + 1$. We focus on the pension plans' position and the value of the industry at the beginning of the planning horizon $\tau + 1$. Investment, funding, and borrowing decisions occur at the last instant of each time period.

Asset investment categories are defined by the set $A = 1, 2, \ldots, I$. Asset category 1 represents cash, and the remaining assets can include broad investment groupings such as stock subindexes, foreign equity, long-term government or corporate bonds, and alternative investments. The categories should track well-defined market segments. To diversify across the asset categories, ideally the co-movements between pairs of asset returns would be relatively low (Kim and Mulvey 2009).

As with single-period models, uncertainty is depicted by a set of distinct scenarios, $s \in S$. Scenarios may reveal identical values for the uncertain quantities up to a certain period $t \in T$: that is, they share common information history up to this time period. This information structure is represented through nonanticipativity conditions. These constraints require that any variables sharing a common history up to time period t must be set equal to each other.

We rebalance the investment portfolio at the end of each period. For each $i \in A, t \in T$, and $s \in S$, we define the following parameters and decision variables.

Parameters

$r_{i,t}^s = 1 + p_{i,t}^s$ where $p_{i,t}^s$ is return of asset i, period t, scenario s (e.g., Mulvey, et al. (2000))

$g_t^s = 1 + \gamma_t^s$, where γ_t^s is the percentage growth rate of the industry in period t, under scenario s

b_t^s Payments to beneficiaries in period t, under scenario s

π^s Probability that scenario s occurs: $\sum_{s \in S} \pi^s = 1$

$v_{i,0}^s$ Amount allocated to asset class i, at the end of period 0, under scenario s, before first rebalancing

z_0 Value of the industry at the end of time period 0

$\sigma_{i,t}$ Transaction costs for rebalancing asset i, period t (symmetric transaction costs are assumed)

Decision Variables

$x_{i,t}^s$ Amount allocated to asset class i, at the beginning of period t, under scenario s, after rebalancing

$v_{i,t}^s$ Amount allocated to asset class i, at the end of period t, under scenario s, before rebalancing

$p_{i,t}^s$ Amount of asset class i purchased for rebalancing in period t, under scenario s

$d_{i,t}^s$ Amount of asset class i sold for rebalancing in period t, under scenario s

w_t^s Asset wealth (pension plan) at the beginning of time period t, under scenario s

z_t^s Value of the industry at end of period t, before a contribution is made in period t, under scenario s

y_t^s Value of the industry after a contribution is made in period t − 1, under scenario s

c_t^s Amount of cash contributions made at end of period t, under scenario s

xb_t^s Amount of borrowing for pension plan at end of period t for use in period t + 1, under scenario s

e_t^s Borrowing costs for period t, under scenario s

Given these definitions, the deterministic equivalent of the stochastic program is

$$\text{(MSP)} \qquad \text{Maximize} U\{Z_1, Z_2, \ldots, Z_k\} \tag{9.1}$$

where the goals are defined as functions of the decision variables $Z_k = f_k(x, v, y, \ldots)$.

Subject to:

$$\sum_{i \in A} x_{i,t}^s = w_t^s \qquad \forall s \in S, \ t = 1, \ldots, \tau + 1 \tag{9.2}$$

$$v_{i,t}^s = r_{i,t}^s x_{i,t}^s \qquad \forall s \in S, \ t = 1, \ldots, \tau, \ i \in A \tag{9.3}$$

$$z_t^s = g_t^s y_t^s \qquad \forall s \in S, \ t = 1, \ldots, \tau + 1 \tag{9.4}$$

$$y_t^s = z_{t-1}^s - c_{t-1}^s \qquad \forall s \in S, \ t = 1, \ldots, \tau + 1 \tag{9.5}$$

$$x_{i,t}^s = v_{i,t-s}^s + p_{i,t-1}^s(1 - \sigma_{i,t-1}) - d_{i,t-s}^s$$

$$\forall s \in S, \quad t = 1, \ldots, t+1, \, i \neq 1, \tau+1 \tag{9.6}$$

$$x_{i,t}^s = v_{i,t-1}^s + \sum_{i=2} d_{i,t-1}^s(1 - \sigma_{i,t-1}) - \sum_{i=2} p_{i,t-1}^s - b_{t-1}^s + c_{t-1}^s$$

$$+xb_{t-1}^s - e_{t-1}^s(xb_{t-2}^s)\forall s \in S, \quad t = 1, \ldots, \tau+1 \tag{9.7}$$

$$x_{i,t}^s = x_{i,t}^{s'}, \quad c_t^s = c_t^{s'}, \quad xb_t^s = xb_t^{s'} \qquad \forall s \text{ and } s'$$

with identical past up to time t $\hfill$ (9.8)

$$Risk\{Z_1, Z_2, \ldots, Z_k\} \leq Risk_{max} \tag{9.9}$$

Constraints (9.2) and (9.3) depict pension wealth accumulation. Constraints (9.4) and (9.5) represent the industry growth and pension funding. Flow balance constraints for each asset categories are given by (9.6) and (9.7). Non anticipativity constraints are represented by (9.8). The risk-based constraints appear in (9.9) and are further discussed in the next section.

Model (MSP) depicts a split variable formulation of the stochastic program. Techniques such as the DQA algorithm by Mulvey and Ruszczynski (1995) have successfully solved the model by taking advantage of this structure. The split variable formulation can be beneficial for direct solvers that use the interior point method.

9.2.2 Alternative Goals

The integrated approach allows for a variety of goals that depict alternative views on the state of the industries and their pension trusts as they evolve over the planning horizon. This approach maximizes the market value of the industry, while putting its pension system on a sound basis.

The utility function (1) depicts a generic multiobjective optimization problem. The goal is to find the best compromise among the competing objectives.

Due to the complexity of integrating an industry with its defined benefit pension system, we propose a set of goals that measures the financial condition of the industry with reference to its defined benefit pension system: (1) the expected industry market value at the end of the horizon; (2) the expected surplus at the end of the horizon; (3) the expected NPV of contributions; (4) the expected sum of (squared) excess contributions; (5) the downside risk for final funded ratio; (6) the probability of insolvency over the planning horizon; and (7) the volatility of future contributions. The measures addressing other interests of different stakeholders can also be added to the model. Setting the priorities of the multiobjectives for the integrated system presents a complex and potentially controversial issue and provides a direction for future research.

9.3   ASSISTING THE DEFINED BENEFIT PENSION SYSTEM

We first analyze all industries in the S&P 500 through forward-looking simulations, locating industries with (potential) financial problems. Stochastic programming is then used to refine rules for industries in trouble.

9.3.1   Industry Projections

Based on the integrated pension/corporate planning framework, we run many simulations under a wide range of assumptions to show the range of plausible outcomes over the 15 years, rather than forecast a single time series. As a preliminary step, we group the S&P 500 companies into 10 industries according to Global Industry Classification Standard (GICS).

Table 9.1 describes the state of the DB system of the S&P 500 companies (as of 2004). In the S&P 500 342 companies have defined benefit pension plans. Among them, 299 were underfunded, and more than one-third of them were severely underfunded (funded ratio < 70%). Pension assets equal $1,004 billion. The ratio of the total industry market capitalization to pension assets is 7.5. This ratio shows that the performance of the DB pension system will bring a sizable impact on the financial health of the whole S&P 500 industry. The system had an aggregate deficit equal to $210 billion. This deficit seems modest as compared with the total industry market value.

If we examine the data industry by industry, we can see that the range of financial conditions is highly variable. The financials sector had a relatively high funding ratio of 93% and also a high ratio of market capitalization to pension assets, 20.7. Of course, the financial sector market capitalization has dropped dramatically during the 2008 to 2009 crash. Consumer staples, energy, and health care had low funding ratios, but their pension plan sizes were small relative to their industry sizes.

Other industries looked less optimistic. Table 9.2 displays the conditions of industries that had potential financial problems. Consumer discretionary seemed the worst, not only because it had a low funding ratio, but also because the size of its pension assets was more than one-third of its industry market value. Looking closer at the companies in the consumer discretionary sector, we can see that the market value for auto companies was only one-third of that of the sector, while both the pension assets and obligations accounted for more than three-fourths of those of the sector. The auto

TABLE 9.1 Status of DB Pensions in S&P 500 Index (2004)

Funding Ratio	Number	Pension Assets (Bil $)	Obligation (Bil $)	Surplus Value (Bil $)	Index Capital Value (Bil $)	Ratio of Index Market Cap to Pension Assets
Total	342	1004.29	1213.80	-209.52	7534.03	7.50
<=1	299	875.34	1102.52	-227.18	6480.23	7.40
1<	43	128.94	111.28	17.67	1053.80	8.17
<=0.7	102	118.91	202.84	-83.93	1828.2	15.37
0.7<<=0.9	151	497.29	625.49	-128.20	3137.93	6.31
0.9<<=1	46	259.14	274.19	-15.06	1514.10	5.84
1<<=1.2	32	71.59	66.34	5.25	643.30	8.99
1.2<	11	57.36	44.94	12.42	410.50	7.16

TABLE 9.2 Status of Industries with Potential Problems (2004)

	Consumer Overall	Discretionary Auto	Industrials w/o GE	Telecom Services
Funding Ratio	73%	72%	82%	95%
Pension Assets (Bil $)	164.6	125.6	205.2	80.6
Obligation (Bil $)	225.0	174.8	250.7	84.5
Surplus Wealth (Bil $)	−60.5	−49.2	−44.6	−3.9
Industry Capital Value (Bil $)	473.4	93.3	715.0	283.3
Ratio of Industry Market Cap to Pension Assets	2.9	0.74	3.5	3.5

industry had a low funding ratio of 72%. The ratio of industry market value to the pension assets was only 0.74. Later we will see that our forward-looking simulations confirmed that the auto industry was in great trouble. And indeed this projection turned out to be correct over the period from 2008 to 2009.

Examining the data for industrials, we find that General Electric stood out as an outlier with a relatively higher funded ratio and more than 30% of the entire sector's market value. When we eliminated GE from industrials, the remaining 48 companies had an aggregate deficit of $45.6 billion, with a market capitalization of $715 billion. Also, pension assets were a substantial percentage of the total market capitalization for this group of companies ($205 billion of $715 billion).

Most companies in the 2004 DB system looked secure with modest deficits relative to market value, but several industries face severe difficulties. We observe a great deal of concentration in the DB problem areas. We project the status of the pension system and plausible values of the sponsoring industries over the 15-year planning horizon from 2005 to 2019. A set of 5,000 scenarios formed the basis for the projections.

Figure 9.2 and 9.3 display two important objectives of the preliminary results for the DB pensions in the S&P 500 over the period from 2005 to 2019.

Firstly, the seven-year amortization rule of the 2005 proposal significantly reduced the amount and volatility of contributions and the chance of making large contributions when compared with a linear contribution rule; see Table 9.3. The top two industries that will need substantial future contributions were consumer discretionary and industrials without GE. Although telecommunication services had a relatively healthy funding ratio in 2004 (95%), it had the highest probability of requiring a large contribution (more than 30% of market capitalization), −5.5% on average and 10%

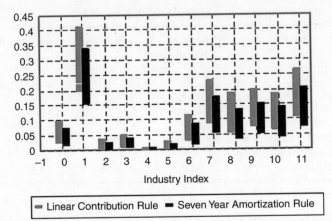

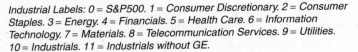

Industrial Labels: 0 = S&P500. 1 = Consumer Discretionary. 2 = Consumer Staples. 3 = Energy. 4 = Financials. 5 = Health Care. 6 = Information Technology. 7 = Materials. 8 = Telecommunication Services. 9 = Utilities. 10 = Industrials. 11 = Industrials without GE.

FIGURE 9.2 The Ratio of Expected NPV of Contributions to Initial Industry Market value

for the worst case even when using the seven-year amortization rule. This was caused primarily by the projected slow growth of the industry relative to other industries and the relatively low ratio of industry market value to pension assets.

The problems of the consumer discretionary sector are concentrated in the auto companies. The simulation results show that the probability

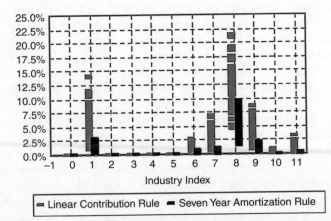

FIGURE 9.3 Probability of Any Excessive Contribution

TABLE 9.3 Forward Simulation Assumptions

Primary Objective	Maintain the funding level to 90% at the end of horizon.
Asset Classes	S&P 500 – EAFE – Treasury Bonds – Cash
Borrowing Funds	5% of the initial industry market value in the first period.
Borrowing Rate	Cash return + 3%
Plan Liabilities	Each year, project a 25-year benefit payment cash flow with the following:
Benefit	(1) Drug pattern (steadily increasing)
Payment	(2) Auto pattern (first increases slowly and then declines)
Patterns	(3)–(5) Linear patterns with growth rate 2.5%, 4.5%, 6.5%
Discount Rates	Long government bond rates
Contribution Rules	(1) Linear Rule: if initial funded ratio < target ratio, use linear contribution rule; otherwise, increase to the target.
	(2) Seven-year amortization rule (Amortization payments are discounted using the AA corporate bond yield curve)

of insolvency ranges from 49% to 91% when using the linear contribution rule (we define insolvency as the company has to make a contribution larger than its market value). Given that insolvency occurs, the conditional expected insolvency time ranges from 10 to 12 years. The new seven-year amortization rule helps to save the auto industry only to certain degree: it delays occurrence of insolvency slightly and reduces the expected probability

TABLE 9.4 Industries in S&P 500

	12/30/1994 to 04/30/2004			Expected Return Used in the Simulation
Index	Expected Return	Volatility	Correlation with S&P 500	
S&P 500 Composite	12.30%	20.80%	100.00%	9.01%
Energy	11.97%	16.48%	80.06%	8.77%
Materials	6.98%	16.31%	48.40%	5.12%
Industrials	12.03%	19.22%	90.46%	8.82%
Consumer Discretionary	12.57%	20.41%	88.45%	9.21%
Consumer Staples	11.53%	17.46%	49.72%	8.45%
Health Care	16.83%	21.90%	76.92%	12.33%
Financials	18.09%	22.17%	81.03%	13.25%
Info Technology	20.27%	43.18%	87.22%	14.85%
Telecom Services	7.08%	31.86%	84.42%	5.19%
Utilities	7.52%	22.66%	59.50%	5.51%

Note: These numbers are adjusted to fit the S&P 500 scenario data.

TABLE 9.5 Projections of Insolvency for the Auto Industry

		Contribution Rule	
		Linear	7-Year Amortization
Probability	Max	91.3%	82.0%
of insolvency	Mean	74.9%	61.2%
	Min	49.1%	34.5%
Expected insolvency	Max	12.0	12.4
year given that	Mean	11.0	11.7
insolvency occurs	Min	9.9	10.9

of insolvency by 13.7%; however, the probability of insolvency is still high, 61% on average. Auto is in great danger and should be listed on the watch list (Table 9.5).

9.3.2 Applying Stochastic Programs to Industries in Trouble

Having identified industries that were potentially in trouble, next we implemented the stochastic program to study the problems of each industry separately.

To save these industries, an urgent question is whether we could discover sound policy rules that could enhance the performance of their integrated corporate/pension systems. By comparing the simulation results of industry projections under two different funding rules (linear vs. seven-year amortization) in last section, we have already seen that employing different policy rules might result in significantly different effects. Industries with differing characteristics generally behave differently with respect to changing policy rules. Therefore policy rules need to be tailored to the type of pension trust, its degree of under/overfunding, and the characteristics of the corporate sponsor.

Stochastic programming conducts a full global optimization without the clutter of many details. More importantly, it provides a benchmark for the comparison of policy rules. If the solution of a policy rule is closer to that of the stochastic program in terms of the objective function values, we propose that the rule is closer to optimal as compared with other rules.

As an example, we evaluated alternative investment strategies for telecommunication services. To pinpoint the problem facing the industry,

TABLE 9.6   Value of Selected Goals of the Stochastic Programs

	Objective Functions (in Bil $, unless stated otherwise)			
	Expected Final Company Value	Expected Squared Excessive Contribution	Expected Final Plan Surplus	Present Value of Contributions
Min Risk	327.55	0	47.27	65.19
Compromise	387.43	0.03	−8.82	27.60
Max Industry Value	388.21	4.74	−10.72	26.59

we aimed to discover investment rules that will lower the risk of large contribution, without worsening other objectives.

We chose a nine-year planning horizon and divided it into three 3-year intervals, with a fourth decision stage at the beginning of year 10. At that point, a hard constraint forces the industry to make a contribution if the funding ratio was lower than 90%. The primary objective was to maximize expected final industry value while preventing the final funding ratio from falling below 90%. The competing objective was to minimize the risk as measured by the expected squared excessive contribution (more than 30% of the industry market capital). We assumed a linear liability pattern with a growth rate of 6.5%. We employed a scenario tree consisting 5,000 scenarios of future paths.

We employed the CAP:Link system for generating future asset returns over the planning horizon (Mulvey et al. 2000). The scenario generator consisted of a set of stochastic differential equations for the principal economic variables, including inflation, interest rates, equity returns, currencies, etc.

The results of solving the stochastic program for telecommunication services appear in Tables 9.5, 9.6, and 9.7. The model consisted of roughly 68,000 variables and 81,000 constraints. It took approximately 14 minutes to solve the program with the quadratic version of the CPLEX solver.

To see the impact of switching strategies on the telecommunication services industry, we compared two investment rules. Strategy I is the conventional 70-30 equity-to-bond fixed mix strategy. Strategy II differs from the first strategy in that it converts to a more conservative strategy when both the pension system and the industry face severe difficulty. Otherwise, if either the pension system stays healthy or the industry is strong enough to support the pension system, we stick to the traditional 70-30 rule. Table 9.8 describes the two investment strategies. Since telecommunication services starts with a reasonable funding ratio of 95%, we followed the

TABLE 9.7   Selected Statistics on Modeling Results

		Characteristics of the Solutions (Bil $)			
		Beginning of Year			
	Expectation of	1	4	7	10
Minimum Risk	Contribution	0.06	60.58	14.36	11.22
	After the Contribution Is Made:				
	Surplus Wealth	−4.23	−13.55	50.75	47.27
	Wealth of the Pension Plan	80.31	102.73	182.99	208.12
	Funding Ratio	95%	88%	138%	130%
	Industry Market Value	283.24	276.25	297.88	327.55
Compromise	Contribution	9.77	0.99	3.12	27.47
	After the Contribution Is Made:				
	Surplus Wealth	−4.23	1.37	−0.09	−8.82
	Wealth of the Pension Plan	80.30	117.65	132.14	152.03
	Funding Ratio	95%	101%	100%	95%
	Industry Market Value	273.53	324.44	363.83	387.43
Maximum Industry Val.	Contribution	6.87	2.06	1.79	30.98
	After the Contribution Is Made:				
	Surplus Wealth	−4.23	−2.42	−3.52	−10.72
	Wealth of the Pension Plan	80.31	113.86	128.71	150.13
	Funding Ratio	95%	98%	97%	93.5%
	Industry Market Value	276.44	326.84	367.78	388.21

TABLE 9.8   Description of Investment Strategies I and II

	Equity Allocation Investment Strategy		
	I	II	
Funding Ratio		If the ratio of Industry Market Cap to Pension Assets < 5 and Funding Ratio < 90%	Otherwise
≤ 70%	70%	20%	70%
70%–90%	70%	30%	70%
≥ 90%	70%	70%	70%

TABLE 9.9 Value of Selected Goals for Investment Strategies I and II

	Objective Functions (in Bil $, unless stated otherwise)			
Investment Strategy	Expected Final Company Value	Expected Squared Excessive Contribution	Expected Final Plan Surplus	Present Value of Contributions
I	347.35	6.61	−7.57	24.57
II	347.08	4.68	−8.81	24.71

simple contribution strategy that makes a contribution to bring the funding ratio back to 90% whenever the ratio falls below this threshold.

The objective function values for telecommunication services employing policy simulation under the two investment strategies are shown in Table 9.9. On average, we switch to the conservative strategy 29.4% of the time under Strategy II. The results of the simulations are less satisfying than that of the MSP model. This is because the policy rules were not able to take full advantage of the scenario structure. Secondly, the goals under Strategy II were closer to the target set by the MSP model. In particular, switching investment strategies under the adverse conditions helped to reduce the amount of excessive contributions.

9.4   CONCLUSIONS

This paper presents a risk-based and anticipatory approach for linking the defined benefit pension system with the sponsoring industries. We have shown that the difficulties in 2004 were concentrated in a few industries. And a similar situation occurred in early 2009. Employing a stylized stochastic program in conjunction with policy simulations is a promising option for exploring policy rules that would help the defined benefit system of an industry in trouble to regain its health.

Formalizing the linkage of stochastic programs and policy simulation is still an area that needs to be explored. Since simulation models appear widely in other domains of operations research, this linkage would help expand the applications of stochastic programming.

Finally, our analysis so far is on an economic basis. Economic analyses can inform decision makers of the consequence of regulatory alternatives. However, a regulatory analysis is needed when dealing with detailed regulation issues.

The recommendations of this research have proven correct over the period since the study was completed. There has been a dramatic reduction in the surplus and commensurate increase in pension deficits since the 2008 to 2009 crash. Again, many DB pension plans did not take adequate action to protect the pension's funding ratio against adverse consequences. Employing an asset-liability planning model can dramatically improve risk management and increase long-term performance.

REFERENCES

Arnott, R., and P. Bernstein. 1990. Defining and managing pension fund risk. In *Pension Fund Investment Management: A Handbook for Sponsors and their Advisors*, ed. F. J. Fabozzi, and N. Mencher. Chicago: Probus, 33–53.

Bader, L. N. 2003. Treatment of pension plans in a corporate valuation. *Fin. Analysts J.* 59 no. 3:19–24.

Birge, J. R., and F. Louveaux. 1997. *Introduction to Stochastic Programming*. New York: Springer-Verlag.

Black, F. 1995. The plan sponsor's goal. *Fin. Analysts J.* 51, no. 4:67.

Dert, C. L. 1995. Asset liability management for pension funds. Ph.D. thesis, Erasmus University, Rotterdam, Netherlands.

Kim, W. C., and J. Mulvey. 2009. Evaluating style investment: Does a fund market based along equity styles add value? *Quantitative Finance*, forthcoming.

Luenberger, D. 1998. *Investment Science*. Oxford: Oxford University Press.

Mulvey, J. M., F. J. Fabozzi, W. R. Pauling, K. D. Simsek, and Z. Zhang. 2005. Modernizing the defined-benefit pension system. *Journal of Portfolio Management* (Winter):73–82.

Mulvey, J. M., G. Gould, and C. Morgan. 2000. An asset and liability management system for Towers Perrin-Tillinghast. *Interfaces* 30, no. 1:96–114.

Mulvey, J. M., and A. Ruszczynski. 1995. A new scenario decomposition method for large-scale stochastic optimization. *Operations Research* 43, no. 3:477–490.

Mulvey, J. M., K. D. Simsek, and W. R. Pauling. 2003. A stochastic network approach for integrated pension and corporate financial planning, In *Innovations in Financial and Economic Networks*, ed. A. Nagurney. UK: Edward Elgar Publishing, 67–83.

Mulvey, J. M., K. D. Simsek, Z. Zhang, and F. Fabozzi. 2008. Assisting defined-benefit pension plans. *Operations Research* 56 (October):1066–1078.

U.S. Department of Labor. 2005. Strengthen funding for single-employer pension plans (February). http://www.dol.gov/ebsa/pdf/sepproposal2.pdf.

Ziemba, W. T., and J. M. Mulvey (eds.). 1998. *Worldwide Asset and Liability Modeling*. Cambridge: Cambridge University Press.

CHAPTER 10

Mortality-Linked Securities and Derivatives

Enrico Biffis
Imperial College Business School, London

David Blake
The Pensions Institute, Cass Business School

10.1 INTRODUCTION

In the last few years, the risk of mortality improvements has become increasingly capital intensive for pension funds and annuity providers to manage. The reason is that longevity risk has been systematically underestimated, making balance sheets vulnerable to unexpected increases in liabilities. The traditional way of transferring longevity risk is through insurance and reinsurance markets. However, these lack the capacity and liquidity to support an estimated global exposure in excess of $20 trillion (e.g., Loeys et al. 2007). Capital markets, on the other hand, could play a very important role, offering additional capacity and liquidity to the market, leading in turn to more transparent and competitive pricing of longevity risk.

Blake and Burrows (2001) were the first to advocate the use of mortality-linked securities to transfer longevity risk to the capital markets. Their proposal has generated considerable attention in the last few years, and major investment banks and reinsurers are now actively innovating in this space (see Blake et al. 2008). Nevertheless, despite growing enthusiasm, longevity risk transfers have been materializing only slowly. One of the reasons is the huge imbalance in scale between existing exposures and willing hedge suppliers. The bulk of longevity exposures is represented by the liabilities

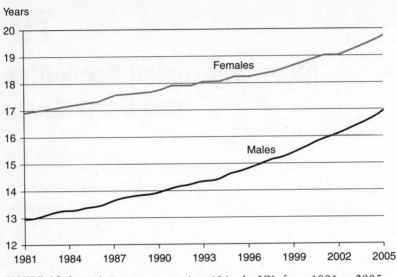

Years

FIGURE 10.1   Life Expectancy at Age 65 in the UK, from 1981 to 2005
Source: ONS (2007).

of defined benefit pension funds and annuity providers.[1] Another reason is that a traded mortality-linked security has to meet the different needs of hedgers (concerned with hedge effectiveness) and investors (concerned with liquidity and with receiving adequate compensation for assuming the risk), needs that are difficult to reconcile when longevity risk, a long-term trend risk that is difficult to quantify, is involved. A third reason is the absence of an established market price for longevity risk.[2] In this chapter we provide an overview of the recent developments in capital markets aimed at overcoming such difficulties and at creating a liquid market in mortality-linked securities and derivatives.

Before outlining the contents of the chapter, we illustrate the magnitude of mortality improvements in recent years using the UK experience in the period from 1981 to 2005. Figure 10.1 shows that male life expectancy at age 65 rose from 13 years in 1981 to almost 17 years in 2005. This corresponds

---

[1]In 2007, these institutions' exposure to improvements in life expectancy amounted to $400 billion in the UK and the US (see Loeys et al. 2007).
[2]There is a useful role for governments here to issue longevity bonds and thereby help to establish the riskless mortality term structure in the same way that governments issued fixed-income and index-linked bonds, which helped to establish the riskless nominal and real interest rate term structures.

to a rate of increase of more than 1% per annum. Female life expectancy rose from 17 to 19.7 years over the same period, corresponding to a 0.6% increase per annum. These increases in life expectancy are not a problem in themselves. They could be properly managed if the mortality improvements were fully anticipated. The real problem is that increases in life expectancy are affected by considerable uncertainty, and changes in mortality rates are often unanticipated. This is what is meant when we refer to longevity risk as being a long-term trend risk.

To understand the implications of longevity risk for pension plans and annuity providers, we look at a longevity fan chart: that is, a plot depicting the increasing funnel of uncertainty around estimates of future life expectancy or, equivalently, around future mortality or survival rates. Figure 10.2 represents the forecast future life expectancies for 65-year-old English and Welsh males. The dark central band provides a 10% confidence level for the central estimate of future life expectancy during the period 2000–2050. Surrounding the central band are bands of increasingly lighter shading, each representing additional 10% confidence intervals for

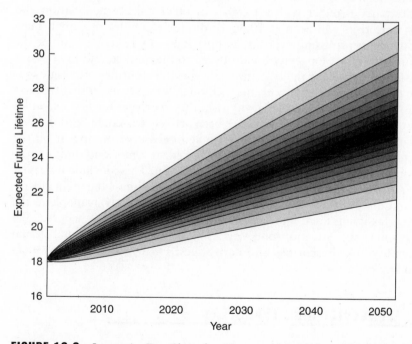

FIGURE 10.2 Longevity Fan Chart for 65-year-old English and Welsh Males
Source: Dowd et al. (2007).

the forecast range of life expectancies. The whole fan chart shows the 90% confidence interval for the life expectancy forecast. The best estimate forecast for life expectancy in 2050 is 26 years, which lies between 21 and 32 years with 90% probability. Since every additional year of life expectancy at age 65 is estimated to add at least 3% to the present value of UK pension liabilities (e.g., PPF 2006; Blake et al. 2008), it is not difficult to see the economic implications of such a huge range of uncertainty. Similarly, if we adopt the perspective of an insurer willing to offer a pension plan protection against longevity risk (or of an investor willing to take on the longevity risk of a pension plan or annuity provider), it is not difficult to see why longevity risk hedges are very capital intensive and command high risk premia.

In the following sections, we provide an overview of the progress that has been made in less than a decade in developing a market in mortality-linked securities and derivatives. We begin in Section 10.2 with a description of the UK pension buy-out market, and of the securitization of insurance assets and liabilities. Pension buy-outs essentially involve transferring pension liabilities to an insurer, while securitizations involve capital market investors, such as hedge funds, endowments, and insurance-linked securities (ILS) investors. In both cases, the longevity risk is typically transferred to a counterparty together with a number of other risks (e.g., inflation and interest rate risks). In Section 10.3, we discuss examples of capital market instruments providing exposure to pure longevity risk. We examine the structure of the first longevity bond offered to the market, and the reasons why it failed, as well as the structure of successful securities offering exposure to catastrophic mortality events. Although these securities involve risks that are the exact inverse of longevity risk, they represent the first examples of mortality-linked securities that have been actively traded. In Section 10.4, we examine the most recent mortality-linked derivatives to appear on the market, namely derivatives with payoffs linked to a mortality index or to the mortality experience of a reference population. These include longevity swaps and mortality forwards. In Section 10.5, we discuss the main advantages and disadvantages of the hedging solutions currently available in the market, classifying them into "cash flow hedges" and "value hedges." We then examine the issues of longevity risk pricing and the optimal design of mortality-linked securities and derivatives. Finally, Section 10.6 offers concluding remarks.

10.2 LONGEVITY RISK TRANSFERS

The most direct way for a pension plan or an annuity provider to reduce its exposure to mortality improvements is to transfer part of its liabilities to a counterparty. The transfer may take the form of an insurance contract, in the case where the counterparty is a life insurer or reinsurer, or of a change of plan sponsor, in the case where the original employer's covenant is ended and the counterparty is another principal employer. An active pension buy-out market has developed in the UK starting in 2006, enjoying formidable growth and attracting the participation of major players in financial markets. We outline the main features of this market in Section 10.2.1 below.

Much older than the pension buy-out market is the traditional reinsurance market, which life insurers have long used to transfer part of their exposures, although the capacity of the reinsurance market to deal in longevity-linked exposures has generally been very limited. A new alternative to the reinsurance market is the transfer of risks to the capital markets via securitization of insurance assets and liabilities. Investors have shown increasing interest in ILS as a way of diversifying their portfolios and earn extra returns that are uncorrelated with traditional equity and bond markets. We examine the most common forms of securitization in Section 10.2.2 below.

10.2.1 Pension Buy-Outs

A common pension buyout transaction involves the transfer of a pension plan's assets and liabilities to a regulated[3] life insurer. A typical example is represented by a company with assets A and liabilities L, valued on an "ongoing basis"[4] by the plan actuary. When the plan's assets are insufficient to cover the liabilities: that is, $A < L$, the company recognizes a deficit of $L - A$. When $A > L$ instead, the company's plan has a surplus of $A - L$. Life insurers are usually required to value liabilities under more prudent assumptions (on future mortality improvements, inflation rates, and market yields) than pension plans, resulting in a valuation $\widetilde{L} > L$ for the liabilities. This increases reported deficits or reduces reported surpluses when a company approaches an insurer for transferring its pension assets and liabilities.

In the case of a deficit, a company borrows the amount $\widetilde{L} - A$ and pays it to an insurer to buy out its pension assets and liabilities. The transaction allows the employer to off-load the pension liabilities from its balance sheet. This means that the volatility of assets and liabilities associated with the pension plan accounts, the payment of management fees on the plan's assets, and any levies charged for members' protection insurance[5] can be avoided. If buy-out costs are financed by borrowing, a regular loan replaces pension

---

[3]E.g., by the Financial Services Authority (FSA) in the UK.
[4]E.g., according to the pension accounting standard FRS17 in the UK.
[5]E.g., the Pension Protection Fund (PPF) in the UK.

assets and liabilities on the balance sheet. From the point of view of the plan members, the pensions are secured in full, subject, of course, to the solvency of the life insurer.

There are alternative solutions to these full buy-out transactions. Partial buy-outs may take different forms, and involve the transfer of liabilities originating from a subgroup of members (e.g., deferred pensions, pensions in payment, etc.) or payable over a limited time-horizon (e.g., liabilities above 10 years' maturity). These buyout deals are usually part of a broader ("de-risking") strategy for reducing the risk exposure of the pension plan or for tilting the investment strategy toward liability hedging (liability-driven investment (LDI)).

Buy-out transactions have become increasingly popular in the UK since 2006. Paternoster, run by Mark Wood, sealed the first buy-out deal with the Cuthbert Heath Family plan in November 2006. A number of transactions followed, involving buy-out startups as well as well-known life insurers. In addition to Paternoster, companies active in the buy-out space include Lucida (run by Jonathan Bloomer), Rothesay Life (owned by Goldman Sachs), the Pension Insurance Corporation (run by Eddie Truell, who secured the largest deal to date in the UK with the $1.1 billion buyout of Thorn's pension fund), Legal & General, Prudential, Canada Life, Aegon Scottish Equitable, and Aviva among others. The reason for such interest in pension assets and liabilities is that insurers have superior expertise in forecasting and managing longevity-linked cash flows and can use the buy-out transaction premium to set up a suitable hedging strategy as well as to earn an attractive return on capital employed. At the time of writing, the return on equity capital for the average buyout transaction is around 15%.[6] On the other hand, the pension buy-out market has become so competitive that margins have reduced considerably. In addition, the new European solvency requirements for life insurers (Solvency II), due to be implemented by 2012, are likely to make the business increasingly capital intensive.[7] For these and other reasons, some new players have pursued the alternative route to the insured buy-out and have opted for a change in the pension plan's sponsor, producing substantial savings on buy-out costs. An example of a so-called non-insured buy-out is represented by Citigroup becoming the principal employer of Thomson Regional Newspapers' closed pension fund in August 2007. However, the UK Pensions Regulator has determined that the change of principal employer weakens the sponsor covenant to an unacceptable degree.

---

[6]Communications at the ILS Workshop held at Imperial College's Centre for Hedge Fund Research on October 31, 2008.
[7]EU told to rethink rules on annuities. *Financial Times*, December 27, 2008.

An Independent Trustee will typically be imposed on the trustee board and this has made non-insured buy-outs less attractive. There have been no such buy-outs since 2007.

10.2.2   Securitization of Life Insurance Assets and Liabilities

The interest in longevity-linked cash flows is not limited to pension liabilities and the pensions buy-out market. Life insurance assets and liabilities have been attracting the attention of investors for at least two decades (e.g., Cowley and Cummins, 2005). The most common form of transaction involves the sale of a pool of assets and liabilities (i.e., rights to a set of future cash flows) to a special purpose vehicle (SPV) and the repackaging of those assets and liabilities into securities traded in the capital markets. The SPV finances the purchase of assets and liabilities by issuing bonds to investors, which are, in turn, secured against the assets and promised cash flows, possibly with some form of credit enhancement (e.g., overcollateralization, credit insurance, etc.).

The earliest and most common form of deals involves the securitization of the cash flows emerging from a block of business, such as a book of life policies. Life insurers are required to set up and maintain adequate reserves to meet liability payments when they fall due. As experience unfolds and liabilities are met, profits can be recognized on the balance sheet. Securitization gives insurers the opportunity to convert to cash the future profits expected to emerge from a block of business.

A related form of life insurance securitization is regulatory reserving securitization, known as Triple-X securitization in the US.[8] Life insurance business is capital intensive, as the costs of writing new policies are incurred up front, and the insurer needs to set up reserves that reflect the value of future liabilities under prudent assumptions. An insurer can "release" the excess of reserves above the realistic valuation through securitization. The capital released can be used to support growth in the same or other lines of business. The key feature of Triple-X securitization is that the insurer's liabilities are not supported by the underlying assets but by the future premium receivables.

A more recent form of securitization involves the sale and repackaging of life settlement portfolios (see Modu 2008). These are portfolios of whole life policies that are sold by the owner to a third party, for a price that is

---

[8]Triple-X regulation (see NAIC, 1999) applies to the valuation of life policies with guaranteed premiums over (part of) the policy term.

higher than the cash surrender value, but lower than the net death benefit. The securitization of senior life settlements (i.e., policies issued to individuals aged 65+) began in 2004, with Tarrytown Second, a transaction involving $63 million of senior life settlements backed by $195 million life policies. In January 2005, the Life Exchange (see www.life-exchange.com) was established with a mission "to provide the secondary life insurance market with the most advanced and independent electronic trading platform available by which to conduct life settlement transactions with the highest degree of efficiency, transparency, disclosure, and regulatory compliance." In April 2007, the Institutional Life Markets Association started in New York, as the trade body for the life settlements industry. In December 2007, Goldman Sachs launched a monthly index suitable for trading life settlements. The index, QxX.LS (see www.qxx-index.com), is based on a pool of 46,290 anonymized lives aged 65+ from a database of life policy sellers assessed by the medical underwriter AVS.

10.3 CAPITAL MARKET SOLUTIONS AND THE DEVELOPMENT OF MORTALITY-LINKED SECURITIES AND DERIVATIVES

As illustrated in the previous section, pension plans and annuity providers can sell their liabilities in the pension buy-out market or transfer them to the capital markets via securitization. However, the cost of selling the longevity risk is bundled up with the cost of selling the other risks, making transactions more expensive and less transparent. Moreover, there are already signs of capacity constraints in the pension buy-out market, as some of the insurers have been unable to attract additional shareholders' funds to expand their capital base. The default of Lehman Brothers in September 2008 has further dampened the exuberance of buy-outs because of the impact on the corporate bond market.[9] It is now recognized that a greater involvement by the capital markets in managing longevity risk could increase market capacity, increase liquidity, and allow a more transparent pricing of longevity risk. Blake and Burrows (2001) proposed the use of long-dated longevity bonds (or survivor bonds) to transfer the longevity risk to the capital markets. These are life annuity bonds with no return of principal and coupon payments declining in line with a chosen mortality index. Their proposal gave rise to a first generation of mortality-linked securities characterized by a bond-like structure. We describe the most relevant examples below.

---

[9]Pension buy-outs slip back on volumes. *Financial Times*, February 9, 2009.

10.3.1   The EIB Longevity Bond

The first attempt to issue a longevity bond was in November 2004 when BNP Paribas announced the issue by the European Investment Bank (EIB) of a 25-year bond with an issue price of $540 million and coupons linked to a cohort survivor index based on the realized mortality rates of English and Welsh males aged 65 in 2002. The initial coupon was set equal to $50 million, while the subsequent coupons would have decreased in line with the realized mortality experienced by the reference cohort of male individuals. A representation of the security cash flows is provided in Figure 10.3; see Blake et al. (2006) for additional details. As the examples in Figure 10.4 show, the higher the number of survivors in the population each year, the higher the coupons paid to investors. Hence the instrument was mainly aimed at pension plans and annuity providers. However, the bond did not generate sufficient demand from investors to be actually launched, and was withdrawn for redesign in late 2005.

Despite its failure, the EIB longevity bond attracted considerable attention for the lessons that could be learned to improve the design and successfully develop a mortality-linked capital market. The main reasons why the EIB bond was poorly received by investors are:

- *Basis risk*: The bond's mortality index covered just a fraction of the average pension plan's and annuity provider's exposure to longevity risk, which spans different cohorts of active and retired members. Furthermore, a large portion of pensions paid by pension funds and life insurers are indexed to inflation. Investors looking at the bond for hedging purposes were therefore concerned about both the considerable degree of basis risk arising from using an index based on a single birth cohort from the national population and the absence of an inflation hedge.

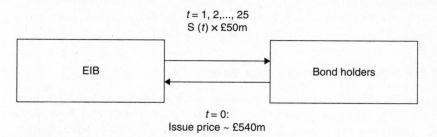

$t = 1, 2, ..., 25$
$S(t) \times £50m$

EIB   Bond holders

$t = 0$:
Issue price ~ £540m

FIGURE 10.3   Cash Flows from the EIB Bond, as Viewed by Investors
$S(t)$ denotes the survivor index at the end of year t.
Source: Blake et al. (2006).

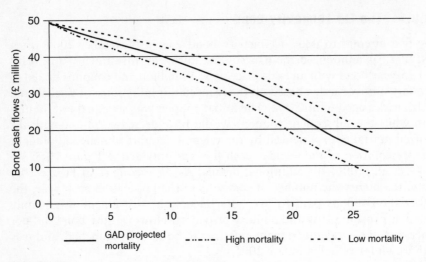

FIGURE 10.4 Coupons on the EIB Bond
Source: Blake et al. (2006).

■ *Capital strain*: As a hedging instrument, the structure of the EIB bond did not offer sufficient flexibility. A considerable upfront payment was required to access the longevity hedge component of the instrument, represented by a longevity swap that paid the longevity-linked coupons. The hedge was bundled up within a bond and provided no leverage opportunities. Furthermore, the size of the issue was too small to create a liquid market in the instrument.

■ *Transparency*: The projected cash flows for the EIB bond (i.e., the fixed leg of the longevity swap) were based on projections prepared by the UK Government Actuary's Department (GAD), but the model used to make those forecasts is not published, and the forecasts themselves are adjusted to reflect expert opinion in a way that is not made transparent. This represented a formidable barrier to investors not familiar with longevity risk and mortality projection models.

10.3.2 Mortality Catastrophe Bonds

Short-term mortality bonds are securities with payments linked to a mortality index. They are very similar to catastrophe bonds and have been successfully marketed in the last few years. The first mortality bond, known as Vita I, was issued by Swiss Re in December 2003 and was designed to reduce Swiss Re's own exposure to catastrophic mortality events, such as major terrorist attacks, avian flu pandemics, or other natural catastrophes.

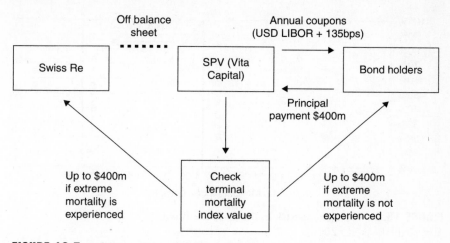

FIGURE 10.5 The Structure of the Swiss Re Bond
Source: Blake et al. (2006).

Vita I had a maturity of three years and an issue size of $400 million. It was issued via an SPV, called Vita Capital, that invested the $400 million principal in high-rated bonds, and swapped the bond income stream for LIBOR-linked cash flows. A scheme of the transaction is reported in Figure 10.5. Income was distributed to investors on a quarterly basis,[10] while the principal repayment at maturity depended on the realized level of a particular index of mortality rates across different countries (the United States, UK, France, Italy, Switzerland) constructed to hedge Swiss Re's book of business. The principal was repayable in full if the mortality index did not exceed 1.3 times the 2002 base level during the mortality bond's life. Reduction in principal payments were 5% for each 1% increase in the mortality index above the base level, with exhaustion of principal at 1.5 times the base level; see Figure 10.6.

The issue of Vita I was very successful and was followed by a number of other bonds, such as Vita II ($362 million) in 2005 and Vita III ($705 million) in 2007, again issued by Swiss Re; Tartan ($155 million) in 2006, issued by Scottish Re; Osiris ($442 million) in 2006, issued by AXA.[11] Investors find these securities attractive because they offer a high income relative to similarly rated floating rate instruments. Several pension funds are investors in mortality bonds. In addition to the appealing income stream,

---

[10] The bond was paying 135 basis points above LIBOR in November 2005.
[11] See Bauer and Kramer (2007) for an overview of recent transactions involving mortality catastrophe bonds.

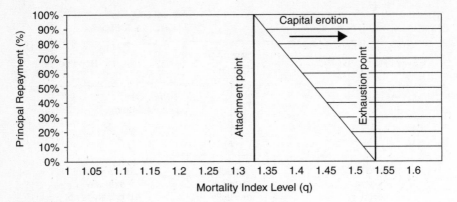

FIGURE 10.6   Principal-at-Risk in the Swiss Re Bond
Source: Blake et al. (2006).

there is a positive correlation of the principal repayments with their active members and pensioners liabilities.

10.4   RECENT TRENDS IN MORTALITY-LINKED SECURITIES

Following the withdrawal of the EIB bond, major investment banks and reinsurers started to work on more transparent forms of mortality indexation and on more effective product designs, giving rise to a second generation of derivative-based products.

    The most important lesson learned was that the survival of a traded capital market instrument depends on meeting the needs of both hedgers and speculators. While the former require an effective hedging instrument, the latter demand liquidity. Reconciliation of these different needs is not straightforward when longevity exposures are at stake, as we argue in the following sections.

10.4.1   Mortality Indexes

The single mortality benchmark underlying the EIB bond was considered inadequate to create an effective hedge by advisers and pension plan trustees. It soon became apparent that a flexible and reliable set of mortality indexes was needed for contracts to be written on. A first attempt was made by Credit Suisse in 2005, with a Longevity Index developed for the US population life expectancy. The index suffered from similar transparency issues as the EIB bond's cohort index, and is no longer actively marketed by Credit Suisse.

A more successful attempt was made by JP Morgan, in conjunction with the Pensions Institute and Watson Wyatt, with the launch of the LifeMetrics Indexes in March 2007 (see www.lifemetrics.com). The indexes comprise publicly available mortality data at population level, broken down by age and gender, for different key countries (UK, US, Holland, and Germany). To foster transparency of the indexes and of mortality projection models, LifeMetrics include an open source toolkit for measuring and managing longevity risk and mortality projections.

Most recently, the Market Data & Analytics department of Deutsche Börse launched the Xpect-Indices in March 2008. Currently published for Germany and the Netherlands, these indexes provide monthly estimates for the life expectancy of a reference group of individuals in a defined cohort or region.

10.4.2 Mortality Swaps and Forwards

The derivatives products that are currently attracting the greatest attention from insurers and investment banks are mortality and longevity swaps. They involve counterparties swapping fixed payments for payments linked to the number of deaths (mortality swaps) or survivors (longevity or survivor swaps) in a reference population in a given time period. The derivative component of the EIB bond described in Section 10.3.1 is a longevity swap, since fixed payments from investors in the bond were intended to be swapped for coupons linked to the annual number of survivors in the cohort of English and Welsh males aged 65 in 2002. More generally, longevity swaps can diversify the exposure to longevity risk of a pension plan or annuity provider, by providing exposure to the mortality experience of different populations. For example, a US annuity provider could swap cash flows indexed on a US mortality index in exchange for cash flows based on a UK mortality index from a UK annuity provider counterparty. The first publicly announced longevity swap took place in April 2007: Swiss Re agreed to assume the longevity risk of £1.7 billion pension annuity contracts written by Friends' Provident, a UK life assurer, in exchange for an undisclosed premium; see also Section 10.5.1.

A mortality swap can be synthesized by combining together several mortality forwards: that is, contracts involving the exchange of a realized mortality rate relating to a specified population at a given future date, in exchange for a fixed mortality rate agreed at the beginning of the contract (this is called the forward rate). Contracts of this type have been marketed by JP Morgan since July 2007, under the name of q-forwards (see Coughlan et al.

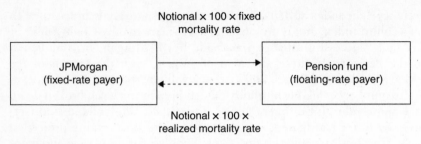

Notional × 100 × fixed
mortality rate

Notional × 100 ×
realized mortality rate

FIGURE 10.7 A q-forward Exchanges Fixed Mortality for Realized Mortality
at the Maturity of the Contract
Source: Coughlan et al. (2007).

2007). Forward contracts, in principle, provide a good basis for developing
a liquid market in mortality derivatives, because they represent the building
blocks of a number of more complex exposures. In addition, they have the
potential to suit the hedging needs of parties that are net short longevity
(pension plans and annuity providers) or net long longevity (providers of
term assurances and whole life policies). Figure 10.7 presents a stylized dia-
gram of a q-forward transaction, while Figure 10.8 provides an illustrative
term sheet for a contract written on a reference population of 65-year-old
English and Welsh men. The payoff from the q-forward depends on the
value of the LifeMetrics index for the reference population on the maturity

Notional amount	GBP 50,000,000
Trade date	31 Dec 2006
Effective date	31 Dec 2006
Maturity date	31 Dec 2016
Reference year	2015
Fixed rate	1.2000%
Fixed amount payer	JPMorgan
Fixed amount	Notional Amount × Fixed Rate × 100
Reference rate	LifeMetrics graduated initial mortality rate for 65-year-old males in the reference year for England and Wales national population Bloomberg ticker: LMQMEW65 Index <GO>
Floating amount payer	ABC Pension Fund
Floating amount	Notional Amount × Reference Rate × 100
Settlement	Net settlement = Fixed amount − Floating amount

FIGURE 10.8 Illustrative Term Sheet for a Single q-forward to Hedge
Longevity Risk
Source: Coughlan et al. (2007).

TABLE 10.1 An Illustration of q-forward Settlement for Various Outcomes of the Realized Reference Rate

Reference Rate (Realized Rate)	Fixed Rate	Notional (GBP)	Settlement (GBP)
1.0000%	1.2000%	50,000,000	10,000,000
1.1000%	1.2000%	50,000,000	5,000,000
1.2000%	1.2000%	50,000,000	0
1.3000%	1.2000%	50,000,000	−5,000,000

Source: Coughlan et al. (2007).

date of the contract. The contract involves JP Morgan providing a hedge to ABC pension fund to cover its longevity risk (i.e., falls in mortality rates) over a 10-year horizon (from 2006 to 2016).

At maturity, the seller of longevity protection pays the ABC Pension Fund an amount related to the forward mortality rate of 1.2%, in exchange for an amount related to the LifeMetrics reference rate that will be available at maturity. The settlement on December 31, 2016 is based on the rate for the reference year 2015, given the 10-month lag in the availability of official data. The settlement amount is the difference between the fixed amount and the realized (floating) amount. Table 10.1 presents possible settlement amounts for different outcomes of the realized reference rate. If the realized mortality is lower than what was anticipated at the inception of the contract (i.e., the LifeMetrics rate for 2015 is lower than the forward rate), the settlement amount is positive, and ABC Pension fund receives from JP Morgan an amount that can be used to offset its higher pension liabilities. If the realized mortality is higher than what was anticipated, it is the hedger who has to make a payment to JP Morgan, but this outflow is offset by a fall in its pension liabilities. The first trade in q-forwards took place in February 2008 between JP Morgan and the buyout firm Lucida; see Section 10.2.1.

10.4.3 Mortality/Longevity Futures and Options

No futures or options markets on mortality-linked securities are active to date. However, considerable effort is being spent by reinsurers and investment banks to explore opportunities for innovation. Natixis, for example, has launched a longevity-driven collar. In addition to the choice of underlying index, a key issue for options contracts is the choice of contract design (underlying, strike levels, tranches, etc.) to maximize liquidity. More details on these issues are provided in Section 10.5.3.

10.5 HEDGING PENSION LIABILITIES WITH MORTALITY-LINKED SECURITIES AND DERIVATIVES

In the previous sections, we highlighted the main features of those mortality-linked securities and derivatives that have appeared in the last few years. A major barrier to the development of a liquid mortality-linked capital market is the different requirements of investors and holders of longevity exposures. We formalize these differences by classifying the hedging solutions currently available to pension plans and annuity providers under the headings of "cashflow hedges" and "value hedges"; see Sections 10.5.1 and 10.5.2.

We also examine the issue of longevity risk pricing and optimal security design. Although considerable progress has been made in understanding mortality dynamics (e.g., Dowd et al. 2008a,b; Gourieroux and Monfort 2008; Jarner et al. 2008; Chen and Cox (2009)), the pricing of longevity risk remains elusive. The pricing models used so far by practitioners are typically based on partial equilibrium arguments (e.g., calibration of risk-neutral valuation models to annuity quotes, or to assumptions used in reinsurance markets; see, for example, Biffis 2005; Bauer et al. 2008) and shed little light on how supply and demand might equilibrate when longevity exposures are exchanged. We address this problem by describing the approaches of Loeys et al. (2007) and Biffis and Blake (2008); see Section 10.5.3.

10.5.1 Cash Flow Hedge Paradigm

Cash flow hedge solutions are similar to the traditional insurance paradigm, whereby the risk exposure is transferred to a counterparty, which continues to pay the required cash flows. Contracts of this kind have the character of indemnification arrangements and typically make payments on a regular basis to cover the periodic liability outflows (e.g., the yearly annuity payments from a book of pension annuities). Examples of such hedges are longevity swaps such as the Swiss Re and Friends' Provident longevity swap described in Section 10.4.2. The advantages of these contracts to the holder of longevity exposures are that the hedge entails no basis risk and, once set up, requires minimal monitoring. On the other hand, as customized hedges, they have some clear disadvantages. Since customized longevity risk solutions are complex and not very scalable or transferable, they involve higher set-up and operational costs. To minimize such costs, cash flow hedges are typically long term and thus have greater exposure to counterparty credit risk. For these reasons, mortality-linked securities and derivatives based on customized hedges are unlikely to be attractive to capital market investors.

This, in turn, reduces their liquidity and drives up the required longevity risk premium.

Despite the limitations and drawback we have highlighted, cash flow hedges seem to be the current preferred solution among pension plan trustees and annuity providers accustomed to the insurance indemnification paradigm. Financial intermediaries, such as investment banks, are actively attempting to enter this space. They offer to take on individual longevity exposures for later repackaging and reselling to capital market investors. One example of this is represented by a recent transaction involving JPMorgan and Canada Life, on the one side, and JP Morgan and the capital market investors, on the other side. The investment bank arranged a longevity swap with Canada Life and simultaneously executed a series of mirror swaps with the capital market investors seeking exposure to longevity risk for a suitable risk premium.

10.5.2 Value Hedge Paradigm

Value hedge solutions are common in capital markets. They are implemented by using standardized hedging instruments written on transparent indexes. The payments are rolled up and paid on the maturity date, at which point they can be used to off set the liability outflows. The standardization and commoditization of these solutions means that they are much cheaper than customized hedges, and have the potential to appeal to a larger investor base, thus increasing liquidity and lowering risk premia. On the other hand, the standardization of value hedge instruments means that hedgers are likely to bear some basis risk.

Examples of these solutions are the q-forward contracts described in Section 10.4.2, and to some extent the EIB longevity bond examined in Section 10.3.1. The structure of the EIB bond was too cumbersome to allow willing investors to exploit the value hedge potential of the longevity-linked coupons. The issue is resolved by mortality forwards, offering opportunities to leverage the exposure to a reference mortality index computed for a range of reference populations (different countries, ages, and gender) and time-horizons (e.g., 5, 10, and 15 years). Although the granularity and transparency of the indexing mechanism make mortality-forwards extremely flexible, the basis risk entailed by a standardized mortality index is still a major source of concern for pension plan trustees and annuity providers, exactly as it was in the case of the EIB longevity bond. Coughlan et al. (2007) and Loeys et al. (2007) show that basis risk can be managed effectively by writing derivatives based on the mortality experience of an entire age range (e.g., from 70 to 79) in a given population ("age-bucketing"), since correlations between mortality improvements in the index and in the longevity exposures of typical hedgers increase dramatically. In addition to mitigating basis risk, the age-bucketing approach streamlines the number of contracts necessary to meet the hedgers' needs and makes it easier to explain the advantages of value hedge solutions. Indeed, Coughlan et al. (2007) argue that a liquid, hedge-effective market could be built around just eight standardized q-forwards, with maturity (say) 10 years, broken down into two genders (male, female) and four age buckets (50–59,60–69,70–79,80–89). The first insurer to adopt a value hedge solution for its longevity exposure was the pension buy-out company Lucida. In January 2008 Lucida completed with JP Morgan a transaction in a mortality forward (i.e., a JP Morgan q-forward contract) written on the LifeMetrics index for England and Wales.

10.5.3   Longevity Risk Pricing and Optimal Security Design

A key issue in the examples of the products covered above, in particular for the mortality derivatives described in Section 10.4.2 and 10.5.2, is the pricing of longevity risk in the absence of a liquid mortality-linked capital market. Currently there is no commonly accepted model for determining expectations about mortality improvements over time. Rather, there is a variety of competing mortality forecasting models available, each of which is subject to a considerable degree of estimation risk; see, for example, Dowd et al. (2008a, b); Cairns et al. (2009).

As a reference point, Loeys et al. (2007) consider the historical volatility σ_q of the relative changes in mortality rates and the forecasts produced by the popular Lee-Carter model. Since longevity risk is virtually uncorrelated with other market risks, Loeys et al. (2007) argue that the required Sharpe ratio on q-forwards (see Section 10.4.2) should be lower than the one available for riskier asset classes such as equities, but high enough to attract investors to the market. They suggest an annualized Sharpe ratio of 0.25 as a possible benchmark. They then use the following expression to compute the forward rate q^{fwd} at which a q-forward contract such as the one described in Figure 10.8 should trade:

$$q^{\text{fwd}} = \left(1 - 0.25\ T\ \sigma_q\right) q^{\text{forecast}} < q^{\text{forecast}}$$

where T denotes the time to maturity (in years) of the forward contract and q^{forecast} is the best estimate for the future mortality rate. This expression results in a forward rate lower than the expected mortality rate, as depicted in Figure 10.9. In other words, the party offering protection against longevity risk is paid a premium equal to Notional $\times$ ($q^{\text{forecast}} - q^{\text{fwd}}$) $\times$ 100 by the hedger (see Figure 10.8). Loeys et al. (2007) show that the required risk

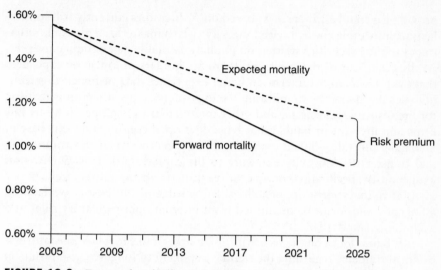

FIGURE 10.9 Expected and (Illustrative) Forward Mortality Rates for 65-year-old English and Welsh Males from 2005 to 2025
Source: Adapted from Loeys et al. (2007).

premium can be reduced by averaging across age groups and time, since volatility in mortality data is affected by factors that are unsystematic to some extent (e.g., measurement error, cohort effects). As an example, they show that trading a mortality (q-) forward for the age range 70–79 in the years 2015–2019 would generate a 40% reduction in risk premium relative to a forward on the mortality rate for age 75 in year 2017.

The volatility of mortality rates is fairly low compared with the uncertainty surrounding changes in mortality trends. Forecasting mortality trends is a challenging exercise that concerns investors willing to take on exposures to longevity risk. Biffis and Blake (2008) (henceforth "B&B") explicitly distinguish the role played by trends and volatility in mortality rates in determining equilibrium risk premia in longevity risk transfers. Specifically, they model future mortality rates as

$$q(X) + \varepsilon \tag{10.1}$$

where ε is an error term, while $q(X)$ represents a trend component that is affected by a vector of risk factors $X = (X^1, \ldots, X^k)'$ or "signals" (e.g., experience data, the outputs of stochastic mortality models, etc.). B&B then consider markets populated by a large number of risk-neutral investors who have no access to the information carried by X, or are unskilled at providing a trend estimate $q(X)$ based on X. Investors currently still seem to be uncomfortable enough with longevity risk to make this a plausible situation, even for securities written on publicly available demographic indexes. At the other end of the spectrum, there are holders of longevity exposures that have access to X (in terms of better experience data or forecasting technologies developed by monitoring the exposures). This situation is realistic for life insurers, reinsurers, and other intermediaries (e.g., pension buy-out firms and investment banks) that have developed considerable expertise in managing mortality-linked cash flows. The incentive to enter a transaction and transfer the longevity exposure to the capital markets is given by an exogenously specified retention cost resulting from capital requirements or alternative investment opportunities. Knowledge of this cost is available to all agents, and it can be quantified from international regulatory rules and accounting standards.

B&B first focus on the securitization market and show how the informational asymmetry regarding the trend component of longevity risk results in a downward sloping market demand for longevity exposures. Consider the securitization of a book of annuity-like cash flows and their backing assets. The presence of asymmetric information means that the holder or originator of the longevity exposure faces a "lemons" problem (as in Akerlof 1970), because investors do not have access to the private signal X. As is common in annuity reinsurance and the securitization of insurance assets and liabilities (see Section 2.2 and Cowley and Cummins, 2005), retention of part of the exposure can be used to "prove" the quality of the cash flows to the market and alleviate the impact of asymmetric information. B&B use a signaling model of market equilibrium as in DeMarzo and Duffie (1999) to determine the optimal retention and securitization levels. As a particular example, consider the situation where a riskless asset valued at $\alpha > 0$ backs a promised payment that depends on the proportion of survivors in a given population at some future date T, say S. Figure 10.10 shows that the optimal securitized fraction of the net exposure $\alpha - S$ is increasing in the trend component $q(X)$: that is, in the private valuation of longevity risk (see the right-hand vertical axis in Figure 10.10). The reason is that a lower private valuation $q(X)$ makes the cash flow $\alpha - S$ relatively less valuable and hence securitization relatively more valuable. On the other hand, investors rationally anticipate that the amount of exposure put up for sale is increasing in the private valuation of longevity risk, and the price they are willing to pay for the exposure is decreasing in the securitized fraction, leading to a lower securitization pay off (see the left-hand vertical axis in Figure 10.10).

B&B then allow the holder of the book of liabilities and backing assets to issue a security that is contingent on the net exposure $\alpha - S$ and examine conditions under which the optimal contract results in tranching of

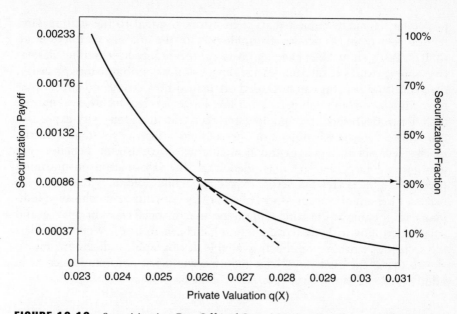

FIGURE 10.10 Securitization Pay Off and Securitization Fraction as a Function of the Private Valuation $q(X)$ of the Trend Component of Longevity Risk (the Plot is Based on the Death Rate of UK Males Aged 75 in the Year 2009)
Source: Biffis and Blake (2008).

the net exposure. By tranching, they mean slicing the net exposure so that, in exchange for a lump sum paid to the originator, investors who buy the tranche put up for sale are entitled to a specific portion of the net exposure's cash flows. The optimal tranching level minimizes the sensitivity of these cashflows to both asymmetric information and the impact of unsystematic risk, both of which are material to risk-neutral agents when pay offs are nonlinear. The optimal tranche is the one that is least risky from the investors' viewpoint, and is equivalent to the senior debt tranche in a debt financing operation. See Sherris and Wills (2008) and Kim and Choi (2009) for numerical examples related to the pricing of similar structures.

B&B extend their analysis to the market for mortality-linked derivatives and examine the issue of optimal contract design under asymmetric information about mortality trends. Under reasonable assumptions on the components $q(X)$ and ε, they find that the optimal securities are put options on mortality rates sold by investors to hedgers wishing to cap their exposure to longevity risk. More interestingly, B&B determine the optimal strike levels for such options. The optimal strikes can be interpreted as the mortality rates at which the marginal benefit to the hedger from purchasing additional protection from the capital market investors is equal to the marginal retention cost of the exposure. By analogy with the analysis of Loeys et al. (2007), B&B show that hedging costs can be reduced by writing derivatives on exposures pooled across age ranges or time periods. More precisely, diversification benefits can be traded off against the detrimental effect of information loss from pooling together low-longevity- and high-longevity-risk cash flows. B&B show that pooling and then tranching longevity exposures can reduce the negative impact of unsystematic longevity risk that is particularly prevalent at high ages and in small portfolios. Also, the benefits from pooling and tranching are magnified when the information on mortality trends is highly correlated across exposures, while residual risk is not. This occurs, for example, when issuers of securities pool different cohorts of individuals belonging to the same geographic area or social class, or pool several small portfolios with similar demographic characteristics. When considering securities written on publicly available demographic indexes, the model shows that "age-bucketing" can reduce asymmetric information costs in addition to mitigating basis risk; see Section 10.5.2.

10.6 CONCLUSION

In this chapter, we have reviewed the main drivers behind the branch of financial innovation that focuses on capital market solutions for managing longevity risk. This new and exciting field has seen major reinsurers and investment banks expending considerable resources in an attempt to develop solutions that successfully bring together both hedgers and capital market investors. Substantial progress has been made in product design, and some key transactions have taken place. The next few years will show which mortality-linked financial securities and derivatives will provide a valid alternative to the more traditional insurance solutions and offer new capacity for the transfer of longevity risk exposures.

REFERENCES

Akerlof, D. 1970. The market for "lemons": Qualitative uncertainty and the market mechanism. *Quarterly Journal of Economics* 89:488–500.

Bauer, D., M. Boerger, and J. Russ. 2008. On the pricing of longevity-linked securities. Technical report, Georgia State University.

Bauer, D., and F. Kramer. 2007. Risk and valuation of mortality contingent catastrophe bonds. Technical report, University of Ulm.

Biffis, E. 2005. Affine processes for dynamic mortality and actuarial valuations. *Insurance: Mathematics & Economics* 37, no. 3:443–468.

Biffis, E., and D. Blake. 2008. Securitizing and tranching longevity exposures. Pensions Institute Discussion Paper PI-0824. Forthcoming in *Insurance: Mathematics & Economics*.

Blake, D., and W. Burrows. 2001. Survivor bonds: Helping to hedge mortality risk. *Journal of Risk and Insurance* 68:339–348.

Blake, D., A. Cairns, and K. Dowd. 2006. Living with mortality: Longevity bonds and other mortality-linked securities. *British Actuarial Journal* 12: 153–197.

Blake, D., A. Cairns, and K. Dowd. 2008. The birth of the life market. *Asia-Pacific Journal of Risk and Insurance* 3, no. 1:6–36.

Cairns, A., D. Blake, K. Dowd, G. Coughlan, D. Epstein, and I. Balevich. 2009. A quantitative comparison of stochastic mortality models using data from England & Wales and the United States. *North American Actuarial Journal* 13, no. 1: 1–35.

Chen, H., and S. Cox. 2009. Modeling mortality with jumps: Applications to mortality securitization. *Journal of Risk and Insurance* 76, no. 3:727–751.

Coughlan, G., D. Epstein, A. Sinha, and P. Honig. 2007. q-forwards: Derivatives for transferring longevity and mortality risks. JP Morgan's Pension Advisory Group.

Cowley, A., and J. Cummins. 2005. Securitization of life insurance assets and liabilities. *Journal of Risk and Insurance* 72, no. 2:193–226.

DeMarzo, P., and D. Duffie. 1999. A liquidity based model of security design. *Econometrica* 67, no. 1:65–99.

Dowd, K., D. Blake, and A. Cairns. 2007. Facing up to the uncertainty of life: The longevity fan charts. Pensions Institute Discussion Paper PI-0703.

Dowd, K., A. Cairns, D. Blake, G. Coughlan, D. Epstein, and M. Khalaf-Allah. 2008a. Backtesting stochastic mortality models: An ex-post evaluation of multi-period-ahead density forecasts. Pensions Institute Discussion Paper PI-0803.

Dowd, K., A. Cairns, D. Blake, G. Coughlan, D. Epstein, and M. Khalaf-Allah. 2008b. Evaluating the goodness of fit of stochastic mortality models. Pensions Institute Discussion Paper PI-0802.

Gourieroux, C., and A. Monfort. 2008. Quadratic stochastic intensity and prospective mortality tables. CREST working paper.

Jarner, S., E. Masotti Kryger, and C. Dengsøe. 2008. The evolution of death rates and life expectancy in Denmark. *Scandinavian Actuarial Journal*, 2008(2–3):147–173.

Kim, C., and Y. Choi. 2009. Securitization of longevity risks using percentile tranche methods. Australian School of Business, UNSW. Available at SSRN: http://ssrn.com/abstract=1349398.

Loeys, J., N. Panigirtzoglou, and R. Ribeiro. 2007. Longevity: A market in the making. JP Morgan's Global Market Strategy.

Modu, E. 2008. Life settlement securitization. Technical report, AM Best Structured Finance.

NAIC. 1999. Valuation of life insurance policies model regulation. National Association of Insurance Commissioners.

ONS. 2007. Valuation of life insurance policies model regulation. Office for National Statistics press release, November 28.

PPF. 2006. *The Purple Book: DB Pensions Universe Risk Profile.* Croydon and Brighton, UK: Pension Protection Fund and the Pensions Regulator (December).

Sherris, M., and S. Wills. 2008. Securitization, structuring and pricing of longevity risk. Australian School of Business, UNSW. Available at SSRN: http://ssrn.com/abstract=1139726.

CHAPTER 11

Asset Allocation and Governance Issues of Government-Owned Pensions

Rachel Ziemba
Roubini Global Economics

This chapter begins by setting out a definition of different sovereign pension funds, discussing how they differ from other public investment funds. It then assesses how well their asset allocation reflects their liability structure over the needed time horizons. It then analyzes a series of governance issues that stem from the public ownership of the funds. Finally, it takes a closer look by region at a selection of key sovereign pension funds to draw some generalized conclusions.

11.1 INTRODUCTION

This chapter looks specifically at the challenges faced by public pension funds around the world. As detailed elsewhere in the book, globally there is a lack of adequate retirement funds, and many governments have been trying to catch up to meet future gaps. These shortfalls affect both developed and developing economies. For emerging market economies, which tend to have less developed pension systems but face aging populations, this challenge has arisen quickly. As such pension funds play a key role in the overall asset allocation strategies of their sponsor governments and have been called on when capital has been required by other parts of the government.

With aging populations in advanced economies, worsening dependency ratios and a need to extend coverage in developing countries, public pension funds sought to make up their funding gap by moving into higher-risk assets and injecting more funds. In practice the asset allocations of public pension funds have become roughly similar to their private sector counterparts and to other institutional investors like endowments and foundations. All have allocated more towards equities and alternative assets which has led to near term losses.

Despite similar asset allocations to other investors, the public ownership of funds poses a special set of issues: even arms-length funds might make investment decisions for not solely economic reasons. Savings earmarked for retirement either of all citizens or public sector workers are but one pool of capital for some governments. As such they may be subject to political pressures, raided to meet other shorter-term liabilities. Utilizing such funds has allowed some governments to avoid taking on substantial short-term debt to finance anticrisis measures. However, the timetable for recapitalizing the funds is uncertain. Moreover, fear of losing public funds could lead to less than ideal investment decisions or lead to pressures to support other key policy goals. While these investments may be in the national interest, it is possible that they might lead to suboptimal policies and lower investment returns.

Table 11.1 shows the assets of selected public pension funds.

TABLE 11.1 Assets of Selected Public Pension Funds Reserve Funds, $ billion

Country	Size of Fund
US Social Security Trust Fund	2,200.0
Japan	1,217.6
South Korea	228.7
China	138.0
Sweden	136.7
Canada	111.3
Australia	49.1
France	47.0
Spain	44.9
Russia	32.4
Ireland	29.0
Norway	20.4
Thailand	11.6
New Zealand	9.5
Saudi Arabia	8.6
Portugal	8.3
Mexico	7.4
Jordan	5.3
Pakistan	2.4
Poland	1.8

Adapted from Sovereign Wealth Funds and Pension Funds Issues.
Source: OECD.

11.2   TYPES OF SOVEREIGN FUNDS

Sovereign pension funds can be divided up into several groups both based on fund structure and the entity to which they report. For the purposes of this analysis, there are three major types of public pension fund. These categories are informed by the work the OECD and others have done on this issue (OECD 2008).

Table 11.2 shows pension reserve assets across the world in 2001, 2004, and 2007.

> **National pension funds based on individual contributions.** These tend to be financed by payroll tax deductions or other individual contributions. Some countries allow the beneficiaries to choose the asset allocation, usually from several choices; others invest the pool. Many of these funds have fairly conservative asset allocations with fixed income dominant. These tend to be pay as you go type operations with today's contributions paying for today's expenditure. Given the changing demographic structure, a pay as you go type

TABLE 11.2   A Selection of Pension Reserve Fund Assets, All Funds $ billion

Country	Type of Fund	2001	2004	2007
Australia	Pension Reserve Fund (PRF)	—	—	4.9
Canada	Social Security Reserve Fund (SSRF)	4.5	5.55	7.89
Denmark	SSRF	0.16	0.46	0.27
France	SPRF	—	1.23	1.91
Ireland	SPRF	6.59	7.87	11.52
Japan	SSRF	29.66	30.11	25.39
S. Korea	SSRF	12.20	17.10	23.86
Mexico	SSRF	0.47	0.74	0.9 (e)
New Zealand	SPRF	—	2.85	7.85
Norway	SPRF	8.76	10.22	5.22
Poland	SPRF	—	0.06 (e)	0.31
Portugal	SPRF	2.94	4.05	4.3 (e)
Spain	SSRF	0.22	2.28	4.5
Sweden	SRPF	24.41	25.23	31.65
US	SSRF	12.04	14.44	16.61
China	SRPF	1.02	1.2	1.88
Jordan	SRPF	1.07	2.09	3.09
Russia	SRPF	—	—	3.28
Saudi Arabia	SSRF	—	2.24	2.5 (e)
Thailand	SSRF	—	—	5 (e)

Source: OECD.

system will be unsustainable as the number of workers falls and the number of pensioners will rise as lifespans lengthen.

National (or Sub-Federal) Pension Reserve Funds. One response to the national pension funds financing gap has been the creation of reserve funds that will eventually be connected to the pension system Many countries have established reserve funds with investment portfolios in an effort to plug funding short falls. These funds, which tend to be under the supervision of the finance ministries, even if the management of capital is outsourced to asset managers, are intended to feed into the public pension system at a later point when pay-as-you-go becomes too costly or when the reserve fund has amassed enough money. Examples include the Irish Pension Fund general reserve, the Australian future fund, and the Chinese national pension reserve fund.

While the ultimate beneficiaries are citizens, the current manager and beneficiary is the government, and the political pressure to use the funds to meet other government priorities may be quite high. Government spending tends to require parliamentary approval. As such, pension reserve funds tend to be functionally similar to some so-called sovereign wealth funds, which are government-owned investment vehicles that manage funds in a variety of asset classes to maximize the long-term value of national wealth.

Pension Funds for Public-Sector Workers. These pension funds, particularly in the US and Canada and often at a subfederal level are based on employer and employee contributions and tend to be defined benefit. These tend to be managed by a board appointed by political leaders. Some of these funds, including Calpers and the Ontario Teachers, were among some of the earliest such investors to expand their asset allocations in alternative assets. Many funds may be a hybrid of the first two structures with a section pay as you go and investment portfolios separated out for longer horizon investment.

In addition to official pension reserve funds, many countries have other assets that are either explicitly or implicitly linked to retirement funding. The sovereign wealth funds of Norway and some other commodity-exporting nations have been earmarked to meet pension liabilities at an undefined point in the future. However, pension funds unlike sovereign funds tend to have defined liabilities. Sovereign funds are also designed to cushion domestic economies from volatile revenue streams as well as preserve the value of national wealth. The link between the future liabilities and current asset management strategy is not necessarily clear, and some governments may choose to spend the funds rather than saving them for the long term. Russia's national wealth fund is one example.

11.3 IS THERE A COMMON ASSET ALLOCATION FOR PENSION FUNDS?

While the asset allocations vary across country and fund type, many public pension funds are coalescing towards a common allocation with a majority in equities, some investment in private equity markets, and many investing in hedge funds or funds of hedge funds. Despite an increased investment in equities especially by pensions in Europe, Canada, Australia and New Zealand, several funds including the US are completely invested in bonds. See Table 11.3 for the asset allocation of several selected funds. This asset allocation not so coincidentally is similar to a common allocation that endowments, foundations, sovereign wealth funds and others have followed. This asset allocation contributed to severe short-term losses in 2008 given the correlated losses of most asset classes, especially public and private equity, corporate bonds and especially any leveraged assets.

Many pension funds, especially from small open economies have increased their exposure to foreign assets especially equities. Funds from Canada, New Zealand, and France all have close to 40% exposure to foreign assets.

It may take quite some time for pension funds to recover from the losses in 2008, particularly if they sold assets at a loss. World Bank research suggests that returns of pension funds, mostly in the developing world suffered losses of 8 to 48% in the year ending in August 2008 (World Bank 2008). Given the performance of global equities and other assets even later in 2008

TABLE 11.3 Asset Allocation of Selected Public Pension Funds

	Equities	Bonds/Cash	Alternative Investment
Australia	25.6	72.8	
Canada	57.9	28.3	13.7
France	64.5	34.7	
Ireland	72.3	21.1	5.9
Japan	37.3	62.7	
Korea	13.7	83.5	
New Zealand	59.9	17.3	17.7
Norway	48.3	51.7	
Portugal	20.8	72.3	
Sweden	53.1	39.8	3.8
China	24.2	63.2	
Jordan	63.5	25.1	7

Source: Adapted from OECD (2008).

(especially September and October 2008), losses were likely far worse than that estimate for the year as a whole. Some funds have regained a significant share of losses.

New capital may be scarce though. Moreover, many governments will likely have more limited funds available to contribute to these funds for many quarters and years to come. US state governments have been underfunding their pensions for some years now, and California will not be the only one to issue further IOUs. Pensions funded in whole or in part by individual contributions will receive lower funding given the reduction in hours worked in many countries.

Many pension funds, especially from small open economies have increased their exposure to foreign assets especially equities. Funds from Canada, New Zealand, and France all have close to 40% exposure to foreign assets.

It may take quite some time for pension funds to recover from the losses in 2008. World Bank research suggests that returns of pension funds, mostly in the developing world suffered losses of 8 to 84% in the year ending in August 2008. (World Bank 2009) Many pension funds, struggling to meet funding gaps expanded significantly into alternative assets, many of which underperformed. They may thus be more cautious (even too risk averse in the future).

Public pension funds are investors with a long-term horizon, given the long-term nature of their liabilities, which means that they may not necessarily have had to assume these losses. In 2008 and 2009 new funds accruing to these funds dropped in several countries, meaning that the new funds able to take advantage of cheap valuations may have been limited.

Many of the assessments on optimal asset allocations for individual and corporate pensions are also applicable to public pension plans. Like other pension systems, public pension funds must start by looking at the size and time horizon of their liabilities in order to pick the most optimal asset structure. Despite long-term investment horizons, some do have near-term cash flow needs. In the developing world, many countries are trying to play a major role of catch up, both in terms of asset management depth and asset value.

The sovereign and state-level public pension funds of several advanced economies have led the charge in investing in equities and alternatives. For example Calpers, Calstrs, Ontario Teachers, and even the Investment part of the Canada Pension plan were among the first to move into these assets. Others have subsequently followed.

However, specific assets and the overall investment strategies are under review. In particular like university endowments, some pension funds are reassessing their allocation in high-fee hedge funds, which on average underperformed indexes (see the discussion in Chapters 4 and 13). The recent market performance underscored the importance of ensuring that assets were really diversified against all risks and of carefully picking managers, whether they be in house or external.

Asset allocation varies by region and should be informed by the risks to the pensions funding streams. As noted by Allianz (2008), many Asian pension funds have maintained a more conservative asset allocation, remaining primarily in cash during 2007 and 2008 despite diversification plans. In the longer term the diversification planned by South Korean, Japanese, and Chinese funds could be significant in the Asian market. As noted below, the Chinese fund is already been being used as a vehicle to help develop domestic capital markets including private equity.

In the Middle East and other oil exporting countries, investing in commodities and commodity-linked assets might be inadvisable given that the government's other revenues stem from these assets. Too large an allocation to assets linked to the commodities that generate government revenue could overexpose these investors to a prolonged downturn.

11.4 SOVEREIGN PENSION FUNDS AND INTERNATIONAL CAPITAL MARKETS

Both government and private pension asset allocation may be contributing to distortions in some investment classes. As argued elsewhere in this book, the increasing flow of funds into financial instruments to meet corporate pension needs led to a change in investment patterns within the US which reduced funds available for real investment, including in infrastructure and instead towards financial investment. Despite the increase in savings by some sectors of the society, in practice most Americans boosted consumption rather than savings.

The desire of pension funds to increase their allocation to real assets, one of several examples in which they have shifted to the endowment model has led to an increase in pension funds investing in commodity funds, including futures. This inflow of capital into futures markets, rather than necessarily contributing to better price discovery may actually lead to bigger swings both in the prices of the underlying assets and the returns on the funds.

However, while asset allocation changes can be significant, it is very difficult to isolate the effect of these public investors. In part their asset allocation decisions are offset by those of other actors. Goldman Sachs noted that increased funds allocated to European Equities by European pension funds actually had limited effect on market dynamics. Adjustments of other investors likely muted this effect. Yet the change in pension fund allocations, coming at a time when other institutional investors were also moving to a asset of common allocations, clearly had an affect.

With the US savings rate finally on the rise after falling to zero earlier this decade, new asset allocation distortions are likely. The most recent data (April 2009) suggests that the US savings rate has quickly climbed to 6.9% from just under 5% in Q1 2009. It may well climb further as households identify a need to increase their savings to offset their wealth losses and financial institutions are reluctant to extend further credit.

11.5 GOVERNANCE ISSUES OF PUBLIC PENSION FUNDS

The different types of funds present different governance challenge, but all types, which may be linked, tend to be subject to political pressures and political oversight. Recent research on sovereign wealth funds (Harvard 2008) suggests that these entities tend not to get lower than expected financial returns despite the goal to maximize them. The researchers argue that the requirement to invest in domestic economies (something very evident in 2008 and 2009!) restricts their ability to choose the best investments.

11.5.1 Intergenerational Borrowing

Governmental saving for retirement or rather public pooling of resources for retirement is a form of intergenerational transfer or lending. In other words, workers contribute today to pay for the needs of current retirees, their descendants will make contributions so that today's workers will have funding. As noted in Chapter 1, this intergenerational transfer is breaking down as demographics have resulted in a lopsided system in which the number of workers supporting each retiree is slipping.

Pension reserve funds may be seen in times of crisis as another pool of unallocated or not yet allocated government funds. In some cases, the link to future pension needs is more implicit than explicit. Russia's national wealth fund is one example. While it is earmarked for future pension needs, it is also being used to fund some of Russia's current spending. Drawing on a pension reserve fund may require fewer legislative changes to draw funds than assets which are already deemed to be pension assets and for which beneficiaries may have some ownership stake. For some countries, the calculation seems simple, why not draw on these assets to finance fiscal stimulus today?

Countries such as Ireland are drawing on pension savings to finance today's fiscal packages. Still others are encouraging pension funds to increase their investment in domestic asset markets, perhaps withdrawing funds from abroad—Saudi Arabia's pension fund (GOSI) has been used as an equity stabilization fund, increasing its share of its domestic assets (Ziemba 2009). It has likewise reduced its exposure to deposits in foreign banks and increased those abroad.

These pools of capital and their asset allocation can significantly shape domestic capital markets, changing the incentives of investors. Many emerging economies tend to lack domestic institutional investors and often are dominated either by domestic retail investors, large corporations, or international investors (depending on how restrictive their investment regime). The introduction of a pension fund or pension reserve fund with a long-term investment horizon could add investors who could at least in theory invest for the longer-term. The sheer number of investment options demanded by those managing public and private retirement could contribute to financial depth in these economies and improve the ability of corporations to seek long-term funding domestically. Doing so would limit some of the exchange rate risks they bear.

Some countries have tried to use their pension funds and other pools of government capital as a tool to lure asset managers and develop their financial sector by entrusting a share of government funds to such asset managers who set up operations domestically. Singapore, for one, used assets from the Government Investment Corporation (GIC) as well as pensions to attract asset managers. Coupled with regulatory changes that increase ease of financial operations, Singapore's seed capital did contribute to its asset management industry development.

The different government revenue streams of the government may be correlated. As noted in Setser and Ziemba (2009), countries like the UAE faced a concurrent fall in investment income and oil revenue as equity, corporate bonds, and alternative asset returns fell, even as the oil price and later oil production reduced revenue.[1] The returns on government savings, as well as resource and tax revenue have fallen even as expenditure demands have increased. The following pressures have emerged even as government pension savings have been in even more demand in a new sort of intergenerational borrowing. Some pension funds and other government savings are being called on to finance both real domestic investment and current government spending today. In other words, some governments are raiding the cookie jar of their pension schemes especially the pension reserve funds.

The political leaders and the population that elects them does at times seek to carry out issues of public and even foreign policy. California's two

---

[1]Non-oil revenue in the UAE also fell as its diversification has primarily been into sectors most vulnerable to the global downturn and credit crunch including real estate, tourism, and trade.

public pension funds (Calpers and Calstrs) have been required to divest of any assets linked to Sudan, going even farther than US sanctions. While one might support the goal of effecting change, this does mean that public pensions funds may be a political tool (Steil 2008). Back when investing in private equity companies IPOs seemed like a great deal, the California legislature tried to limit co-investment of Calpers and others in private equity firms partly owned by sovereign wealth funds whose sponsoring governments had not passed certain human rights requirements. While not passed, this amendment is reflective of political debates surrounding public pension funds, and others that may arise in the future.

Some of these issues may be more murky in countries where the "owners of the fund" are government ministries directly rather than individual beneficiaries represented by the government asset manager.

Other public pension funds like that of Norway black-list certain investments to meet ethical and environmental standards. With Norway's government pension fund global (GPF-G) now the largest single holder of European equities being left off is significant. Norway's GPF-G is a hybrid between a public pension fund and a less than defined sovereign savings fund the assets are destined to be capital for Norway's retirement needs as the name suggests, but the time frame is long-term, and funds could be used on other purposes in the interim in 2009 some of the funds are going to fund the non-oil budget deficit.

Public pension funds, especially those of Norway, Canada, Ireland, and others are key activist investors, frequently participating in shareholder activities to improve the performance of their assets.

Not only might public pension funds be used as a tool of persuasion, governments might also hope to use their funds to promote economic and especially financial development. In 2007, the Chinese Pension reserve fund was given permission to invest in domestic private equity. Motivations were multifold: increase returns on savings to boost the capital available for pensions but perhaps more significantly to provide seed capital for the domestic industry. Other countries, such as Singapore, have used seed capital from their sovereign funds including pensions to lure foreign asset managers to their jurisdiction, helping to develop the domestic asset management industry. In Singapore's case the combination of financial deregulation, changes that made it cheaper to open a trading operation, and the seed capital helped contribute to industrial growth. Others such as South Korea have tried to follow such paths.

Many Asian oil-exporting nations allocate investment capital for resource investment. While these investments may respond to long-term resource demands of these energy and metal importers, they also may be good financial investments, given the likelihood that the lack of investment may lead to high commodity prices in the long term. Yet, as with other sovereign investors, some investments may reflect longer-term economic or even strategic goals not just financial returns: for example, recent investments by some of Abu Dhabi's investors.

11.6   REGIONAL TRENDS

The following section evaluates recent trends in several key sovereign pension funds, with a focus on those in emerging market economies, which may experience the largest growth and largest potential diversification into equities, alternative assets etc in coming years. This survey is not comprehensive but illustrates many of the themes across public pension funds.

Asia

Several Asian countries have a significant share of savings earmarked for retirement either through individual savings or those of government pension funds. Many of these could be dedicated to riskier assets over time. However, the losses such investments faced in 2008 may defer any such diversification.

The more developed Asian economies like Japan and South Korea have significant retirement savings, quite high on a per capita basis, even though these tend to be relatively conservatively managed; Singapore reformed its pension system and now lets its residents choose between a variety of investment fund options. Overall, aging populations create a pension burden for many corporations and imply that there are a lot of the national wealth invested in low yielding assets (either domestic or foreign long-term bonds). The less-developed economies tend to be less prepared for retirement needs, though some, including China, are rapidly trying to respond to the challenge.

In Japan, the Government Pension Investment Fund (GPIF) is the largest government pension fund globally with well over $1 trillion in assets under management, mostly in Japanese government bonds. The GPIF is one of several investment funds in Japan that might be diversified in the future. Others include the individual savings in the Postal Bank as well as Japan's foreign exchange reserves. However, the rather risk averse Japanese might draw back given the losses the fund faced in 2008 and early in 2009.

South Korea's funds, which are also predominately invested in domestic government securities, have also been earmarked for diversification. The pension fund has increased its exposure to equities and overseas investment in the last few years. They have planned some co-investment with the Korean Investment Corporation, the country's sovereign wealth fund. The South Korean pension fund is among several Asian investment funds that have been interested in investing in energy and other commodity producers, perhaps in tandem with the country's overseas oil corporation.

Despite China's high national savings rate, its retirement finance has many gaps. Only a small share of workers are covered by the existing corporate or national systems, and the payouts tend to be quite small, much lower than would be sufficient to meet retirement needs. Moreover, Chinese demographics, engendered by the one child policy suggest the share of elderly to working population is growing, increasing the need for individuals to self-insure for retirement as they already need to do for their health care, education needs, and in case of job loss. China set up a reserve fund for the national pension system in 2000 to try to narrow the shortfall, though further funds would be needed.

China has also tried to use its fund to help develop the its financial sector, allowing and encouraging the National Social Security Fund to invest in local private equity and requiring state-owned enterprises to issue it block shares. The SOE stake issuance seems to meet several policy goals, adding capital to the NSSF, helping create institutional investors with longer-term horizons to reduce the speculative nature of the market as well as creating a new set of shares that could not be sold immediately.

Singapore has one of the more developed pension systems in the region. The Central Provident Fund (CPF) allows Singaporeans some choice between funds to allocate their funds. These funds, as well as those from Singapore's sovereign wealth funds were used as seed capital to try to attract foreign investors to the city state.

Australia and New Zealand have likewise set up reserve funds that are trying to increase retirement assets through judicious investments. The Australian Future fund, Australia's sovereign fund, is expected to be used to meet retirement shortfalls, though it could be spent on other investments in the interim if needed. A vast majority of its assets continue to be invested domestically, especially in fixed income, but it plans to increase its foreign holdings.

Middle East

As a whole the Middle East tends to have low levels of pension coverage, limited to those in the formal sector and especially public sector workers. In general, there are different trends across the energy-exporting and energy-importing countries. The latter, tending to be poorer, tend also to have lower national savings as a whole. In fact some countries like Egypt and Lebanon are particularly reliant on the financing from foreign sources. Jordan, however, is an exception; the assets of its fund are equivalent to 36.7% of GDP according to the OECD and ILO.

These economies, as rentier states, tend to have high levels of transfer payments and pensions are a prime vehicle, especially in the GCC. Despite the young population, the unemployment rates tend to be high, meaning the amount saved in public retirement funds may be insufficient. Meanwhile with the labor force small, and women in particular inadequately represented, retirement needs are ticking time bombs.

Some of these undercapitalized systems have benefited from the oil boom. Some countries allocated a share of the surplus to bolster retirement savings. Kuwait used the opportunity of high economic growth and great savings to provide transfers to start putting their pension funds on sounder footing. It made transfers of as much as 10% of GDP in 2008 but subsequently stopped transfers as oil prices fell. It is unlikely to make transfers in 2009. However shortfalls still remain both for national funds as a whole and public sector workers in particular.

The Abu Dhabi Retirement Pensions & Benefits Fund was set up in 2001 and collects 26% of funds earned by any Emirati: 5% is paid by the employee, 15% by the employer, and the remainder is paid by the government. However, the government may have been prepaying the fund. IMF data assessed in Arnold (2008) suggested that the government contributed more than the 6% share in 2005.

Given the reduction in growth, contributions from individuals may well fall along with wages. However, throughout the region, nationals tend to be more protected from job losses. Foreign workers, who bear most of the job losses, tend not to be contributers to these state schemes

Overall, these funds tend to be relatively conservative, and tend to have little international exposure (ILO 2009). Several such as the pension funds of public workers in Abu Dhabi have become rather sophisticated, drawing on the expertise of internal and external asset managers. Increasingly, funds are being invested in foreign bonds and stocks as with other government assets. Some countries like Saudi Arabia actually have fairly established pension funds that are significant holders of domestic equity in addition to foreign currency assets. These, though, are small as a share of GDP and in comparison to the overall asset of the government

Overall pension fund asset allocation tends to be more conservative than that of their sovereign funds, and in some countries pension funds tend to be used as a tool for recapitalization of domestic asset markets. For instance, the GOSI, one of the two main Saudi Arabian pension funds, not only increased their holdings of domestic equities as a market stabilization tool but also shifted many of its deposits in foreign banks to those held in local banks, likely helping shore up their capital base (Ziemba 2009). The Saudi pension funds also bought a significant amount of the debt the government issued during the 1990s (it repaid much of it from 2003–2008). Other pensions like that of Jordan allowed beneficiaries to borrow against their savings (ILO).

Europe

Public pension coverage and asset allocation varies quite widely across Europe, which also has well established and large private pension funds. Yet public funds still account for close to a majority of retirement savings, particularly for public sector workers. Most funds have significant exposure to equity markets and a small allocation to alternative assets. As such they are significant participants in European equity markets. There are some exceptions to the shift to riskier assets. Spain keeps 100% of its assets in bonds and cash. Their size also varies. The largest fund, as a ratio of the size of the economy is in Sweden. Sweden, with one of the most developed social welfare systems, also has the largest amount of public pension assets as a share of GDP 31.6% according to the OECD.

Norway has both a dedicated pension fund, which includes many domestic assets, and a much larger sovereign wealth fund called the government pension fund global (GPF-G). This fund, whose goal is to save Norway's wealth for future generations and to cushion the domestic economy from high and volatile hydrocarbon revenue. This fund, as indicated by the name is intended to meet long-term funding needs of the pensions. However, these assets (over $330 billion at the end of April 2009) may also be spent on other purposes. In 2009, a portion will help finance Norway's fiscal stimulus. Norway's fund has increased from under $50 billion in 2000 to well over $400 billion in mid-2008. The loss in value since then is partly attributable both to exchange rate volatility as the value of its predominately European assets fell in US dollar terms over the past year. However, the fund also faced significant losses on its investments, especially on its equity holdings but also on some of the higher risk bonds. The fund, which now has a target asset allocation of 60% equity and 40% bonds, underperformed its benchmark in H2 2008 and Q1 2009. It has been going through a process of improving its risk management and assessing its asset allocation.

Russia also intends to use a share of the foreign exchange accumulated in the oil boom to meet its retirement needs. In early 2008, it split its stabilization fund into a Reserve fund, intended to provide budgetary support when revenues fall and a National Wealth fund to save the funds for future generations. Russian officials intended to invest these funds to meet pension funding gaps. However, given Russia's financial vulnerabilities, these funds may well be used for other purposes. Already the value of the reserve fund has fallen from a peak of over $130 billion in early 2009 to under $100 billion in June 2009. With Russia at risk of running a low double digit as a share of GDP fiscal deficit in 2009 and a 5–6% of GDP deficit in 2010, it may exhaust both of its funds, leaving little for the future. Russia has continued to be conservative in its asset allocation, despite initial ideas that the wealth might invest in equities. Instead it is restricted to AAA-rated government bonds and restricted from agency bonds. However, future asset allocation changes are possible.

US and Canada: Public pensions in the US and Canada tend to be co-funded by payroll deductions from employees, contributions from employers, including the government in the case of public sector workers. The largest source of retirement funds in the US comes from social security, which is completely invested in US treasury bonds, despite some diversification suggestions. The political debate on the underfunded liabilities of social security and Medicare will revive in coming years, but for now concerns have taken a back seat to shorter-term financing worries. By contrast the public funds of individual states for their public employees have tended to increase their allocation to equities and other riskier assets. As noted above, the funds for California's public workers, some of the largest public pensions, were quick to move into these assets. Some may be reducing their allocations, particularly given that they have faced losses on some of these assets. Some investments have been sold at a loss, especially property holdings, and private placements relied indirectly on leverage.

State and local governments have been underfunding their pensions for some years now as their fiscal positions weaken. This trend has worsened in 2009 when public workers were also forced to take furloughs, reducing their work hours and thus their contributions. Moreover, such authorities may continue to underfund their pensions for several years, given that revenues may be slow to recover even as short-term liabilities mount.

Unlike US social security trust fund, the Canadian pension plan (CPP) set up an investment portfolio about a decade ago to try to grow its assets. Eventually these assets or the return on their investment are intended to be deposited into the main fund of the CPP. These assets, prefunded by the government have been invested in equities, foreign and domestic as well as alternative assets. The same reform boosted the share of assets that could be invested outside of Canada. Large public pension funds for provincial workers like Ontario Teachers fund have followed the lead of their US counterparts, emerging as key activist investors.

11.7 CONCLUSION

By virtue of their increase in assets and diversification to increase their risk-adjusted return, public pension funds have become a more significant investor in global, regional, and national capital markets. The creation of reserve funds by both developed and emerging economies to help meet the retirement funding shortfall has boosted the size of these assets. In 2009, these funds are trying to process the lessons of the credit crisis and global asset market correction. Several may take the lesson to increase the share of liquid assets in their portfolios to have funds available should the government or beneficiaries claim funds. Moreover, given the political pressures inherent in investment losses, some sovereign investors may further try to minimize losses.

Thus, sovereign pension funds must be seen as one of several pools of capital managed by governments. Despite different goals and time horizons, many of these varied types of sovereign capital are being managed with a similar asset allocation. Over time, should pension funds continue to attract assets, their asset allocation may adjust slightly. In particular, given their long-term horizon, it could be in the interest of financial markets, pension beneficiaries, and other citizens, if sovereign pension funds filtered more investments into real investment, particularly infrastructure. Not only might such investment lead to long-term economic benefits, but it should also bring a financial return, which should hold its value even in the case of rising inflation.

REFERENCES

Allianz Global Investors. 2008. Funding unfunded pensions: Governance and investments of Asian reserve funds. Allianz Global Investors.

Arnold, W. 2008. Wealth funds draw profits and attention. *The National* [Abu Dhabi], July 13. www.thenational.ae/article/20080713/BUSINESS/923178969.

Behrendt, Christina, Tariq Haq, and Noura Kamel. 2009. The impact of the financial and economic crisis on arab states: considerations and social protection policy responses. International Labor Organization. Beirut, Lebanon.

Bernstein, S., J. Lerner, and A. Schoar. 2009. The investment strategies of sovereign wealth funds. Harvard University.

Blundell-Wignall, A., H. Yu-Wei, and J. Yermo. 2008. Sovereign wealth and pension fund issues. OECD.

Monk, A. 2008. Is CalPERS a sovereign wealth fund? Boston College, Boston, MA.

Setser, B., and R. Ziemba. 2009. GCC funds: Reversal of fortune. Council on Foreign Relations.

Ziemba, R. 2009. GCC: Sovereigns a bit better. Roubini Global Economics, New York.

CHAPTER 12

Issues in Individual Asset-Liability Management for Retirement

12.1 OWN COMPANY STOCK

The stock market decline of 2000 and 2003 was very hard on pension funds in several ways:

- Shortfalls were created in defined benefits programs.

  General Motors at the start of 2002 had obligations of $76.4 billion and assets of 67.3 billion for a shortfall of 9.1 billion. Despite contributions of $3.2 billion in 2002, the shortfall was projected to be $23 billion at the end of 2002.

  Ford had an underfunding of $6.5 billion on September 30, 2002, projected to be about $10 billion at 2002's year end.
- If a defined contribution plan, company image, and employee morale are hurt.

The Enron collapse in late 2001, when the stock fell 99% from $90 to under a dollar and employees lost their jobs and also lost most of their pensions, pointed to something well known to professional analysts. There is a lot of risk in having a pension fund largely in one asset, and the risk is even larger if that asset is correlated with one's income as well. Enron employees lost over a billion dollars in total, some 60% of their 401(k) pension. This is a classic example of overbetting and lack of diversification.

Table 12.1 shows that for many major companies, their own company stock is a very high percent of 401(k) plans.

In total, according to Mitchell and Utkus (2002), there are about five million 401(k) plan participants that hold 60% of their assets in company stock, but those that do generally have large amounts. In total, company stock is about 19% of assets. But for those who have any company stock,

TABLE 12.1 Share of Own Company Stock in 401(k) Pension Plans

Company	Shares in Own Company as % of 401(k) assets	Share Price Performance 2001, %	2002, %
Procter & Gamble	94.7	−2.2	11.5
Pfizer	85.5	−12.3	−22.0
Coca Cola	81.5	−25.1	−5.5
General Electric	77.4	−23.3	−37.4
Enron	57.7	−99.1	−85.4
Texas Instruments	75.7	−34.5	−46.1
McDonald's	74.3	−22.1	−39.3
Ford	57.0	−28.9	−38.3
Qwest	53.0	−69.7	−64.6
AOL Time Warner	52.0	−8.1	−59.2

Source: Updated from *The Economist*, December 15, 2001, p. 60.

it's 29%. Not surprisingly, employees have a lower percentage of stock, 22%, when they have free choice versus 53% when the company decides.

Why do companies and employees invest so much of their own company stock in their pensions? Companies can either purchase shares in the open market, as some like Microsoft do, or they can just issue shares just like options to key employees slightly diluting thir stock price. The latter is economical for the company. In the words of *The Economist* (December 15, 2001, p. 60),

> Employees who invest in their company's shares solve two problems, in theory. They resolve the issue of agency costs that arises between shareholders and the people hired to work on their behalf. And, ... they reap the benefits of capital appreciation, a fundamental component of capitalism.
>
> The results can be spectacular. America is filled with tales of people who held jobs as cash-register clerks at Wal-Mart, or on the diaper-making line at Procter & Gamble, who survived on their wages but have made fortunes through steady accumulation of company stock in retirement plans.

There are many other spectacular positive examples such as Microsoft, Intel, and Nokia.

Employees can frequently purchase own company shares at a discount to current market price or acquire the shares through options given for free.

Also, there is the pressure of corporate culture. Bill and Sandra saw that in Japan from 1988 to 1989 where employees of the Yamaichi Research Institute were obliged by moral suasion and peer pressure to buy Yamaichi Security stock, which later went bankrupt in 1995. Enron has refocused this risk that has been around a long time.

Most likely there will be rule changes enacted. A key is the risk bearer position of employees and employers. In 1942, laws were passed to limit own company stock to 10% in defined benefit plans that bore employer risk. The 401(k)s are defined contribution plans that shift the risk to the employees. At Procter & Gamble, the company says that the welfare of the company and the employee are inseparable. That may be the American way, but at 95% plus job risk, employees are taking a lot of risk. This concentration usually leads to either very high or very low returns.

What is the real risk of the own stock and job risk concentration? Douglass, Wu, and Ziemba (DWZ) (2004) have estimated this using mean-variance and stochastic programming assets-only models. Before discussing this, Mitchell and Utkus (2002) remind us how volatility destroys wealth. They consider three workers who earn $50,000 per year and contribute 10% to a 401(k) with contributions and inflation at 3% per year. The stock market index and company stock are assumed to return 10% per year with annual standard deviations of 20% and 40%, respectively. After 30 years, the median employee, who invested 100% in the market index had $830,000, with 50–50 splits it was $615,000 and with 100% in company stock, it's $411,000. This is because of the geometric-arithmetic inequality caused by the volatility: gaining 50% and then losing 50% does not make one even; 100 becomes 75, with a rate of return of -13.4%. The greater the volatility, the lower the geometric mean, which determines long-run wealth gains, for constant arithmetic mean.

DWZ consider the following situation: an investor chooses between the market index (S&P 500), a bond index (Lehman Brothers US aggregate), cash and own company stock. The parameter assumptions, estimated from 1985 to 2002 monthly data from Datastream, mirror long-run stock, bond and cash returns from Constantinides (2002), Dimson et al. (2002), and Siegel (2002). Yearly mean returns are 1.10, 1.05, 1.00, 1.125 for these four assets, respectively. Standard deviations are 0.20, 0.04, 0.01, 0.50 and the covariance matrix is

$$
\begin{bmatrix}
1.000 & 0.750 & 0.058 & 0.500 \\
0.750 & 1.000 & 0.250 & 0.550 \\
0.058 & 0.250 & 1.000 & 0.029 \\
0.500 & 0.550 & 0.029 & 1.000
\end{bmatrix}.
$$

These assumptions have mean returns relative to cash, and higher expected returns, but with much higher volatility for own company stock (two and a half times the S&P 500 which is typical for mid-cap equities). Figure 12.1 shows the results from the mean-variance model as a function of investor risk aversion with (12.1.b) and without (12.1.a) company stock and as a function of company stock mean return (12.1.c). The shaded regions indicate portfolio weights (leftscale). The diamonds indicate the expected return of the optimal portfolios. When risk aversion is 8, there is a 60% stock, 40% bond mix.

This optimal portfolio has no own company stock holdings. Hence, without trading constraints, it is not optimal with risk aversion of 8 to hold own company stock. However, for investors with trading constraints, such as the inability to short sell, owning some company stock can be optimal.

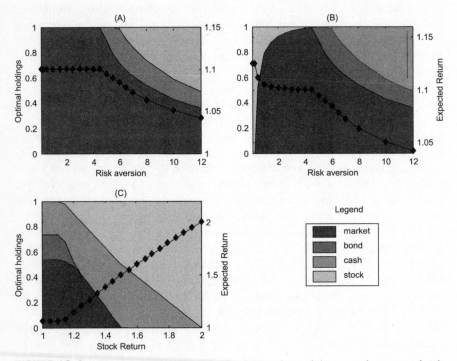

FIGURE 12.1 Mean-Variance Model. The optimal portfolios as a function of risk aversion (A,B) and expected return on company stock (C). Shaded regions indicate portfolio weights (left scale). The line represents the expected return on the optimal portfolio (right scale). Diamonds indicate values of independent variable for which calculations were made. Results for the three asset cases, with no own-company stock, are in (B). Results for the four asset cases are in (B) and (C)
Source: Douglass, Wu, and Ziemba (2004).

Company stock appears as an optimal portfolio choice if investor's risk aversion is very low or their expected return for the stock is high . At a risk aversion of five, the short-selling constraint becomes binding and the optimal portfolio begins to shift to the riskier stock investment (Figure 12.1b). To obtain company stock holdings above 50%, as observed in Table 12.1, requires a risk aversion parameter below 0.5. Alternatively, company stock holding of 50% is obtained if the employee is presumed to have an expected return for company stock over 50% (Figure 12.1c). Own company stock begins to enter when its mean return approaches 20%, that is double the S&P 500. The expected return of own company stock must be over 50% or five times the S&P 500 for the optimal allocation of own company stock to reach 50%.

This analysis assumes that all employee wealth is contained in the company pension plan. This assumption is reasonable considering that many North Americans save little beyond what enters their tax-sheltered accounts. However, Figure 12.1b shows what proportion of wealth would have to be held outside the plan in order to support a 50% own stock holding within the plan. An employee with risk aversion of 8 and 50% of their pension plan in own stock company stock would have to have 50% of their retirement savings outside the company plan.

12.2 THE ROLE OF ANNUITIES

Annuities are the purchase of a steady stream of income in the future. They are defined by the characteristic that the time between the purchase and the first payment is no more than the time between payments. They provide a way for an individual to shift the longevity risk that comes with the conversion of defined contribution pension savings.

There are a number of types of annuities designed to split the longevity and investment risk between annuitant and provider in different ways. Annuities can have payments fixed as a percentage of the contract or variable, based on the returns of the assets (this does not provide a full shift of the risks). Guaranteed annuities provide a certain period over which payments will be made even if the annuitant dies earlier but continuing to pay beyond that date as long as the annuitant lives. As the fear that led to the choice of an annuity is to avoid outliving your savings, it is generally not recommended to have a long "certain" period annuity, as this significantly lowers the monthly payout. Joint annuities include joint-life and joint-survivor benefits enabling couples to determine whether payment continues until the last spouse dies. Impaired life annuities make payment on medical diagnosis of severely reduced life expectancy. The variants are limited only by the imagination of the contractors and the ability to value the risks.

TABLE 12.2 Monthly Payout from $100,000 Invested under Various
Assumptions Regarding the Annuitants and Different Types of Annuities

Income Payment Options		Monthly Income					
	Fixed	Male, 65	Female, 65	Couple, 65	Male, 70	Female, 70	Couple, 70
SL: Single Life Income, No Payments to Beneficiaries		668	625	548	757	697	614
5CC: Single Life Income, Up to 5 Years Paid to Beneficiaries	1,757	662	621	548	745	707	614
10CC: Single Life Income, Up to 10 Years Paid to Beneficiaries	1,000	643	610	547	707	680	611
15CC: Single Life Income, Up to 15 Years Paid to Beneficiaries	757	615	593	543	654	641	600
20CC: Single Life Income, Up to 20 Years Paid to Beneficiaries	645	582	569	535	600	596	577
IR: Single Life Income, Installment Refund Paid to Beneficiaries	567	632	600	544	696	669	606

Source: www.totalreturnannuities.com

Table 12.2 shows the various payouts from the purchase of a $100,000 annuity. This was calculated on June 30, 2009, for California residents. The first column has the fixed-term payouts for comparison. The other columns each have a form of longevity insurance without or with various term guarantees. The columns are for males and females retiring at 65 or 70, for individual or joint longevity coverage.

Some countries have requirements for the conversion of retirement savings like 401(k)s into annuity by a certain age; for instance, in the UK it is 75. Countries with required conversions have been changing the age.

In general annuities are very expensive with relatively high fees for the insurance that they provide if in the end you do not survive.

In 2009, there is much distrust of financial institutions so buying an annuity for say $500,000 now to provide income for the next 20 to 30 years till death has default risk in it as well as the high cost due to low interest rates.

12.3   THE ROLE OF INSURANCE

Insurance is equivalent to an annuity in which you pay a premium overtime for a one-time lump sum in the future. Insurance has several advantages. First, the payout is tax free, and it can be a large sum in the millions. Second, it is a security blanket for many people. A spouse can feel more secure with a policy on their partner that will cover his income should he die or be unable to work. Third, it is a portfolio hedging vehicle and reduces risk in a portfolio of assets. Fourth, an insurance policy can be used to cover inheritance taxes. These advantages are to be balanced by the cost of insurance, which is generally high and any insurance company credit risk. Being an insurance company is like being a put seller who collects the premium now and invests that money now and pays off the claim later or in some cases does not have to pay. It is known that the expected value of puts is negative for buyers and positive for sellers; see Figure 12.2 from Tompkins, Ziemba, and Hodges (2008). So as an insurance purchaser, you are paying a premium for these advantages.

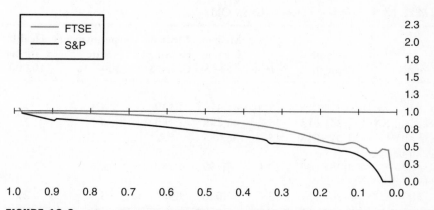

FIGURE 12.2   Mean Return per Dollar Bet vs. Odds Levels: One-Month Stock Index Futures Puts, 1985 to 2002
Source: Tompkins, Ziemba, and Hodges (2008).

12.4   THE ROLE OF MANAGED
WITHDRAWAL PLANS

12.4.1   Mandatory Withdrawals

Rules vary by country but there is generally a mandatory withdrawal schedule for tax-sheltered savings such as IRAs, 401(k)s, etc. In the US those 70.5 and over must have a plan for withdrawal; in Canada the age is 71. If one does not buy an annuity but manages the portfolio, a loss in value such as occurred in 2008 can make it difficult to meet the withdrawal requirement without greatly lowering the asset value and thus creating added longevity risk. A good news, bad news item: the US Congress in December 2009 voted on a one-year waiver for 2009 but not for 2008. Following a year in which retirement savings lost much value, retirees were still required to withdraw based on the end of 2007 balances.

12.5   WHERE AND HOW TO RETIRE?

U.S. News and World Report has a section ranking places to retire on various criterion including healthiest, low-cost, brainiest, outdoorsiest, greenest as well as special interests, such as political party, sports enthusiast, etc. Sherrian (2009) also reports on research that has selected the five best places to grow old based on costs, climate, and access to life-style desires. Not all five are in warm places; see Table 12.3.

TABLE 12.3   Five Best Places to Grow Old

County	Total Population	% 65+	Median Income 65+, $	Median Housing Costs, $	Unemployment Rate 2008, %	Health Care per 10,000
Montgomery, PA	778,048	14.9	41,323	1,539	4.4	2
Nassau, NY	1,361,625	15.0	48,848	2,140	4.7	2
Pima, AZ	1,012,018	15.2	36,635	972	5.1	2
Palm Beach, FL	1,265,293	22.1	37,799	1,250	6.6	4
Honolulu, HA	905,034	15.4	53,020	1,566	3.5	2
US average						

Source: Adapted from Sherrian (2009).

12.5.1   New Type Retirement Communities

Baby boom retirees are likely to want a different type of retirement community from past generations.

Andrew Carle, directior of the assisted living/senior housing administration program at George Mason University feels that retirement communities will spring up to match a variety of needs and wants (*US News and World Report*, 2009). Though undoubtedly there will be many types, he suggests five types:

1. Campus living: more than 100 retirement communities have been located near major universities to take advantage of a variety of facilities offered, including good medical care, continued learning programs, concerts and plays, easy access to sports as participant and spectator.
2. Feng shui: Aegis a well-known administrator of retirement and assisted living communities, has designed Aegis Gardens based on the principles of Feng shui and geared to Chinese and Japanese speakers.
3. Gays and Lesbians: RainbowVision in Santa Fe is attractive to gay, lesbian, bisexual, and transgender residents. They have a cabaret instead of a golf course, for example.
4. Country music lovers: The Crescendo to open in 2013 near Nashville will cater to those who made country music their career and now want it as part of their retirement.
5. Assisted RV living: the Rainbow's End RV Park in Texas has services provided by CARE (Continuing Assistance for Retired Escapees) so that retirees can live in their RVs and have help with meals, laundry, getting to medical appointments, and changing propane tanks. They also have access to an activity center.

12.5.2   Assisted Living

When health deteriorates, it may become necessary to consider an assisted living option. This option might require prior purchase of insurance to cover the costs or sufficient savings.

Retirees are moving out of elder care facilities to live with their children. This trend has been encouraged for economic reasons including unemployment among adult children so the senior income and wealth is needed; 77% of US wealth is held by those 50 and older (Sherrian 2009).

12.5.3   Reverse Mortgages

Reverse mortgages help retirees to retire in their own homes. A reverse mortgage, a form of an after-tax annuity, is a hybrid instrument. Like an annuity for a given amount upfront, equity in your home, you receive a fixed monthly payment. However, as you receive the monthly payment, you are accumulating interest on the loan. The equity in the home must in the end be sufficient to pay back the loan and the accumulated interest. So is is also akin to a loan with monthly payouts.

An *Intentionally Defective Trust* is a way of structuring a reverse mortgage within a family trust. This instrument includes the ability to pass on assets to heirs (children or grandchildren) thus avoiding estate taxes and at the same time continue to pay any taxes due (in effect a second gift). It is also possible to lend the trust money to, say, buy your home, and then the trust would pay you interest. In the end the trust owns the home rather than a bank or other provider of the reverse mortgage. Though a potentially useful instrument, the IRS has yet to rule on the legality of these trusts (Spector and Tergesen 2009).

12.5.4 Does It Pay to Have Multiple Residences?

Having multiple residences would help retirees to split the year at different places.

In Canada there was less leveraging and less speculation and banks do not make subprime loans to Canadian customers. However, the banks (the few of them that are all very powerful) have some US and other toxic assets, some from US subprime investments. But none of these banks is in serious trouble like many US and UK banks.

Let's now look at a case study that's farily simple, that being the case of a person call Cynthia having two residences. This is based on Attentuck (2009). The idea is that one residence is for working now and one is for retirement and in this and most other similar cases, the second home is in another city. In this case, a 58-year-old woman runs a business out of a rented apartment in Toronto. But she also owns a condo in British Columbia, where she plans to retire. She has no debt, $325,000 in registered retirement plans which are taxable only when they are taken out, $715,000 in investments and a car, worth $15,000 for a net worth of Cdn$1,605,000. She would like to remain in both communities for the next 10 to 15 years. But the cost of maintaining both houses and other expenses is much more than her annual $29,808 after-tax income. So she has had to deplete her investments to cover this shortfall.

What should she do?

The opinion of a financial planner, Mike Cherney, follows and then there are our thoughts.

Mike advises as follows:

- Give up one of the two residences. Their cost is $5,168 monthly more than twice her monthly after-tax income.

  Property taxes $350, condo fees $250, utilities and phones $230, rent on Toronto apartment $2,100, food $450, restaurant $250, entertainment $200, clothing $250, car fuel $50, travel $200, car and home insurance $188, misc $350, charity and gifts $300 for a total of $5,168.
- If she were to give up her Toronto apartment, her monthly expenses would decrease to $3,068 which still exceed her after-tax monthly income.
- She could consider selling her $550,000 valued BC condo for say $500,000, thereby increasing her investments to $1,215,000.

Mike assumes investment return of 4% and inflation of 2.5% per year and estimates her income from taxable and registered retirement savings with the assumption that she exhaust both at her actuarially expected death at 94.

- Taxable assets would provide $4,556 a month or $54,675 a year.
- Registered retirement savings could provide $12,840 a year.
- For a total of $67,515.
- On turning 60 she could add $5,944 or $495 a month from her early retirement Canada Pension Plan. Bringing her income from 60 to 65 up to $73,459 a year or $6,122 a month.
- At age 65 she could add Old Age Security for $ 6,204 a year. This would bring her post 65 income to $79,663 a year or $6,639 a month, which would more than cover her current expenses and provide a cushion for emergencies.

Cynthia rejects the idea of giving up one residence. That was our conclusion, too! She prefers to work more hours on her business and raise her income by nearly $30,000 per annum some four times her present income from self-employment. But this is risky, and she could suffer from injury or illness; plus there is a lot more work.

The planner suggests that if she wanted to sustain the two homes she could work longer hours and perhaps move to a lower cost apartment in Toronto and she could consider renting either home when she is not using it.

Cynthia fortunately did not lose money in the 2007 to 2009 stock market decline because most of her investments were in guaranteed income certificates, which have returns that averaged 4.75% per year. But current GIC rates are lower so she might consider other alternatives such as annuities, preferred stocks, or depressed common shares. For example, in early 2009, the Bank of Montreal had a dividend over 9% and at $30 is well below a previous $50 share price. (Later in 2009, the stock moved back to the $50 area.) Government bonds had low returns and seem to be a bubble. The $5,000 per year tax free savings account can shelter a little bit.

Cynthia and her advisor concluded that at some stage she may have to move to BC and give up the Toronto rental apartment. Working more might help in the short term.

What can we add to this analysis?

Cynthia's risk attitude is probably low, given the investment in the GICs. She is debt free and has considerable assets. She has the flexibility to either work more or spend less. She is not depleting her $1.6 million net worth much each year. It seems she should enjoy herself in the Toronto and BC residences, and, possibly, sublet or rent in longer periods away and not worry too much. She is actually in pretty good shape. If in later years she needs more spending money, she can dispose of some of her assets or the condo.

There is a general issue here, which is that assets to hold to cover liabilities safely with low risk. In Chapters 7 and 14 to 16 we, present a general model to analyze such situations and discuss a number of applications.

12.5.5   Interest-Free Loan

There is currently a loophole in the social security legislation that allows an individual to start taking benefits at one age, say, 62, and then at 70, say, change their minds, repay the cash amount they received and start over. This is without accumulating interest (Munnell et al. 2009).

REFERENCES

Attentuck, A. 2009. Two houses are not so sweet. *Globe and Mail*, January 17, B8.

Douglass, J., O. Wu, and W. T. Ziemba. 2004. Stock ownership decisions in DC pension plans. *Journal of Portfolio Management* (Summer): 92–100.

Sherrian, L. 2009. These counties offer retirees comfort and opportunity, but also financial peace of mind. *Forbes*, March 21.

Spector, M., and A. Tergesen. 2009. Unusual trusts gain appeal in unusual time. *Wall Street Journal*, April 10.

Starr, C. 1999. The ultimate uncertainty: Intergenerational planning. Paper for Workshop on an Application of Planning under Uncertainty, Electric Power Research Institute, Palo Alto, CA, July 12.

Tompkins, R., W. T. Ziemba, and S. Hodges. 2008. The favorite longshot bias in S&P 500 futures options: The return to bets and the cost of insurance. In *Handbook of Sports and Lottery Investments*, ed. D. B. Hausch and W. T. Ziemba. North Holland, 161–180.

U.S. News and World Report. 2009. Next-generation retirement communities. May 15.

Modeling the Issues

CHAPTER 13

Learning from Other Models

This chapter concerns learning from models for managing wealth such as university endowments, foundations, family trusts, and other nonprofit organizations.

13.1 PRESERVING ENDOWMENT SPENDING

Major foundations such as the Carnegie, Ford, and Rockefeller and universities such as Harvard, Princeton, Stanford, Yale, and Columbia have large multibillion dollar endowments. These funds, which came from wealthy donors, are used to improve and preserve educational institutions. Since typically there is inflation, endowment spending is also usually increasing. The endowments must manage their funds so that current spending is increasing without depleting very much of the capital to be used for future spending. Capital campaigns occur from time to time, as do bequests, and there is income from tuition, grants, research contracts, and other sources. However, to maintain this spending, a good investment performance is crucial.

Yale University has approached this problem with a heavy emphasis on private equity rather than publicly traded equity; see Swensen (2000). Yale's endowment made 19.1% on its private equity portfolio and 17.6% on the whole portfolio over the 16 years from 1982 to 1997, which is higher than US bonds, US equity, development equity, emerging equity, real estate, and cash Adding two more years for the 18 years 1982 to 1999, the annualized return was 16.9%, which was in the top 1% of institutional funds during this period. Their asset allocation as of June 1997 was domestic equity, 22.5%, domestic fixed income 12.5%, foreign equity, 12.5%, private assets, 32.5% and other marketable securities, 20.0%. The high amount of private assets reflects the belief that large-scale inefficiencies frequently exist in illiquid markets simply because the illiquidity provides a premium, so positions can

TABLE 13.1 Net Returns from Various Asset Classes, 1982 to 1997

	US Bonds	US Equity	Developed Equity	Emerging Equity	Real Estate	Cash	Yale's Absolute Return	Private Equity
Years	72	72	38	13	21	72	20	16
Arith. return, %	1.2	9.2	6.3	11.1	3.5	−0.4	17.6	19.1
Standard dev	6.5	21.7	18.9	27.9	5.1	4.1	11.8	20.0
Growth rate	1.0	7.0	4.7	7.7	3.4	−0.5	17.0	17.5

be entered at discounts and that these markets are not well understood. So Yale is an example where private equity can have high returns over long periods that include bear markets; see Table 13.1. Yale's returns from private equity were statistically significantly higher than the other asset classes.

Table 13.2 compares the Yale and Harvard Endowments with the S&P 500 for the years 2000 to 2008.

The best venture capital managers (which include Swensen at Yale) are extremely careful and have very good returns but most others have poor returns. See Tables 13.3 and 13.4.

Table 13.5 shows how four funds do in bull and bear markets and during two market crashes.

TABLE 13.2 Comparison of Returns for Yale, Harvard, and the S&P 500, %

Year	Economic Cycle	Yale	Harvard	S&P 500
2000	Tech bubble	41.00	32.00	7.00
2001	Tech bubble bust	9.20	−2.70	−14.83
2002	Tech bubble bust	0.70	−0.50	−17.99
2003		8.80	12.50	0.25
2004		19.40	21.10	19.11
2005	Real Estate bubble	22.30	19.20	6.32
2006	Real Estate bubble	22.90	16.70	8.63
2007	Real Estate bubble bust	28.00	23.00	21.00
2008	Real Estate bubble bust	4.00	8.60	−14.80
Average return, 2000–2008		17.80	14.40	1.60
Volatility, 2000–2008		12.40	11.30	14.60
2009		−25.00		

Source: WSJ (2008).

TABLE 13.3 Dispersion of Active Management Returns Identifies Areas of Opportunity, January 1988 to December 1997

Asset Class	First Quartile	Median	Third Quartile	Range
US fixed income[†]	9.7	9.2	8.5	1.2
US equity[†]	19.5	18.3	17.0	2.5
International equity[†]	12.6	11.0	9.7	2.9
Real estate[*]	5.9	3.9	1.2	4.7
Leveraged buyouts[‡]	23.1	16.9	10.1	13.0
Venture capital[‡]	25.1	12.4	3.9	21.2

[*]Institutional Property Consultants.
[†]Piper Managed Accounts Report of December 31, 1997.
[‡]Venture Economics. Venture capital and leveraged buyout data represent returns on Funds formed between 1988 and 1993, excluding more recent funds so that mature investments will not influence reported results.
Source: Swensen (2000).

Table 13.6 shows the current June 2009 situation at Harvard, Yale, Stanford, and Princeton. These endowments probably fell 25 to 30% in the past year so that guaranteed commitments to private equity funds and others are a greater proportion of assets. Large increases in endowments from trading gains, donations, and fund raising expanded these assets. But

TABLE 13.4 Comparison of Asset Classes: Investment Fund Returns, 1980 to 1997

	Real Estate[*]	Venture Capital[‡]	Leveraged Buyouts[‡]	Domestic Equity[†]	Foreign Equity[†]
Maximum		498.2	243.9	18.1	19.5
First quartile	9.9	17.1	23.8	16.6	16.1
Median	7.8	8.1	13.2	15.5	14.9
Third quartile	5.9	0.6	1.1	14.9	14.0
Minimum		−89.7	−65.9	13.2	11.1
First to third quartile range	4.0	16.5	22.7	1.7	2.1
Standard deviation	2.5	30.0	35.7	1.3	2.1

[*]Institutional Property Consultants.
[†]Piper Managed Accounts Report of December 31, 1997.
[‡]Venture Economics, 1998 Investment Benchmark Report: Buyouts and Other Private Equity and 1998 Investment Benchmark Report: Venture Capital.
Source: Swensen (2000).

TABLE 13.5 How Four Funds Did in Bull and Bear Markets, 1977 to 2001

	Bull and Bear Markets		Crashes of 1987 & 1998		Market Volatility	
	Average Monthly Return in Excess of Benchmark (%)		On-Month Return in Excess of Benchmark (%)		Correlation of Monthly Returns in Excess of Benchmark with Volatility Measure	Sharpe Ratio, Jan 1980– Mar 2000
	Bulls	Bears	Oct-87	Aug-98		
Berkshire Hathaway	1.21	1.70	0.40	0.89	−0.14	0.786
BGI TAA	0.10	0.73	20.38	−1.74	0.54	0.906
Ford Foundation	0.11	−0.08	−1.11	−2.11	−0.09	0.818
Magellan	0.52	0.88	−5.46	−1.20	−0.04	0.844

Source: Clifford, Kroner, and Siegel (2001).

the recent losses have ushered in a new austerity of tight budgets, stopped projects, caused hiring freezes, etc.

Table 13.7 shows the asset allocation mix of these four university endowments along with the estimated July 2008 to June 2009 returns from the various asset classes. The private equity and real asset returns were about −50% versus excellent previous returns. Despite large recent losses, these four endowments have excellent long-term records, which is what counts, as they are long-term investors targeting to spend about 5% of the portfolio

TABLE 13.6 University Endowments and Annual Budgets

	Harvard	Yale	Stanford	Princeton
Endowment, $ bil				
June 30, 2008	36.9	22.9	17.2	16.3
June 30, 2009 (est)	25.0	17.0	12.0	11.4
Change (est), %	−30	−25	−30	−30
Budget, $ bil	1,100*	2,280	3,500	1,360
From Endowment				
$ bil	600	850	1,000	653
Percent	55	37	29	48
Academic year	2008 to 2009	2007 to 2008	2008 to 2009	2008 to 2009

*Faculty of Arts & Sciences only.
Source: Barron's (2009).

TABLE 13.7 Asset Allocations of Four Major University Endowments

Asset	Harvard	Yale	Stanford	Princeton	Average Educ Endowment	Est Return June 2008 to 2009
Hedge funds	18	25	18	24	22	−20
Domestic equity	11	10	37	7	22	−27
Bonds	11	4	10	2	12	6
Foreign equity	22	15	na	12	20	−31
Private equity	12	20	12	29	9	−50
Real assets	26	29	23	23	14	−47
Cash	−3	−4	na	2	2	2

Source: Bary (2009).

per year. For the ten years to June 30, 2008, Yale's annual return was 16.3%, Harvard's 13.8%, and Princeton 14.9% vs. the S&P 500 of 2.9%.

13.1.1   Cloning the Yale Approach

A description and results of the Yale endowment approach up to June 2007 is in Ziemba and Ziemba (2007). Harvard, Princeton, and Stanford have had similar portfolios of assets and success up to fiscal 2008 with large gains of about 16% per year since 1985 but substantial losses in 2008 and 2009. The basic idea is to follow Siegel's (2008) *Stocks for the Long Run* as discussed in Chapter 4 with a modification that the equity categories are expanded to include private equity, real assets, commodities, and similar assets, and there is extensive, careful research in-house and by the active managers. These are pseudo-equities, so the idea is to invest in those equities when they are good but diversifying the asset portfolio. Faber (2007) shows how one could clone the Yale approach using ETFs. This does not mean that the results of Yale's careful and outstanding research work of their own and other superior managers can really be duplicated. But with very low transactions costs of about 0.40% per year versus much higher costs by Yale and others, this approach has merit. Also adding Mulvey's (2009) idea of equally weighting then rebalancing other EFTs to fixed mix provides a useful strategy. We can clone Yale's 2007 portfolio, which gained 28% or Yale and Harvard's combined as shown in Table 13.8, which shows the results as of June 30, 2008, the only day that they mark-to-market for the years 2000 to 2008. The portfolio for various reasons is only market-to-the-market at the end of the fiscal year on June 30.

TABLE 13.8 Endowment Investing Harvard and Yale and
ETFs, 2007, %

	Harvard	Yale	ETFs
Domestic stocks	12	11	SPY
Foreign developed stocks	12	6	EFA
Foreign emerging stocks	10	9	EEM
Bonds	9	4	AGG
TIPS	7	0	TIP
Real estate	9	14	IYR
Commodities	17	14	GSP
Private equity	11	19	PSP, PFP
Hedge funds	18	23	
Cash	−5	0	

Source: Faber (2008).

13.1.2 Dealing with Liquidity the Yale Way

Swensen was asked how endowments should deal with liquidity issues in
the current crisis (Hettena 2009). Some endowments have floated bonds
in an attempt to avoid selling assets that have fallen dramatically in value.
Swensen agreed that selling assets might not be the best way if an endowment
is properly positioned. He mentioned the easy liquidity from dividends on
stocks, rents on real estate, logging income from timber holdings, coupons
on bonds. Assets can be pledged for loans. Sales of assets should be more a
question of asset allocation rather than liquidity.

13.1.3 Swensen's Rule and Others

Can individual investors mimic the great investors and do as well in their
investment choices? Many economists think not. Even when regulated, there
is always, if subtle, insider-type and special-relationship information and
access to large-scale deals that set the great investor apart.

> *You can't make the level playing field. What you tell people
> is that this is very unlevel, there are land mines everywhere
> and Joe-6-pack doesn't have an equal chance as Warren Buffett.
> Anyone who tells Joe-6-pack he does is lying to Joe-6-pack...
> Thurow (1989).*

Thurow (1987) suggested that there is no level playing; indeed if there were, the game would not be any fun as there would be no special gains to be made. Samuelson as well has always argued that point.

Swensen suggests that there are two choices for asset management: as he sees it, the distinction is not between institutional investors and individual investors but between those who can take an active role in management and those that take a passive role. In this regard, he suggests there is no middle. The active group includes those with high quality investment teams: Yale, Harvard, Princeton, Stanford. Swensen suggests that the passive group should include most investors! In his book—he proposed that individuals use ETFs with low fees. Swensen is very good at what he does; that's for sure. So his opinion must be considered carefully.

Faber (2007) takes a different approach to the problem of whether individuals can invest well. Like Swensen she cautions against taking an active approach if one does not have a qualified team. Her research shows that if one tries to mimick the best portfolios passively using the same asset allocations you are likely to end up with a portfolio in the bottom 30 to 40%. Faber suggests focusing on the asset classes where you can best leverage your knowledge. El Erian (2008) suggested that it would be harder for followers to gain the same level of return as the leaders in the alternative asset universe. So those who venture here should be careful; perhaps the experts deserve their fees!

13.2 DEVISING A RULE SO THAT SPENDING NEVER FALLS

An important way to preserve capital is to not lose it during weak markets. Table 13.5 shows that the Ford Foundation, Berkshire Hathaway, Fidelity Magellan, and Barclays Global Investor Tactical Asset Allocation fund were able to do this during 1977 to 2001. Bear markets are defined as July 1977 to February 1978, December 1980 to July 1982, September to November 1987, June to October 1990, and July to August 1998. Other periods are defined as bull markets, even if there was little gain, as in 1984 and 1994.

The problem of how to invest in risky assets and cash dynamically in time so that a given spending rule will allow spending to never decrease has been considered by Dybvig (1988, 1995, 1999). This problem is very similar to the constant proportional portfolio insurance model of Black and Perold (1992) and is illustrated in Figures 13.1 to 13.3.

Figure 13.1a is the performance during 1946 to 1996 of a fixed mix strategy with equal proportions of large cap US stocks and three-month index linked T-bonds (assumed to be a risk-free asset in real terms). The

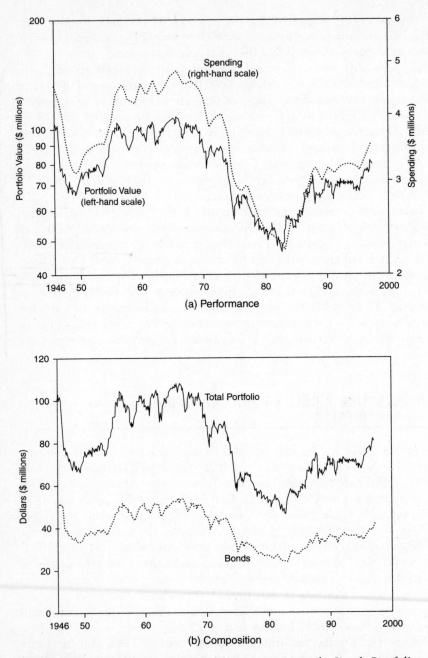

FIGURE 13.1   Performance and Portfolio Composition of a Simple Portfolio
Strategy and Spending Rule, 1946 to 1996
Source: Dybvig (1999).

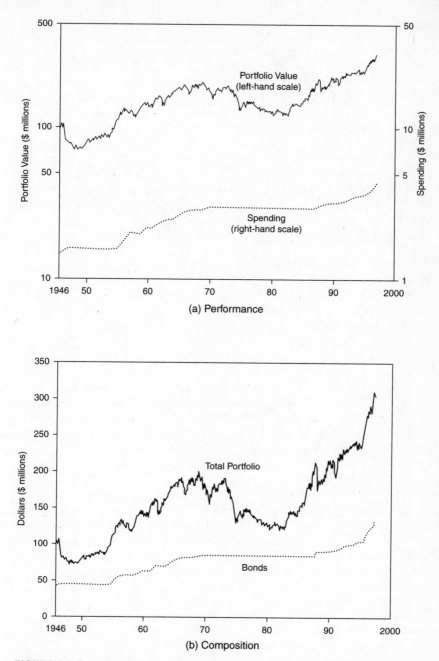

FIGURE 13.2 Performance and Portfolio Composition of the Proposed Expenditure Protected Policy, 1946 to 1996
Source: Dybvig (1999).

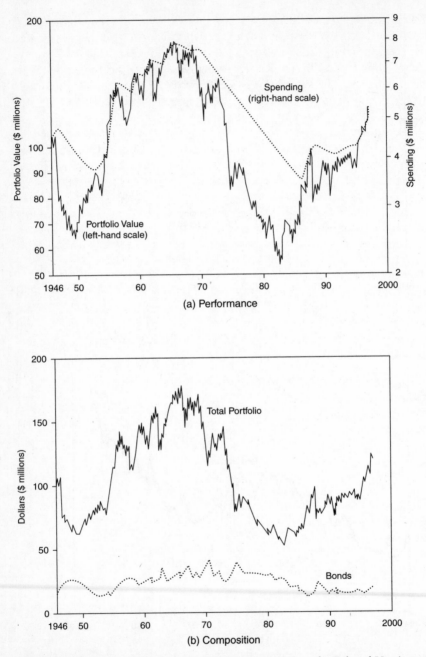

FIGURE 13.3 Performance and Portfolio Composition of a Diluted Version of the Expenditure Protected Policy, 1946 to 1996
Source: Dybvig (1999).

spending rate is 4.5% of beginning initial wealth each year with an initial endowment to $100 million. With the fixed mix strategy, the weights change as the stock portfolio rises and falls as shown in Figure 13.1b. There is a protected part that is invested in the Treasuries, and the remainder is in stocks. The protected strategy, like portfolio insurance, moves into safer assets when the market falls. The strategy avoids spending cuts while still allowing significant participation in rising equity markets.

One can smooth the spending pattern in Figure 13.1a and base spending on the average wealth levels over several years, but this is an ad hoc approach. Figure 13.2 shows Dybvig's approach where spending never decreases, even in periods in which the portfolio value declines. The strategy does require low spending rates that may be below current spending for some plans. Many variants are possible, such as beginning with higher spending rates and allowing the spending rate declines at a small continuous rate. Figure 13.3 is one such example. In that example, spending fell nearly a half during the poor stock market years following the 1973 to 1974 oil price crisis in stock prices and then increases.

This is an interesting strategy, which will perform best in rising or falling markets and not so well in choppy markets. As with all continuous time models, the choice of parameters is crucial, and the portfolio weights will change dramatically as market expectations, especially the means, change.

13.2.1   A Protective Spending Model

Dybvig's (1988, 1995, 1999) protective spending model is an extension of Merton's (1973) continuous time portfolio choice model with the additional constraint that spending can never fall. The spending rule $\frac{s_t}{r}$ and the risky portfolio investment α_t are chosen to

$$\text{Maximize } E\left[\int_0^\infty U(s_t)exp^{-\delta t}dt\right]$$

subject to $s'_t \geq s_t$ for all $t' > t$ and $w_t \geq 0$ for all t,
where w_t solves the budget equation

$$dw = w_t r\, dt + \alpha_t(\mu dt + \alpha dz_t - r\, dt) - s_t dt,$$

subject to the initial wealth constraint $w_0 = W_0$.

The endowment's preferences are represented by the power utility function

$$u(s_t) = \frac{s_t^{1-\gamma}}{1-\gamma}$$

where relative risk aversion $\gamma > 0$ and $\gamma \to 1$ gives log utility. The objective function is to maximize the discounted sum over time of instantaneous benefits weighing the benefits at t by a weight that is declining in time so that later spending at the same level is valued less than earlier spending. The non-negative wealth constraint ensures that the fund cannot borrow forever without repayment and rules out doubling strategies.

The budget constraint is the riskless return from cash investments plus the random return from risky assets less the spending per unit of time. The optimal solution is to invest

$$\alpha_t = k \left(w_t - \frac{s_t}{r} \right)$$

in the risky portfolio and the remainder

$$w_t - \alpha_t = \frac{s_t}{r} + (1 - k) \left(w_t - \frac{s_t}{r} \right)$$

in the riskless asset.

The portfolio has the cost of maintaining current spending forever $\frac{s_t}{r}$ invested in the riskless asset and the remainder $w_t = \frac{s_t}{r}$ invested in fixed proportions of k in the risky portfolio and $1 - k$ in the riskless asset. The constant

$$k = \frac{\mu - r}{\gamma^* \sigma^2}$$

where

$$\gamma^* = \sqrt{\frac{(\delta + k^* - r^*)^2 + 4r^* k^* - (\delta + k^* - r^*)}{2r^*}}$$

is a number between 0 and 1,

$$k^* = \frac{(\mu - r)^2}{2\sigma^2} \quad \text{and} \quad r^* = r \left(\frac{\gamma - \gamma^*}{\gamma} \right)$$

If the strategy is to allow spending to fall at a rate d, then the part of the endowment in risky assets is

$$\alpha_t = k \left(\frac{w_t - s_t}{r + d} \right)$$

and the amount in riskless asset is

$$w_t - \alpha_t = \frac{s_t}{r+d} + (1-k)\frac{w_t - s_t}{r+d}$$

Spending declines by the proportion d per unit of time and is increased as necessary to maintain $s_t \geq r^*w$ where $r^* < r + d$. The protected part of the endowment is smaller than with $d = 0$. The investment required to maintain constant spending forever is less in this strategy as the endowment can spend a proportion of the original investment in addition to the riskless return. Consumption is also different as it declines when the endowment is not at the minimun proportion, r^*. Another difference is that the minimum spending rate may be larger than the riskfree rate as long as it is less than $r + d$.

The estimation of the endowment's relative risk aversion parameter can proceed by the certainty equivalent or other methods as discussed in Ziemba (2003). Dybvig's (1999) estimate is 0.498. This assumes that this year's budget is \$10 million and there is a 50–50 chance of an increase of zero or one million and the fund's certainty equivalent is \$10.3 for sure.

This uses the equation

$$\frac{10.3^{1-\gamma}}{1-\gamma} = 0.5\frac{10^{1-\gamma}}{1-\gamma} + 0.5\frac{11^{1-\gamma}}{1-\gamma}$$

Now if the fund is indifferent between spending \$10.45 this year and next year and spending \$10 million this year and \$11 million next year. That is, the fund is willing to spend less in total if it can spend more earlier. Then the time preference parameter δ is 0.177 as the solution to

$$\frac{10.45^{1-\gamma}}{1-\gamma} + exp^{-\delta}\frac{10.45^{1-\gamma}}{1-\gamma} = \frac{10^{1-\gamma}}{1-\gamma} + exp^{-\delta}\frac{11^{1-\gamma}}{1-\gamma}$$

REFERENCES

Bary, A. 2009. The big squeeze. *Barron's*, June 29.

Clifford, S. W., K. F. Kroner, and L. B. Siegel. 2001. In pursuit of performance: The greatest return stories ever told: Investment insights. *Barclays Global Investor* 4, no. 1:1–25.

Dybvig, P. H. 1988. Inefficient dynamic portfolio strategies, or how to throw away a million dollars in the stock market. *Review of Financial Studies* 1, no. 1:67–88.

————. 1995. Duesenberry's ratcheting of consumption: Optimal dynamic consumption and investment given intolerance for any decline in standard of living. *Review of Economic Studies* 62, no. 2:287–313.

————. 1999. Using asset allocation to protect spending. *Financial Analysts Journal* (Jan.–Feb.):49–61.

El Erian, M. 2008. *When Markets Collide*. New York: McGraw-Hill.

Faber, M. 2008. Endowment investing 2008. Yale-style. *Seeking Alpha*.

Hettena, S. 2009. Yale's financial wizard, David Swensen, says most endowments shouldn't try be like Yale, ProPublica. www.propublica.org, February 18.

Siegel, J. 2008. *Stocks for the Long Run*, 4th ed. New York: McGraw-Hill.

Swensen, D. W. 2000. *Pioneering Portfolio Management: An Unconventional Approach to Institutional Investments*. New York: The Free Press.

Thurow, L. 1989. Comment in Anatomy of a hostile takeover. PBS. Ethics in America.

WSJ. 2008. Harvard endowment returns 8.6%. September 17.

Ziemba, W. T. 2003. *The Stochastic Programming Approach to Asset Liability and Wealth Management*. AIMR.

CHAPTER 14

The Innovest Austrian Pension Fund Financial Planning Model

14.1 HOW SHOULD COMPANIES FUND THEIR LIABILITIES AND DETERMINE ALLOCATIONS AMONG ASSET CLASSES AND HEDGING INSTRUMENTS?

In this chapter, we describe an approach to asset-liability modeling using discrete time stochastic linear programming. The application is to the Siemens Austria pension fund, and the model has been in use since 2000. The model has had considerable success and has been used by regulators to determine the effect of various possible pension fund policy changes as well as by pension fund advisors who deal with uncertain assets and liabilities subject to various legal and policy constraints. In Chapters 15 and 16 a similar model is developed and applied to individual ALM decision making.

Siemens AG Österreich, part of the global Siemens Corporation, is the largest privately owned industrial company in Austria. Its businesses with revenues of €2.4 B in 1999, include information and communication networks, information and communication products, business services, energy and traveling technology, and medical equipment. Their pension fund, established in 1998, is the largest corporate pension plan in Austria and is a defined contribution plan. Over 15,000 employees and 5,000 pensioners are members of the pension plan with €510 million in assets under management as of December 1999.

Innovest Finanzdienstleistungs AG founded in 1998 is the investment manager for Siemens AG Österreich, the Siemens Pension Plan and other institutional investors in Austria. With €2.2 billion in assets under management, Innovest focuses on asset management for institutional money and pension funds. This pension plan was rated the best in Austria of 17 analyzed in the 1999 to 2000 period. The motivation to build InnoALM, which is described in Geyer and Ziemba (2008; see also Geyer et al. 2002), is part of their desire to have superior performance and good decision aids to help achieve this goal.

Various uncertain aspects; possible future economic scenarios; stock, bond, and other investments; transactions costs; liquidity; currency aspects; liability commitments over time; and Austrian pension fund law and company policy suggested that a good way to approach this was via a multiperiod stochastic linear programming model. These models evolve from Kusy and Ziemba (1986), Cariño and Ziemba (1994, 1998a,b), and Ziemba and Mulvey (1998). This model has innovative features such as state-dependent correlation matrices, fat-tailed asset return distributions, and simple computational schemes and output.

InnoALM was produced in six months during 2000 with Geyer and Ziemba serving as consultants with Herold and Kontriner being Innovest employees. InnoALM demonstrates that a small team of researchers with a limited budget can quickly produce a valuable modeling system that can easily be operated by nonstochastic programming specialists on a single PC. The IBM OSL stochastic programming software provides a good solver. The solver was interfaced with user-friendly input and output capabilities. Calculation times on the PC are such that different modeling situations can be easily developed and the implications of policy, scenario, and other changes seen quickly. The graphical output provides pension fund management with essential information to aid in the making of informed investment decisions and understanding the probable outcomes and risk involved with these actions. The model can be used to explore possible European, Austrian, and Innovest policy alternatives.

The liability side of the Siemens Pension Plan consists of employees, for whom Siemens is contributing DCP payments, and retired employees who receive pension payments. Contributions are based on a fixed fraction of salaries, which varies across employees. Active employees are assumed to be in steady state; so employees are replaced by a new employee with the same qualification and sex so there is a constant number of similar employees. Newly employed staff start with less salary than retired staff, which implies that total contributions grow less rapidly than individual salaries. Figure 14.1 shows the expected index of total payments for active and retired employees until 2030.

The set of retired employees is modeled using Austrian mortality and marital tables. Widows receive 60% of the pension payments. Retired employees receive pension payments after reaching age 65 for men and 60 for women. Payments to retired employees are based upon the individually accumulated contribution and the fund performance during active employment.

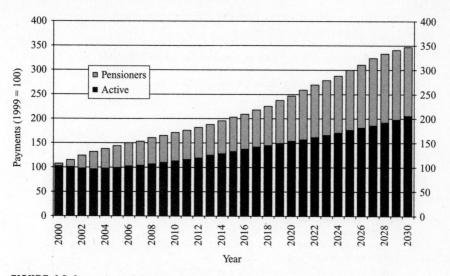

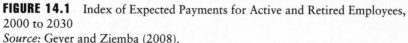

FIGURE 14.1 Index of Expected Payments for Active and Retired Employees, 2000 to 2030
Source: Geyer and Ziemba (2008).

The annual pension payments are based on a discount rate of 6% and the remaining life expectancy at the time of retirement. These annuities grow by 1.5% annually to compensate for inflation. Hence, the wealth of the pension fund must grow by 7.5% per year to match liability commitments. Another output of the computations is the expected annual net cash flow of plan contributions minus payments. Since the number of pensioners is rising faster than plan contributions, these cash flows are negative so the plan is declining in size.

The model determines the optimal purchases and sales for each of N assets in each of T planning periods. Typical asset classes used at Innovest are US, Pacific, European, and Emerging Market equities and US, UK, Japanese, and European bonds. The objective is to maximize the concave risk-averse utility function expected terminal wealth less convex penalty costs subject to various linear constraints. The effect of such constraints is evaluated in the examples that follow, including Austria's limits of 40% maximum in equities, 45% maximum in foreign securities, and 40% minimum in Eurobonds. The convex risk measure is approximated by a piecewise linear function, so the model is a multiperiod stochastic linear program. Typical targets that the model tries to achieve, and if not is penalized for, are wealth (the fund's assets) to grow by 7.5% per year and for portfolio performance

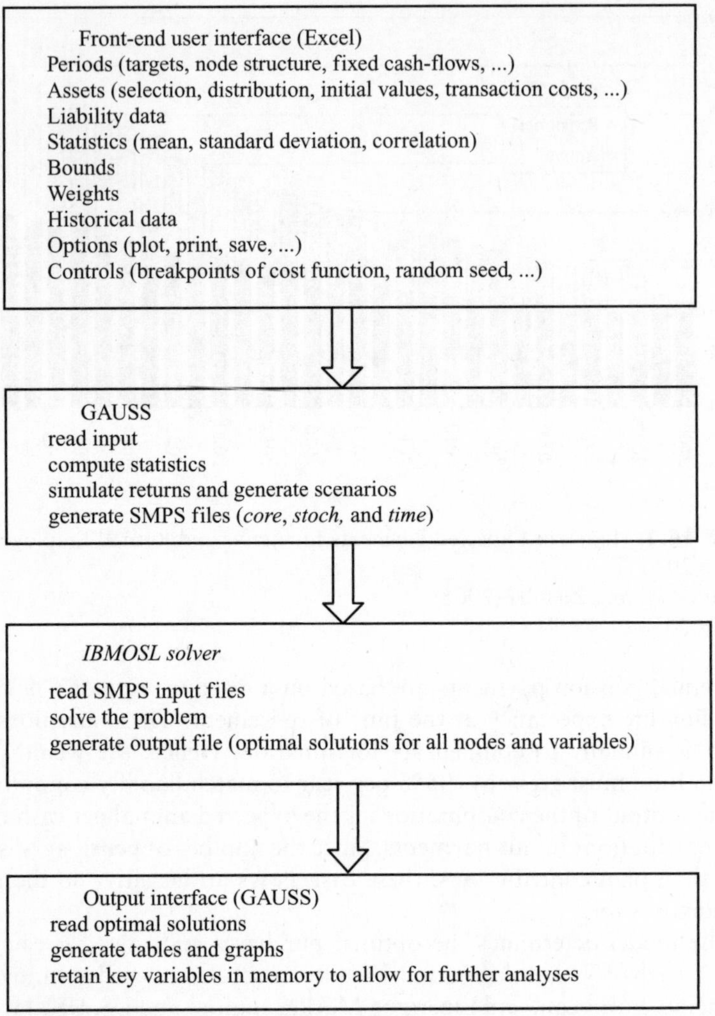

Front-end user interface (Excel)
Periods (targets, node structure, fixed cash-flows, ...)
Assets (selection, distribution, initial values, transaction costs, ...)
Liability data
Statistics (mean, standard deviation, correlation)
Bounds
Weights
Historical data
Options (plot, print, save, ...)
Controls (breakpoints of cost function, random seed, ...)

GAUSS
read input
compute statistics
simulate returns and generate scenarios
generate SMPS files (*core, stoch,* and *time*)

IBMOSL solver

read SMPS input files
solve the problem
generate output file (optimal solutions for all nodes and variables)

Output interface (GAUSS)
read optimal solutions
generate tables and graphs
retain key variables in memory to allow for further analyses

FIGURE 14.2   Elements of InnoALM
Source: Geyer and Ziemba (2008).

returns to exceed benchmarks. Excess wealth is placed into surplus reserves, and a portion of that is paid out in succeeding years.

The elements of InnoALM are described in Figure 14.2 The interface to read in data and problem elements uses Excel. Statistical calculations use the program Gauss, and this data is fed into the IBM0SL solver, which generates the optimal solution to the stochastic program. The output, some of which is shown in the next section used Gauss to generate various tables and graphs and retains key variables in memory to allow for future modeling calculations.

14.2 FORMULATING INNOALM AS A MULTISTAGE STOCHASTIC LINEAR PROGRAMMING MODEL

The non-negative decision variables are wealth (after transactions costs) and purchases and sales for each asset $(i = 1, \ldots, N)$. Purchases and sales take place in periods $t = 0, \ldots, T - 1$. Except for $t = 0$, purchases and sales are scenario dependent. All decision variables are non-negative.

Wealth accumulates over time for a T period model according to

$$
\begin{aligned}
W_{i0} &= W_i^{init} + P_{i0} - S_{i0}, & t &= 0 \\
\tilde{W}_{it} &= \tilde{R} W_{i0} + \tilde{P}_{i1} - \tilde{S}_{i1}, & t &= 1 \\
\tilde{W}_{ii} &= \tilde{R}_{it} W_{ii,t-1} + \tilde{P}_{it} - \tilde{S}_{it}, & t &= 2, \ldots, T - 1 \\
\tilde{W}_{iT} &= \tilde{R}_{it} W_{ii,T-1}, & t &= 2, \ldots, T - 1
\end{aligned}
$$

where W_i^{init} is the initial value of asset i. There is no uncertainty in the initialization period $t = 0$. Tilde denote random scenario-dependent parameters or decision variables. Returns $\tilde{R}_{it}$ $(t = 1, \ldots, T)$ are the gross returns from asset i between $t = 1$ and t.

The budget constraints are

$$
\sum_{i=1}^{N} P_{i0}(1 + tcp_i) = \sum_{i=1}^{N} S_{i0}(1 - tcs_i) + C_0 \quad t = 0 \qquad \text{and}
$$

$$
\sum_{i=1}^{N} \tilde{P}_{it}(1 + tcp_i) = \sum_{i=1}^{N} \tilde{S}_{it}(1 - tcs_i) + C_i \quad t = 1, \ldots, T - 1
$$

where tcp_i and tcs_i are the linear transaction costs for purchases and sales, and C_i is the fixed (nonrandom) net cash flow (inflow if positive).

Since short sales are not allowed, the following constraints are included

$$
\begin{aligned}
S_{i0} &\leq W_i^{init} & i &= 1, \ldots, N; \ t = 0, \qquad \text{and} \\
\tilde{S}_{it} &\leq \tilde{R}_i \tilde{W}_{i,t-1} & i &= 1, \ldots, N; \ t = 1, \ldots, T - 1
\end{aligned}
$$

Portfolio weights can be constrained over linear combinations (subsets) of assets or individual assets via

$$\sum_{i \in U_t} \tilde{W}_{it} - \theta_U \sum_{i=1}^{N} \tilde{W}_{it} \leq 0 \qquad \text{and}$$

$$-\sum_{i \in L_t} \tilde{W}_{it} - \theta_L \sum_{i=1}^{N} \tilde{W}_{it} \leq 0, \, t = 0, \ldots, T-1$$

where θ_U is the maximum percentage and θ_L is the minimum percentage of the subsets U_j and L_l of assets $i = 1, \ldots, N$ included in the restrictions j and l, respectively. The θ_U's, θ_L's, U_j's and L_l's may be time dependent. Austria, Germany, and other European Union countries have restrictions that vary from country to country but not across time. Austria currently has the following limits: max 40% equities, max 45% foreign securities, min 40% Eurobonds, max 5% total premiums in noncurrency hedge options short and long positions. The model has convex penalty risk function costs if goals in each period are not satisfied. In a typical application, the wealth target $\overline{W}_t$ is assumed to grow by 7.5% in each period. This is a deterministic target goal for the increase in the pension fund's assets. The wealth targets are modeled via

$$\sum_{i=1}^{N} (\tilde{W}_{it} - \tilde{P}_{it} + \tilde{S}_{it}) + \tilde{M}_t^W \geq \overline{W}_t \qquad t = 1, \ldots, T$$

where $\tilde{M}_t^W$ are wealth-target shortfall variables. The shortfall (or embarrassment) is penalized using a piecewise linear risk measure based on the variables and constraints

$$\tilde{M}_t^W = \sum_{j=1}^{m} \tilde{M}_{jt}^W, \qquad t = 1, \ldots, T$$

$$\tilde{M}_{jt}^W \leq b_j - b_{j-1}, \, t = 1, \ldots, T; \, j = 1, \ldots, m-1$$

where $\tilde{M}_{jt}^W$ is the wealth target shortfall associated with segment j of the cost function, b_j is the jth breakpoint of the risk measure function $b_0 = 0$, and m is the number of segments of the function. A quadratic function works well, but other functions may be linearized as well. Convexity guarantees that if $\tilde{M}_{jt}^W \geq 0$ then $\tilde{M}_{j-1,t}^W$ is at its maximum, and if $\tilde{M}_{jt}^W$ is not at its maximum then $\tilde{M}_{j+1,t}^W = 0$.

Stochastic benchmark goals can be set by the user and are similarly penalized with a piecewise linear convex risk measure for underachievement.

The benchmark target $\tilde{B}_t$ is scenario dependent. It is based on stochastic asset returns and fixed asset weights defining the benchmark portfolio

$$\tilde{B}_t = W_0 \sum_{j=1}^{t} \sum_{i=1}^{N} \alpha_i \tilde{R}_{it}$$

with shortfall constraints

$$\sum_{i=1}^{N} \tilde{W}_{it} + \tilde{M}_t^B \geq \tilde{B}_t \qquad t = 1, \ldots, T$$

where $\tilde{M}_t^B$ is the benchmark-target shortfall.

If the total wealth implied by the allocation is above the target, a percentage γ, typically a conservative 10%, of the exceeding amount is allocated to the reserve account. Then the wealth targets for all future stages are increased. For that purpose, additional non-negative decision variables $\tilde{D}_t$ are introduced, and the wealth target constraints become

$$\sum_{i=1}^{N} (\tilde{W}_{it} - \tilde{P}_{it} + \tilde{S}_{it}) - \tilde{D}_t + \tilde{M}_t^W = \overline{W}_t + \sum_{j=1}^{t-1} \gamma \tilde{D}_{t-j}$$

$$t = 1, \ldots, T - 1, \text{ where } \tilde{D}_1 = 0$$

Since pension payments are based on wealth levels, increasing these levels increases pension payments. The reserves provide security for the pension plan's increase of pension payments at each future stage. The fund had accumulated such a surplus by 2000.

The pension plan's objective function is to maximize the expected discounted value of terminal wealth in period T net of the expected discounted penalty costs over the horizon from the convex risk measures $c_k(\cdot)$ for the wealth and benchmark targets, respectively,

$$Max\ E \left[d_T \sum_{i=1}^{N} \tilde{W}_{iT} - \lambda \sum_{t=1}^{T} d_t w_t \left(\sum_{k \in \{W, B\}} v_k c_k(\tilde{M}_t^k) \right) \right]$$

Expectation is over T period scenarios S_T. The v_k are weights for the wealth and benchmark shortfalls, and the w_t are weights for the weighted sum of shortfalls at each stage. The weights are normalized via

$$\sum_{k \in \{W, B\}} v_k = 1 \qquad \text{and} \qquad \sum_{t=1}^{T} w_t = T$$

The discount factors d_t are defined on the basis of an interest rate $r : d_t = (1 + r)^{-t}$. Usually r is taken to be the three- or six-month Treasury-bill rate. However, Campbell and Viceira (2001) argue that, in a multiperiod world, the proper risk-free asset is an inflation-indexed annuity rather than the short dated T-bill. Their analysis is based on a model where agents desire to hedge against unanticipated changes in the real rate of interest. Ten-year inflation-index bonds are then suggested for r as their duration closely approximates the indexed annuity.

The shortfall cost coefficients are based on the least-cost way to make up the shortfall-embarrassments, which may be the product of an optimized combination of borrowing, equity, short- and long-term debt, and other financial instruments. Cariño and Ziemba et al. (1994, 1998a,b) and Consiglio et al. (2001) discuss this.

Allocations are based on optimizing the stochastic linear program with IBM's optimization solutions library using the stochastic extension library (OSLE version 3).[1] The library uses the Stochastic Mathematical Programming System (SMPS) input format for multistage stochastic programs (Birge et al. 1987). The OSLE routines require three input files: the core-, stoch- and time-file. The core-file contains information about the decisions variables, constraints, right-hand-sides and bounds. It contains all fixed coefficients and dummy entries for random elements. The stoch-file reflects the node structure of the scenario tree and contains all random elements: that is, asset and benchmark returns, and probabilities. Non-anticipatory constraints are imposed to guarantee that a decision made at a specific node is identical for all scenarios leaving that node so the future cannot be anticipated. This is implemented by specifying an appropriate scenario structure in the stoch input file. The time-file assigns decision variables and constraints to stages. The required statements in the input files are automatically generated by the InnoALM system.

14.3   SOME TYPICAL APPLICATIONS

To illustrate the model's use we present results for a problem with four asset classes (Stocks Europe, Stocks US, Bonds Europe, and Bonds US) with five periods (six stages). The periods are twice 1 year, twice 2 years and 4 years (10 years in total). We assume discrete compounding which implies that the mean return for asset i (μ_i) used in simulations is $\mu_i = exp(\overline{y})_i - 1$ where $\overline{y}_i$ is the mean based on log-returns. We generate 10000 scenarios using a 100-5-5-2-2 node structure. Initial wealth equals 100 units, and the wealth

---

[1]For information http://www6.software.ibm.com/sos/features/stoch.htm.

target is assumed to grow at an annual rate of 7.5%. No benchmark target and no cash in- and outflows are considered in this sample application to make its results more general. We use $R_A = 4$, and the discount factor equals 5%. which corresponds roughly with a simple static mean-variance model to a standard 60-40 stock-bond pension fund mix; see Kallberg and Ziemba (1983).

Assumptions about the statistical properties of returns measured in nominal euros are based on a sample of monthly data from January 1970 for stocks and 1986 for bonds to September 2000. Summary statistics for monthly and annual log returns are in Table 14.1. The US and European equity means for the longer period 1970 to 2000 are much lower than for 1986 to 2000 and slightly less volatile. The monthly stock returns are non-normal and negatively skewed. Monthly stock returns are fat tailed whereas monthly bond returns are close to normal (the critical value of the Jarque-Bera test for a = .01 is 9.2).

However, for long-term planning models such as InnoALM with its one-year review period, properties of monthly returns are less relevant. The bottom panel of Table 14.1 contains statistics for annual returns. While average returns and volatilities remain about the same (we lose one year of data, when we compute annual returns), the distributional properties change

TABLE 14.1 Statistical Properties of Asset Returns

	Stocks Eur		Stocks US		Bonds Eur	Bonds US
	1/70	1/86	1/70	1/86	1/86	1/86
	–9/00	–9/00	–9/0	–9/00	–9/00	–9/00
Monthly returns						
Mean (% p.a.)	10.6	13.3	10.7	14.8	6.5	7.2
Std.dev (% p.a.)	16.1	17.4	19.0	20.2	3.7	11.3
Skewness	−0.90	−1.43	−0.72	−1.04	−0.50	0.52
Kurtosis	7.05	8.43	5.79	7.09	3.25	3.30
Jarque-Bera test	302.6	277.3	151.9	155.6	7.7	8.5
Annual returns						
Mean (%)	11.1	13.3	11.0	15.2	6.5	6.9
Std.dev (%)	17.2	16.2	20.1	18.4	4.8	12.1
Skewness	−0.53	−0.10	−0.23	−0.28	−0.20	−0.42
Kurtosis	3.23	2.28	2.56	2.45	2.25	2.26
Jarque-Bera test	17.4	3.9	6.2	4.2	5.0	8.7

Source: Geyer and Ziemba (2008).

dramatically. While we still find negative skewness, there is no evidence for fat tails in annual returns except for European stocks (1970 to 2000) and US bonds.

The mean returns from this sample are comparable to the 1900 to 2000 one hundred and one year mean returns estimated by Dimson et al. (2002). Their estimate of the nominal mean equity return for the US is 12.0% and that for Germany and UK is 13.6% (the simple average of the two country's means). The mean of bond returns is 5.1% for the US and 5.4% for Germany and the UK.

Assumptions about means, standard deviations, and correlations for the applications of InnoALM appear in Table 14.3 and are based on the sample statistics presented in Table 14.2. Projecting future rates of returns from past data is difficult. We use the equity means from the period 1970 to 2000 since 1986 to 2000 had exceptionally good performance of stocks that is not assumed to prevail in the long run.

The correlation matrixes in Table 14.3 for the three different regimes are based on the regression approach of the 1996 paper of Solnik et al. Moving average estimates of correlations among all assets are functions of standard deviations of US equity returns. The estimated regression equations are then used to predict the correlations in the three regimes shown in Table 14.3. Results for the estimated regression equations appear in Table 14.2. Three regimes are considered and it is assumed that 10% of the time, equity markets are extremely volatile, 20% of the time markets are characterized by high volatility, and 70% of the time, markets are normal. The 35% quantile of US equity return volatility defines *normal* periods. *Highly volatile* periods are based on the 80% volatility quantile and *extreme* periods on the 95% quartile. The associated correlations reflect the return

TABLE 14.2 Regression Equations Relating Asset Correlations and US Stock Return Volatility (monthly returns; Jan 1989–Sep 2000; 141 observations)

Correlation Between	Constant	Slope w.r.t. US Stock Volatility	t-statistic of Slope	R
Stocks Europe—Stocks US	0.62	2.7	6.5	0.23
Stocks Europe—Bonds Europe	1.05	−14.4	−16.9	0.67
Stocks Europe—Bonds US	0.86	−7.0	−9.7	0.40
Stocks US—Bonds Europe	1.11	−16.5	−25.2	0.82
Stocks US—Bonds US	1.07	−5.7	−11.2	0.48
Bonds Europe—Bonds US	1.10	−15.4	−12.8	0.54

Source: Geyer and Ziemba (2008).

TABLE 14.3 Means, Standard Deviations, and Correlations Assumptions

		Stocks Europe	Stocks US	Bonds Europe	Bonds US
Normal Periods	Stocks US	.755			
(70% of	Bonds Europe	.334	.286		
the Time)	Bonds US	.514	.780	.333	
	Standard deviation	14.6	17.3	3.3	10.9
High Volatility	Stocks US	.786			
(20% of	Bonds Europe	.171	.100		
the Time)	Bonds US	.435	.715	.159	
	Standard deviation	19.2	21.1	4.1	12.4
Extreme Periods	Stocks US	.832			
(10% of	Bonds Europe	−.075	−.182		
the Time)	Bonds US	.315	.618	−.104	
	Standard deviation	21.7	27.1	4.4	12.9
Average Period	Stocks US	.769			
	Bonds Europe	.261	.202		
	Bonds US	.478	.751	.255	
	Standard deviation	16.4	19.3	3.6	11.4
All Periods	Mean	10.6	10.7	6.5	7.2

Source: Geyer and Ziemba (2008).

relationships that typically prevailed during those market conditions. The correlations in Table 14.3 show a distinct pattern across the three regimes. Correlations among stocks tend to increase as stock return volatility rises, whereas the correlations between stocks and bonds tend to decrease. European bonds may serve as a hedge for equities during extremely volatile periods, since bonds and stocks returns, which are usually positively correlated, are then negatively correlated. The latter is a major reason why using scenario-dependent correlation matrixes is a major advance over sensitivity of one correlation matrix.

Optimal portfolios were calculated for seven cases: with and without mixing of correlations and with normal, t- and historical distributions. Cases NM, HM, and TM use mixing correlations. Case NM assumes normal distributions for all assets. Case HM uses the historical distributions of each asset. Case TM assumes t-distributions with five degrees of freedom for stock returns, whereas bond returns are assumed to have normal distributions. The cases NA, HA, and TA use the same distribution assumptions with no mixing of correlations matrices. Instead the correlations and standard deviations used in these cases correspond to an "average" period where 10%, 20%, and 70% weights are used to compute averages of correlations and standard deviations used in the three different regimes. Comparisons of the average (A) cases and mixing (M) cases are mainly intended to investigate the effect of mixing correlations. TMC maintains all assumptions of case TM but uses Austria's constraints on asset weights. Eurobonds must be at least 40% and equity at most 40%, and these constraints are binding.

14.4 SOME TEST RESULTS

Table 14.4 shows the optimal initial asset weights at stage 1 for the various cases. Table 14.5 shows results for the final stage (expected weights, expected terminal wealth, expected reserves, and shortfall probabilities). These tables show a distinct pattern: the mixing correlation cases initially assign a much lower weight to European bonds than the average period cases. Single-period, mean-variance optimization, and the average period cases (NA, HA, and TA) suggest an approximate 45–55 mix between equities and bonds. The mixing correlation cases (NM, HM, and TM) imply a

TABLE 14.4 Optimal Initial Asset Weights at Stage 1 by Case (percentage)

	Stocks Europe	Stocks US	Bonds Europe	Bonds US
Single-period, mean-variance optimal weights (average periods)	34.8	9.6	55.6	0.0
Case NA: no mixing (average periods) normal distributions	27.2	10.5	62.3	0.0
Case HA: no mixing (average periods) historical distributions	40.0	4.1	55.9	0.0
Case TA: no mixing (average periods) *t*-distributions for stocks	44.2	1.1	54.7	0.0
Case NM: mixing correlations normal distributions	47.0	27.6	25.4	0.0
Case HM: mixing correlations historical distributions	37.9	25.2	36.8	0.0
Case TM: mixing correlations *t*-distributions for stocks	53.4	11.1	35.5	0.0
Case TMC: mixing correlations historical distributions; constraints on asset weights	35.1	4.9	60.0	0.0

Source: Geyer and Ziemba (2008).

TABLE 14.5 Expected Portfolio Weights at the Final Stage by Case (percentage), Expected Terminal Wealth, Expected Reserves, and the Probability for Wealth Target Shortfalls (percentage) at the Final Stage

	Stocks Europe	Stocks US	Bonds Europe	Bonds US	Expected Terminal Wealth	Expected Reserves at Stage 6	Probability of Target Shortfall
NA	34.3	49.6	11.7	4.4	328.9	202.8	11.2
HA	33.5	48.1	13.6	4.8	328.9	205.2	13.7
TA	35.5	50.2	11.4	2.9	327.9	202.2	10.9
NM	38.0	49.7	8.3	4.0	349.8	240.1	9.3
HM	39.3	46.9	10.1	3.7	349.1	235.2	10.0
TM	38.1	51.5	7.4	2.9	342.8	226.6	8.3
TMC	20.4	20.8	46.3	12.4	253.1	86.9	16.1

Source: Geyer and Ziemba (2008).

65–35 mix. Investing in US Bonds is not optimal at stage 1 in any of the cases, which seems due to the relatively high volatility of US bonds.

Table 14.5 shows that the distinction between A and M cases becomes less pronounced over time. However, European equities still have a consistently higher weight in the mixing cases than in no-mixing cases. This higher weight is mainly at the expense of Eurobonds. In general the proportion of equities at the final stage is much higher than in the first stage. This may be explained by the fact that the expected portfolio wealth at later stages is far above the target wealth level (206.1 at stage 6), and the higher risk associated with stocks is less important. The constraints in case TMC lead to lower expected portfolio wealth throughout the horizon and to a higher shortfall probability than any other case. Calculations show that initial wealth would have to be 35% higher to compensate for the loss in terminal expected wealth due to those constraints. In all cases the optimal weight of equities is much higher than the historical 4.1% in Austria.

The expected terminal wealth levels and the shortfall probabilities at the final stage shown in Table 14.5 make the difference between mixing and no-mixing cases even clearer. Mixing correlations yields higher levels of terminal wealth and lower shortfall probabilities.

If the level of portfolio wealth exceeds the target, the surplus $\tilde{D}$ is allocated to a reserve account. The reserves in t are computed from $\sum_{j=1}^{t} \tilde{D}$ and as shown in Table 14.5 for the final stage. These values are in monetary units given an initial wealth level of 100. They can be compared to the wealth target 206.1 at stage 6. Expected reserves exceed the target level at the final stage by up to 16%. Depending on the scenario, the reserves can be as high as 1800. Their standard deviation (across scenarios) ranges from 5 at the first stage to 200 at the final stage. The constraints in case TMC lead to a much lower level of reserves compared to the other cases, which implies, in fact, less security against future increases of pension payments.

Summarizing we find that optimal allocations, expected wealth, and shortfall probabilities are mainly affected by considering mixing correlations, while the type of distribution chosen has a smaller impact. This distinction is mainly due to the higher proportion allocated to equities if different market conditions are taken into account by mixing correlations.

The results of any asset allocation strategy crucially depend upon the mean returns. This effect is now investigated by parameterizing the forecasted future means of equity returns. Assume that an econometric model forecasts that the future mean return for US equities is some value between 5 to 15%. The mean of European equities is adjusted accordingly so that the ratio of equity means and the mean bond returns as in Table 14.3 are maintained. We retain all other assumptions of case NM (normal distribution and mixing correlations). Figure 14.3 summarizes the effects of these mean changes in terms of the optimal initial weights. As expected, see Chopra and Ziemba (1993) and Kallberg and Ziemba (1981, 1983), the results are very

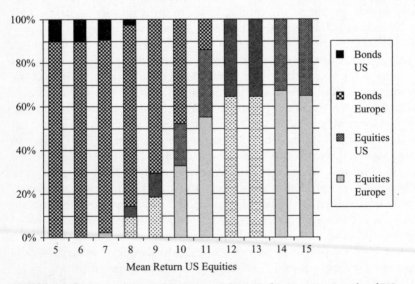

FIGURE 14.3 Optimal Asset Weights at Stage 1 for Varying Levels of US Equity Means
Source: Geyer and Ziemba (2008).

sensitive to the choice of the mean return. If the mean return for stocks is assumed to equal the long-run mean of 12% as estimated by Dimson (2002), the model yields an optimal weight for equities of 100%. However, a mean return for stocks of 9% implies less than 30% optimal weight for equities.

14.5 MODEL TESTS

Since state-dependent correlations have a significant impact on allocation decisions, it is worthwhile to further investigate their nature and implications from the perspective of testing the model. Positive effects on the pension fund performance induced by the stochastic, multiperiod planning approach will only be realized if the portfolio is dynamically rebalanced as implied by the optimal scenario tree. The performance of the model is tested considering this aspect. As a starting point, it is instructive to break down the rebalancing decisions at later stages into groups of achieved wealth levels. This reveals the "decision rule" implied by the model depending on the current state. Consider case TM. Quintiles of wealth are formed at stage 2, and the average optimal weights assigned to each quintile are computed. The same is done using quintiles of wealth at stage 5.

Figure 14.4 shows the distribution of weights for each of the five average levels of wealth at the two stages. While the average allocation at stage 5 is essentially independent of the wealth level achieved (the target wealth at stage 5 is 154.3), the distribution at stage 2 depends on the wealth level in a specific way. If average attained wealth is 103.4, which is slightly below the target, a very cautious strategy is chosen. Bonds have the highest weight in this case (almost 50%). In this situation the model implies that the risk of

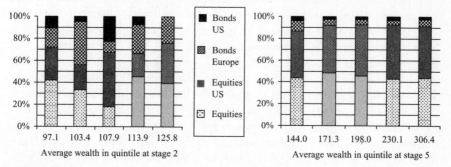

FIGURE 14.4 Optimal Weights Conditional on Quintiles of Portfolio Wealth at Stages 2 and 5
Source: Geyer and Ziemba (2008).

even stronger underachievement of the target is to be minimized. The model relies on the low but more certain expected returns of bonds to move back to the target level. If attained wealth is far below the target (97.1), the model implies more than 70% equities and a high share (10.9%) of relatively risky bonds. With such strong underachievement there is no room for a cautious strategy to attain the target level again. If average attained wealth equals 107.9, which is close to the target wealth of 107.5, the highest proportion is invested into US assets with 49.6% invested in equities and 22.8% in bonds. The US assets are more risky than the corresponding European assets, which is acceptable because portfolio wealth is very close to the target and risk does not play a big role. For wealth levels above the target, most of the portfolio is switched to European assets, which are safer than US assets. This "decision" may be interpreted as an attempt to preserve the high levels of attained wealth.

The decision rules implied by the optimal solution can be used to perform a test of the model using the following rebalancing strategy. Consider the ten year period from January 1992 to January 2002. In the first month of this period we assume that wealth is allocated according to the optimal solution for stage 1 given in Table 14.4. In each of the subsequent months the portfolio is rebalanced as follows: identify the current volatility regime (extreme, highly volatile, or normal) based on the observed US stock return volatility. Then search the scenario tree to find a node that corresponds to the current volatility regime and has the same or a similar level of wealth. The optimal weights from that node determine the rebalancing decision. For the no-mixing cases NA, TA, and HA the information about the current volatility regime cannot be used to identify optimal weights. In those cases, use the weights from a node with a level of wealth as close as possible to the current level of wealth. Table 14.6 presents summary statistics for the complete sample and the out-of-sample period October 2000 to January 2002. The mixing correlation solutions assuming normal and t-distributions (cases NM and TM) provide a higher average return with lower standard deviation than the corresponding nonmixing cases (NA and TA). The advantage may be substantial as indicated by the 14.9% average return of TM compared to 10.0% for TA. The t-statistic for this difference is 1.7 and is significant at the 5% level (one-sided test). Using the historical distribution and mixing correlations (HM) yields a lower average return than no-mixing (HA). In the constrained case TMC, the average return for the complete sample is in the same range as for the unconstrained cases. This is mainly due to relatively high weights assigned to US bonds, which performed very well during the test period; whereas stocks performed poorly. The standard deviation of returns is much lower because the constraints imply a lower degree of rebalancing.

TABLE 14.6 Results of Asset Allocation Strategies Using the *Decision Rule* Implied by the Optimal Scenario Tree

	Complete Sample 01/92–01/02		Out-of-Sample 10/00–01/02	
	mean	std.dev.	mean	std.dev.
NA	11.6	16.1	−17.1	18.6
NM	13.1	15.5	−9.6	16.9
HA	12.6	16.5	−15.7	21.1
HM	11.8	16.5	−15.8	19.3
TA	10.0	16.0	−14.6	18.9
TM	14.9	15.9	−10.8	17.6
TMC	12.4	8.5	0.6	9.9

Source: Geyer and Ziemba (2008).

To emphasize the difference between the cases TM and TA, Figure 14.5 compares the cumulated monthly returns obtained from the rebalancing strategy for the two cases as well as a buy and hold strategy, which assumes that the portfolio weights on January 1992 are fixed at the optimal TM weights throughout the test period. Rebalancing on the basis of the optimal TM scenario tree provides a substantial gain when compared to the buy and hold strategy or the performance using TA results, where rebalancing does not account for different correlation and volatility regimes.

Such in- and out-of-sample comparisons depend on the asset returns and test period. To isolate the potential benefits from considering state-dependent correlations, the following controlled simulation experiment was performed. Consider 1,000 ten-year periods where simulated annual returns of the four assets are assumed to have the statistical properties summarized in Table 14.3. One of the ten years is assumed to be an extreme year, two years correspond to highly volatile markets, and seven years are normal years. We compare the average annual return of two strategies: (a) a buy and hold strategy using the optimal TM weights from Table 14.4 throughout the ten-year period, and (b) a rebalancing strategy that uses the implied decision rules of the optimal scenario tree as explained in the preceding in- and out-of-sample tests. For simplicity it was assumed that the current volatility regime is known in each period. The average annual returns over 1,000 repetitions of the two strategies are 9.8% (rebalancing) and 9.2% (buy and hold). The t-statistic for the mean difference is 5.4 and indicates a highly significant advantage of the rebalancing strategy, which exploits the information about

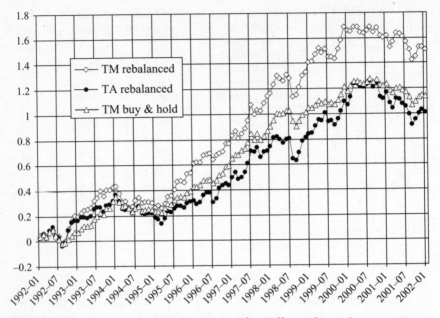

FIGURE 14.5 Cumulative Monthly Returns for Different Strategies
Source: Geyer and Ziemba (2008).

state-dependent correlations. For comparison the same experiment was repeated using the optimal weights from the constrained case TMC. We obtain the same average mean of 8.1% for both strategies was obtained. This indicates that the constraints imply insufficient rebalancing capacity. Therefore knowledge about the volatility regime cannot be sufficiently exploited to achieve superior performance relative to buy and hold. This result also shows that the relatively good performance of the TMC rebalancing strategy in the sample period from 1992 to 2002 is positively biased by the favorable conditions during that time.

14.5.1 Final Comments

The model InnoALM provides an easy to use tool to help Austrian pension funds' investment allocation committees evaluate the effect of various policy choices in light of changing economic conditions and various goals, constraints, and liability commitments. The model includes features that reflect real investment practices. These include multiple scenarios, non-normal distributions, and different volatility and correlation regimes. The model provides a systematic way to estimate in advance the likely results of particular policy changes and asset return realizations. This provides more confidence and justification to policy changes that may be controversial such as a higher weight in equity and less in bonds than has traditionally been the case in Austria.

The model is an advance on previous models and includes new features such as state-dependent correlation matrices. Crucial to the success of the results are the scenario inputs and especially the mean return assumptions. The model has a number of ways to estimate such scenarios. Given good inputs, the policy recommendations can improve current investment practice and provide greater confidence to the asset allocation process. The following quote by Konrad Kontriner (Member of the Board) and Wolfgang Herold (Senior Risk Strategist) of Innovest emphasizes the practical importance of InnoALM:

> The InnoALM model has been in use by Innovest, an Austrian Siemens subsidiary, since its first draft versions in 2000. Meanwhile it has become the only consistently implemented and fully integrated proprietary tool for assessing pension allocation issues within Siemens AG worldwide. Apart from this, consulting projects for various European corporations and pensions funds outside of Siemens have been performed on the basis of the concepts of InnoALM.
>
> The key elements that make InnoALM superior to other consulting models are the flexibility to adopt individual constraints and target functions in combination with the broad and deep array of results, which allows to investigate individual, path dependent behavior of assets and liabilities as well as scenario based and Monte-Carlo like risk assessment of both sides.
>
> In light of recent changes in Austrian pension regulation the latter even gained additional importance, as the rather rigid asset based limits were relaxed for institutions that could prove sufficient risk management expertise for both assets and liabilities of the plan. Thus, the implementation of a scenario based asset allocation model will lead to more flexible allocation restraints that will allow for more risk tolerance and will ultimately result in better long term investment performance.
>
> Furthermore, some results of the model have been used by the Austrian regulatory authorities to assess the potential risk stemming from less constraint pension plans.

REFERENCES

Campbell, J. Y., and L. M. Viceira. 2002. *Strategic Asset Allocation*. Oxford: Oxford University Press.

Cariño, D. R., T. Kent, D. H. Myers, C. Stacey, M. Sylvanus, A. L. Turner, K. Watanabe, and W. T. Ziemba. 1994. The Russell-Yasuda Kasai model: An asset/liability model for a Japanese insurance company using multistage stochastic programming. *Interfaces* 24, no. 1:29–49.

Cariño, D. R., D. H. Myers, and W. T. Ziemba. 1998. Concepts, technical issues, and uses of the Russell-Yasuda Kasai financial planning model. *Oper. Res.* 46:450–462.

Cariño, D. R., and A. L. Turner. 1998. Multiperiod asset allocation with derivative assets. In *Worldwide Asset and Liability Modeling*. ed. J. M. Mulvey and W. T. Ziemba, 182–204. Cambridge: Cambridge University Press.

Cariño, D. R., and W. T. Ziemba. 1998. Formulation of the Russell-Yasuda Kasai financial planning model. *Oper. Res.* 46:433–449.

Chopra, V., and W. T. Ziemba. 1993. The effect of errors in mean and covariance estimates on optimal portfolio choice. *J. Portfolio Management* 19:6–11.

Dimson, E., P. Marsh, and M. Staunton. 2009. *Global Investment Returns Yearbook*. London: ABNAmbro.

Geyer, A., and W. T. Ziemba. 2008. The Innovest Austrian pension fund planning model InnoALM. *Operations Research* 56, no. 4:797–810.

Kallberg, J. G., and W. T. Ziemba. 1981. Remarks on optimal portfolio selection. In Methods of Operations Research 44, ed. G. Bamberg and 0. Opitz, 507–520. Oelgeschlager: Gunn and Hain.

Kallberg, J. G., and W. T. Ziemba. 1983. Comparison of alternative utility functions in portfolio selection problems. *Management Sci.* 29:1257–1276.

Kusy, M. I., and W. T. Ziemba. 1986. A bank asset and liability management model. *Oper. Res.* 34:356–376.

Ziemba, W. T., and J. M. Mulvey, eds. 1998. *Worldwide Asset and Liability Modeling*. Cambridge: Cambridge University.

CHAPTER 15

An Individual ALM Model for Lifetime Asset-Liability Management

Marida Bertocchi, Vittorio Moriggia, and William T. Ziemba

In this chapter we develop a scenario-based, stochastic programming optimization model in discrete time to provide an approach to individual asset/liability modeling over time. This model enables us in the next chapter to use this tool to evaluate different individuals, and family office's lifetime asset-liabilities situations to determine their chances of achieving their preferred targets, given their asset mix and liability committments. Since both assets and liabilities are stochastic, exact targets cannot be determined with certainty. The model gives advice regarding the characteristics of the life plan and the chance of achieving these targets.

The objective function of our model reflects the tradeoff between expected return and risk. The individual investor usually aims at achieving, with a given preference function, a number of intermediate and final goals under a rich set of individual and regulatory constraints, which depend on their age, the composition of their family, the taxes they pay, the changing employment conditions over time, and other elements; see Mulvey (1996), Berger and Mulvey (1998), Mulvey and Thorlacius (1998), Consigli (2007). Following Kusy and Ziemba (1986), Cariño and Ziemba (1998), Cariño et al. (1994), Cariño, Myers, and Ziemba (1998), Geyer and Ziemba (1998), Hoyland and Wallace (2007), Consigli (2007), Wallace and Ziemba (2005), Zenios and Ziemba (2007), and the survey by Ziemba and Ziemba (2007), we associate to every target a shortfall with a cost, the shortfall cost function measures the cost of shortfall of different magnitudes; usually convex cost functions are chosen: the larger the target violations, the larger the penalty cost: that is, we have an increasing marginal penalty in our objective function.

The model provides realistic strategies on how one should choose asset mixes over time to achieve targets and to cover liabilities. Return and risk are balanced to achieve period by period targets as well as a long-run goals. The model allows for diversification and, by considering all relevant scenarios including extreme ones, protects individuals from the effects of bad scenarios, and also performs well in normal situations (Ziemba 2003).

The model maximizes a concave risk-averse utility function composed of the expected final wealth in the final period less a convex risk measure composed of a risk aversion index times the sum of convex penalties for target violations related to several individuals' goals in various periods, opportunily capitalized at the final horizon.

Discrete scenarios that represent the possible returns and other random parameters outcomes in various periods are generated from econometric or stochastic models, expert modeling past data, and other sources. Rockafellar and Ziemba (2000) justify the convex risk measure in an axiomatic way.

Let

$t = 0, \ldots, T$ be the discretization of the planning horizon

$\bar{t} \in \bar{T}$, with $\bar{T} \subseteq T$, $\bar{t}$ the time points for targets

$k = 1, \ldots, K$ the indexes of the different income sources

$l = 1, \ldots, L$ the indexes of the different debt sources

$s = 1, \ldots, S$ the indexes of the various scenarios

$j = 0, \ldots, J$ the indexes of the different investment classes: $j = 0$ identifies cash and $j = 1, \ldots, J_1$ identifies asset classes, $j = J_1 + 1, \ldots, J$ identifies different target funds

$X_j^{init} = \alpha_{j0} \sum_{k=1}^{K} I_{k0}$ the initial holding of asset j, $j = 1, \ldots, J_1$ (in face value)

τ_j the transaction cost for asset j, $j = 1, \ldots, J_1$

x_{j0} and y_{j0} are the purchases and the sales (in face values) of assets j, $j = 1, \ldots, J_1$ at time 0; the initial fair prices p_{j0} is scenario independent; $\zeta_{j0} = p_{j0}(1 + \tau_j)$ are the purchasing prices, $\xi_{j0} = p_{j0}(1 - \tau_j)$ are the selling prices

X_{j0} the value of asset j, $j = 1, \ldots, J_1$ at time 0

z_0 the cash at time 0

d_{l0} the debt of type l, $l = 1, \ldots, L$ at time 0

W_0 the surplus or total wealth at time 0

X_{jt}^s the value of asset j, $j = 1, \ldots, J_1$ at time t under scenario s; where $X_{j0}^s = X_{j0}$

p_{jt}^s the fair price of asset j, $j = 1, \ldots, J_1$ at time t under scenario s; $\zeta_{jt}^s = p_{jt}^s(1 + \tau_j)$ are the purchasing prices, $\xi_{jt} = p_{jt}^s(1 - \tau_j)$ are the selling prices

x_{jt}^s and y_{jt}^s the purchases and the sales of assets j, $j = 1, \ldots, J_1$ at time t under scenario s

r_t^s the risk-free short rate at time t under scenario s; R_t^s the gross return at period $(t, t + 1)$; where r_0 is a known constant

$\tilde{r}_{jt}^s$ the short rate for fund j, $j = J_1 + 1, \ldots, J$ at time t under scenario s; $\tilde{R}_{jt}^s$ the gross return for fund j, $j = J_1 + 1, \ldots, J$ in the period $(t, t + 1)$; where $\tilde{r}_{j0}$ is a known constant

ψ_{jt}^s the exchange rate for asset j, $j = 1, \ldots, J_1$ at time t under scenario s; notice that ψ_{j0} is known

f_{jt}^s the cash flow of asset j, $j = 1, \ldots, J_1$ at time t under scenario s

d_{lt}^s the debt (or liabilities) of type l, $l = 1, \ldots, L$ at time t under scenario s

d_t^{-s} the borrowing at time t under scenario s

d_t^{+s} the lending at time t under scenario s

I_{kt}^s the income from source k at time t under scenario s; where I_{k0} for each k is a known constant

inr_t^s the inflation rate at time t under scenario s

g_t^s the growth rate at time t under scenario s

$F_{j\bar{t}}^s$ the value of target fund j, $j = J_1 + 1, \ldots, J$ at time $\bar{t}$ under scenario s

$B_{j\bar{t}}$ the fixed value of target fund j, $j = J_1 + 1, \ldots, J$ at time $\bar{t}$

W_t^s the surplus or total wealth at time t under scenario s

α_{jt}^s the percentage of income spent for asset j, $j = 1, \ldots, J_1$ or left in cash ($j = 0$) along scenario s; α_{j0}^s is scenario independent, i.e., $\alpha_{j0}^s = \alpha_{j0}$; usually $\alpha_{jt}^s \geq \bar{\alpha}$, where $\bar{\alpha}$ is a parameter

β_{jt}^s the percentage of income spent for target fund j, $j = J_1 + 1, \ldots, J$ along scenario s; β_{j0}^s is scenario independent, i.e. $\beta_{j0}^s = \beta_{j0}$

γ_t^s the percentage of income spent for consumption along scenario s; γ_0^s is scenario independent, i.e. $\gamma_0^s = \gamma_0$; usually $\gamma_t^s \geq \bar{\gamma}$, where $\bar{\gamma}$ is a parameter; where $\sum_{j=0}^{J_1} \alpha_{jt}^s + \sum_{j=J_1+1}^{J} \beta_{jt}^s + \gamma_t^s = 1$, $\forall t, s$

π^s the probability of scenario s with $\sum_{s=1}^{S} \pi^s = 1$

The first-stage decision variables $x_{j0}, y_{j0}, X_{j0}, \alpha_{j0}, \beta_{j0}, \gamma_0$ are nonnegative and satisfy the constraints on conservation of holdings

$$y_{j0} + X_{j0} = X_j^{init} + x_{j0} \quad \forall j, j = 1, \dots, J_1 \qquad (15.1)$$

and on balancing of cashflows

$$W_0 = z_0 + \sum_{j=1}^{J_1} \psi_{j0}\xi_{j0}y_{j0} - \sum_{j=1}^{J_1} \psi_{j0}\zeta_{j0}x_{j0} - \sum_{l=1}^{L} d_{l0} \qquad (15.2)$$

where the non-negative variable W_0 denotes the initial wealth, $z_0 = \alpha_{00}\sum_{k=1}^{K} I_{k0}$, with $\alpha_{00} = 1 - \gamma_0 - \sum_{j=J_1+1}^{J} \beta_{j0}$, and I_{k0}^s is scenario independent, i.e. $I_{k0}^s = I_{k0}$.

Equations 15.1 and 15.2 do not depend on scenarios.

The second-stage decisions on rebalancing the portfolio, borrowing or reinvestment of the surplus depend on individual scenarios. They satisfy the constraints on conservation of holdings in each asset at each time period and for each of scenarios

$$X_{jt}^s + y_{jt}^s = X_{j,t-1}^s + x_{jt}^s \quad \forall j, j = 1, \dots, J_1, \forall s, t \geq 1 \qquad (15.3)$$

as well as on balancing of cash flows at each time and for each of scenarios

$$\sum_{j=1}^{J_1} \psi_{jt}^s \xi_{jt}^s y_{jt}^s + \sum_{j=1}^{J_1} \psi_{jt}^s f_{jt}^s X_{jt}^s + W_{t-1}^s(R_{t-1}^s - \delta_c) + d_t^{-s} + \sum_{j=0}^{J_1} \alpha_{jt}^s \sum_{k=1}^{K} I_{kt}$$

$$= W_t^s + \sum_{j=1}^{J_1} \psi_{jt}^s \zeta_{jt}^s x_{jt}^s + \sum_{l=1}^{L} d_{lt}^s + d_t^{+s}, \quad \forall s, t \qquad (15.4)$$

with non-negativity of all variables, $\sum_{j=0}^{J_1} \alpha_{jt}^s = 1 - \gamma_t^s - \sum_{j=J_1+1}^{J} \beta_{jt}^s$, and with $d_0^{-s} = 0$. Variables d_t^{+s}, d_t^{-s} describe the (unlimited) lending/borrowing possibilities for period t under scenario s and the non-negative spread δ_c is a model parameter to be determined. Nonzero values of δ_c account for the difference between the returns for stock and bonds and for cash.

The following constraints describe the evolution of funds, of income over time:

$$F_{jt}^s = F_{jt-1}^s \tilde{R}_{jt-1}^s + \beta_{jt}^s \sum_{k=1}^{K} I_{kt}^s \quad \forall j, j = J_1 + 1, \dots, J, \forall t, \forall s \qquad (15.5)$$

with $F_{j0} = \beta_{j0}\sum_{k=1}^{K} I_{k0}$ is scenario independent;

$$I_{kt}^s = I_{kt-1}^s(1 + inr_{t-1}^s + g_{t-1}^s) \quad \forall k, \forall t, \forall s \qquad (15.6)$$

We also impose the following constraints so that fund j fulfills target j at time $\bar{t}$

$$F_{j\bar{t}}^s + D_{j\bar{t}}^s \geq B_{j\bar{t}} \quad \forall j, j = J_1 + 1, \ldots, J, \forall s, \forall \bar{t} \tag{15.7}$$

where $D_{j\bar{t}}^s$ indicates a non-negative shortfall variable used to penalize the objective function when the target cannot be reached.

The optimization problem is to maximize the expected concave utility of the final wealth at the planning horizon T

$$\sum_{s=1}^{S} \pi^s U(g_T^s) \tag{15.8}$$

subject to (15.1)–(15.7), the nonnegativity constraints on all variables with

$$g_T^s = W_T^s - \lambda \sum_{\bar{t} \in \bar{T}} \omega_{\bar{t}} \left(\sum_{j=J_1+1}^{J} \mu_j (\prod_{t=\bar{t}}^{T} \tilde{R}_{jt}^s)(D_{j\bar{t}}^s)^2 \right) \tag{15.9}$$

where λ is the risk aversion of the individual, μ_j represents the weight on target j not reached and $\sum_{j=J_1+1}^{J} \mu_j = 1$, $\omega_{\bar{t}}$, $\sum_{\bar{t} \in \bar{T}} \omega_{\bar{t}} = \bar{T}$ is a weight on the importance of each time instant corresponding to a target.

To reduce our model to a multiperiod stochastic linear programming problem, we approximate the shortfall quadratic term, representing the cost function related to the shortfall, by a piecewise linear convex risk measure using the variables and constraints

$$D_{j\bar{t}}^s = \sum_{m=1}^{M} D_{mj\bar{t}}^s \quad \forall j, j = J_1 + 1, \ldots, J, \forall s, \forall \bar{t} \tag{15.10}$$

$$0 \leq D_{mj\bar{t}}^s \leq b_{mj} - b_{(m-1)j} \quad \forall j, j = J_1 + 1, \ldots, J, \forall s, \forall \bar{t}, m = 1, \ldots, M \tag{15.11}$$

where $D_{mj\bar{t}}^s$ is the non-negative target shortfall associated with segment m of the cost-function, b_m is the mth breakpoint of the risk measure function ($b_0 = 0$), and M is the number of segments of the function.

Consequently, equation (15.9) becomes

$$g_T^s = W_T^s - \lambda \sum_{\bar{t} \in \bar{T}} \omega_{\bar{t}} \left(\sum_{j=J_1+1}^{J} \mu_j (\prod_{t=\bar{t}}^{T} \tilde{R}_{jt}^s)(\sum_{m=1}^{M} c(D_{mj\bar{t}}) D_{mj\bar{t}}^s) \right) \tag{15.12}$$

where $c(D_{mj\bar{t}})$ is the marginal cost corresponding to segment m.

In the next chapter we will use this model to evaluate retirement strategies for five different type of individuals and family offices:

1. Wealthy people with a net worth of 10+ million dollars
2. Wealthy family offices with different individuals with different tax rates and other characteristics with net wealth of 10+ million dollars
3. Middle-class individuals with net wealth of 0.5 to 5 million dollars
4. Family offices for those with net wealth of 0.5 to 5 million dollars
5. Poor and modest-income people with net worth in the range [*debt*, 500,000] dollars

We identify the following investment classes among which these categories of individuals and family offices can make their dynamic investment and other choices. They are

- Fixed-income, including domestic bonds (taxable or tax-exempt) and foreign bonds
- Inflation-indexed bonds
- Equities (domestic and/or international)
- Emerging markets debt and equity
- Commodities
- Hedge funds
- Real estate (personal and/or commercial)
- Private equities
- Leveraged buyouts
- Venture capital
- Real assets
- Closed-end funds
- Exchange-traded funds (ETF)
- Restricted stocks
- Insurance
- Limited partnerships
- Illiquid assets from company business and other sources
- Family trusts
- Cash

For liabilities, we consider the following classes:

- Credit cards and short-term loans
- Margin loans
- Commercial real estate loans
- Personal real estate loans

- Unfunded equity commitments
- Compulsory retirement commitments
- Insurance commitments.

In our implementation, for the scenario generation (see Dupačová, Consigli, and Wallace (2000)), we adopt a model for the risk-free rate evolution (see Bradley and Crane (1972) and Vašíček (1977)) and relate the other rates (inflation rate, growth rate, fund rate) to it through fixed different spreads. The same strategy is adopted for computing purchasing and selling asset prices. We use historical correlations among returns on asset prices. One can build more complex scenarios, including more sophisticated models together with an appropriate correlation structure (Consigli 2007). For the exchange rate volatility we use a GARCH(1,1) model based on historical data, and the forecasted model is generated using a regression equation on CBOT volatility. Eventually, t-Student innovations may be used to handle fatter tails.

The risk aversion coefficient λ represents the absolute risk aversion of Arrow (1995) and Pratt (1964), and it is fixed according to which of the above-mentioned classes the individual or family offices belong to. Typical values are $\lambda = 2$ the aggressive investors in classes 1 and 2, and $\lambda = 4$ for the moderately conservative investors in classes 3 and 4 and $\lambda \in [2, 8]$ for people in class 5 (Ziemba 2003).

The final horizon may coincide with the time of retirement or with some other important future date. The number of stages may vary depending on the length of the time horizon and on the complexity we want to deal with. More stages yield more complexity. There are a number of suggestions in the literature on the number of stages Bertocchi, Dupačová, and Moriggia (2005, 2006), and the references therein, even if the determination of an appropriate number of stages is certainly problem-oriented.

Many examples are reported in the literature, see Bertocchi, Dupačová, and Moriggia (2000); Cariño and Turner (1998); Fleten, Hoyland, and Wallace (2002); Kouwenberg and Zenios (2005); Topaloglou, Vladimirou, and Zenios (2002); Ziemba (2007); Consiglio et al. (2009) and references therein, where it is shown that the stochasting programming approach is superior to the buy and hold and the fix-mixed models.

REFERENCES

Arrow, K. J. 1965. Aspects of the theory of risk bearing. Technical Report. Yrjö Jahnsson Foundation.

Berger, A. J., and J. M. Mulvey. 1998. The Home Account Advisor™: Asset and liability management for individual investors. In *World Wide Asset and Liability Modeling*, ed. W. T. Ziemba and J. M. Mulvey, 634–665. Cambridge: Cambridge University Press.

Bertocchi, M., J. Dupačová, and V. Moriggia. 2000. Sensitivity of bond portfolio's behavior with respect to random movements in yield curve: A simulation study. *Annals of Operations Research* 99:267–286.

Bertocchi, M., J. Dupačová, and V. Moriggia. 2005. Horizon and stages in applications of stochastic programming in finance. *Annals of Operations Research* 142:63–78.

Bertocchi, M., J. Dupačová, and V. Moriggia. 2006. Bond portfolio management via stochastic programming. In *Handbook of Asset and Liability Management*, vol. 1, *Theory and methodology*, ed. S. A. Zenios and W. T. Ziemba, 305–336. Amsterdam: North Holland.

Bradley, S. P., and D. B. Crane. 1972. A dynamic model for bond portfolio management, *Management Science* 19:139–151.

Cariño, D. R., T. Kent, D. H. Myers, C. Stacy, M. Sylvanus, A. L. Truner, K. Watanabe, and W. T. Ziemba. 1994. The Russell-Yasuda Kasai model: An asset/liability model for a Japanese insurance company using multistage stochastic programming *Interfaces* 24:29–49.

Cariño, D. R., R. Myers, and W. T. Ziemba. 1998. Concepts, technical issues and uses of the Russell-Yasuda Kasai financial planning model. *Operations Research* 46:450–462.

Cariño, D. R., and A. L. Turner. 1998. Multiperiod asset allocation with derivative assets. In *World Wide Asset and Liability Modeling*, ed. W. T. Ziemba and J. Mulvey, 182–204. Cambridge: Cambridge University Press.

Cariño, D. R., and W. T. Ziemba. 1998. Formulation of Russell-Yasuda Kasai financial planning model, *Operations Research* 46:433–449.

Consigli, G. 2007. Asset-liability management for individual investors. In *Handbook of Asset and Liability Management, Volume 2, Applications and Case Studies*, ed. S. A. Zenios and W. T. Ziemba, 751–827. Amsterdam: North Holland.

Consiglio, A., S. Nielsen, S. A. Zenios. 2009. *A Library of GAMS Models*. Chichester, England: Wiley Finance.

Dupačová, J., and M. Bertocchi. 2001. From data to model and back to data: A bond portfolio management problem. *European Journal of Operations Research* 134:261–278.

Dupačová, J., G. Consigli, and S. W. Wallace. 2000. Scenarios for multistage stochastic programs. *Annals of Operations Research* 100:25–53.

Fleten, S. E., K. Hoyland, and S. W. Wallace. 2002. Stochastic dynamic and fixed mixed portfolio models. *European Journal of Operations Research* 140, no. 1:37–49.

Geyer, A., and W. T. Ziemba. 2008. The Innovest Austrian pension fund financial planning model InnoALM. *Operations Research* 56, no. 4:797–810.

Hoyland, K., and S. Wallace. 2007. Stochastic programming models for tactical and strategical asset allocation study from Norwegian life insurance. In *Handbook* of *Asset and Liability Management, Volume 2, Applications and Case Studies*, ed. S. A. Zenios and W. T. Ziemba, 591–625. Amsterdam: North Holland.

Kouwenberg, R. R. P., and S. A. Zenios. 2006. Stochastic programming models for asset liability management. In *Handbook of Asset and Liability Management, Volume 1, Theory and Methodology*, ed. S. A. Zenios and W. T. Ziemba, 253–304. Amsterdam: North Holland.

Kusy, M. I., and W. T. Ziemba. 1986. A bank asset and liability management model. *Operations Research* 34:356–376.

Mulvey, J. M. 1996. Generating scenarios for the Towers Perrin investment system. *Interfaces* 26:1–13.

Mulvey, J. M., and E. Thorlacius. 1998. The Towers Perrin global capital market scenario generation system. In *World Wide Asset and Liability Modeling*, ed. W. T. Ziemba and J. M. Mulvey, 286–312. Cambridge: Cambridge University Press, Cambridge, England.

Mulvey, J. M., and S. A. Zenios. 1994. Capturing correlations of fixed-income instruments. *Management Science* 40, no. 1:1329–1342.

Mulvey, J. M., and W. T. Ziemba. 1998. Asset and liability management for long-term investors: Discussion of the issues. In *World Wide Asset and Liability Modeling*, ed. W. T. Ziemba and J. M. Mulvey, 3–38. Cambridge: Cambridge University Press.

Pratt, J. W. 1964. Risk aversion in the small and in the large. *Econometrica* 32, no. 12 (January–April):122–136.

Rockafellar, T., and W. T. Ziemba. 2000. Modified risk measures and acceptance sets. Working Paper, University of Washington (July).

Topaloglou, N., H. Vladimirou, and S. A. Zenios. 2002. Constructing optimal samples from a binomial latticea models with selective hedging for international asset allocation. *Journal of Banking & Finance* 26, no. 7:1531–1561.

Vašíček, O. 1977. An equilibrium characterization of the term structure. *Journal of Financial Economics* 5:177–188.

Wallace, S. W., and W. T. Ziemba (eds.). 2005. *Applied stochastic programming*. SIAM Mathematical Programming Society.

Zenios, S. A., and W. T. Ziemba, (eds.). 2007. *Handbook of Asset and Liability Management, Volume 2, Applications and Case Studies*. Amsterdam: North Holland.

Ziemba, R. E. S., and W. T. Ziemba, 2007. *Scenarios for Risk Management and Global Investment Strategies*. Chichester, England: John Wiley & Sons.

Ziemba, W. T., ed. 2003. *The Stochastic Programming Approach to Asset, Liability, and Wealth Management*. The Research Foundation of AIMR, Charlottesville, VA.

———. 2007. The Russell-Yasuda Kasai, InnoALM and related models for pensions, insurance companies and high net worth individuals. In *Handbook of Asset and Liability Management, Volume 2, Applications and Case Studies*, ed. S. A. Zenios and W. T. Ziemba, 861–962. Amsterdam: North Holland.

Implementation and Numerical Results of Individual ALM Model for Lifetime Asset-Liability Management

Marida Bertocchi, Vittorio Moriggia, and William T. Ziemba

In this chapter we implement the scenario-based multiperiod, stochastic programming optimization discrete time model of Chapter 16 to provide an approach to individual asset/liability modeling over time. This model enables us to evaluate different individuals and family offices' lifetime asset-liabilities situations to determine their chances of achieving their preferred targets, given their asset allocation mix and liability committments. Since both assets and liabilities are stochastic, exact targets cannot be determined with certainty. The model gives advice regarding the characteristics of the life plan and the chance of achieving these targets.

The objective function reflects the tradeoff between expected final wealth and risk. The individual investor usually aims at achieving, with a given preference function, a number of intermediate and final goals subject to individual and regulatory constraints, which depend on their age, the composition of their family, the taxes they pay, the changing employment conditions over time, and other elements. We associate to every target a shortfall cost function that measures the cost of shortfalls of different magnitudes. A convex cost function is used so the larger the target violations, the larger the penalty cost. Thus we have an increasing marginal penalty in our objective function.

We thank Riccardo Pianeti for helping us in collecting data and running the econometric package OxMetrics.

The model based mainly on Geyer and Ziemba (2008) and other references listed in Chapter 16 provide realistic strategies on how one should choose asset mixes over time to achieve targets and to cover liabilities. Return and risk are balanced to achieve period by period targets as well as long-run goals. The model allows for diversification and, by considering all relevant scenarios including extreme ones, protect the individuals from the effects of bad scenarios and also performs well in normal situations.

The model maximizes a concave risk-averse utility function composed of the expected final wealth less a convex risk measure, which is a risk aversion index times the weighted sum of convex penalties for target violations related to the individual's goals in various periods.

Uncertainty is modeled using multiperiod discrete probability scenarios that represent the possible returns and other random parameters outcomes in various periods generated from econometric and statistical models based on past data and other sources. These scenarios are approximations of the true undelying probability distributions. The scenarios construction is critical for the model success. The multiperiod stochastic programming model leads to superior performance with respect to other approaches because the scenario's modeling effort tries to cover well the possible future evolution of economic and financial environment.

We discuss this model's implementation for a typical individual with net wealth of 0.5 to 5 million dollars.

It is assumed initially that individuals utilize the following assets for their investment choices:

- Fixed-income instruments, including domestic bonds (taxable or tax-exempt) and foreign bonds
- Equities (domestic and/or international)
- Cash

The liabilities are:

- Family expenses
- Insurance commitments

To test the models, we adopt a scenario generation model for the risk-free rate evolution and relate other rates (inflation rate, growth rate, fund rate) to it through fixed different spreads. We assume full correlations among these rates. The scenarios for purchasing and selling asset prices are modelled taking into account the correlation structure among them. For the exchange rate volatility we use a GARCH(1,1) model based on historical data, and the forecasted model is generated using a regression equation on CBOT volatility. The test results shows the type of investments that should be utilized by investors in various stages to maximize the objective function of risk adjusted expected final wealth.

The risk-aversion coefficient λ represents the Arrow-Pratt absolute risk aversion, which varies reflecting individual preferences and attitude towards risk. The choice of $\lambda = 4$ represents moderately conservative investment behavior.

We consider the following situation. We assume a 50-year-old individual with $300,000 in wealth, a net yearly salary of $100,000, and a yearly net income of $18,000 from house rent, yearly adjusted for inflation and growth rate. The individual time horizon is 10 years. Five years from now $20,000 per year is needed for three years for university fees and costs for their daughter and $4,000 per year for insurance commitments for the next 10 years. The final horizon coincides with the time of retirement at age 60. The number of stages has to be fixed at the beginning, what is typically 2–6; see Bertocchi, Dupačová, and Moriggia (2005, 2009) for suggestions on the number of stages. We test 2 and 6 stages. When it is fixed to 6 with a yearly time discretization equal to 0,1,2,4,6,10, this means that periods 1 and 2 are one year in length, periods 3 and 4 are two years in length and period 5 is four years long. This reflects the rebalancing strategy of this specific individual who adjusts the portfolio once per year at the very beginning of the planning horizon and then rebalances the portfolio less frequently. We can increase the rebalancing stages which increases the decision variables and consequently the computational time.

We work with returns, and we use discrete compounding within the year.

We generate 2,000 scenarios using a $20 - 5 - 5 - 2 - 2$ node structure, which provides sufficient details about the assets distribution, while still keeping reasonable computing times.

To represent the various classes of assets we use the following bench-mark indexes:

- JPMorgan Government Bond Index (JPM GVI) for domestic fixed-income
- DowJones (DJIA) for domestic equities
- DAX for German equities

The weekly returns for DAX and DJIA are far from normally distributed. The JPM GVI based both on 2000 to 2006 data and on 2000 to 2009 data did not pass the normality test based on the χ^2 test ($\chi^2 = 19.925$ for 2000

TABLE 16.1 Statistical Properties of Asset Returns during 2000–2006

	DAX	DJIA	JPM Global Bond Index USD
Weekly Returns			
Mean (% p.a.)	2.285	2.541	5.51
Std. dev. (% p.a.)	23.13	16.77	2.94
Skewness	−0.1268	−0.6793	−0.6057
Kurtosis	4.2405	7.6262	3.9586
Annual Returns			
Mean (%)	2.378	0.939	6.321
Std. dev. (%)	35.012	16.457	2.676
Skewness	−0.06108	0.81007	0.62617
Kurtosis	1.79814	2.93566	1.70172

to 2006 data, $\chi^2 = 16.168$ for 2000 to 2009 data). The order of magnitude of returns shown in Tables 16.1 and especially in 16.4 confirm what was reported in Chapter 5.

The individual utilizes three asset classes plus cash. Lower bounds are introduced on the percentage of income to be used for cash, for targets, and for consumption.

Assumptions about the statistical properties of index returns are based on a sample of weekly data from 2000 to 2006 and from 2000 to 2009. Summary statitstics for weekly (annualized) returns are in Table 16.1, and the related distributions are presented in Figure 16.1.

For a medium-long-term planning model, as in our case with a one-year rebalancing period, properties of weekly returns are not relevant. However, we prefer to use the annualized data taken from weekly return, because the second panel of Table 16.1 containing statistics for annual return is characterized by a number of observations that are too small. Due to the difficulty with choosing an appropriate parametric distribution for annual return, we adopt a nonparametric approach to generate random samples reflecting the shape of historical return distributions. One may also choose to draw random samples from multivariate t-distributions or skewed t-distributions to better take into account returns with fat tails.

To simulate the historical distribution for a single asset, we standardize the annual return r_t. We use overlapping annual returns from weekly data rather than weekly data, since the planning intervals we want to use are in years. An element of the simulated historical return distribution is computed as follows. A random number u is drawn from a uniform distribution in the

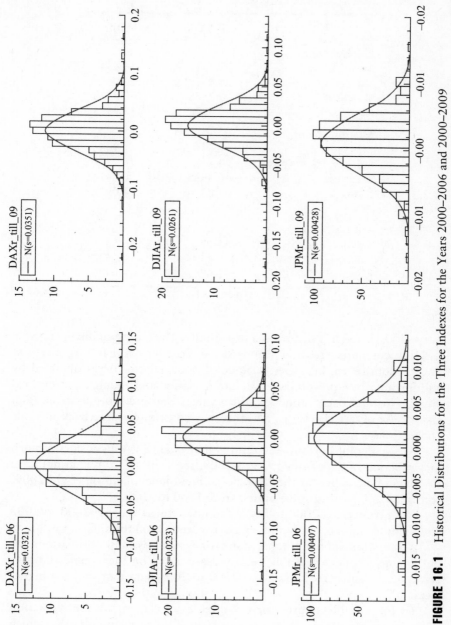

FIGURE 16.1 Historical Distributions for the Three Indexes for the Years 2000–2006 and 2000–2009

TABLE 16.2 Statistical Properties of Asset Returns in the Period 1928 to 2009

	DAX	DJIA
Weekly Returns		
Mean (% p.a.)	8.261	6.434
Std. dev. (% p.a.)	23.87	20.06
Skewness	−0.2828	−0.2722
Kurtosis	6.0276	13.4473
Monthly Returns		
Mean (%)	7.535	5.944
Std. dev. (%)	21.84	18.78
Skewness	−0.4938	−0.08145
Kurtosis	3.8376	11.0931
Annual Returns		
Mean (%)	10.67	6.334
Std. dev. (%)	25.77	19.88
Skewness	−0.4506	−0.15205
Kurtosis	2.6062	4.0776

interval [0,1], and it is treated as a probability. The corresponding percentile z is then computed from the standardized returns such that $P(r_t < z) = u$. The random return in a specific node of our scenario tree is obtained by multiplying z by a prespecified standard deviation and adding a prespecified mean. This approach cannot produce values that are more extreme than historically observed returns, and this may constitute a drawback in some applications.

We also point out how the returns may change if we consider a much longer period of data from 1928 to 2009; see Table 16.2. We do not have the longer data series for the JPM global bond index. Dimson et al. (2009) report a 4.2% return for the period from 1900 to 2009.

The period from 2000 to 2006 had low returns because 2000 to 2003 had a double market crash and a recovery from 2003 to 2007.

Assumptions about means, standard deviations, and correlations for our example appear in Table 16.5 and are based on the sample statistics presented in Table 16.3 related to 2000 to 2007 data that shows a higher mean.

To forecast the returns for the three asset classes, we use regression equations relating asset correlations and CBOT volatility index (VIX), which is considered a good indicator of the investor sentiment.

TABLE 16.3 Statistical Properties of Asset Returns from 2000 to 2007

	DAX	DJIA	JPM Global Bond Index USD
Weekly Returns			
Mean (% p.a.)	5.35	3.67	6.09
Std. dev. (% p.a.)	17.52	16.77	3.08
Skewness	−0.1680	−0.6877	−0.5375
Kurtosis	4.3627	7.4922	3.8999
Annual Returns			
Mean (%)	3.088	1.5836	5.68
Std. dev. (%)	29.904	11.342	2.8259
Skewness	−0.5617	0.3839	0.3548
Kurtosis	2.159	1.8336	3.8999

Using weekly time series, we compute moving average (window length of 34 weeks) estimates of correlations among assets and CBOT index volatility. The estimated regression equations are computed for the three regimes as they appear in Table 16.4.

Once we have the regression coefficients, we can create our forecasted scenarios as belonging to three different volatility regimes (see Geyer and Ziemba (2008)).

The three different regimes, to which a probability of occurence is assigned, correspond the the following equity market situations:

- Normal, when 70% of the time equity markets are normal
- Volatile, when 20% of the time equity markets are volatile
- Extremely volatile, when 10% of the time equity markets are in a violent crash mode

TABLE 16.4 Regression Equations Coefficients Relating Asset Correlations and CBOT Volatility Index (Weekly return; July 2000 to December 2007; 416 Observations)

Correlation Between	Constant	Slope w.r.t. CBOT Vol. Index	t-Statistics of Slope	R^2
DAX—DJIA	0.735886	0.231468	6.17	0.113133
DAX—JPM	0.000615	−1.90436	−17.9	0.476864
DJIA—JPM	−0.0393277	−1.36044	−9.83	0.247316

TABLE 16.5 Standard Deviations and Correlations Assumptions, 2000–2007

		I. Stock US	I. Stock EU	I. Bonds US
Normal (70% of	I. Stock EU	0.75511	1.	
the time)	I. Bond US	−0.22607	−.26047	1.
High volatile (20%	I. Stock EU	0.79353	1.	
of the time)	I. Bond US	−0.36939	−0.47386	1.
Extreme (10% of	I. Stock EU	0.82551	1.	
the time)	I. Bond US	−0.48868	−0.65146	1.

Having the distribution of CBOT index volatility,

- The 35th percentile located at the center of the 70% normal range defines the normal market.
- The 80th percentile defines the volatile market.
- The 95th percentile defines the extremely volatile market.

The correlation matrixes corresponding to the three different regimes are used to generate scenarios of the asset returns.

For each asset, we generate n_t standardized random numbers z_{ti} where n_t is the number of nodes in period t, where z has been chosen with the procedure described above in order not to be too far from historical asset returns. Those vectors are used to fill the $n_t \times N$ matrix Z. The correlation among assets is modeled by multiplying the matrix Z by the Cholesky decomposition of the correlation matrix C^j obtaining matrix Y^j, the index j corresponding to one of the three regimes. The number of nodes for each regime is determined by multiplying the total numer of nodes n_t by the probability p^j of the three regimes.

The simulated gross returns of each asset are obtained by multiplying each column of Y with the standard deviation of asset i and adding the asset's mean μ_i, both adjusted for the length τ_t of the planning period t

$$R_{ti}^j = (1 + \mu_i)^{\tau_t} + Y_{ti}^j \sigma_i \sqrt{\tau_t} \tag{16.1}$$

The simulated gross returns belonging to each regime are randomly distributed among nodes.

We have structured the rebalancing strategy of our individual investor assuming different number of stages. In Table 16.8 we report results for the single-stage solution (the buy and hold solution), the two-stage solution with period 1 one year in length and period 2 nine years in length and a

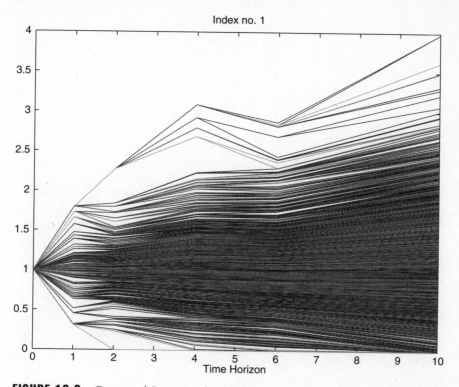

FIGURE 16.2 Generated Scenarios for DAX Index for the Years 2006 to 2016

node structure of $5 - 5 - 2 - 2 - 2$ that produces 200 scenarios, the six-stage solution with periods 1 and 2 one year in length, periods 3 and 4 two years in length, period 5 four years in length and two other node structure: the $10 - 5 - 5 - 2 - 3$ that produces 1, 000 scenarios and the $20 - 5 - 5 - 2 - 3$ that produces 2, 000 scenarios. Figures 16.2, 16.3, 16.4 show the generated scenarios with the procedure described above for the $100 - 5 - 5 - 2 - 3$ structure.

We use the Libor-3months as risk-free rate. We use the historical weekly data from 2000 to 2009 and compute the historical weekly volatility. We regress those data on the VIX lagged 30-days, and we obtain significant coefficients of the regression as shown in Table 16.6. The model used to generate the forecasted risk-free rate is

$$dr_t = \mu dt + \sigma_t dW_t \qquad (16.2)$$

where dr_t is the variation of the risk-free rate in the interval dt of one week, W_t is a Wiener process, and μ is the expected value of dr_t.

Index no. 2

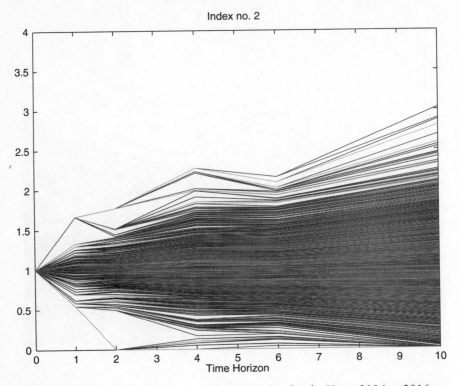

FIGURE 16.3 Generated Scenarios for DJIA Index for the Years 2006 to 2016

Using the model and the estimation of the volatility we generate scenarios for risk-free rate for our planning horizon as shown in Figure 16.5.

The weekly exchange rates USD/EUR for 2000 to 2006 pass the normality test while those for 2000 to 2009 do not pass the test; see Figures 16.6 and 16.7.

To forecast the exchange rate, we use regression equation relating exchange rate volatility and CBOT volatility index (VIX); see Table 16.7.

The values for the first-stage variables are shown in Table 16.8 for an increasing number of stages and different number of scenarios. The changing in the number of stages increases the complexity of the problem, and it allows rebalancing when we expect new information are coming at disposal. For the two-stage case, the first stage solutions shows investment in stocks, due to the fact of high liabilities in closed periods; this behavior is similar to the single-stage case, when a sufficient number of scenarios is considered. The six-stage case uses much information coming in and the choice becomes more conservative investing in bonds. We know that assuming different

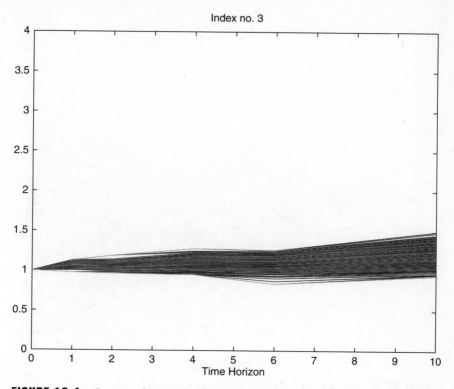

FIGURE 16.4 Generated Scenarios for JPM Index for the Years 2006 to 2016

means in the stock index will influence the behavior of our investor. With a long-run mean of 8.3% for US stocks as estimated by Siegel (2008) and also in Geyer and Ziemba (2008) the percentage investment in equities is 100%, while with a mean around 9%, the optimal weights are 30% on stocks and 70% in bonds.

One further example follows. (See Table 16.9.) Guglielmo Zimbini is a 50-year-old manager working for a law office as a senior attorney (annual

TABLE 16.6 Regression Equations Coefficients Relating Historical Libor-3months Volatility and CBOT Volatility Index (Weekly rates; July 2000 to December 2009; 440 Observations)

Libor-3months Volatility	Coefficients	Standard Error	t-Statistics	R^2
Constant	−0.0023	0.000369	−6.22	0.0813
Slope w.r.t. CBOT Vol.	0.035597	0.001612	22.1	0.5268

Index no.1

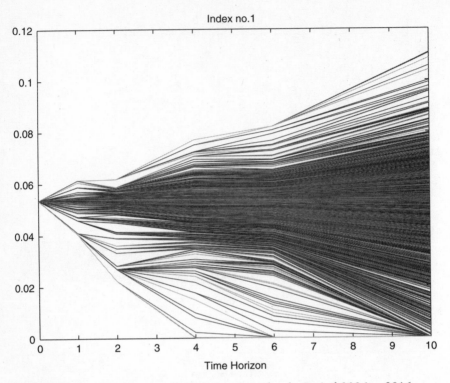

Time Horizon

FIGURE 16.5 Scenarios for the Risk-Free Rate for the Period 2006 to 2016

gross income around €80,000, estimated to rise with inflation). His wife Alessandra is an employee working for an insurance company (annual gross income around €40,000, estimated to rise with inflation). They live in Italy. Zimbini's family consists of their son Cesare and daughter Maria. He is a first-year student at a private university specializing in economics and finance. Maria is a high school student. Longer-term, the Zimbinis wish to assure not only their own financial security and standard of living but that of their children as well, regardless of what professions their children end up in. The investment portfolio (€600,000 net in total, with 15,000 in stocks, 285,000 in bonds, 300,000 in cash in a bank) has to pay at least half of the Cesare's college fees in addition to the inflation offsetting on what will ultimately be their children's inheritance. A €10,000 residual mortgage debt must be returned at an amount of €2,500 per year for the next for 4 years. The Zimbinis have a good wealth position, so their ability to deal with the risk aspects of their situation is good. The Zimbinis are relatively risk-averse by nature. They have historically held a large portion of their liquid

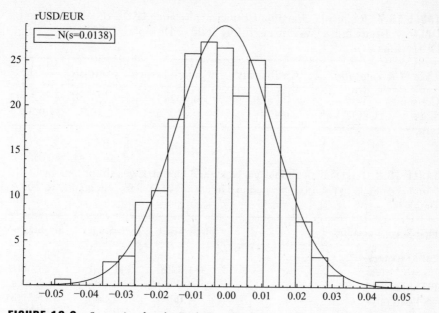

FIGURE 16.6 Scenarios for the Risk-Free Rate for the Period 2006 to 2016

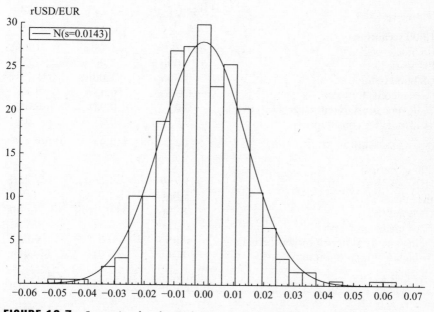

FIGURE 16.7 Scenarios for the Risk-Free Rate for the Period 2006 to 2016

TABLE 16.7 Regression Equation Coefficients Relating USD/EUR Volatility and CBOT Volatility Index (Weekly rates; July 2000 to December 2009; 440 Observations)

USD/EUR Volatility	Coefficients	Standard Error	t-Statistics	R^2
Constant	0.0629	0.00243	25.9	0.6041
Slope w.r.t. CBOT Vol.	0.17495	0.01050	16.7	0.3879

TABLE 16.8 First Stage Optimal Variables and Optimal Wealth for Different Number of Stages (Values Expressed in Thousands of Dollars Using 2000 to 2007 Data)

First Stage Variables	Single Stage	Two-Stages	Six-Stages
2,000 scenarios:			
US Stock (b/s)	341.78(b)	341.78(b)	1.00(s)
EU Stock (b/s)	1.00(s)	1.00(s)	1.00(s)
US Bond (b/s)	1.00(s)	1.00(s)	341.71(b)
% income for cash	0.31	0.31	0.31
% income for different targets (average)	0.05	0.05	0.05
% income for consumption	0.01	0.01	0.01
Optimal wealth	1,254.04	1,260.14	1,338.24
1,000 scenarios:			
US Stock (b/s)	341.78(b)	341.78(b)	1.00(s)
EU Stock (b/s)	1.00(s)	1.00(s)	1.00(s)
US Bond (b/s)	1.00(s)	1.00(s)	341.71(b)
% of income for cash	0.31	0.31	0.31
% income for different targets (average)	0.05	0.05	0.05
% income for consumption	0.01	0.01	0.01
Optimal wealth	1,253.43	1,258.98	1,399.83
200 scenarios:			
US Stock (b/s)	341.78(b)	1.00(s)	341.78(b)
EU Stock (b/s)	1.00(s)	1.00(s)	1.00(s)
US Bond (b/s)	1.00(s)	341.71(b)	1.00(s)
% of income for cash	0.31	0.31	0.31
% income for different targets (average)	0.05	0.05	0.05
% income for consumption	0.01	0.01	0.01
Optimal wealth	1,250.67	1,177.57	1,326.95

TABLE 16.9 Zimbinis' Assets and Liabilities Data

	Tax Basis	Value	Cash Flow
Assets			
Cash and marketable securities		300,000	120,000
Closed-end funds			
Restricted stock		15,000	
Bonds		285,000	
Insurance			
Limited partnership			
Commercial real estate			
Total assets		300,000	120,000
Liabilities			
Credit cards and ST			
Loans			
Margin loans			
Commercial R/E loans			
Personal R/E loans		10,000	
Unfunded			
Total liabilities		10,000	

assets in money market accounts. Furthermore, the Zimbinis do not want a portfolio value decline of more than 10% in nominal terms in any given 12-month period. So, their willingness to take risk is below average ($\lambda = 6$). The Zimbinis' targets are

- Purchase of a new car €30,000 (within two years)
- Purchase of a second home €400,000 (next three to five years when Cesare will finish university)
- Net annual expenses including the Cesare's college fees €66,000 (estimated to rise with inflation)
- Required annual net return 1.5%
- Expected annual inflation 2.0%
- Annual net return objective 3.5%

Zimbinis investment liquidity options are

- Restructuring their first home €80,000 (within one year)
- Cash bank TIPS (Treasury inflation protected securities)

Aside from the liquidity events listed above, the Zimbinis have a long-term multistage time horizon of 20 years, and they are subject to their country's tax code.

TABLE 16.10 Zimbini's Portfolio: First Stage Optimal Variables and Optimal Wealth for Different Number of Stages (Values Expressed in Thousands of Euros. 2000 to 2007 data)

First Stage Variables	Single Stage	Two-Stages	Six-Stages
2,000 scenarios:			
US Stock (b/s)	15.00(s)	15.00(s)	15.00(s)
EU Stock (b/s)	501.37(b)	503.5(b)	0(b)
US Bond (b/s)	282.87(b)	285.0(b)	219.13(b)
% income for cash	0.0	0.0	0.0
% income for different target1	0.0	0.0	0.0
% income for different target2	1.0	1.0	1.0
% income for consumption	0.0	0.0	0.0
Optimal wealth	2,106.01	2,165.47	2,323.8
1,000 scenarios:			
US Stock (b/s)	15.00(s)	15.00(s)	15.00(s)
EU Stock (b/s)	490.58(b)	219.15(b)	0(b)
US Bond (b/s)	272.05(b)	0.0(b)	219.13(b)
% income for cash	0.0	0.0	0.0
% income for different target1	0.0	0.0	0.0
% income for different target2	1.0	1.0	1.0
% income for consumption	0.0	0.0	0.0
Optimal wealth	2,126.1	2,175.68	2,462.85
200 scenarios:			
US Stock (b/s)	15.00(s)	15.00(s)	707.98(b)
EU Stock (b/s)	0.0(b)	0.0(b)	0.0(b)
US Bond (b/s)	219.13(b)	219.13(b)	285.00(b)
% income for cash	0.0	0.0	0.0
% income for different target1	0.0	0.0	0.0
% income for different target2	1.0	1.0	1.0
% income for consumption	0.0	0.0	0.0
Optimal wealth	2,174.66	2,238.44	2,492.9

The following portfolio constraints are active:

- The Zimbinis' second home will represent an illiquid portion of their total net worth. They have decided to not consider that home as part of their actively managed investment portfolio. The second home could carry a mortgage if necessary or convenient.
- The Zimbini's want only a limited exposure to stock investments (no more than 30%).

TABLE 16.11 Zimbini's Portfolio: First Stage Optimal Variables and Optimal Wealth for Different Number of Stages (Values Expressed in Thousands of Euros. 2000–2007 Data)

First Stage Variables	Single Stage	Two-Stages	Six-Stages
2,000 scenarios:			
US Stock (b/s)	15.00(s)	15.00(s)	15.00(s)
EU Stock (b/s)	0.0(b)	0.0(b)	0.0(b)
US Bond (b/s)	24.09(b)	87.3(b)	221.64(b)
% income for cash	0.0	0.0	0.0
% income for different target1	0.05	0.05	0.05
% income for different target2	0.82	0.82	0.82
% income for consumption	0.1	0.1	0.1
Optimal wealth	1,878.8	1,949.83	2,128.69
1,000 scenarios:			
US Stock (b/s)	15.00(s)	15.00(s)	15.00(s)
EU Stock (b/s)	0.0(b)	0.0(b)	0.0(b)
US Bond (b/s)	48.52(b)	67.43(b)	221.64(b)
% income for cash	0.0	0.0	0.0
% income for different target1	0.05	0.05	0.05
% income for different target2	0.82	0.82	0.82
% income for consumption	0.1	0.1	0.1
Optimal wealth	1,898.67	1,960.8	2,260.83
200 scenarios:			
US Stock (b/s)	15.00(s)	15.00(s)	707.98(b)
EU Stock (b/s)	0.0(b)	0.0(b)	0.0(b)
US Bond (b/s)	221.64(b)	86.49(b)	285.0(s)
% income for cash	0.0	0.0	0.0
% income for different target1	0.05	0.05	0.05
% income for different target2	0.82	0.82	0.82
% income for consumption	0.1	0.1	0.1
Optimal wealth	1,983.56	2,025.84	2,296.39

The values for the first-stage variables are shown in Table 16.10 for an increasing number of stages and different number of scenarios. The value of the new information along the 20-year horizon shows up with a stability reached for the six stages and the suggestion is to sell US stocks and invest in US bonds. This result does not include any constraint on consumption either in cash in the first stage and this is the reason why the second target becomes more important. We can also impose lower bounds on the value of variables that manage the percentage of income spent on cash, assets, target funds, and consumption (see Table 16.11). Choosing a lower bound for consumption of 0.10, for target funds of 0.05, for cash of 0.0, and for assets of 0.01, the optimal value of β_{2t} becomes very high in order to cope with the target of the house which requires a large yearly investment.

We notice that a sufficient number of scenarios has to be generated to obtain a reliable solution and the number of stages is important to put more emphasis on the arrival of new information. The model we have proposed results in a very general setting where we can easily add ad hoc constraints to fulfill the investors needs.

In our model the role of targets is significant, and we allow each individual investor to calibrate their portfolio depending on how much importance they give in reaching the targets. The model has a very broad range of applications, and it may be applied and adjusted to various different situations. We have just given few examples; more elaborate ones can be implemented adding various categories of assets. If one wants to work with scenario-based programs, it would be necessary to introduce a factor analysis identifying the main factors that drive the various asset evolution.

REFERENCES

Bertocchi, M., J. Dupačová, and V. Moriggia. 2005. Horizon and stages in applications of stochastic programming in finance. *Annals of Operations Research* 142:63–78.

Dimson, E., P. Marsh, and M. Staunton. 2002. *Triumphs of the Optimists: 101 Years of Global Investment Returns*. Princeton, NJ: Princeton University Press.

Dimson, E., P. Marsh, and M. Staunton. 2006. *The Global Investment Returns Yearbook*. Amsterdam: ABN-Ambro.

Dupačová, J., M. Bertocchi, and V. Moriggia. 2009. Testing the structure of multi-stage stochastic programs. *Computational Management Science* 143:161–185.

Geyer, A., and W. T. Ziemba. 2008. The Innovest Austrian pension fund financial planning model InnoALM. *Operations Research* 56, no. 4:797–810.

Siegel, J. 2008. *Stocks for the Long Run, 4th ed.* New York: McGraw-Hill.

CHAPTER 17

Conclusions

In this book we have covered the key issues in retirement. There is a conflict between living longer and paying for it in an era of low interest rates and very risky equity and other places to invest one's savings. There is much counterparty risk, so having long-termed annuities and other asset choices has this additional risk of default. Meanwhile, health and other costs continue to rise, and, even though working longer is important, there is much unemployment.

For some, good asset allocation and modest liability commitments put them in good shape. But planning for a long retirement is difficult at best. The US, UK, and other countries also face a potential inflation problem by 2012 as a result of the huge debts created to stem the 2007 to 2009 credit crisis.

The various chapters in the book cover aspects of these issues.

Chapter 1 discusses the key issues in retirement. This includes the root of the problem from a social desire to avoid poverty in the elderly population when they are too old or unable to work. This is in an era of changing demographics with fewer workers supporting more retirees. Meanwhile, pensions arose by trading off future pension benefits for lower current wages in labor negotiations. Chapter 2 discusses macro economic costs for retirement and highlights the shift from DB to DC pension schemes, which shifts portfolio and longevity risks from employers to employees who become retirees. Chapter 3 discusses the pillars of retirement in different (mainly OECD) countries and how they are being transformed to meet both the impact of changing demographics and the changing economic and political institutions in an attempt to improve the distribution of risk among companies and retirees. Chapter 4 discusses various asset classes and presents their historical returns, volatility, correlations, and risks and how they might be used for saving for retirement. Chapter 5 discusses the 2007 to 2009 economic crisis and its impact on retirement assets and future retirement practice.

Part II includes more in-depth analyses of some of these issues. Chapter 6 shows that investment in equities tends to grow at middle age after establishment in career and housing. To reflect this, retirement plans should be defined in a way to allow sheltering of greater balances at this period rather than flat throughout the working life. Chapter 7 presents a continuous time Merton-type asset-liability model of intergenerational surplus management applicable for life and other insurance companies, pension funds, and other organizations. Using the model, we can calculate asset weights as a function of the funding ratio of assets over liabilities. Chapter 8 discusses a possible shift from final salary to career average pensions. There are a number of advantages in these schemes including improved pension equity among different types of workers and the possibility of reducing the disincentive to continued work after peak income has been earned. Chapter 9 discusses a multiperiod stochastic programming model to help the DB pension system survive. It uncovers substantial industry concentration of the DB problem with industry problems and pension funding issues impacting each other, something that was confirmed by the bankruptcies in the auto industry. Policy simulations help create rules to aid for the troubled industries. Chapter 10 discusses the use of various capital market derivative instruments to more effectively deal with the longevity risk imposed on pensions and insurance companies. This offers additional capacity and liquidity to the market and more transparency. Chapter 11 considers the long-term retirement funding of national and state-level governments, which have been adopting two strategies: contributing more money and increasing their risk profile in the hopes of increasing net returns. Chapter 12 investigates issues relating to decumulating assets on retirement and includes a study of the risks and returns of own company stock, housing, annuities, and insurance.

Part III brings the various issues together in an all-encompassing modeling framework. Chapter 13 describes the important lessons in successful investment for the long term, including lessons from endowment management and the great investors. Chapters 14 to 16 provide a multiperiod stochastic optimization model to evaluate long-term asset allocation, subject to liability commitments and policy and other constraints with targets for intermediate goals. While complex to implement, such models provide a good way to plan and take various future scenarios into account.

We also have the following broad conclusions.

1. More and more pension plans are being converted from DB with guaranteed retirement income and benefits to DC plans that are subject to the vagaries of the market. Given the nature of so-called DC pension, they should no longer be called *pension plans* but should be considered *tax-protected savings plans*. This would help individuals better assess

their actual preparation for retirement and would be a cleaner distinction between current income and deferred income, and clarify vesting and ownership in the plans and help in the reform of retirement savings.

2. Rather than set a retirement age we suggest as a society to reconsider retirement as a phase that depends on ability to work, gets phased in, and lasts a limited time until expected death. This would be a reversion to long-held life-cycle ideals. In doing so, we would likely need to create a path for work that could continue as strength declines. We would definitely need to get off the track of expecting a continuing increase in wages as we age; something the Japanese had attempted to do in the 1980s when the retirement age was 55 (without social security or corporate pensions) and workers were expected to be rehired at lower salaries with less job security.

3. Retirement consumption in the aggregate can only ever be secured from production that is current at the time. Goods and services must be available when you want them. Some things can be stored away in your freezer; you can prepare by having a suitable home paid off . . . but much of what you will want to consume must come out of current production: food, medical services, entertainment. Both the retired and the workers draw on the same pool of goods and services, current GDP. If there are not sufficient goods to satisfy all at a reasonable price, there will be much inflation from bidding up the pool of goods that are available.

In turn, if there are not sufficient desired savings to replace the withdrawals of the retired, their assets will fall rapidly in value as they convert them to cash for consumption. This is the other side of the relationship; savings represent current production that is not consumed by those doing the producing!

4. This means that retirement is only ever really funded on a PAYG basis, that is pay-as-you-go. To put this in context: social security was originally set up as PAYG. And originally there were many workers per retiree so this system looked good. Then about a decade or so ago analysts began to worry about the aging of the population. Demographics is something that can be analyzed a couple decades ahead as the babies born today become the retirees 65 years from now give or take migration, death, and so forth. In economic terms this is a pretty reliable system for estimation! Looking ahead we could see that the age shape of the population distribution would change from bulging with workers to becoming more heavy with retirees who would need to be supported by the workers. This led to creating a trust fund to store the money for future retirement (and similar things happened for company pensions, often with companies putting aside shares to be sold later and then more sophisticated funds). To do this, social security insurance payments had

to rise. Even with the trust fund there is a concern that the money in the trust fund will run out by approximately 2050. So what to do? This is more than 30 years away. There are as yet no promises made to these workers, so we have the time to change the contract and make the system work better. Here we come to a fork in the road.

5. Saving is good, but there is a paradox of thrift known to economics that if everyone suddenly saves, there is not enough consumption, and in old-style economics inventories would accumulate and eventually production would fall to cover the lowered demand and of course people would be unemployed. In "Just in Time" economies there is a tighter lag and we do not have to wait for accumulated inventories, or at least we would have thought that but look at the auto companies' lots filled with unsold cars; guess they did not get the message and that is how they ran through so many billions!

6. Fork A: what does the financial savings get us? We can think of these savings funds as vouchers that will entitle us to bid on items in current production, and if that production falls short, inflation will result. So, yes, it's good to save, and much of the book is devoted to improving the vouchers we bring to the market on retirement.

7. Fork B: so do something good with the savings. That is where financial institutions are supposed to come to the rescue and funnel these savings into real investment; economists, real economists, must take back the word investment: it once meant using things currently produced as plant and equipment, seeds, R&D, and so on for future consumption. Unfortunately we thought that we were investing when we put the savings aside, but we were only buying slips of paper. We suggest training doctors, nurses, care workers, investing in constructing care homes and hospitals. We must do R&D and improve productivity. These things will make retirement easier to access.

Index